NEW HARVEST

NEW HARVEST:

JEWISH WRITING IN ST. LOUIS, 1998–2005

Edited by Howard Schwartz
and Barbara Raznick

Missouri Center for the Book

🙢 🙢 🙢

Missouri Authors Collection

The Brodsky Library Press

St. Louis

2005

This book was brought to publication with generous assistance from the
Ethel and Lawrence Sagarin Memorial Publication Fund
of the Central Agency for Jewish Education.

New Harvest: Jewish Writing in St. Louis, 1998-2005

ISBN 0-9657880-1-6

The Saul Brodsky Jewish Community Library and the Central Agency for
Jewish Education are supported by the Jewish Federation of St. Louis

Visit the Saul Brodsky Jewish Community Library online at
www.brodskylibrary.org
the Central Agency for Jewish Education at
www.cajestl.org
or visit the gateway to the Jewish community of St. Louis at
www.jewishinstlouis.org

With much love, we dedicate this book to our niece,
Elizabeth Ann Sagarin

The Sagarins

Contents

II FICTION

Foreword

What a propitious time this is! We begin the New Year with the publication of a new book, symbolic of renewal and promise in the year that has yet to unfold.

The High Holy Days in themselves express an amalgam of the best of the "old" and "new" as both realities are culled in such events as the creation, the Binding of Isaac, the giving of the Law atop Mt. Sinai, the Prophets call for repentance. Each of these is worthy of study and further interpretations—the *hidushim*, new thoughts and insights in our tradition.

With *New Harvest* we continue to move into the future, striving to take the best of our former selves while "donning new clothing," never being fully content with the status quo.

Some of *New Harvest's* contents have been taken from the 2002 edition of the *Sagarin Review*, including writings among others by Donald Finkel, Jeff Friedman and Shelly Fredman. In addition, there is an abundance of heretofore unpublished works by St. Louisans Allison Creighton, Andrea Jackson, Cheryl Maayan, Jane Schapiro, Steven Schreiner, Rabbi James Stone Goodman and many others. With such diverse authors and subjects, *New Harvest* remains a most absorbing and eclectic volume.

Personally, I would like to thank the indefatigable efforts of Howard Schwartz and Barbara Raznick, whose energy and time brought this rich anthology to fruition. I would also like to extend thank you's to CAJE and the Saul Brodsky Jewish Community Library for their continuing and unflagging support.

L'shanah Tovah,

Rabbi James L. Sagarin
October 2005
Tishrei 5766

Introduction

The Jewish community of St. Louis has the unusual distinction of being the first to have created its own journal, *The Sagarin Review*, which published six issues starting in 1991, and the first to edit an anthology of the Jewish writers of their city, *First Harvest: Jewish Writing in St. Louis, 1991-1997*. At the time that *First Harvest* was published in 1997 we agreed that we would try to aim for a sequel seven years later. Although it took eight years, we now present that sequel, *New Harvest: Jewish Writing in St. Louis: 1998-2005*. We are grateful for being able to reach this landmark, and proud to present this new anthology, rich with poetry, fiction, life stories and essays.

Readers of *New Harvest* will find considerable continuity, as well as many welcome surprises. As in the earlier anthology and literary journal, well-established writers are side by side with previously unpublished ones. The academic community is well-represented, with contributions from most of the major universities, and the older generations are accompanied by the younger ones. Of course, some of the writers from the previous anthology, such as Larry Eigner, Stanley Elkin, Bert Minkin, Howard Nemerov, and Constance Urdang, are no longer with us, while many new writers have been included who have emerged in recent years. We are proud to have been the first to publish Naama Goldstein, whose first book of stories, *The Place Will Comfort You,* has been widely heralded. And we are pleased to be the first to publish several younger authors whose work is exceptionally promising. See, for example, the wonderful story "Swirling Souls" by Adina Talve-Goodman. And readers will find that *New Harvest* is full of surprises, such as the magnificent poems of Edward Londe, one of our best-kept literary secrets, and the remarkable biblical and family poems of Jeff Friedman, a St. Louis native who is now emerging as an important nationally recognized poet. Readers should be sure to look into our section of essays, where the history of Serah bat Asher, the legendary figure who lived longer than anyone else, can be found, along with an important essay on the Golem.

We want to thank Jerred Metz, who spent many hours interviewing older members of the St. Louis community about their lives. The stories he collected from Minnie Appel, Freda Berns, Sophie Dricker, Frank Fershter and Yetta Schneider (all of whom are no longer among us) are vivid recollections of what life was like in the Old Country and the New World for them. These stories are among the highlights of our section of Life Stories, always everyone's favorite. This section also include Robert A. Cohn's fascinating essay, "My Past Life Experience."

The inspiration and support for *The Sagarin Review* and the two anthologies that have gathered the work of St. Louis Jewish writers came from Rabbi James L. Sagarin. Without him this unusual project would never have taken place. We are also grateful for the support of the Brodsky Library and the Central Agency for Jewish Education.

Above all, we are grateful to our contributors, who have not only contributed to this collection, but are a vital part of the literary life of St. Louis.

Howard Schwartz
Barbara Raznick

I
Poetry

Gloria Attoun
Posture

The day I came out of the blood red,
rhythmic, rocking darkness
of my mad mother's
middle
I was curled tight
clenching my own skin
until my doll–like hands
were white like bone.
I unfolded.
A slow–motion movie of a purple orchid's tongue
was I
digging itself out of spring–moist soil
welcoming its way
into the world
of light.

I am still opening.

Others have revealed their soft, pale undersides
with unshakeable confidence
an evolutionary dance
in a matter of minutes.
It has taken me half a lifetime.
My peak
is approaching
My Equinox, my high tide climax crescendo
When my head reaches its highest sun
My feet their strongest roots
MY WILL BE
My own face of vulnerability
will feel safe
In the open straightness
of
I AM
I AM
uncurling.

The Darkness

My mama sits alone in bed.
She sways and rocks to the sound of voices in her head.
The lighted lamp looks old and gray
I want to touch her but she seems so far away.
I slowly walk up to her side
I wonder if I could fill the emptiness inside
And take her nightmares all away
I'd solve it all and then let in the light of day

Chorus
But she says:
"Don't look for easy answers they've been buried or destroyed
Don't try to fix my problems like you would a child's broken toy
Just look at my eyes and hold them like a candle holds your gaze
Let my words flow through you and then listen to the pain."

My mama's gone and I am here
My mind is slipping down, I'm holding back the fear.
It's no one's fault there is no key.
These thoughts keep sifting up through ancient memory.
And now you wonder what to say
To make this suffering and sadness go away
You know I'm out here all alone
But stand by me and hold me and I'll fight it on my own.

Don't look for easy answers they've been buried or destroyed
Don't try to fix my problems like you would a child's broken toy
Just look at my eyes and hold them like a candle holds your gaze
Let my words flow through you and then listen to the pain.

I'm digging it up.
The darkness
I'm digging it up.
And letting go at last.

Thaw

I crash through the crust of ice into the water below
and sink to the bottom in
seven
slow
seconds.
You watch with shocked eyes and disappear,
looking for a rope.
The softness of the muddy bottom calls me,
promising gold and emerald mysteries.
I dig and dig but find only shards and rusty metal bait cans
left over from a fisherman's long, lazy, Sunday afternoon.
I try to swim, to float, to reach, but the water is changing
to ice
and I expand from the inside out
my heart frozen, held in place for minutes
or years.

When the sun is released from the clouds of February,
water will creep around the melting edges,
covering it with a slippery wetness.
You
will crawl carefully to the middle, aware of its
creaking.
On your hands and knees, you will peer into the green, frozen
hardness,
looking for an eye, a flailing arm, a bubble...
rope dangling by your side.
I will float up with the thaw
and break the ice from below with my head
like a chick looking for the light of life.
Slimy, wet and wrinkled, I will pull up to the surface.
Though my arms and legs will be weak,
I will wrap my self around you
And we'll climb up the hill
in the warm
changing
air.

Leah F. Silberman Bernstein
Concentric Circles

2am
My daughter's round *keppie*
with her crown of thick, auburnred hair tipped with gold
cradled heavily in my arms
as her almond–round eyes
open and close and
open and close making sure that
my large brown areola remains in view
Delicate little forefinger and thumb
crudely pushing and poking and encircling to grasp
in amusement at her new fine skill
Sweet, warm milk stretching my ballooning breast
cradled in her little hug
as she learns to manipulate my nipple to her searching
round mouth latching furious with hunger
needing comfort and the warmth of her mother's love
as I gaze upon her with my mother's almond–round eyes
Protected by the nestle-spooning of the husband and father
the most beautiful scene
greeting me 'round the clock
framed by my chestnut-streaked-silver curls
as the fullest moon shines a sliver of light
and smiles upon us
in her lunar slow–dance.

Lorry Blath
Praying for a Beach

I lay on the table in a sterile room.
Oh, they try to warm it with vistas of beaches,
but I know where I am and why I am here.

I await the doctor whom I've never met.
Or maybe a resident, eager and earnest,
accompanied by a name-tagged student.

The lights are florescent, unable to mimic
the shoreline locales at all. I am cold, then hot.
I wear long pants, sandals, and a hospital smock.

The chairs catch my eye—a pretty print
with brown foliage. Decay? The seats are narrow.
Their wooden arms seem to hinder comfort.

Water trickles from the faucet into the steel sink.
Tears trek along my cheek toward my hair
needing to be combed. Heels click in the hall outside.

The doctor at last opens the door, smiling,
chart in hand, hair in place. Confident.
But I am curled on my side, uneasy about
her news, or, perhaps, praying for a beach.

Louis Daniel Brodsky
At Sundown

Tomorrow night, at sundown,
I, a Jew who's lost his direction,
A melancholy soul wandering in the wilderness,
Trying to make his way, as Abraham did,
From the Ur of myriad gods, to Canaan,

Will enter the house of the Lord, contrite,
Recite the sacred, ancient Hebraic prayers,
Hum the cantor's plaintive strains
Of Kol Nidre and *O-Seh Shalom*,
And beg silent forgiveness from the congregation.

Tomorrow night, at sundown,
I'll fill the temple with my meditations,
Entreat God to find my expiations acceptable,
Exculpate me for my imperfections,
And grant my soul another *Shana Tova*.

Where to Begin?

Where to begin?
Today, at about three in the afternoon,
We buried our father,

Laid him to rest, recited Kaddish,
Tossed roses on his vault,
Honored him with snow-covered dirt

Shoveled, from a mound, by his wife,
Children, grandchildren, close friends,
Sent him on his destiny's way.

Where to begin?
Between noon and one, at the visitation,
Four hundred mourners filled the temple—

Those he'd touched with his generosity,
His modesty, his nobility, his dignity—
Wanting to be close to him one last time.

Where to begin?
I can't fathom what my life will be like
Without him in it.

After all, my sixty-one years
Bear his imprint, his influence, his spirit.
That he's no longer alive diminishes me.

This afternoon, the snow stung my toes;
Tonight, they're still cold.
I sense myself beginning where he ended.

Ghosts

Tomorrow will mark three weeks
Since my father's parting.

I still can't gain my footing,
Locate myself, determine my destination,

Decide who I am,
Now that he's a ghost among the ghosts

Of my paternal ancestors—peddlers from Kiev,
Peasants from rural Ukraine.

Tonight, I raise my wineglass,
Pray for his safe passage to Heaven,

And say *l'chaim* to the afterlife.
Dad, will you show me the way home?

Jan Garden Castro

Genesis

After a performance by *Himiko Minato*

When we come into being,
eyes, sinews and muscles are
wet, half-formed. Love is
lapping waters, a bath,
the genesis
of the soul. We pour our
energies into the dark,
lighting spaces of naked longing.
The color machine is twirling,
twirling. We have survived
the storm. We have survived.
Now it is one of many and
winter has begun. So dance . . .
hold me in your arms . . .

Grandfather

My Grandfather
Is silver and golden
Like Aztec coins
Which bring good luck at weddings.

Through wrinkling brow he watches
Life increasing in me.
I watch his sun-baked skin grow loose
Around his tiger bones.

He is the warrior
Shining in my eyes.

Poem for the Lunar Eclipse

We celebrate darkness as we celebrate light:
by being lotus buds inside its silky, silty
incantatory depths just as the moon

caressed by earth's shadow mocks
the body double gliding over
her numinous moorland.

And we, we skitter across surfaces too
obliquely, forgetting the grace of moving
in space. Seeing light years enfolded
in earth's specter is an illusion.

Forms slow, then free motion.
Circles mesh in the eye, then
unmask vision.

The Classics

Madame Bovary is reading *The Cherry Orchard* and
dying so that Flaubert may parade before society
its own judgment in the guise of a beautiful strumpet.

Julius Caesar is being stabbed by Brutus because one
loved fame more. Power is passing from the pen
to the people here and in Hamlet, the son framed

again and again. Nora is walking out and
slamming the door, leaving her husband and son,
leaving a mindless doll's life—for no life at all.

Love has flown early and often from hearts
frozen with fear and longing! The sorrows
we live form the classics, those tents of emotions

pitched above our heads. We long to touch the
magnets of love radiating from voices, strings—
the Stradivarius that breathes and talks the way

Love talks—with an ageless grace that flies us
to vistas, unfurls the heart.

Michael Castro
Hasdai Ibn Shaprut

"Prince of the Jews,"
in Cordoba, at the end of the first millennium,
knew the antidotes for poisons—
Doctor Hasdai—
found himself
in demand
by the royal & ruling families—

Who was this Jew with clout who
translated the pharmacology—
saw deeply into human nature—
wrote poems,
organized soirees,
practiced healing arts &
embarked on diplomatic missions
to Baghdad & Bergundy,
to Otto Uno of Germany
for Abdl al-Rachmann?—

Hasdai!
A Jew with personality,
a healer,
a man of knowledge—
a talker, a guy
who could converse with anyone, anywhere, highborn or low—
existing or even, maybe no—
Hasdai, projected
imagination into space,
as "Prince of the Jews"
wrote to Joseph, King
of the legendary Khazars,
somewhere out there
(maybe)
beyond the Empire's boundaries—

Did His Majesty really exist? he inquired.
What was his tribe? His Judaism like?
Did he know when the Messiah was coming?
Wasn't his arrival long overdue?

"O Blessed is the Lord of Israel," intoned Hasdai,
from Spain, to his desire, "who would never leave us
without an independent kingdom. . . ."

Hasdai, centered once, but now on the margins—
emissary,
liaison, foreign
minister,
connection,
great tree
rooted deep in Spanish soil,
but branching out,
embracing other branches, shading
as it reaches for the heavens, spreading
the dream—of peace—
the dream of Hasdai—
dream of a Jew,
dream splattered & streaming
in all directions,
portable dream,
bearing the home inside
the dream—
the central fire,
burning bush, embers glowing
into letters, kindling, lighting,
fueling the survival—shaping
words,
poems, illuminating
the suffering—the burning
Temples, charred scrolls,
acrid cinders, powdery bones,
the headaches, the glow
between the brows, the dream

of life. Transcending.
Transforming. Hasdai

the healer
repairs damage,
founds schools for Jewish children,
spends his wealth buying old manuscripts
so that the Word would never be lost,
protests directly to the Bishops of Burgos
their Easter-time ritual humiliations of the Jews:
God,
he reminds them, sees everything,
& never forgets;
Hasdai,
the right hand man,
gathers a courtyard full of poets & philosophers
a chorus of Muslims, Christians, & Jews—
to please His Majesty—

Shapes the dream
of a golden age,
the idea of
a beautiful garden
in Cordoba's courtyard, a garden
filled with intermingling fragrances,
harmonic voices,
multi-colored flowers of every description,
a garden not in some distant land,
some distant, mythical past,
a garden here & now in Sepharad;

Hasdai planting, nurturing,
the dream
seeds of Hasdai,
a cosmopolitan Jew,
a Jew who knew
the antidotes for poisons,
the sweetness of the tongue, the sharing
of the soul-stuff,

a healer,
a Jew who delivered
the royal birth

Hasdai stoops,
gathering sparks
to light the way.

2.

A thousand years later,
at the end of the second millennium,
I write your name, Hasdai,
I write 'Sepharad,' opening its gates of mind,
living a kind of dream
that might have been yours,
beaming on my screen in letters of light
a kind of creation, projecting
clusters of sparkling
singers, bards of every complexion.
A courtyard, a cafe, a dark bar,
a magazine.
A living room.
Is this what it is to be poet—
a unified effort
cutting through time?
a ceremony of mending & healing?
a language so precise
it blurs all boundaries?
the more you are yourself,
the more you are not?
one mind?
a march of names?
shards of light?

Sepharad gleams at the end of the highway.

Lily Heart

She rose, a creature of light,
a lily, rising in her dewy bed, stretched
her body of light & 13 rays shot out,
13 rays of consciousness materialized in the void
between sleeping & waking,
she rose & wrapped herself in 13 petals,
a Lily of the West, rising in morning's eastern light
above the saloon, rose to dance in the warm wind
of barroom bluster below, a dance hall gal,
a Lily, a flower among the thorns
in the Wild West of Creation.

                    ★

O the rednecks & roughnecks & rubber necks
that clattered through the swinging doors!
How they whistled & stomped & brawled & bled
for beauty & booze. How they cut the decks of destiny
with dung-flecked fingers & gun-greased hands
how they reached out to pluck every fruit & flower
wavering before them in the bloodshot smoky light.

O how Lily danced!
O how her 13 leaves, her 13 feathered fans, rose
& fell, revealing & concealing her loveliness &
luminous core. How she engulfed the mind & soul as she
eluded their grasp. How her hair flamed red as fire,
how she flared off warmth & glow,
& could not be held in hands or arms or mind.

O Lily of the West. I conceive your memory.
I saw you dance on the sawdust stage of the Golden Slipper.
I was among the rollicking miners who lay bags of treasure
alongside the footlights, who showered you with powdered gold.
O you were powerful & radiant.
I saw your eye-beam humble a heckler,
your darting glance make a groper grovel,
your flash of disdain straighten up a crook.

O Lily, Lily. O holy flower, wholly
out of reach. How you stripped each petal
& glided with amazing grace in the soft eye of spot,
how you teased us, bumping & grinding down
to your bare
essentials,
how when the thirteenth feather floated
into the gaping pit of the awed orchestra,
it revealed you

gone. Just traces
of your movements
etched in the light

that darkening morn.

Homage to Ten in Ten Lines

I stood on ten toes
I prayed with ten fingers
I witnessed the ten plagues devour Egypt
I descended from the ten lost tribes
I bowed before the ten commandments
I opened the Torah's ark as part of a *minyan*
I walked in the creation uttered by ten powerful words
I wandered in a universe structured by the ten *sephiroth,* the divine
    program
String theory & Mahayana Buddhists placed me in the ten dimensions
I collaborated with the nine muses to write my poems

Guide to the Perplexed

Moses ben Maimon,
Moses the Spaniard,
Moses the Jew,
Maimonides, Moses
ben Maimon ha-Sepharadi,
The Rambam, giver

of the essence
of the law—
Mishnah Torah—gentle
in manner, but fierce in intellect, endurance, sheer nerve—
"from Moses to Moses,
there is no one like Moses:"

Cordoba 1135, Sepharad,
where this life begins,
amidst war & woe, caught
between one interpretation & the other—

Allah, Allah,

the Almohades insist
on their version of the name
of God who is beyond
names (we say), they don't
listen, in the name of Allah,
the Almohades burn down
the corrupted Islamic mosques
of those whose accent's off;
we don't even speak
the same language,
& the synagogues burn too on general principles—
Jews must swear allegiance to Allah,
must pay lip service
& through the nose—

It's not the names we fear, it's the sticks, the stones,
          the fire—
Amidst flames—not of a burning bush—
but of burning books,
scorched scrolls, smoking letters,
my wanderings began—

pero
          ningun encarcelado, se puede descarcelar.
          No one is a prisoner if he can escape.

& so we left our home, our wealth—

si los anios calleron, los dedos quedaron—
if the rings fell off, at least the fingers stayed,

we fled through Sepharad, from town to town, to Almeria.
the Almohades hot on our heels—

(*Cominos macarones, alambicos corazones.*
We ate macaroni, & licked our hearts.)

& when the Almohedan armies stormed Almeria's gates,
we set sail for Africa—Morocco.

Thus began my journey—Fez, Acco, the Holy Land,
    Alexandria, Cairo. *My mind was troubled,*
& amid divinely ordained exiles, on journeys by land
    & tossed by tempests of the sea . . .

Sepharad was our Jerusalem, our jewel, a garden
we had tended, transplanted trees,
& put down roots. . .
       we knew the bite
of the olive and the fig, the land's strange fruits
      we tried to live
amidst the Christians, amidst the Muslims, to work through our
   tikkun—& now
     another wound to heal . . . another burning
                 temple

I think of those round Andalusian hills,
    the play of God's light off the green leaves
after a cleansing rain—
                 as I watch

   the gray waves
      rise & fall,
the horizon flat
    as unleavened bread.

Quien no sabe de mar,
          no sabe de mal.
He who knows nothing of the sea,
     knows nothing of suffering.

                    ★

Since we went into exile,
          the persecutions have not stopped.
I have known affliction since childhood,
          since the womb.

Ah, the sun, the beautiful sun
that creates this desert—the aching beauty
of these desert flowers. . .

               The greater the pain,
                    the greater the reward.

Fez is a labyrinth, its streets reflect its soul.
Everything is hidden: the faces of its women
behind dark veils, the sumptuous interiors
of its white-walled, shuttered homes

Here we hide in plain sight.
Tired of running.

The Almohades approach the city gates.
Some say, resist, refuse, martyr yourselves—
     as others have. But I say, be calm,
when the Almohedes come to your door,
listen carefully to their conditions—
     If they are as we hear,
submit &
take the vow.

               Before you protest,
Think it through:
In the earlier religious persecutions

we were forced to violate certain *shalls* and *shall nots*
through our deeds. In the present persecution, however,
no deed is demanded of us,
only *words*. A *name*.

I am a man of words, but listen to me O Jews.
We do not need martyrs. Resist
the long winded foolish babbling & nonsense
of those who argue for unflinching death.
Use your heads.

      Live *your name*
behind closed doors—cover your windows.
After all, if someone wishes to observe
all 613 laws in private, no one hinders him.

Now, if they tried to force us to commit a forbidden act,
of course, we would rather be killed than carry it out.
But there has never been so strange a persecution
in which we are forced to transgress only verbally.

Lie then, & live
the truth.

      Submit, for now,

    Faste a amigo con el huerco,
              hasta ques pases el ponte.
                   Befriend the hangman,
                         till you are over the bridge.

    but remember:

Quien muncho se aboca, el culo se le vee.
        He who bends down too low, exposes his rear end.

   ★

I was of *"the exile of Jerusalem*
that was in Sepharad," as the book of *Obadiah* describes us.
And now we were doubly exiled. We
who had lived in Sepharad
before the Visigoths & the Vandals invaded,
before the Christians or the Muslims
were conjured up by their prophets,
before the Almohades, who were Berbers from Morocco,
began their righteous pillage, we
who were part of the soil & soul of that place,
    who helped to make a Golden Age, we

abandoned our ancient villages & ourselves
to God's will, without any signs
save those of danger, took up the challenge
with Hope & Faith—& if truth be told,
with fear
for ourselves & for those
who remained behind—

I landed in Fez, in the heart
of the beast.

                ★

My desire & my quest
was to know God
so far as this is possible for a human being.

I mastered first mathematics, then the natural sciences,
especially to familiarize myself with their patterns
& subtle perfections,
before I grappled with metaphysics. My brother,
David, sailed around the world buying & selling
to support my efforts—this was his way
of worship & of love—& I studied, & I taught, & wrote.

I wrote many books, among them the *Mishnah Torah:*
here I put into one book
the unraveled strands, the distilled opinions,

the essence of Talmudic wisdom.
Someone had to resolve the disputes, the split hairs,
the rabbinic quibbling, & testing—
Who could really read through the whole *megillah*
of the Talmud, that weighty treasure chest,
every time another dispute arose?
Here it is, I said, & people listened & read:
the naked heart
of the matter.

I wrote from mind, & breath, & source—
from God, seeking God.

My only master was Aristotle.
Reading him encouraged me to live
in the mind, showed me
that thinking is godly,
implying
that even a master, an Aristotle,
is not to be followed
blindly. Blind dedication,
   blind faith, blind obedience
      leads to blind fanaticism, blind persecution,
        blind hatred.

What's a mind for, I thought,
       if not to help us
          see?

      ★

Some call me "Rabbi."

      ★

I advise my neighbors & friends:
     never eat except when hungry, or drink except when thirsty.
     Observe moderation. Don't go out in the cold after bathing.
     Avoid constant bloodletting.

Be guided by *hesed*: loving-kindness & compassion;
    tsedekah: righteousness;
    mishpat: judgment.

    For stating the obvious,
        I am called 'wise.

Everyone wants to obey
someone.

We are too immersed in tradition,
too bogged down in faith, too frozen
in ritual. In our exile
we have forgotten
  how to think.

    And therefore, we must train the mind,
      as we do the body:

Think of God
        as a King.
& think
         how, in a kingdom,
some have more direct access than others.

In the Kingdom of God,
those who have studied
the mathematical sciences & logic,
& who have studied the Talmud,
but who have not asked
whether the propositions found there
are actually true, these seekers
wander around the walls of the palace,
looking in vain for the entrance.

And those who have studied the mathematical sciences & logic,
& who have studied the Talmud
& *the natural sciences*
& actually thought about them,
these seekers enter the palace's forecourt.

But those who have studied the mathematical sciences & logic,
who have studied the Talmud,
the natural sciences,
& *metaphysics*, & who have thought
about all of them,
    & understood what can be understood—
    these seekers arrive
    in the interior of the royal palace.

Thinking is a way to God.

   Consider this:
The prophet who "sees" God
does not really see in form
He who is beyond form.
The prophet is thinking
of God.

And when God is said to see
something, as He doesn't have sense organs, truly
He is contemplating the world.

God is a perfect intelligence.
The thinking that pours out from God
upon us is the link between Him & us.

We must solidify this link
& make it more intimate,
or it will gradually loosen
& dissolve altogether.

I am a doctor, attending at the birth
& rebirth of philosophy, metaphysics,
imagination, & prophecy.
I labor at preparing the way
to the *Protecting King*, the *Active Intellect*.
I teach the burnishing & restoring,
the lighting of the inner lamp—
the bond of light between God & us—

The more active the mind, the more open
to God.

For just as we know God by the light
that he has streaming out to us,
thus does He look through us
by means of this light.

This light is what makes everything
we see or do possible.

& yet this light is so brilliant
no one alive can
stare directly into it.

★

There have been times when I have lost the light.
I dwelt in darkness
when my beloved brother, David, died at sea;
my world collapsed.
There were days I moaned in despair.
What was the logic of the bad happening to the good?
Why is it that each of us is Job?
How do we fill the loss of love?
My friends & family gathered & we wept.
We cursed & praised, we remembered, & we prayed.
We chanted *Kaddish*.
Its mystic sounds & rhythms
gave us a music to calm the soul.
We could not understand its ways & power,
or the ways & power of our God.
We pictured David in our minds, where he would always live.
Rains came, & we thought it was David, cleansing & renewing
            our shattered reality.
We felt his presence.
& the presence of God.

★

I say to you, there is nothing
but God and His works. & His works include
everything in existence except God.
God is One—his own source
& the source of everything else.

God be thanked for all conditions,
whose universality is to be found
in the universe of existences
& whose specificity is to be found
in every single individual.
May the praise for every single condition
be constant, no matter what the situation may be.

★

To support myself, & others,
I became a Doctor. For many years
I have worked
long hours to improve the human condition.

Now, even in my old age,
I go to Cairo every morning
at the crack of dawn to treat the Sultan
& his family, and if nothing unforeseen happens,
if nothing keeps me there, I can come home in the afternoon
but never earlier. Here, starving as I am,
I find the antechamber full of people: Jews
& non-Jews, nobles & lowly people, judges & officials,
friends & foes, a motley company awaiting me
with impatience. I dismount from my horse, wash,
& enter the waiting room with the plea that they
may not feel offended if I have to make them wait a bit longer
while I partake of a hasty light meal, which normally happens
once every twenty-four hours. Then I go out to them again,
treat them, & prescribe medicine on notes.
Thus the people go in & out of my home until late in the evening.
Sometimes, I swear on the Torah,
it is 2 a.m. or even later before I manage to consume anything.

I am then so worn out that I collapse on my bed;
I have to say good-night. I am totally exhausted
& incapable of speaking. Only on the Sabbath
can anyone speak to me alone, or can I be alone with myself,
if only for an instant. Then the members of my community
gather in my home after the morning prayer.
I indicate what is to be done in the community
during the coming week; then they listen to a lecture
until noon, go home, and return in smaller number
for another lecture. Thus do my days go by.

I teach & I heal. I give all I have
    to continue, to improve, to perfect
       the creation.
         This is our purpose.
         I think.

There are four perfections:
     the perfection of wealth—a king's perfection—
     illusory because transient;

     the perfection of health—the body's perfection—important
     because a well-tuned instrument
       keeps the mind clear;

   But these things we look upon as the basis of happiness—
     riches or health—are not
       the purpose of life.

   There is the third perfection—perfection of character—
     moral perfection, which contributes
       to the social good.

This perfection improves mankind,
& provides important training for the mind;

   for only a person whose character is pure, calm,
    & steadfast can attain to the fourth—

intellectual perfection:

the ability to acquire correct conceptions;
the perfection of the highest intellectual qualities;
    training the mind to a rigor & openness

    capable of receiving divinity;
    capable of expanding to God.

★

            The Lord of the Universe
knows in what condition I write these lines.
I have withdrawn from people & sought peace
& quiet in order to remain undisturbed. At times,
I lean against the wall; at times, I continue my writing.
I am so feeble that I mostly have to lie down;
a weak body has joined forces with my age.

My body aches & breaks, but still I work, still
I study, still I think, still I try to heal & improve.
I observe, remember, make notes, logical connections.

But logic cannot tell us where creation comes from,
    or why nothing leads to something. Knowing God
        is beyond thought, beyond words &
                    their source.
How can you compare 100 cubits
    to the sharpness of pepper?

Know that there is a level that is higher
than all thought, than all philosophy:
Call it "prophecy."

Prophecy is a different world.
Arguing and investigating are out of place here;
no evidence can reach prophecy;
        any attempt to examine it in a scholarly manner
        is doomed to fail. It would be like trying to gather
        all the water in the world in a single cup.

★

When the Bible says, "And God said,"
it means, "A Prophet understood."
God chooses prophets
from among those
whose minds are finely honed,
& whose imaginations
are vital: those who are open
to seeing new forms & combinations.

A prophet must be able
to actively think,
& then to rationally convey
& defend his experience.

Prophecy is not learning.
It breaks on you like a lightning storm.
It is like the weather.
The wisest man can go through life
and never experience the whirlwind.

★

My whole life I have tried
to be a guide to the perplexed.

        You have doubtless heard about the controversies I have had,
against those who come before me with my tongue,
against those who attack from afar with my pen.
There was a time I would obtain satisfaction for myself
with my tongue and quill
even against the great & the wise
when they polemicized against me.
But now I know that pride & anger are very ugly qualities.

Then, if someone said I am neither pious nor religious,
it would infuriate me. Now, I would not resent it—on the contrary
I would speak good gentle words to them, or hold my

tongue, depending on the circumstances. I seek no victory
for the honor of my soul; character
consists in deviating
from the paths of fools,
not in conquering them.
        If a man wanted to wax wroth
about the ignorance of men, he would never stop
being angry, & would lead a life of grief & affliction.

                ★

Know then,
I have set myself the goal of behaving humbly
in every action, even though it damages me
in the eyes of the world.
If someone wishes to flaunt his own excellence
by demonstrating my failings, then I forgive him,
though he may be one of the most insignificant students.
Our leaders along the paths of good have said:
If one is to help both a friend and an enemy,
then one is required to help the enemy first
in order to subdue and to tame passions.

Anyone who wishes to be a human being
should work toward perfecting his character
& acquiring knowledge, he should not occupy his mind
with stupidities.

Remember, the necessary things are few in number.
while the superfluous things are unlimited.

                ★

Thoughtfulness outlives each & all.

Allison Creighton
*Shemirah

After your body had been through
the ritual washing—
gently cleansed
and dressed in white shrouds,
the watcher took his place beside you.

Did he see your life in a flash
and then more slowly,
the letters that fell
from between thin yellow pages,
weightless
as your footsteps
light in love?

Did he hear your begging
questions, your final wishes,
echoes of your dying breath?

Did he comfort your soul
with psalms
by candlelight
until sunrise seeped in
through veiled windows?

Did he bow his head
in a silent prayer of his own,
before departing

into dazzling sunlight—

*The title refers to a practice, known as Shemirah, that is part of traditional Jewish death ritual in which the body is "guarded" or "watched" from the time of death until burial.

The Field Goddess

This evening the sun dangles low.
She wants it to set on her shoulders.

She is dying to grow old.
Each morning she rises
with the sun in her field
and dreams of death
dressed in green.

She imagines the ground
opening,
her body falling
deep into the earth,
falling hard against other bodies.
The dirt coming down on her.

Time passing.
Her body's slow decay.
Green shoots sprouting.
The blossoming.

She dreams of bearing fruit.

Wedding Dance

The stars had stolen my breath that night
and I wondered what it feels like to return again to dust.
To become a single light in an endless span of stars.
I imagined rising far above my body, straight out of my satin shoes.
I saw us dance through many seasons in the center of the garden.
The frail evening shadows. How thin our skin was.
Its frightened translucence. I heard our hearts pumping,
saw the blood coursing through our veins, the garden spinning
like a carousel before the eyes of the child I once was,
pole after pole wrapped in a spiral of vines. Your face
in the paper lantern light. My pale dress swaying.

Its constellation of creases. Below the hem of small red roses,
I saw a single satin slipper, and it was then I knew—
my own dark shadow traveling the universe
with one fragile shoe.

Drawing Down the Moon

At dusk I stare through my kitchen window.
The sky is still touched with blue.
I see the moon's broad face.
A somber mouth and deep-set eyes.

The moon watches me too.
It tries to lean closer,
so tired of the unrelenting distance.
I slowly dim the kitchen light,
make my way to bed.

The moon now stares
through my open bedroom window.
I slip into my nightshirt.
The moon sees me blush.
I lift a book from the shelf,
lean back on pillows piled high.

I read to the moon.

Its gentle force tugs at the letters on the page.
The words begin to rise.
They swirl into sentences
flowing out the window.
Countless stories
weave constellations
through the evening sky.

The moon swallows every word—
becomes a perfect circle.

I dream of the smallest moon falling into my hands.

Donald Finkel
Parable

Up in the apple tree, the woman reaches for the boulder.
She can barely brush the surface with her fingers.
You'd think she was stroking the stone this evening.
As a matter of fact she's steadying it for the man
who lifts it to her.
                Feet planted in the earth,
he takes the weight evenly on wrists and shoulders.
Long wedded to the stone, his fingers have penetrated
the stone like petrified roots. Perhaps the strain
is beginning to tell. He's only human.
                     Now out
on a limb, belly down in the failing light, she's reading
the stone with her fingers. The tree is whispering
to her of mysterious needs, of deep green ardor,
renewal and loss. The message of the stone, however,
is simple and insistent. The man can hear it singing
in every tendon.
                They've juggled the stone between them
one more day. His fingers have sunk a hairsbreadth
deeper into the stone, hers softly stroke its brow.
The sun sets, the birds go silent.
                   And now the night.

The Invention of Meaning

In the beginning was the hand
and the poem of the hand,
a breathless trope, a floating hieroglyph,
seamless as water.

Then the hand spoke, and the hand said
"Let there be meaning," and the meaning sang:
"Let there be love," and the hand
shaped itself another hand of clay.

Now, where there had been
but one meaning, there were two.
So the hands wrestled all night
till they saw it was pointless.

So together they shaped themselves
a cunning tongue, to arbitrate.
Now, where there had been two meanings,
there were three.

And the hands wrung one another,
abashed, and the tongue took over.

Lot's Wife

Rabid as his uncle he was,
with his covenants and his
revolting rites, cringing before those
wretched Sodomites, whining,
"Take my daughters, heart-breakers,
chaste as the day they were born.
Do what you must, friends—
only spare my angels!"

There, by the gates of Zoar,
she turned away from him at last,
from that fixed grin of obeisance,
yearning over her shoulder
that wrenching homeward gaze
the Greeks call *nostalgia*,
as if home were still there,
waiting back on the plain—

the girls intact, and the man
she remembered marrying,
arms outspread for her,
framed in the igneous glare,
the purgative rain.

The Last of Her Friends

There wasn't a crevice in her flesh pain did not dwell.
There were nights it huddled in one misshapen toe
and sang till she thought its tiny heart would break.
The two were never apart in their snug asylum,
fast companions, sharing the selfsame thought,
one nestled inside the other like Russian dolls—
not so plump, of course, nor apple-cheeked,
but lank and haggard.
                              And while the old woman
shrank from the world outside like a withered leaf,
the last of her friends took root and ramified—
her ungrudging, steadfast, staunch, familiar pain.

Jacob and the Stranger

Wrestled a stranger all night to a draw,
they say. Over what, they do not. Amen,
no two ways about it: this slyboots, this mama's boy,
this agile fantast wrestled a putative angel
from sundown to sun-up.
                              And when, at long last,
the stranger changed tack and tweaked his rival
in that occult place in the hollow of his thigh,
Jacob lost the leg-lock. Though he still had hands
(one of them cunning enough the day he was born
to keep its grip on his brother's hairy shank
as they wriggled into the light).
                              Yet finally,
despite Jacob's notorious lust for benediction,
despite the stranger's clever moves, the deadlock
broke at break of day. And, as the sun
lifted his molten brow to watch our hero
limp off after his wives, his women-servants,
his herds, his flocks, and his eleven presumptive
sons, escaping with his skin (though under
a pseudonym),

presumably, the inscrutable
stranger vanished, leaving Slyboots to tell the tale.

Babel

One of that pack of deputies last week,
breathless from the climb,
wheezed at me, "Now, that's more like it!"
Like what? I'd like to know.

Up here, some words have lost their virtue.
Higher, for instance, and *farther*, *nearer*,
there. We need new words,
but all they send us now are bricks and slime.

Nothing changes, here in the stratosphere.
We breathe today what we exhaled yesterday.
Good thing—the staler it grows,
the fainter it gets.

At night, giddy, splayed on the scaffolding,
one word begins to sound like any other.

Merle Fischolowitz
Soup

When my wife makes soup,
to warm her lost child years,
she cuts potatoes and carrots,
adds a great big bone,
brings them to a boil,
not in the heavy black iron pot
her grandmother used
in the Hungarian village,
but in the huge steel clad one
her mother gave her thirty years ago.

She stirs in caraway seed, the flavor
of Budapest childhood winters,
adds more potatoes,
as many as a week's ration
at Bergen-Belsen;
a handful of pasta,
curved and stout as the women
whose pictures fill the photo albums
rescued from beneath the floor
of the bombed out home.

She made enough for the two of us tonight,
for leftovers too,
so we'll never be starved for memories.

Jeff Friedman
The Lives of Isaac

I was born a Jew
who could sell a riddle
to the sphinx. In my mouth
nouns married adjectives
and entered the world
as a sales pitch—
a quick hard sell,
offer driven,
Big Value for a Buck.
I had fleshy features,
small sturdy hands
and sawed-off white teeth
that could tear small
pieces of meat easily.
I carried no insurance
and died eating.
Then I was born a dog
who lived off scraps
and sniffed the messages
the wind delivered.
Each time I stole
from my master
my tail betrayed me.
When the herds dwindled to wind
and the tents collapsed
like a city of matchsticks
I ran with jackals
warning off intruders
with low deep growls
as we ripped apart carrion
and snapped flies
from the dust-laden air.
Before I was 20,
my heart gave out.
Then I was born a laugh
and came out of a parched orifice.

I died in mid–air.
And I was born a mixed blessing.
My sighs grew persistent
over the years
like a cramp in the intestines.
My face grew pinched,
my mouth distended
around an endless vowel.
I passed away in sleep.
Then I was born 2 dice
rolling across pavement.
I came out snake eyes.
I came out a bad decision.
I was born an invisible bird
that nested in the chest
of a prophet
and flew out of his mouth
in guttural ejaculations,
aiming for the eyes of his enemies.
I broke down into molecules,
into atoms, into electrons
spinning out of control,
shot down a racetrack—
broke down into quarks.
And then I was born a desert,
a promise never fulfilled.
My tongue thickened.
My mother sacrificed herself
again and again
while the soup boiled.
My father laid me out
on a table, brandishing his blade.
He lifted the knife
above his head and I
could see the sincerity
in his dark brown eyes.
And so I lived on
as words live,
blocks of print

on parchment.
My mother conceived me
well into her 90s
and on the night of my birth
the star of my kingdom
lit up the heavens.
With each telling
I grow stronger.

Taking Down the Angel

As he ticked off numbers—
how many sheep
I'd pilfered from Laban
and their rate of reproduction—
he opened and closed
his fists, cracked
his knobby rough-
skinned knuckles.

An angel on the take, I thought,
and he stinks like a goat.
While my white wooly profits
bleated their blessings,
I rose from my perch,
took him down
so hard the breath
went out of him.

He touched the hollow
of my joint and threw
my hip out of whack,
but I put him in
a choke hold he never
escaped from, buried his
crumpled carcass in the hard
white sand.

Memorial

It's nice to remember the houses
floating on water. It's nice
to stand on shore and sing
a hymn of praise
while candles burn
in the windows.
It's nice to dream the loaves
rising in ovens
and the floors dusted with flour,
the women with beautiful
hair falling like cities
into darkness, the long
nights of love. It's nice to
pretend we could have saved them.
It's nice to say a few
words as spring turns to fall,
as fall turns to winter, and winter to spring.
It's nice to return again
and stare at the stars
so bright and forgettable.
It's nice to remember laughter
spilling into the wind,
roses sprouting from their fleshy mouths
as children fall down
and down into the dirt.
It's nice to remember the voices
calling for you, calling
back the curtains, calling
through the long sleeves, the hollow places.
It's nice to remember the feast
of speckled blackbirds
huddled on the rims
of roofs, the stars
drawn in ash on the doorways,
the lament of uncles—
the long dance that kicked
up the dust and crinkled leaves,

the bodies waiting to burn,
the ash drifting on water.

Two Salesmen
   (Sunday Night, Fall 1961)

"Work hard," my uncle Harold says
"and you'll get somewhere, boy"
and my father nods his head
of black curly hair.
With drinks cradled in their hands
they sit side by side
on two throne-shaped swivel
chairs, staring at the small black
screen set in the tan console,
carved wood doors
pinned back against blond wood.

Harold sips the scotch
slowly, but my father drinks it down
then rattles the ice in his glass.
I sit on the carpet in front of them
playing solitaire Vegas-style
while they repeat the same stories,
how Galvani made a fortune
in Houston, how Klein's went
under because of bad management,
how Challoff declared bankruptcy
but not before he put away
"a pretty penny" for himself.

"I lost a 25,000-piece order,"
my father says, "because Henry
couldn't ship it on time."
"That's crazy." Harold's clipped
thick mustache tickles his
long hawkish nose
whenever he smiles or laughs.

He can make a quarter disappear
from his hands and pull it out
from behind my ear. He can shuffle
a deck in one hand
and turn over an ace of spades
anytime he wants to. I tell him
I've gone out twice in a row.
"Amazing," he says,
but my father looks down at me
with his sad tired eyes.
"Quit cheating—play it right."

Outside the wind tears at the trees
and fading red and gold,
the leaves tumble in a shower of leaves
and one more fall passes.
The wasps curl in their white
paper house shaped
like a large beautiful shell.

And the cedar bushes bunch
together like broccoli. In fall
my father died in a car accident
practically penniless
and my uncle went to sleep
forever in a hotel room
hundreds of miles from home,
staring at a picture of the sea
and three white gulls frozen on the shore.

"Work hard," Harold says
and my father nods his assent
cracking the ice between his teeth
while I cheat at solitaire
pulling a card from the bottom
of the deck when I need it
to keep my run going.
The swivel chairs squeak
and groan as my father and uncle

lean together and whisper
their plans to make it big.
Then they toast each other and touch
the empty glasses to their lips.

My Father Out of the Wind

My father comes to me as a little
bit of dust swirling in the wind.
He no longer slumps when he walks
or scrapes his heels on the pavement
as he lugs his two beaten canvas grips.
He is no longer anxious
and tired, stretching his hairy arms toward
the ceiling and crumpling into a
loud slumber in his chair. He has
survived yet another Egypt
and a thousand Pharaohs. He comes
to me as a little bit of dust
that flares in the wind like a swarm of locusts.
I see his bearded face, born in the
time of Isaac, streaked with tears.
He has survived the gnashing of teeth,
the punishing blows, the hammering hoofs
that pound the desert floor,
the violent diasporas. I hear him
rising with the ferocity of a hyena,
a gleam of light in its yellow eyes
as it crunches the neck bones of its prey.
He swirls in the air above the yellow
wildflowers in the shadow of the mountain—
a little bit of dust, some words
to the wise, an exhortation
to the wicked, a new covenant,
and his legend grows mighty on the tongues of strangers.

In the Kingdom of My Palm

From far away
my mother calls out to me,
a thread of voice
that floats through air,

words breathed
into the darkness.
Near death
she sits in a room

with all her things
and calls out to me
with her hands curled
like irises,

with the pain spreading
along the ridges of her shoulders,
with the soft touch
of her tongue on her lips.

She wants me
to come back to her
before she closes her eyes,
before she lies down

and gives up her body
to dust and ash.
She calls out to me
from the blue blush of light,

from the swirl of molecules
colliding in the kingdom
of my palm, from the roads
that rip through me.

I am the son
who kicked his feet

and splashed in the dark waters
of her womb, and made her cry.

I am the son she set into motion
like a small planet orbiting around her,
the son she taught
to lift a spoon and eat.

Now a wind enters her room.
The metal chimes jangle.
The gold swans
reach toward the flames.

I sit with her one last time,
close her eyes
with my fingertips,
and call her "mother."

Rabbi James Stone Goodman
Learning With Rashi
*Rashi, Bible scholar, poet, (1040–1105 CE),
lived in Troyes, France*

I was visiting with Rashi the poet
on a hillside in eastern France,
it was winter. Snow on the ground.
We were sitting on bales in a circle
as the sun began to make its way home in the west.
Rashi lit some candles. He also gave us grapes about then,
they were translucent dark, blue–black,
almost lapis,
I had never seen such grapes.
During our discussion, Rashi's daughter,
I think her name was Miriam,
was speaking in quiet tones from behind a screen
to her father.
"My daughter reminds me,"
Rashi used a word in medieval French for reminds,
"that the first light, created day one,
the light that sustains—
is hidden away for the future."
The candles had burned all the way down,
there were none left.
Rashi asked me to collect some icicles
from across the field.
I brought back four or five icicles,
Rashi put them in the candle holders,
lit them, and we continued learning.
As he spoke, he gathered light with his hands,
like he was moving air around above the flames,
as if he was gathering light into his arms.

I Keep Three Weeks

There is a hilltop in Jerusalem
Where heaven and earth touch

After the destruction the bride began to weep
The ground wept too
The bride returned
As a bird
Perched at the wall

For three weeks in summer
I sat low in sadness
I planned to bleed
To wash myself clean

This I have been taught:
After a river of tears
Expect the messiah

The Divine Coupling on the Feast of Weeks

The night before the wedding
all the companions adorned the bride
all of them necessarily present.
She had been preparing these seven weeks
to meet her lover.
The repairs would be made later.

Day of the wedding, the supernal mother descended.
All the souls would be expressly named by God,
blessed, the interpretations would all seem new.
The principles and the stories united in one
seamless document, integrated.
All of this would be told
through the radiating light.
The telling would be a lightning
of words.

Prayer #13
On a Yahrzeit

We measure our grief in years:
one year, two years, twenty.
I soften to my sadness daily, in a year of days
I remember I don't remember every minute.
I want the seconds back,
I am making a coat of my memories.
These are the chapters of my life, I remember
and cry for all that I love the most.

O God, master of all the worlds,
do not save me from my tears.
Let them pour forth
like a fountain.

Let my tears wash me clean:
salt, heart, blood, bones, hands.

Prayer #17
On the New Moon

Master of Mirrors,
let me see with the unclear mirror, the dark images,
the images that are only discerned at night,
by moonlight.

God of the light and the dark,
release me from distractions,
bind me with invisible fibers of connection
to the deep story, the right words, not the simple words,
not the easy ones not even the sweet words,
I want the true ones.

God of the right and wrong,
don't sweet talk me, draw me into the deep.
Carry me not in your pocket but sling me like a satchel

over your shoulder.
Let the truth plump like the moon,
the dark moon, the dark candle,
the candle at the hearth with all its shadows,

it's the moon, it's the moon, the dark candle,
the reflected dark dark dark—
light.

The Prince and The Rooster

Remembering Rebbe Nachman, 1772–1810,
the Chassidic story master

I ran into Jimmy in Detroit.
There was a wildness in Jimmy's coal-black eyes,
from within a dark thatch of Rebbe Nachman beard
that had overgrown his face.
"Hey Jimmy, you're Rebbe Nachman," I said,
he had no idea what I was talking about but he smiled
and instructed me to take off my shoes daily
and walk through the grass,
which confirmed to me
what I had seen in his face.

Jimmy then told me that not too long ago
he had lost his mind
and thought he was a rooster.
"Where was this?" I interrupted,
"California. I took off all my clothes," Jimmy said, "lived under a table,
wouldn't eat anything but grain and chicken food.
All the best physicians tried to help me,
Even Dr. Rabbits prescribed the strong medicine.
Then Prince the guitar player came,
took off all his clothes,
got under the table and began to act
like a rooster too.
I said to Prince, 'what are you doing?'
'I'm Prince, the rooster, I promise I will never leave you.'

We swore friendship to each other,
and slowly slowly, Prince began the healing.
He put on a shirt, I put on a shirt.
I said to Prince, 'do you really want to be a human being?'
You know what Prince said to me?"

"I think so, but tell me anyway."

"Prince said just because you dress like a human being
doesn't mean you have to cease being a rooster.
The next day we ate at the lunch counter in the bowling alley.
Prince ordered a tuna sandwich.
'You gonna eat like a person too?' I asked Prince.
'You can eat like a human being and still be a rooster,' Prince told me.
'You can do anything and still be the rooster you are.'"

"That's how it worked for me,"
Jimmy said, "Prince saved me slowly slowly.
He taught me I can do anything and still
remain the rooster
that I am."

Maurice L. Hirsch, Jr.
Escape Hatch

I'm not sure what frightens you.
I only write about my life
And this cancer,
Which for me is neither morbid
Nor depressing.
It helps me get on,
Enjoy each instant.

I spend my days in peace
With horses and dogs,
Clean stalls,
Work outside, in,
For community, home.
There's lunch with my children.
Dinner with my wife,
Playtime with my grandchildren.
I sit silent in the woods
On the back of a horse,
Watch pastures green up,
New plants push
Through winter soil.

Writing shows me
Who I am, where I am,
Where I was, where I am going.
If anything, I am saner
Now than ever, enjoying
The whole timeline of my life.

Jane Ellen Ibur
Mrs. Abraham

Neither consulted nor considered, obligation
bound me to obey, observe, believe blindly
subdued while you steered our brightest boy
up the slope. Our shining son—our—yet
did you abide barren ninety years, the prayer
of birth buried, boiling in your bosom?
Did your belly blossom? Did your breast beat
for both, a being buoy in your sacred seed
to surface at the source? Now the blood
that once bathed my hands will blacken
yours. Now your tongue will burn like ash,
your breath wither. The sky brightens
as I bolt bearing my tiny bundle of belongings,
my love bludgeoned. I am adrift bereft
as Hagar, Noah, Cain, the yoke of shame
bowing my shoulders. My head bends
forever and I dwell in the valley
of the shadow of death, believing evil.

Mrs. Stand-In
for Betsy

Not sorry I loved her, a servant
Seduced by sisterhood, stabbed
In my stomach when she swelled,
My usefulness spent. How do I say
Sibling to Ishmael? How do I spell
A life stolen?

I swallowed his seed, squatted
Out a son, and now am spat out,
A peach pit, scratching subsistence
Like some desert squirrel, slipping away
Skinned, despised, left with nothing,
Not even pleasure.

Shooting Stars
for my brother, John

Steamy summer days
wetness hangs in the air.
Still only June and John
swims like crazy reaching
for the stars with every stroke.
Slow down, I tell him.
You'll get there soon
enough. I tread water,
not even tired yet.
Sometimes I float on
my back staring at the night
sky and for the first time
in my life I hate the stars
because I know the next
shooting one will be John.

Mom and Frank

At least this one made sense.
He had her on a string
sitting on a rainbow
with that string around her finger,
but, finally, she was the gal
that got away. I see his face
in the picture; fedora cocked back
on his head, crooning, sweeping
her, and all the rest, even me, off
our feet, mine grounded, opposed
to Mom's whose were horizontal
that one time with him. He came
to her that very good year, either
before Dad or during, unbeckoned,
out of the old blue. Frank took Mom
to the Summit, the tables empty,
the dance floor deserted, the same love
song, the 10th time she'd heard it.

Andrea Jackson
The Danger of Journaling

Perhaps you think you can hide the diary under your skirt
the way your mother smuggled arms to Palestine,
concealing your thunderous thoughts
in the soft folds of domesticity
as the fiery gasses of space configure themselves,
for us, in homespun, earth-bound zodiac shapes:
a fish, a virgin, a water-pourer, a goat.
Do you not know what happens
when a person harbors explosives?

She acted not from any clear conviction
but because she'd been asked and was ashamed to flinch
and because she was young and immortal, and already there,
on board, en route to rejoin the Zionist boyfriend—
an escapade unreal even to her,
though it had cost her six months' salary.
She could enjoy the bluff
only so long as she didn't believe in the danger.

Finally the swallowed resentments, the silent criticism,
erupted into a quarrel that ended it all.
Back in America, she married the other guy,
and in spite of all her conniving, her life settled back
to the begetting of you, which seems, in your hindsight at least,
to have been its major purpose from the beginning.

However you might try, you can never know
whether the ammunition will explode
just as you reach the bottom rung of the ladder
as you disembark from the cargo ship at Haifa.

Lynn Levin
Sundry Blessings

On awaiting an important phone call, an invitation, or other good news

Blessed are You, O Lord, who allows me to live in the brief world of
   the possible.

★ ★ ★

On seeing a person who has one foot on the ground and is trying to
   put the other down

Blessed are You, O Lord, who causes the earth to fall away from a man's
   step.

★ ★ ★

On having someone see in your work something deeper than what you
   intended

Blessed are You, O Lord, who has not made me my only interpreter.

★ ★ ★

On being rejected by a school, an employer, or by voters

Blessed are You, O Lord, who has not required me to change my life.

★ ★ ★

On hearing of a massacre, a comet strike, or a family burned in a house
   fire

Blessed are You, O Lord, who has created forces beyond Your control.

★ ★ ★

On standing before a tree that bends with fruit

Blessed are You, O Lord, who causes happiness to weigh heavily upon
    me.

★ ★ ★

On seeing a fledgling drop from a crow's mouth

Blessed are You, O Lord, who surprises from a great height.

★ ★ ★

On being unable to sleep

Blessed are You, O Lord, who gives the night legs.

★ ★ ★

On arising

Blessed are You, O Lord, who has given me another opportunity to
    show courage.

★ ★ ★

On not being recognized

Blessed are You, O Lord, who has given me another face.

Edward Londe

The Magic of Colors

Indigo and Orange, and perhaps a dash of yellow
    Now cocoa, peach and purple
Magenta, cobalt, mahogany and umber
    Velvet, silk, lace, and cashmere
Hold the cashmere to your cheek and
    your infant's new born skin pressed
to your lips, in a loving kiss, only a mother & father
    can bestow in a paternal embrace
Remembered for a life time, deep in the recesses
    of our souls, until the day we breathe our last
Tasted all, seen it all, breathed it all in just
    one large inhalation and exhalation
Lasting, deeply secured in our immortal souls
    God loves colors and created all these hues
Mimicked in the Garden of Eden, locked in

The Way of Angels

They dwell in a sphere of light and harmony
    and there is a calmness, as of a sea at rest
There all is a balance of truth and spirit
    Welcomed here, are all who have loved and given charity
in their lives, and revere justice and truth
    Handmaidens to God are they, and never falter in their Holy quest.
So may it ever be, for you and me

The Beach

The waves break upon the sandy beach,
    Erode, and nibble away, each yard by
yard, it's length and breadth,
    As the years have assailed our skin and bones,
We are no longer young, but the mind my friend,

the mind, that fortress on the bluff beyond the beach,
Unscathed by all assaults below, still flourishes in a
    mellow afterglow, as that primordial light, never extinguished
will shine, as yet another star, in the vast heaven, which
    is eternal home to all souls, who perish here below.

An Invitation

I dream of an invitation to a most Holy place.
    It is the Heavenly Tabernacle where He holds court
When young I was not worthy, not clean mentally,
    now cleansed by the fire of life's trials,
Stand ready, to enter those Heavenly Portal,
    Just for a visit Pray you, for prefer not to stay
forever, mind you, long enough to become One
    with the minion gathered there and hear the
Chorus of those angelic voices echo throughout the Heavens.
    So Aaron help me don the breast plate, the tallith, and
usher me into His court, I will not be afraid. as I stand
    and bow before my Father, as a tear falls from my face.
I am home.

Adam

And Adam whispered, from Earth I have come,
    to Earth I will return
Thus was sealed the fate of one and all.
    Not too bad, considering the gift of life
from Sunrise to Sunset, we enjoy each breath,
    inhaling the sweet fragrance of Eden
the love by your side, on cold dark nights, and
    a child whispering, soft and low, daddy, daddy,
I love you so.
    Now the child grown, full of years, remembers the
embrace, of his mother and father, and a tear of
    joy, falls silently into a sea of memories of a time
so long ago. and gently we go into the book of ages,

Whose author, we no longer remember but still revere.
Oh so many Kaddishes to recite, in memory of so
   long ago. and the memories like a once beautiful rose
now withered falls, and scarcely is heard the echo,
   As another life begins.

My World

My world stretches from here to there,
   it is in and out, and all about
Burning sunsets, and dusty trails, by bubbling streams,
   leaping salmons, fighting upstream, to spawn,
Feasting bears, and eagles, descend upon their quarry,
   I turn from the TV in horror, at a another car bomb explodes,
My pain intense, from present and past wounds to my body and soul
   Shrug them aside, these pains of mine, and turn to Chanel nine,
and Beethoven, Bach, Mozart, brings some sanity to it all.
   Not quiet ready to don, my pack, and start the trek, that will
forever erase the memory of this World.
   Have stories yet to tell, songs to sing, and love to give,
to those who love me and I them.
   So good and bad, I will embrace this only world I know,
until, the guards to Eden will beckon me to enter,
   His World, the most perfect world of all.

Jered Metz
Even a Vision

Even a dream likes to
dip its stiff finger in honey.

Even a prophesy
wants to clasp the girl splashing and singing in a brook.

Even memory loves
the fluttering of smoke.

Even a vision needs
a stick to lean on when

it climbs down through the sky.

Sabbath

The still parlor beckons the hours.
A sickle rusts in a corner propping a drowsy angel's arm.
Until something transpires the celebrants lounge on the
davenport, stand and sit again in turn. Suddenly, this
is the seventh of days, the hour of weaving and unraveling,
of lamplight swaying out of the lamp.

Over the ironwork   and over the nightwork
cranes fly and   light on chimney pots
and sing in the   language of
tongueless creatures   the song
the wind plays along   their wings,
this is the seventh   of days, moment of
tearing and making,   of a door closing to
one side and opening   on the other.

Divination

by
birds
bird flocks
oracular utterance Bible
ghosts crystal shadow
cloud forms birth
star meteor wind
fish animal and
human entrails mice
their bedding or feces or
edges of books they
have chewed grain
a rooster pecked
snakes herbs fountains
red-hot iron
pool stream wand
altar smoke fire
dough meal barley
salt lead dice
arrows hatchet
sieve ring suspension
random dots precious
and semi-precious
stones pebbles pebble
cairns mirrors ash
writing dreams palm
nail rays finger
rings numbers passages
from books names
lettering the manner
of laughing ventriloquism
circle walking wax
hidden springs wine
and shoulder blades.

Stolen Wood

Woodcutters kneel before a tree,
its branches filled with angels
whose gullets brim with fiery gold,
whose backs mirror the Forest in Paradise.
The angels warn:
"The bark of every tree hides a faces;
no man can profit from stolen wood."

II

A new stove that burns stolen wood
falls to pieces, each piece turning
to rust in even the driest air.

An old stove where a thief burns wood
will always be cold, no matter
how hot the fire.

IIII

Nor may a wood thief sit in a tree's shadow
nor may he pass on a public road
nor may you plant vegetables where
a wood thief has passed.

David Millman
Cossack Dance

1906.
Grandpa stands his ground.
Refusing to name names.
Solitary in confinement.
Refusing to answer questions. And (no evidence later)
for crimes against the czar—given three Arctic Circle years.

Three hundred now wait in Bootierska Prison's dark
great hall under one instruction—
silence or the dungeon.
Spotlights of thin windowed sun reach
to touch a hand
or cheek.
The train ready to travel its tracks toward
Siberia.
Legs waiting for leg cuffs.
The guards watching their guns.
The prisoners watching
the guards.

A hatless Cossack in boots and vest jumps
upon a table.
And begins to dance soundless.
Leaping to the ceiling, landing weightless on the tips
of his feet. Whirling, twirling,
tickling the dark.
Taking control of the air.   Master
of the dance of endurance.
Regaling guard and guarded with a spring of the cat unfettered,
a soar of the bird unbound, a beat
of the heart unconfined.

1976.
At the St. Louis Jewish Home for
the Aged,
Grandpa stands his ground.

Sometimes when
embedded linoleum floor-cracks
of hallway aged urine
defeat the smell of Clorox.
When Grandma dream whimpers
from her fetal position.
When the air is overstuffed
by people
shuffle-clutching metal walkers.
Grandpa leaps
silently onto the small table
in his room
and does a Cossack dance.

Scrubbing Floors

Down here
scouring pad in hand
erasing black scuff marks
from time's dragging heels.
My grandmother
spent too many mornings
walking the wood with
her knees. Waxing
perfection for company to see
and even not for company to see.
The order of cleansing out chaos
passes hands
from my mother
to my aunt
to the way my fingers carefully ascertain specks
not related to the tile pattern
to the way my daughter
now appraises and scolds
the smudges
of all the
floors in her life.

Unicycling the Universe

My father wheeled the world
on a one circled
embellishment of stories.
Riding past
tortuous days of
same old same old,
elaborating over
years and years of
flat planed highways,
finessing the trip worthwhile.
And whiling away,
he created a whole new
time and
space.

Niki Nymark
Lilith

Do you cringe when I howl and shriek,
when I snap my fingers at your domesticity,
or dare you to think
what it would be like
in the desert,
ultimate, arid, in-your-face, personal
responsibility?

My Father (or was it my Mother?)
said I was the first
of my kind—unique,
that I could do anything, be
not an angel, but a Being
with breath, life, a soul.

So I believed.
I studied, watched
how tenderly the grass
grows up in Spring,
pale and blushing green,
how the petals of the rose unfold
to show its hidden, central sex,
how the mare runs
in the field, stops
to nurse her foal, then
runs freely, fiercely.

I stood naked in the rain
with my face upturned,
eyes and mouth   open
wide to receive the blessing.
I shook my wet braids out
to shiver water over—
whats-his-name.
Oh, I'm getting to that.

My Mother (or was it my Father?)
told us both—yes,
I'm sure it was both,
"I have created you *Adom*, Woman
and Man as helpmates to one another."
But that Man, what a sulky child,
did not, would not,
belligerently could not play fair.
How self-important,
acting as if he were
the last Man on Earth instead of the first.
Setting such a bad example for Humanity.
So I left; moved out
on my own.

I hear he married again,
someone more suitable to be
The Mother of Mankind.
They tended the Garden for awhile,
then moved on to live an ordinary life;
children, grandchildren.

My life, on the other hand,
is chaotic.   I live in the desert,
clean and alone,
at night I prowl the dreams of Men,
rub their sex, whisper, "Catch me
if you can."
That I suck the breath from babes
is a lie, though sometimes I do
peek into the nursery
to kiss their lips, their fingers,
because I have no Other,
no children of my own.

I enjoy my solitude,
the desert, my nightly flights
into the dreams of Men,
my reputation, especially in these times.

Now, at least, Women understand me.
And I have never been sorry
that I left the Garden.

Tourist In Jerusalem

In the Old City
I seek
the Golden Cord
that binds us
to the World to Come,
connects us to the Rock of Torah
the altar of the Binding of Isaac,
the place where other prophets, some say,
stepped incarnate into Heaven.

I cannot walk
where they walked,
where the Holy of Holies stands
invisible, sealing this world
to the next.
This is forbidden to me
by culture,
and by my own eyes
not fine enough to see.
I can only wail at the Wall,
Leave a folded paper message
for a city of peace .

If this is the place
where we and G-d attach,
if this reflects the mercy of
the World to Come, surely
that Cord connects
each crying Sarah and Hagar.
Nothing has changed.

History is merciless.
Now, this is the place
where buildings fall,
busses explode, mothers
weep bloody tears
while I, a tourist,
sit in a fine hotel
with a TV and a pastel
sketch of the Old City on my wall,
with money and an
American passport in my purse
my belly filled with
beguiling hotel food,
my soul filled with sorrow,
knowing the Messiah
isn't coming this week,
again.

Jerry Perkoff
Family Tree
Rosh Hashonah 2002

I felt the sand and the
lightning and thunder,
Moses was there, and
Rachel and Leah,
their spirits swirled
with the rhythm
of those who
walked the desert
and read the tablets
and built the temple
that lives in the wall,
who lived in the Pale
and escaped the ovens
and stifling steerage,
and came in a line
that ran thru me
to this tall red-haired grandson
who stood by me and
closed his eyes and
moved his heart
in the ageless rhythm
of an unbroken stream,
and I knew
in that instant
I could answer
the eternal question,
"why?"

Lilian's Birthday
May 31, 2004

She is a
thin grey shadow now,
a moth flirting with fire,

moving in, moving out,
singed but not yet burned,
the knife-edges of her mind
nicked but still sharp
between the notches,
an ancient Yiddish song
quavering on her lips,
the reed-like tune
riding shoulders of time back
to a tiny kitchen
where the strudel dough
was so thin the
glistening northwest light
shone thru, ready for
raisins and nuts,
currency of a life paid out in
ninety-six installments,
the number of coupons
left in the book
hidden from view,
as it always
is.

Chanukah Lights

I dissolve in the
dusk-dark centers
of the yellow lights,
and flow downward to
the catacombs of childhood,
those clay-hewn berths
that hold all means of
self-deprecation and
pride

I search
the slotted shelves
for keys to

my inner cauldron, where
love and fear,
humility and ego,
create mortal
awareness.

Oh candles, signs
of introspection and
symbols of life,
burn bright or burn pale,
burn even with
the flickering of
near extinction,
but burn!

Vickie E. Pickle
My Mother's Pen

I cross my t's
and dot my i's
with my mother's pen.

Throughout the house
echoes of her.
Whole notes on playbills,
half notes on newspapers,
quarter notes on menus
with reminders:
Call the bakery,
send a baby gift.

Her address book
banded with rubber
for safe keeping,
an ensemble of friends
and family. Recipe cards
composed for holidays;
brisket, chicken soup—
"You need onion soup mix."

Her postcards chant the rhythm of camp.
Dear Mom,
         Having a wonderful time at Hawthorne.
Audrey Sue is my bunkmate. Last night
a snake crawled under the door! Don't worry,
the counselors rescued us. Please give my
love to Daddy, and give Michael and Allison
a kiss for me. Next week is our big dance
with the boys. Our counselors are teaching
us to foxtrot. I will write again soon.
                         Your loving daughter,
                           Suzanne

P.S. Send my gray skirt.

Her life, written in measures,
the scored directed. Grateful parents
sang her praises. Children and
grandchildren recite cards and letters,
the important words underlined.

And now, my mother passes her pen
like a conductor's wand
to this writer of stories,
moving these words and sentences,
the strength of her hand on mine.

Lady Liberty

Drawn to her majestic torch,
he follows her illustrious light.
For miles the flame mixes
with the sky. She continues pulling
him closer to freedom. Her safe harbor
protects him, her open shores
his refuge. His journey over her
open waters wash away all transgressions.
His identity lays in her hands. Unblinded,
he grasps for land. The island fortress
awaits his promise, engulfed by hot sand
and stone, her embrace strong, sustained.
In the background the flame signals sailors
to the new land. Waves of change
hit the shores with relentless power
and possession. He grabs for the milk
and honey in the faint glow of the flame.

Nancy Powers

Lost in the Woods

Poor Hansel and Gretel. Spellbound
between cruelty and desire
they can't stop themselves
from seeking the promise
of something better, sweeter
than everything they know.
Jealousy behind, who-knows-what
ahead; how do they find the way
through woods so dark,
so ravening with peril?

It is how one thing
leads to another thing,
how we never stop
clutching the string we're following,
stop ourselves
from stooping close to the ground,
desperate to spy the gleaming pebble
or next crumb of bread
before cruel birds swoop
to dine on our salvation,
our only hope to slip the grasp
of such elaborate danger.

No One's Daughter

In all my dreams you're young again,
sparkling in that way you had,
laughing with someone I don't know
at all. You don't notice me or else
we try to talk but something comes between us.
Sometimes I hear you calling
out the backdoor of my childhood,
still whistling me home before dark.

I want you to see me now,
see how I listened after all.
I was afraid I'd never forget
the sound of your labored breath,
how your lungs filled, drowning you.
I held your swollen hands, waiting,
longing for that familiar banter, your lively eyes
flashing mother-code, tangible signals
I'd learned to read like Braille. Suddenly

you woke, looked straight through me.
I'm trying to get across, you said,
but I can't find the way.

How He Dried Himself

Some days she lets herself remember
the way he dried himself: his hair, face
and chest, then his arms and thighs.
He always flipped the towel behind his back,
let it slide from his thick shoulders
like a cashmere wrap.

He knew the exact distance
from the end of his thumb to the tip
of his little finger, used the span
to measure things: the height of a bed,
width of a door, a mirror's frame.
In his right eye a freckle floated,
a chip of mica sharp against a field of bronze.

She knew his voice the moment
he inhaled to speak, could tell
how drunk he was by the cadence.
She became skilled at assessing his moods.

When she catches sight of him now,
in the cereal aisle at the grocery store

or waiting in the post office,
it's like running into a boy she knew
in high school. She can't figure out
how she's supposed to feel
after all this time. She wonders
if he thinks of her at all.

Waking Early: The Lost-Wax Method

*A method of sculpting; molten metal is poured into a wax
mold, which is lost (melted away) during the process. The
resulting object is perfected by smoothing and polishing.*

Her eyelids are sun–reddened;
blindness of desire. She swallows,
listens to the sound. It's an echo
from somewhere muffled, secret.
He sleeps on, tranquil breathing
alternately heating then cooling
the pulse at the base of her throat.

He is heavy against her breast,
thigh lolling carelessly across her,
holding her still. A damp sheen
polishes her skin everywhere his skin
touches her skin. She imagines
she has been wrought
as from a lost–wax mold.

How does he know what to keep?
What to smooth away?
She is unsure what might be left
if she is fired to an even higher fervor.
All she is might melt away.

The Custom of Roses

You were there at my door
with roses. I already wanted you
to stay, watch them open
as I opened, surrendering
to such tender urgency.

Your body, thin, carved bone
pressed into my softest hollows,
your hands, dark against my pale skin—
fingers slender, hesitant—
slid over me, learning,
remembering. You whispered
I want to be inside you;
Now you are in ways I can't explain.

Once I fooled everyone,
looking happy
without knowing what happy should feel like.
I only imagined something better for me,
something that could hold me,
free me, burn into me
so the center would fuse.

Marilyn Probe

Letting Go Desire in the Month of Av

The Hebrew month of Av (or Menachem-Av, the consoler of Av) is the fifth of the   twelve months of the Jewish calendar. (July / August)   The name Av literally means "father." It derives from the root which means "to will" or "to desire."

After dovening to the moon at dawn, I strode
to the cabin cooking alcove, threads of silken web,
trailing me to the sink, as tenuous a cover
as a lover's wink, as if I were still entangled
in the aura I had lured from lunar orbit,

Where the orb of Av broke through
morning's charcoal dust, as I blessed
my daughters and son and released
the tendrils that entwined me that bend

but do no shatter, when only with binoculars,
I saw the crimson sequins on Mars as earth's star,
as clearly as dewdrops on a spider's maze.

Before the Exodus

Let go the grooves worn by your carved rocker of walnut,
a grounded color, where you cradled each child's dreams.
Separate from the skin of your beloved, breaking the blueprint
of rulers, and fly into tomorrow.

Watch swarms of butterflies mate on Valentine's Day,
flutter flushing your face, a healing tingle of Monarchs,
kingly in their name. Erase the need to solidify. Refresh
like thousands of the order of Lepidoptera, breaching
their chrysalis wombs. The males, only a few days to float
before they're spent.

Thrown off by climatic changes, loosen commitments that bind,
The pride of finishing what you've begun to slide into

declining decades, letting go of the brain to feel butterflies
in your marrow.

Be the one who kneels into earth, awash with bulbs and worms
and peat moss, moist to sense the place you will return. Inhale
the hyacinth's presence. Caress Shasta daisies, lemon balm
and tarragon and know it will be safe to be among the tang
of licorice and lemon.

Miriam Raskin
Maker of Peace

A lifetime ago, in that far-off place
where gossamer dreams turned to solid ash
my mother and I were children together

and we played and sang and made Shabbat
with that adorable grandfather of hers,
soaking in the words he chanted

and the tune of the *Oseh Shalom Bimramov*
that he sang, wine glass raised
to the heavens, humbly asking for peace

from the One on High Who Wasn't Listening
so that what happened happened and
no Maker of Peace came along to save the day.

But as luck would have it, and we had it,
we grew old, and now, sometimes confused,
she calls me mom when she needs something

and if that fails to bring her what she wants,
she cries out Mutter, Mutter, Mutter,
for the other mother, the one they killed,

the one she never wept for, until now,
and then I hum to her that ancient song
whose lilting words, unwitting threnody,

even our enfeebled synapses can recall
so that the long-gone Opa Karl still
makes her smile and sing along in peace.

Oseh shalom bimramov...........

Ann Lesley Rosen
A Brother's Kiss

And Esau fell upon Jacob's neck,
a neck suddenly ivory against
Esau's grinding canines. Bone
flaking bone in an awful kiss,
the divided twins wolf and ram,
howling pain, terror, years no damper
for stolen blessings. And their howls rise,
filling the land, families divided
by unshared destiny.

Reuben Returns to the Pit

The pit is still, dark,
he creeps to its sandy edge,
his brother's cries echoing,
condemning in his mind,
sun accusing at his back.

On his knees, he bows
into the pit, eyes shut
as ears strain for any
sound of life, a slight
rustle of breath, a dry
cough, sobs,
but only the scratch
of snake skin.

"Joseph!" His own voice
pushes him back, oldest son
too weak to save the youngest,
so afraid of his brothers
to suggest only the pit
instead of death, his own fear,
no, his own pride, too strong
to save the boy completely.

Tearing his clothes, he flings
himself to the pit, and his body
falls, turning through darkness
to the damp floor,
brother long gone,
and in the dark, he prays,
snakes coiling
around his ankles.

Numbers

"I was forced to memorize and recite . . ."—Michael Harper

1. Seven Days of Creation

From darkness and light
to the seventh day of rest,
I could never remember
if the sun, moon, and stars
or vegetation to cover the land
appeared on the fourth day.
And how strange
that animals to fill the sky—winged creatures
of every kind to traverse the heavens—
and animals to fill the sea—sea monsters,
great sea monsters!—
both emerged the same day.

2. Joseph's Eleven Brothers (and One Sister)

The same men who flung their brother
into a pit to die and sold him
to a desert caravan
slaughtered an entire city to defend
their sister's virtue.

3. Ten Plagues

I still don't know all ten,
translations different in every book,
though I recite them twice a year
spilling drops of wine to symbolize
sorrow I'm not sure I feel.

4. Ten Commandments

I never had a problem remembering
the order, until I learned Christians
counted them differently,
then I didn't know what to think.
I thought it was simple math.

5. Forty Years

I have lived only half
and cannot imagine wandering
for this long and more.
Even with a gray-bearded leader,
clouds of protection during the day,
pillars of fire at night,
what hope can I find
in a long-imagined land
just beyond that river
and so far out of reach?

First Burial

My friend had buried a dead bird
in her front yard. The two sticks
taped in a cross interrupted
the green lawn, but I was five—
my friend had it, so I wanted it.

I watched the birds on telephone wires
as we walked to school, black shadows
against blue sky, eyed brown sparrows
hopping in neighbors' lawns. Surely,
some would be dead by three o'clock.

At the arts and crafts table I made a case,
brown construction paper and tape,
imagined slipping the still bird inside,
feathers crackling against the paper,
the weight of no life, the cold.
I started making a cross with popsicle sticks,
my friend said I couldn't.

On the way home I spotted
a dark figure on the corner,
took out my case. I tiptoed,
but as I got close, it hopped
three times, took flight.
My friend laughed.

The next morning I approached her house,
saw the shallow grave empty,
an open mouth in the green,
and in the street the flattened cross,
dirt stuck in the transparent tape,
and feathers, black feathers,
like ash around the small body
smeared with mud.

Jane Schapiro
Habit of Discontent

I dreaded camp but backwards
day I enjoyed: kids running
around with pajamas, their shoes
on the opposite feet.

It seemed such a grand idea
yet I would always remain
intact, afraid to stray
from familiar terrain.

This fear is why
in the midst of good fortune
I continue to cling
to discontent. Once habits settle

they harden like asphalt, pave
the paths we've been treading on.
Brooders like me travel
best at night.

Our compasses fixed
on the nearest black hole, we follow
worries like bearings ahead.
Why try and change

the route, pretend
there's nothing to fear? At my age
it's safer to stay
on course, inside the shadow

of malaise. That way
when darkness lifts
we aren't blinded
by happiness.

Saturday

We can win this one, my daughter announces
while putting on her shin guards and cleats.
As we drive to yet another field our ritual begins.
Stay focused, I remind her. Find the open space.
Clean passes. Anticipate. Make every move count.
I finish my sermon, then pause, as we each imagine
our own perfect plays. On these roads, possibility
rises with each blind crest. I prefer these moments
before when faith and hope envelop us,
much as they do during the Days of Awe
when we beat our breast as the *shofar* sounds
and recite our sins, promising
no more gossip and lies,
next year we won't commit any fouls.
When the whistle blows, I rise from my chair,
join the chorus of parents.
Be aggressive. Fight for it.
Our raised fists pound the air.

Oklahoma Hero

Truth is
he didn't want to go back in
but *The Towering Inferno*
haunted him.
He was standing half-dazed
by the bombed-out ruin
when Richard Chamberlain
flashed through his mind.
Over and over
scenes replayed
until he told himself
I am not like him
and climbed five floors
to help save a man.

He hadn't known this Hollywood film
had been buried in him.
Preserved through the years,
it had smoldered like a forgotten scent.
Who can predict what will rise
from the rubble?

It was his wife who had chosen the video.
He remembers that Friday night.
Settling back with a can of beer,
he had looked forward to escape.

Black Hole

Eventually the universe must end.
With these words
the planetarium lights dimmed.
Too old to take my mother's hand
I stared at the dark.
Expand forever, contract and burst.
What's a billion years
give or take? To a girl of ten
the message was clear.
Who was this Prophet, this Cosmic
Oz whose voice kept circling
like a hawk?

I had always sensed
some other force
lurking outside
my bedroom door.
Supernova, white dwarf . . .
on he went, pausing
only to let cymbals crash.
When the last star blinked
off, my mother turned,
The world is still here, she whispered,
her words weightless.
Don't worry.

Steven Schreiner
An Unfinished Life

At five, I'm wearing a bow tie
and wristwatch, dressed with decorum
as a young man bearing
a sign of my future
politeness, my notable reputation
for being eager to please
and willing to suffer.
My mother seems to know
all, her hand on my father's
shoulder, giving him a slight push.

My father's wrists rest on my waist,
my brother stands beside him
proud to be the oldest,
as if he doesn't want to touch
the handle of the cane.
My sister on my mother's lap
completes the scene in patent leather
Buster Browns and a dress
like sea foam with lace frilling
the tops of her socks.
My beautiful mother smiles
desirably, a dim, hopeless gesture.

As we gaze into the past
at the last family photograph to arrive
from my mother's fading archive,
I insist to my wife that I know
the portent of the portrait.
She can see as well as I
the long lips I would inherit
sliding to one side, the semblance
of his wise smile, his justified
scorn, forced to fulfill
his fate. He's been given
the awareness of a man

never to see the children grown,
to know his wife will sleep and belong
in another husband's bed.

I say I can tell
why we've been assembled
as if to attend
a birthday party, as if to celebrate
an unfinished life. At forty-eight
my father looks eighty.
I say you can see the shadow
my eyes cast, still the same today;
you can see the displeasure
a premonition
of foreclosure brings;
you can even see how I forbear
his leaving of which I have no
recollection. I'm taking note
of love's presumption
to remain with us
in our weakness.

Backrub

I've just come from a place
where the shadows are inappropriate
for the middle of the day. My stepfather's bedroom
has its shades pulled, air conditioner on
and king-sized bed made except for
his portion, where he has climbed in naked
after undressing in silence,
unseen, laying his barreled chest and massive arms
against the chilled sheets, his slender
legs trailing down almost invisible
like a fold in a curtain. Soon he will begin
to snore, dreaming as a shark dreams,
moving through dark water, swimming to stay
alive. He will sweeten the air around him

with breath that smells of bananas. But before
he falls asleep he will call out one of our names,
today mine, tomorrow my brother's. I go
because he is a shark and there's no escape.

When I reach his room atop the stairs
I enter softly and close the door,
the air cold as a path through snow,
and go around his bulk and lie beside him
hoping he is asleep. Then I ask
"Daddy, where does it hurt?"
and he tells me to rub his back
all around, shoulders and thick neck, lower
where the shrapnel entered
before I knew him and before he knew us,
lodged where the spine curves
like a tail between his legs. I make circles
on his back with my fist, folding the flesh
like a tailor's cloth; he tells me
use both hands and I work harder
till he calls out for punches and chops
and I am pounding away at him
because he doesn't budge or talk and still
he will not snore.

He lies there, like a god
I no longer believe in.
Beyond the shades
a day is wasting. When I try
once more to rise he stirs
and I know it is too soon to leave,
that I must go on running my fist
up and down his spine in a futile effort
to heal him.
                    Finally his snores begin, growing louder,
a sign that soon they will break on shore
and he will turn and go deeper, heading out
to the colder waters in his dream;
and I think of a day when I will be released,

though it means he is dying. His snores
catch like cloth torn in mourning
as I speak to be free.

Barren

I found the tick there
in the loose skin,
days after returning from the woods
of a state park in Missouri.
It was full summer, signs warned hikers
to stay away from the brush, to wear
pants tucked into socks, and to explore
the body you bathe when you return;
for even a speck of dirt
that you can't flick away
or even a freckle
can turn inward and grow.

Like the poppy-thin skin of man's cheek
whose old body has puckered,
like the milky pod
that dangles from a sapless limb,
like the fig tree Jesus withered,
like passion flower and breadfruit
but not a flower and not a fruit
my body was barren.

I thought a miracle might happen.

Sarah must wait forever, it seems,
and learning she will bear a son
laughs and barely escapes
more wrath. Rebecca's womb
is closed for a time
though in a world where time
stretched on and on
it seemed forever

she was denied children
as numerous as the sand
or the stars that cover heaven
or the dust that spreads across
the dry and barren land.
Like Jacob I labored
to make someone mine.
For a time we believed
God would grant us children
if only I forgave. But
unlike Jacob I was mistaken.
The stone upon the well
was very heavy, and
she who married me waited
while I moved it aside, but
the well was dry. Dear
tick, hanging black as a seed,
suck deep, drink, grow fat
from me, be a life
that I have fed, that found
its way to my body,
then fall, be fruitful, and multiply.

Orange Sweater

My mother knitted an orange sweater
for me when I was just a boy,
cables woven down the front
of the wiry mohair cardigan.
There was so much strength
in having gotten it to fit, in choosing orange
and being brave enough to wear it.
My mother was thankful
for her own victory, keeping us
safe until all her grief was gone.
Your life will last, she said
to me with the gift of this
sweater. She brought forth

a burning brand from her needles
clicking away her tears
which could never drown the fire
taking shape on her lap. When
Mother later cried through the nights
paying penance for the crime
that would go unpunished,
I was so skinny, my sweater
gave me strength to bear
the cold dust, the trembling fist,
my mother's wounds, but I could not
bear to outgrow the fond love
that was kindled in her gift.

And then he was gone.
His death seemed mingled
with my unweeping mother, with heaven
for taking its mistake away,
but the pain grew more fierce,
the mourning unceasing, white ashes
settling upon orange embers
as a fire cools still glowing.

Desolated

It's possible to live on the surface
of life, as on a pond,
the way De Niro does as Travis Bickle
in *Taxi Driver*. Alone in his room
he takes notes, keeps a journal
on all that he abjures.
as if the war we never see him fight
outfits him to stay awake
and keeping distances, between himself
and the next likely victim. One snowy night
the weather made us close, as in a carriage,
and next day, bundled into sausages,
we crunched through high, new snow

into the destined park.
A few giddy drivers
rewarded themselves
for buying jeeps and trucks.
The woods were quiet, but the wind burned.
We were indivisible in our task
to climb a small hill.
Alike on the landscape though apart
we let the breath out of the snow
with each heave
as we fell step by step
through the crust that had formed
in the hour of the ice.
The muscles of your thighs were tired,
your ankles warm with pain;
there were your dark enormous eyes,
the same untiring face
that never expressed resolve or dismay
as though you'd absorbed blows
and shuddered surprise
into stillness like a fighter
learning where the pain came from
and how to avoid it.
When we crouched down
at a windbreak, between
the frozen stems of tow-headed reeds
bent over by the ice,
I wished, simply, that we had
kissed. But I did not kiss you
and you did not kiss me.
What good, then, was that storm
for all its change?

Joan Schultz
Invitation
Modigliani 1917 *Nu Au Coussin Blanc*

Come touch my skin that is the white
of throbbing suns in quivering light
glistening with warmth and wet with life
watching in the honeysuckled night

Serenely content, curved on my bed
pillows like clouds encircle my head
my body caresses the blood red spread
staring in space, I delight and invite

Longing and lusting with passive desire
listening in silence in smoldering fire
patiently waiting for the weight of you
gazing, wondering and wanting you

Past Remembering
Modigliani 1918 *Femme a la Robe Noire*

Wearing the melancholic cloth
of the mourning of the dark
choked by a collaring of white
that never fades in deepening night
thick with dank airless voids
crushing sound and searing sight
preparing for the final loss of light
lost to the sacred future
blocked by the gargoyled past
passivity binds and surrounds me
weighted weariness drowns me
sealing my soul in brown and black
that soon will swallow reality
and I will be past remembering

Henry Schvey
I Dreamt I Was a Jew in Prague

I dreamt I was a Jew in Prague
Searching for Franz Kafka.
I hunted him through winding streets
Leading all the way up to Hradcany Castle;
I looked for him in the Jewish Cemetery,
Picking my way among crooked stones;
I even tried to see him at the
Arbeiter-Unfall-Versicherungs-Anstalt,
The Insurance Company
Where he designed the handbook
"Accident Prevention Regulations in the Use of Wood-Planning
     Machines,"
But had no luck.
Then, when I thought my search in vain,
I saw him vanish
Round the corner
From my hotel.
His gray suit hanging from his bony shoulders,
His felt hat was
Pulled down
To avoid detection.
He muttered something,
Winked,
And disappeared into the fog.

Next morning I awoke,
Packed up my things,
And returned home.
My first night back in the States
The dream returned.
Only now
I searched for Kafka
At Wal-Mart,
Walgreen's,
And the Galleria.
He was not at any of those places.

I announced I was quitting my job:
>My fiancé left me,
>My family stopped seeing me,
>My friends told me I badly needed to see a shrink.

The next morning
There he was
At my writing table.
"You see," he said in perfect English, "it wasn't so hard after all."
"What wasn't so hard?" I said.
"Finding me," Kafka said, smiling.
"I knew you would."
"What are you talking about?" I said, "I'm only dreaming this."
Then he picked up a pen that was lying on my desk,
Not the Mont Blanc,
But an old Bic with the end chewed off,
and gave it to me to eat.
I swallowed hard.
He disappeared after that.
Next morning,
I awoke,
Rested,
Refreshed,
The happiest
I have felt in years.

Howard Schwartz
Waking Too Late

How many winters
did I sleep
without waking,
the image of the moon
fading
in my eyes?

You woke me
with gentle, insistent questions.
There was something in your voice
that recalled
the rain
falling through branches,
the sound of the wind in the leaves,
the way a tree breathes
in the dark.
Little by little
the world took form
and we were the only
inhabitants.

Yet this was not the same world
I had left behind,
but another,
far crueler,
where even the rising of the moon
was just a rehearsal,
and we were only
ghosts
who had never lived.

The First Eve

Male and female He created them.
Genesis 1:27

As Adam watched,
the first Eve
was created
from the inside out—
first her bones,
then her flesh;
finally she was covered
with skin.
But when God offered her to Adam,
he fled,
in disgust.

So the first Eve
was taken away,
never to be heard from again.
And Adam was put to sleep.
And when he awoke
there was another woman,
one created from his own rib,
a woman close to his heart.
But what of the first Eve?
No one knows
her fate—
whether she was taken into paradise
or uncreated.

Even now
she haunts us
from the shadows,
calling Adam's name.

Out of Egypt

At first
I was your master,
you,
my slave.
But we traded places,
and I have been your slave
ever since.

You taunt
and tantalize me,
command me to come closer,
then cast me out.
How long
will I have to mourn in the desert
this time?

At night
the locusts insist
it is time to take leave
of you,
to abandon your embrace.
But I have been a slave so long
I cannot bear
to go.

Yehuda Amicahi in the Heavenly Jerusalem

On earth,
in his beloved Jerusalem,
he could often be found in that tiny cafe
on King George,
sipping black coffee.
Everyone knew who he was,
but they all left him alone.
Later
he would shop in the *shuk*

like everyone else,
take a seat in the back of the bus,
put down his bags of fruits and vegetables,
and dream a little
till the bus reached his stop.

Everyone else was asleep
when he rose at four in the morning
to jot down the poems hidden in the corners
of his city
that no one else seemed to notice.
This was his secret life.

On his seventieth birthday he whispered,
I am tired of giving birth,
And it seemed to be true.
His face was tired,
even his eyes,
and yet something continued to burn.
I have learned the secret
Of fertilizing myself,
he told me.
I supply both egg and seed.
But I am tired of giving birth.

At seventy-six
he took leave of this world
quietly,
as one would expect of such a modest man.

Presidents and prime ministers spoke at his funeral;
thousands gathered to pay their respects.
When he reached heaven,
he was greeted by his heroes,
King David and Shmuel ha-Nagid,
along with hundreds of his poems,
their flying letters swirling around him.
The angels,
delighted to welcome him,

offered him a pair of wings,
but he declined, saying,
"It's enough if my words have wings.
Tell me, where are the cafes?"

Other souls
wander the streets of Paradise
like tourists,
staring at the heavenly temple
or taking a seat at the back of Rashi's class.
Not Yehuda.
He is still longing for the ruins
of the earthly temple,
for the ancient stones of his earthly city,
for all the sheets hung out to dry,
flapping like sails in the wind.

Miriam Schwartz
Ancient Dust

As I walk alone
In the vast terrain
I remember my ancestors
Who walked these same deserts
For forty years
Dragging their tired camels and crying children,
Through the never-ending dunes of time.

My well followed
As they searched for the holy land
Its waters sustained them.
As they drank, the people of Israel
Found wisdom in its sweet drops
That contained the secrets
Of both heaven and earth.

As the sun fades into the earth
The desert silence overtakes the night
And the winds sing
Like a golden dove
Hidden beneath wandering steps
Of sand and time,
Sings to be remembered, and felt,
Both in its beauty and sadness.

Remembered
Like our ancestors
Who wandered until they found their home
Beyond the realm
Of ancient dust.

Kristalnacht

1. Shattering

In the beginning
There was light
A bright light
Which encompassed
God's presence
And filled the universe
With divine power

This light was contained
In a powerful vessel
Filled with the entire cosmos
Of the Universe
And this vessel continued
Growing and growing
Until there was no more space
For all the light to exist

Bursting with God's light
The vessel shattered
And shards of light
Dispersed
To all corners of the Universe
Especially to Earth
Where God's light
Was sent
To every Soul

2. Darkness

Kristalnacht
The night of crystal
Encompasses the darkness
Of human nature
The jagged edges
Of despair
Resound in the clinking of broken glass
Against the hard ground

Shattered glass
Is strewn across
The synagogue floor
The jagged, broken shards
Try desperately to capture
The light of the moon
In their glossy reflection
Yet can only reflect back
Darkness

The *Torah*
Our holy scripture
Has been killed
Just like they killed
90 innocent people
On that fateful night
Families, homes, shops
All shattered
The synagogue
Our house of learning
Burnt down
Destroyed
The ashes
Of the burnt books
Rise to the sky
Hebrew letters in
An eternal dance
Black fire against white

3. Gathering the Light

Each soul, each shattered piece
Yearns deeply, to be back together
As part of the Whole, once again
We will each return back to God,
As we heal the World
For Tikkun Olam
Will Bring back
The shattered pieces

That have spread upon
This home, This earth

Winds carry our prayers
To the four corners
Of the earth,
And high up to the heavens
Where *Adonai*, posited on a throne of Glory
Listens to each prayer;
Collects them
In large loving hands
Kisses them, and sends them back to this earth

So continue collecting
The shards of light
That come your way
Grasp them in your hands,
Kiss them,
And never let them go.

She Glows Above

Silver moon rises high above the mountaintops
To light the way,
For the small children and stray cats
Who wander her cobblestone streets.

The wind whispers her song,
In unison with the singing crickets and birds;
Ode to the Sabbath queen
Bless the evening with a touch of *Adonai*.

White stones form the streets and
Carry wisdom in their cracks, as
Stained glass windows catch her light,
And reflect back ruby glimmer.

Voices of prayer resound in the distance
Echoing and rising up
As the silver crescent, shadow of the earth
Lights up this mystical place,

She glows above the sacred city of Safed.

Shira Schwartz
Children of the Holy Land

Today is our first chance
As the sun spreads
Warmth to the land

So too shall the children of the
Holy Land send light
To the nations

Not through war
But through peace
Not through hatred and fear
But through forgiveness and love

Two nations shall rise up together
Out of the level of survival
Together we must grow
Together we must allow ourselves
To envision change

Together we must learn
To love ourselves
And one another

The Soul Jewel

Eyes, the jewel of her soul,
Staring into divinity.
Opal, worn green, oceanic aquamarine
Her eyes, green-eyed, jeweled jealousy.
Blue, watered down, emptying
Into the river,
And when the meager shaft of wood
Reaches the jutting shore,
The course-sharpened rocks melt
Into rounded stones.

Silk sand falling through his calloused palm,
Opals, jewels, sparkling,
Guiding her into the circle of life.
There, the child continues to laugh,
There, her soul is placed in his palm.
Lines of fate, drawn upon his hand,
Intertwining like streams which
Empty into the river, and
Finally end,
In her eyes.

Thank You Note

I thank the Universe for the following:

For carrying me in calm waters
For protecting me from all danger
For allowing me to see beauty
To stand by a mountain
To play by an ocean

Where could I begin to count all the
Blessings you have given me

For every surprise
For every memory which makes me
Smile.

Laya Firestone Seghi
Before and After the Rain

I. Before the Rain

Space moves in
The day darkens
And the skies reach down
To remind you:
Even clouds get heavy
Trying to carry more
Than they can bear.

Sometimes you wait:
Ready to welcome
The cracking whip
(If only it would strike already!)
Wanting to break
With the thunder
Splatter in all directions
Just to let the burden down.

II. Rain

Here it comes.
You can sense it
Before you can see it
Smell it
Before you touch it

What the air
Held in
Takes aim
Riding in dotted rivulets
Down from the sky

Hear it:
It's the rain
Wringing out the atmosphere
Rattling everything from there to here

Finally breaking loose
Never worrying where it falls.

III. After the Rain

Is it over yet?
The pressure is gone.
Leaves are breathing again.
The trees are calm.

What happened here
Just a short while ago?
Heaven leaned over
And touched the ground

Can it be denied
That what was up
On high
Came down?

Look now and see
Where the earth was touched:
The trace
Still shimmers.

A Stiff-Necked People

We all long,
Though only a few admit it.
For some,
It is easier not to speak
That loneliness,
Nor feel it.

Many are called,
That is to say: we all long.
But few are chosen,
Which means those lonely ones

Who openly carry
The yoke of that longing.

A stiff-necked people,
The chosen ones,
Who try to hold their heads up
While the burden of longing
Bends them down,
Again and again.

But after long enduring the yoke,
Even the ox feels tenderness
For the master that drives it.
And so too, the time may come
When the chosen feel their burden
Has been a blessing.

Thank You for Being

There's more to be said,
But where to begin
Becomes a question
Open as the shore—
Starting here, then there
Or later
Somewhere else again—
Moving, always moving
To tell you something
Maybe you already knew

But better not assume.
The words need to be said
For what is felt to be
Known, more accurately,
As in using a compass
To find the way that's true
Or tide tables to tell
The highs and the lows—

Just to be sure, and then
To go from there.

So do you know
How your wordless actions
Have spoken?
Let me tell you—
They continue to echo
Like a spiraled shell
Penetrating silence
Or like waves greeting water
As they return
To the sea.

All this by way of saying
Thank you for being
More than a friend,
For who you are,
At home by the sea,
Reaching us who wonder
How you know to give
What has been missed
And how, inasmuch as we receive,
We find ourselves.

Jason Sommer
Adam's Call

> *"Man is the only animal that laughs and weeps: He is . . .*
> *struck with the difference between what things are and what they*
> *ought to be."*
> —William Hazlitt

Morning it must have been
for the Angel's sword seemed
flame only behind them
turning at the gate.
Also like a blade before them,
the river bending the light
thinly down the ranks of hills
serried each behind the other
cutting then through tawny plains.
On its banks he pauses
to decipher the one feature on the flats,
which at first he thought incised,
creases in the earth:
a dark line splaying into lines
splaying into lines and lines—
scrawled over its own shadow
though, bowed almost to the ground,
wintry even in the heat,
stinted of fruit, of leaf.
It takes him a moment,
which is what it may be to have
a mind for Eden and an eye full of the world,
but then what starts in his belly
shakes his chest,
wind coming from his stretched
mouth, gaped jaws.
Head thrown back he brays
barks crows neighs roars
laughter until tears
channel the dust of his face.
So the animals name him,
and though each now has its own

call, cry, song according to its kind,
one in the hills or circling
unseen in the sun above
gives out with what may be reply.

The Laughter of Adam and Eve: A Detail

As has been established in Midrash
elsewhere, the first hilarity in the world
occurred as they were making their way east
along one of the branches of the river Nod
in a near-desert place: ochre dust-
devils and shale, scrub grass and the sun
whirling light down as off the flat
of that sword burning behind them,
                              and Adam
struck with a kind of fit, shaking and stamping,
doubling over, rocking back, hinging, unhinging,
making sounds he could only have gotten
from the beasts of the field—
over what?
              She doesn't quite know and yet
she starts to get it, take it from him,
him up from a bow with his head
thrown back, the whatsit stuck
midway in his craw now bobbing
interestingly—almost before she sees
her belly gives some sympathetic twitches

as *etz* he says to her in the original, *etz,*
tree, tree, gasping this,
                          what the scrawny
item baking on the banks
turned out to be on inspection.
So pathetic a thing it was compared
to those majesties that knowledge
first depended from, and life:
all green hands turning, over

and back, light side, dark
side, slatting a glimpse of the red
suns of the fruit—
                    all green wings rising, banking,
stalling aquiver with God's garden
wind, unseeable but good,
ambling about in the heat of the day,
all green tongues whispering where are you,
what have you done?
                 Tree?
This thing? And she lets go
to the sky in her pitches higher than his,
birds of the air more like, turns to him then,
a rough breathing, a half-voiced,
an almost nothing itself to be opening
and closing the jaws on.
The curse notwithstanding,
this first fruit of exile he offers her,
plucked bodily but with some ease
from the barren land, is sustenance forever:
a knowledge of evil that is good.

Exegete to Nymph

*Man before his birth, being pure spirit, knows everything; but at the moment
he sees the light of day, an angel strikes him on the mouth and he forgets the
whole Torah.*   —Ludwig Blau, "Angelology,"
                                    The Jewish Encyclopedia.

       ★

*Between morning and evening the angel carries the soul around, and shows
her where she will live and where she will die . . . and he takes her through
the whole world, and points out the just and the sinners and all things.*
                         —Louis Ginzberg, *The Legends of the Jews*

That every mark upon the soul is made
upon the body, I know and I can prove,
if you allow your mouth and mine persuade.
My people say—above the lips, that groove's

an angel's, who taught our souls before the earth
all we would know here. Then his finger left
us dumbstruck and disremembering for birth,
and living to recall what we again forget.
Note how instinctively the finger fits
that space still when it's silence we request,
the soul's soft clay mnemonic on the lips.
So if I seek your silenced lip's impress
to match with mine, it's that I wish to wake
a memory of heaven, and for knowledge's sake.

⋆

Heaven, lips, soul! A practical poem made
to win you. We can all the pleasures prove
is what I mean to say, mouths persuade
indeed. The needle's wearing out the groove
in my head where you're recorded. Remember-earth
we-come-to-in-the-end is suasion better left,
with young girls, alone, strictly. You're the birth
of the blues in thirtyish me, singing forget
it, rightly maybe, except I feel it fits—
your fawn coloring leggily makes requests
of its own, and sweet downturn of your lips
natural refusal. Who'd not impress
you with love songs, sonnets, anything to wake
beside you? Girl, give in for heaven's sake!

⋆

The Rabbinic version of the tale is made
less for etiology than to prove
knowledge determinate, and to persuade,
too, that it's heaven sent. The charming groove
in your lips aside, presumably the earth-
bound, carnal knowing I infer is left
a place in lore, not just allied with birth,
elsewhere. The knowledge we're lip-struck to forget
is word-bound. The efficacious word fits

behind all this. *Let there be light* requests
the world to make itself by word of lips,
as by words the angel's teaching must impress.
But by fingers we're dumb, by mouth's breath clay wakes
to words which would be breath again for our sake.

David

In Somerville, Mass., "All American City"
(title holder nineteen seventy-two)
tonight it is Palestine in the doldrums
within *hamsin*: when air baked in a desert
settles in town, sits square in rooms, oblong
in the corridors, presses flat against the sides
of our houses, penned in the alleys between,
so even the curtains hold their feathery breath
in the windows, and night is a room crowded
with the feverish, sweat like sudden tears starts
at the least motion.
                    Nevertheless, I wander
my apartment till, across the way, below
a little, illumined by the yellow moon
of a bulb, a woman turns in her shower slowly,
hooked on a line of sight, in a silver-bead
curtain of water, flat streams of dark hair
and pursed lips as she figureheads into the spray,
then arching down to tend one ankle,
her back breaks the water, her droplet breasts
lead rivulets from their tips, and her hands flow
all over in the veils of water as she performs
her privacy for me.
                    I keep as still
as hunter and quarry both, for sound travels
in the heat as over water. Desire that surged
now goes to ground in a heat that pushes lust
beyond enactment, into mind.
                    Had I
come upon her husband in that window or

another, delaying then to observe the oddity
of my nakedness confirmed as human, seen
in him, what acts might he make natural
for me?
       I may look in on him as he
looks in on someone else, on anyone
but me, or in a book, and reads aloud
gesturing strangely—or does, alone or not,
what I would do. Or wouldn't. What can he
hold back, not knowing we're here?
                                  To look unobserved
into another life and make other lives
grandiose persistence of old story:
Later, when it cools a little, bring her
to me; send him to where the fighting is.

Arlene Rubin Stiffman
Thoughts Before the Exodus

There is no "me."
A slave is but a master's tool.
"I" becomes a lightening rod,
inviting destruction.

Another master leads now
Into the searing sand.
Death by sand, death by whip
Both hard.

Too late. Too old

But,—
Perhaps,—
My children's children will be "I"
—And remember the "not me"

Philip Sultz
Talmud Torah

When you get there
you play step ball.
Two points, liners,
one point, bouncers.
Everyday I sit between
a girl and a window cactus.
The teacher comes down
the aisle with his stick.
You crouch down a little.
You don't know who's
been misbehaving.
A student is reading
to the class.
The teacher is waving
his stick. My brother is
sitting behind me.
It's my turn to read.
You go everyday except
Sunday. If you get there
early, before Saturday
morning services,
you can sit with the
teachers and have a
hard roll and cocoa.

Maria Szapszewicz
They Left the Shoes

Wherever you look
You see shoes,
Piles and mountains of shoes.
Some of them were once squeaking;
They were almost brand new.
Some had holes and leaked.
Some shoes were beautifully polished
And some were completely demolished.
Shoes of almost all colors
And shoes of all sizes—
Narrow, wide, bright, light, tight.
Shoes with high heels;
Shoes with low heels.
Shoes for display.
Shoes with nails.
Some even had skates.
And some were single,
Without a mate.
Shoes very fancy,
With beautiful bows.
Some were so worn out,
They were patched.
Some didn't match.
Some shoes had laces.
There were even shoes with braces.
Other shoes had beautiful good looks.
There were men's shoes, women's shoes,
Children's shoes, and even babies' shoes.
These shoes were worn by people
To walk, to run, to kick.
Some were for happy occasions,
Some for sad.

When I looked at them,
I became very angry.
Those babies' shoes,

Those poor babies' shoes
In which babies tried to take
Their first steps,
In which they tried
To learn to walk
And did take a few steps
Before falling into their mothers' laps.
Those fancy shoes worn by women
Who walked with such grace.
And I can see each face.
Shoes and shoes and shoes—
Where are all the people
Who wore those shoes?
What a terrible shame that
There is nobody to claim
Those shoes.
And we all know
Who is to blame.
Yes, those shoes belonged
To our mothers, fathers, sisters, and brothers,
And to our children.
What is left of those piles of shoes
Can't talk. Their masters are dead.
It is a very sad and tragic tale.

Shlomo Vinner
The Melody Lingers

1. The Thing is Known

Even my little daughter
Has already understood
That one day
I'll die.

Surely the thing is known.

Now,
Like Moses in Egypt,
I'll have to flee to the desert
To seek some other form of life:
In the dust,
In the wind,

In words.

2. Gifts

Deep asleep
My daughter clings to her dolls:
A gift from her father,
A gift from her mother,
A gift from her grandfather,
May his memory be a blessing.

In the other room
I am trying to conquer my fears
By peaceful thoughts
And memories:
A gift from my mother,
A gift from my father,
A gift from my grandfather,
May their memories be a blessing.

3. A Memory of Others

I've already forgotten
But my daughter still remembers
How
When she was two years old
I carried her on my shoulder
And sang to her:

Little Rabbit.

Thus,
Erased from my own memory,
I become a memory of others.

Thus,
In spite of all,
We continue.

4. Two Voices

September evening in a park:
Half the world is asleep
And half the world
Is awake.
Sleep
As a temporary death,
Awakening
As a temporary eternity,
Alternating.

Children slide
On the last sun beams
And climb again
To the top of the tower.
All at once
The moment seems to last
A thousand years.
In two voices

I'm singing with my daughter:
The days pass,
The year ends.

Two voices.
The melody lingers.

Translated by Howard Schwartz

The Philosophical Stage
  for Howard Schwartz

I.

At the beginning of the famous essay
The statement that three words suffice:
for the world
for the law.

The world—
it is said,
is all but
a narrow bridge.
But if that is all,
then between what and what
is the bridge?

The Law—
love your neighbor
(as yourself).
But
what is Love?
If you must ask,
go and study.
This too is
Law.

II.

On the banks of the frozen lake
we sat.
A man who insisted on fishing
under any condition
bore a hole in the ice
and sank his line.
Geese licked up crumbs
from the palms of our hands.
Time out for winter
and a question.

Are the Divine Presence, the Holy Spirit
        and the Heavenly Voice
just different aspects of God
Or is it possible
separate entities?
If they are not just aspects,
What about the Lord
our God the Lord is One?

This way or that,
one must tell stories
must
write poems.

III.

And more questions:
Were there once spirits and demons?
Are there now?
Everyone with conviction
held his own opinion.
Friendship alleviates the pain
of arguments of that order.
At a nearby airport
planes took off and landed,
like angels on Jacob's ladder.

Concerning Lilith,
men of our experience
agreed.
Each has encountered
more than one.

IV.

And during all this time,
the runners
passed by us,
back and forth,
running themselves to death.
I too,
now observing from the side,
once,
until the last breath,
ran,
on rocks and stones,
afterward
on grass and tracks of dust;
and in running,
as in life,
the moment in which it seems
that one can go one forever
is the right moment

to stop.

Translated by Laya Firestone Seghi.

Jane O. Wayne
Time Exposure

We don't know the place or country
in this blurred photograph
my grandmother left in a box of documents,

or the white-bearded relative,
who stands tall before a sunlit column,
the man himself a column, feet together,

hands pocketed in the open overcoat he wears
above another full-length coat,
or why just then he stopped

whatever he was doing
to have his picture taken in his hat—
eyes narrowed for the sun, brows lowered

in what seems a frown till at closer look
the way he holds our gaze
shows something mild, something easy in a man

who wears a tie knotted at the throat,
but whose half-buttoned vest
droops open in the middle,

whose too-long-sleeves are stacked
with creases wrist-to-elbow.
His shoes are worn, some tired second skin

that barely hides its bones.
He could be tired, too. And there's a hint,
I think, of gentleness around his mouth

which might have widened to a smile
or words perhaps—some levity
beyond the camera's reach.

Before? After?
Conjecture, of course, when what survives
is only this enlarged photograph

reducing him to moments.
Think, then, of stopping on that street,
a letter not yet posted

or travel papers to fill out,
and standing by that wall—
the cold of idleness, of interruption,

the open lens and how long it must have seemed
before some other hand
capped off a certain measurement of light.

Bookmarks

Hard bound, soft bound, even magazines you visit
have your calling cards.
You never slam a door behind you.

On these shelves in almost every book you've read,
assorted scraps stick out
like loose threads from a carpet's fringe.

Cardboard leans like tombstones;
softer papers bend like banners
in a wind that no one notices.

Postcards, envelopes,
movie tickets, shopping lists,
you leave anything in reach that's flat enough—

some strings, some ribbons,
and here's a nail file
wedged into a dictionary.

When you turn pages,
moving forward in a book
you must struggle with a counter urge

that slows you down, some stealthy child
who's trailing bread crumbs.
Each flap of paper leads you back:

a passage underlined, a circled word or phrase, a chapter
like an island-paradise you left
hoping to return.

A Quick Lesson

You might have left it out overnight,
the way it's lying in the shade near your swing,
its brindled fur smooth as a new toy animal's.

It lets you hunker down to get a closer look,
even lets you nudge it in the side—the same prod
you'd use to wake the cat

though this sleeper doesn't startle
toward the privet-hedge. Nothing happens
until you claim it with both hands,

then what was docile on the ground
takes on a cardboard-stiffness—
some stronger hold than yours already on it.

There's a moment—still cradling it—
when whatever stopped in the garden
makes you stopæand in the hush

though you're far too young
to ask if it weighs now what it did before,
if the life in it weighed nothing

you must be weighing
something in your mind
before you let it go: rabbit and all.

Nati Zohar
Primal Scent

the sound of shattering glass is like fire being frozen
echoing through the dense air
where immense breath burns through each of my veins
the surreal drops of dew penetrating
through the darkening silence
rising to see a figure
my eyes cannot see anything
but the radiant smell that suffocates them
with apathetic ignorance of my own nature
the fragrance of the air smells like dew to my tongue
I melt under the empty heat
trying to reach a place where nothing grows anymore
not even the lustful maple trees
that died out already after years of crying
with their thick sap tears
where the rocks laugh with inanimate ecstasy
a laugh that burns through my own veins

II
Fiction

Allison Creighton
The Night Temple

When I discovered that you could visit the temple at any time of the day or night, without following any set order of prayers, and without any-one instructing you when to stand and when to sit, when to read respon-sively and when to pray in silence, I decided to make my way back— although it had been years.

My decision to return to the temple was not for any of the reasons one might expect. I wasn't attempting to strengthen my floundering faith or to enrich my character in the hope of becoming a better person. All I really wanted was a quiet place where I could escape my own life for a while, a place where I could be invisible.

I came to the temple late at night, always hoping to be alone. But the same woman was constantly there, sitting in the corner of the last row. She wore a silver scarf on her head and a sheer, flowing shawl around her shoulders. She never seemed to notice my arrival or departure, and I began to wonder if she could see me at all. Sometimes when I entered I could hear her singing or chanting in soft low murmurs. Once she was sitting with her eyes closed, rocking back and forth and holding her prayer book tightly to her chest, as if she was cradling a baby.

As I sat in my familiar chair, not far from the holy ark, the sound of her distant prayers actually comforted me and helped me let go of all the thoughts that had crowded my mind all day.

Every evening, the time came too quickly when I knew I had to go home. I'd rise from my warm chair and walk slowly to the door at the back of the temple, feeling like part of myself had evaporated into the sanctuary's hazy glow.

I'd get into my car and open the moon roof, even in the coldest weather, so that the wind would rouse me. Upon returning to my house, I'd quietly slip into bed. My husband was always sleeping soundly.

One freezing night, I drove to the temple well past midnight. By the time I arrived, my gloved hands were numb from the cold. The strange woman was there as usual, sitting in the same chair and holding her prayer book open. Without even thinking, I walked over to her. She reached out and gently squeezed my hand. The cold instantly fell from my body.

I made my way to the front row and sat down. I stared above the holy ark, straight into the temple's eternal light. For a moment I saw the light flicker.

I don't know how much time passed before I ventured back out into the frigid night air. Just as I was crossing the street to my car, a pair of headlights shone through the darkness, blinding me for a few seconds. The car disappeared and I began to shiver. I realized I'd left my coat in the temple, so I went back inside.

I walked to my seat in the front row, but my coat was no longer there. I looked around and saw that for the first time, the woman in the corner of the back row was gone. But there, on her chair, I could see it—the nubby silhouette of my worn winter coat.

Shelly R. Fredman
Isaac, My Laughter

He was always *shlepping* home strangers, that one. So when he came running into the tent that day yelling, "Sarah, put on the stew! Milk the goat! Bring bowls for the almonds and figs!" I didn't move so fast. At ninety-two, I'd seen enough of the world's comings and goings to know a minute here or there makes little difference. We were living in the land of Canaan, nearby Mamre's oak grove. Although it was the heat of the day, our tent remained cool and dark. There was panic in Abraham's voice. "Do you hear me?" he said. "They're here."

I moved slowly, gathering my long silver hair, twisting it into a rope and binding it to the top of my head with a tortoiseshell comb he'd given me the morning after the first night he slept with her.

Hagar. The dark one. You know the story—how, unable to give him a child, I'd urged him to lie down with her. A risk, I know. But I had big things in mind—the destiny of our people, God's promise, his line about our descendants becoming as stars in the sky, as sand on the seashore. Survival. All that. What I hadn't counted on, couldn't imagine, was how the little things would undo me. The spring in his step the morning after he slept with her. The way her sheath clung as she sashayed by me on her way to the well, the thin cotton outlining the swell of her breasts. And then, the look in his eyes when he handed me the tortoise-shell comb, as if that was enough.

"Sarah! Why are you dreaming? I told you to hurry." His words came to me dimly, as if through a veil of oak leaves. He'd designed our tent so the flaps could be open on all four sides, so he shouldn't miss a thing. My Abraham, the guest lover. It wasn't his voice, but the light that roused me. It crept slowly into the cool darkness of the tent, as if the sun had tumbled from the heavens, rolled down the ravine, through the sagebrush and sabras and stopped outside our door. It wasn't the sun, though. It was them. Angels.

"Hagar," I whispered, under my breath. "Where is that damn girl when you need her?" Always around when you least want to see her and never there when the guests arrive.

Abraham washed their feet. He was an infinitely tender man. He invited them to sit down. "Let me get you a bit of bread. Rest a little. Relax," he said. There they were at my table and not all that extraordinary, to tell you the truth, except for the third one. The first was short and round and a troupe of flies circled his head. He stuttered terribly, but he did all the talking. The second was loaded down with pots and rugs and candlesticks, as if he'd just lit out of town to avoid an angry mob. The third's features were so perfectly formed he was hard to look at. He was hairless except for his thick, dark eyelashes and there was something girlish in the curve of his arms. Though he said nothing, his lips were slightly parted, as if he knew great secrets he wasn't quite ready to reveal.

They looked like ordinary men, but the light gave them away. And less a light, in fact, than a kind of white fragrance like freesia you could see and touch. It clung to their skin, moist, warm, and rose from their bodies in waves. The tent was no longer cool and dark. The heat they gave off filled my nostrils. I wanted to climb between them, lay my head down in their laps. I wanted to run as far as my creaking knees would carry me. The other side of the Euphrates wouldn't be far enough. Instead, I ladled the lamb stew into bowls. The sweat pooled in my armpits and dampened my inner thighs as I gathered the oranges and almonds and figs.

"Sarah, we're out of milk," Abraham said, holding up the empty pitcher. I hesitated before taking it from his hands. As they ate, I went out to milk the goat. Perhaps I could find Hagar. Instead, there was Ishmael crouched down, hiding within the herd. The top of his bristled head was barely visible among their woolly hides. Always hiding, that no good son of hers. And his, too, I told myself, as I did almost daily, still trying to make it real, though it should have been by now. The boy was nearly thirteen.

"We have guests, Ishmael. Unless you're going to help me here, run off and find your mother. Tell her I need her." He rose slightly and stared at me, as if for one moment he was actually considering helping me out. I held his gaze. "Come on, Ishmael," I said. It wasn't his fault, after all. None of it. The day he was born, I was the one who lifted him from the dark, wet circle at the edge of her body. I watched as she smoothed his matted hair and placed his mouth to her brown nipple. Though I didn't want to feel it, a pressure rose in my chest. My dry breasts swelled, grew full and hard, as if there were milk there, endless pitchers of cream. He had a small, round, beautiful face and tiny fingers that moved through the air slowly, as if still in the watery bliss of the womb. Her womb.

Ishmael looked away, toward the green hills. Then he ran off, dragging his bow in the sand. I sat, squeezing the goat's teats roughly. "Hurry, damn it," I whispered, "I've got angels inside."

The freesia scent again, mixing with the animal smell of the herd. I turned around. The silent one was behind me, mouth open. High and shrill as a reed his voice came. "Sarah. You remember the promise?"

"Of course I do. We're to be as the stars in the sky, as the sands on the seashore. You're a little late, though. About fifty years."

"It's never too late. When the moon shrinks and grows nine times, you will have a son."

Moons, sons, who did he think he was talking to? And yet . . . a vague image of Abraham's old body and mine moving the way we used to, like fish, like dogs, like lions, came to me. I laughed out loud. This startled the goat, who went running from my hands. Three drops of milk spilled into the dirt.

I looked up at him. "You're joking, aren't you? You expect me to believe this old body is going to carry a child?"

His placid expression didn't change. In the distance, lightning broke the sky and a chill purple darkness spread like a bruise across the land. I looked away, and when I gathered the courage to raise my eyes again, he was gone.

Would you believe me if I told you that as I walked back to the tent, the half-full flask of goat's milk still in my hand, I felt my legs growing strong and supple, like the branches of the tamarind, saw the tiny cracks of my hand disappear, as if I'd just emerged from the finest, most fragrant waters and had been massaged with almond oils and myrrh? Would you believe if I told you that as I reached the opening of the tent, I felt the rough gray rope of my hair unfurl, felt my scalp tingle and buzz, and whole tresses lengthened, becoming fine scarlet silk in my hand? I glanced down and saw my toenails, no longer yellowed and rough, but white, paper-thin, as the wings of a moth.

When Abraham and I lay together that night I watched his leathered face become soft. His eyes were the eyes of long ago, the ones that first met mine across the circle of my father's well. Did it really happen? Were we really young again in each other's arms, or had that angel worked his spell in our heads, so we only saw each other this way? I do not know. I can only tell you how it felt. We lay together as we did that first night when he took me from my father's home, lay entwined like two vipers, our rough skins sloughed, lying in a heap at the edge of the bed.

Nine new moons later, I pushed Isaac into the world. Abraham, though he meant well, was no help whatsoever. Pacing like a crazy man round and round the tent, asking a hundred questions we couldn't begin to answer. Hagar finally had to chase him out. It was she who breathed with me and told me when to bear down. Throughout the long night, as she and I breathed together like that, I thought of my sister, whom I hadn't seen in sixty years . . . the way we used to whisper together, lying on our beds of straw, when everyone else in the tent was asleep.

As Hagar and I breathed as one, I remembered how it had been between us just weeks ago down at the wadi, when I was full with child. I rubbed Abraham's robe back and forth against the rock, cleaning away the rough desert sand, when suddenly I had the impulse to tell her about the changes taking place inside, the miracles. Now that I was pregnant it didn't seem to matter so much, about her and Abraham. As we washed the clothes, I told her about how the vague, stirring motion, little more than a thought, had become the flip flops of a butterfly fish, which had become the jab of a new elbow, just beneath my rib. Abraham had looked at me strangely when I tried to describe what seemed to me a world, inside, but when I told Hagar, she stopped dipping Ishmael's shirt into the water, held it there dripping, and something distant and close moved across her face like a breeze. When she lowered her hands, she let the shirt fall, and held her belly, silent.

Now Hagar told me to push one last time, as she wrenched my Isaac from his liquid home. Her two coffee-colored hands lifted him into the world. She placed him at my breast. I recalled how I once had to lay Ishmael at hers. How empty my hands felt as I let him go. "I want Abraham," I said. "Tell him to come."

Her nostrils flared. The tenderness was gone. She left and soon Abraham came to me, a new look on his face, just when I thought there were no more expressions to be added to the kaleidoscope I'd seen over the past sixty something years. We laughed and cried together, our hands moving over Isaac's toes and shoulders and rosebud mouth. The baby's hair was the color of the sun, nothing like Abraham's or mine, as if the angels, for their amusement just before sending him from heaven had lowered him by the ankles and dipped his head into a vat of gold. He was the most beautiful thing I had ever seen. Promised and promise in one. I named him laughter.

For the next four years, he was my lover. I lavished kisses on his small body, fondled the plump roundness of his sturdy legs, and nursed him endlessly. When my nipples blistered and cracked, after days of feeding him at his first cry, Hagar told me of how she had rubbed hers with aloe and had lain out in the sun to heal. That afternoon, I stole past our servant, Eliezer's, tent at the edge of camp and went into the desert, taking Isaac with me. I placed him in the shade of a rock, took off my robes and stretched out upon the face of the boulder. The sun beat down on my body and I arched my back to meet it, ripe and full. Thinking of him, my Isaac, my laughter, I felt a warmth and completeness I'd never known before. God had kept his word.

Or so I thought. One Friday night in the month of Sivan, Abraham announced he was giving a party in honor of Isaac's weaning. I stared into the flame of a Sabbath candle.

"But I'm not ready," I said. "He's not ready."

"It's been too long already." The green bunch of grapes in Abraham's large hands nearly matched the color of his eyes.

"Too long? What are you saying?"

He slipped a grape into his mouth. "It's time."

The day of the party, they came from Tzo'ar, from Kadesh and Shur and Gerar. We served lamb stew and goat's milk, almonds and figs, just like on the day of the angels. Though everyone got drunk and the ground seemed to shake with their laughter, I spent the day in the tent, alone. Their laughter came to me like a poisoned melody, insidious and shrill.

For a time though, Isaac remained mine. Abraham couldn't touch us, no matter how he tried. When Isaac stumbled it was me he came running to, and as he grew and his father began taking him off hunting, though they were gone for days at a time, I was the one whose face he sought when he came running across the rough sands with his prize.

One day when I went out to check on the herd, I saw a lamb pinned between two rocks at the top of the hill. I climbed up slowly, stepping carefully, and as I did I heard the thin voices of Isaac and Ishmael, arguing.

"Who came first?," Ishmael screamed.

"You did."

"Who's the oldest?"

"You are."

"Who is his father's first son?"

"You. You. You," yelled Isaac. I spotted them just as I reached the lamb. Ishmael had Isaac pinned beneath him. Isaac's thin arms were covered in sand. The lamb bleated in pain. I lifted it, and as I held it trembling in my arms, its mouth brushed my ear. "Send them away," it whispered.

That evening, over steaming bowls of couscous and onions, I told Abraham that Ishmael and Hagar had to go.

"What are you saying, Sarah?" The horror in the shadows around his eyes chilled me even more than seeing Isaac pinned beneath Ishmael. "He's my son."

"Don't you think I know that? But your destiny lies with Isaac. You may not admit it, but deep within you know it's true." A cold wind came rushing through the tent. There was the rustling of tamarind leaves, and the tent flaps whipped back and forth.

Abraham didn't come to bed that night. The next day they were gone. No arguments. No fighting. Did God himself descend and show him the way? Did He whisper it in his ear—the future? I don't know. I only know Abraham took them in the night, so quietly I never heard them pack their things. We ate breakfast beneath the tamarind tree—hot, sweet loaves and a lovely Turkish coffee Abraham had traded something precious for. Three times Isaac asked where Ishmael was. "Have more bread," I told him, passing the warm loaf. "It's delicious."

When Abraham lay next to me that night, he turned to face the tent wall where the odd shadows of the herd played against the canvas. His spine was stiff and I suddenly knew that though I had won, a part of him had traveled a bow's length with them, leaving Isaac and me behind.

I was sitting in the sun, kneading cakes, my old hands turning and turning the warm dough, when God came to us yet again. "Abraham," God said. He was always calling out, like a father seeking his lost child. On the other side of the tamarind, He spoke to Abraham in low tones, both of them so caught up in their conversation they didn't realize I was nearby.

"Abraham," He said, "Take your son, your only one, whom you love." I leaned in closer to the tree. "And go to the land of Moriah, and offer him there as a sacrifice."

Here I stopped kneading. What kind of God would ask such a thing? Give—only to take away? My hands rested, and yet I still felt the ghost rhythm of turning circles. You're not really going to listen to this, I thought. This is a crazy, mixed-up God. This is not God at all. This is the ghost voice of your father, Terah, who delivered you into the fire after you smashed his idols. Tell Him, I whispered. Speak up, Abraham. Tell Him he's gone too far this time. Enough with the tests, endlessly proving ourselves.

I strained my ears, forcing myself not to creep closer to the rough bark of the tree. Silence. Where is my Abraham, I wondered, the one who stood up to Him and argued on behalf of that wretched lot in Sodom. The Abraham who pleaded for their puny lives. This is no time for weakness, for humility. Abraham! I wanted to scream, are you sleeping?

Nothing. I heard his footsteps and I saw him walk away, toward the lavender hills, where Isaac played.

I ran toward Eliezer's tent. He was off with the herd. I stole inside, found his thick brown cloak, wrapped it around myself, drew the hood over my head, and stepped into his boots. I was still tucking strands of hair behind my ears when Abraham called.

"Eliezer," he yelled, as I knew he would. Live with a man for one hundred years and you know what he will say before he says it. I hastily packed some bread and water, fetched the donkeys, and went out to meet them. Abraham was already walking, as if in a dream, toward Moriah and Isaac followed close behind.

You will wonder how we journeyed three days without my being discovered. And I will tell you, on that last journey, as I pretended to be Eliezer, they too, were not themselves. Abraham walked as if he'd had a heart attack yet somehow still lived. He sleepwalked through the days and tossed and turned at night beneath the half light of the moon. And Isaac, though Abraham said not a word, seemed to know already, following along as if already slaughtered.

On the third day, Abraham looked up and saw the mountain. He froze, gazing, and I knew he was having one of his visions. That look came into his eyes that I'd seen so many times over the years. It was uncanny the way he could tell us the future, startlingly detailed and vivid, as if he'd already painted it.

"Do you see?" he asked.

"Yes, father," Isaac said, obedient, somber. "I see a ring of fire over the mountain."

"Do you see it, Eliezer?"

I had to admit I saw nothing.

"You see nothing and the donkeys see nothing," Abraham said. "You stay here with the donkeys."

My heart began to tear then, a small seam unraveling at the edge. They walked on without me. How could I save him from down here? I stood still for a few minutes and then, as in every other moment in my life, when I couldn't bring the answer up from within my blood, the voice came. That still, small voice Abraham and Isaac and Jacob, the whole lot of them, are so famous for having heard.

Follow, Sarah, the voice said, unspeaking. Follow behind and at the right time you will know what to do.

And so we climbed. They were fifty feet away, close enough so I could see Isaac's white robe in glints and flashes, ascending. They never looked back.

Near the top, the air was thin and cool. I gulped it in, straining to breathe. As they reached the summit, Abraham began to lay down the logs he had split himself, one upon another. I moved in closer. Things were misted and blurry here, in the realm of clouds. Isaac said, "Here is the fire and the wood, but where is the lamb for the offering?"

"God will see for himself to the lamb, my son," Abraham said. I kneeled behind a rock. I watched Abraham stare into Isaac's face. Say it now, I whispered. Turn to the heavens and scream it out. God, it is too much. You ask the impossible.

He said nothing. Instead, he reached down to his side and drew the knife from its sheath. I couldn't breathe. The small seam ripped apart. He held the blade against the blue sky.

I stood. "Abraham!" I screamed and as I did, I heard another voice behind mine, barely recognizable. That angel. The girlish one. The one who had promised Isaac. He held Abraham's large hand in his own delicate one, high against the patient sky. "Do not stretch out your hand against the lad," he said.

As I clutched my chest, I heard the bleating of a ram.

When I awoke, there was the iron smell of blood. There was not much left of the fire—a thin pillar of smoke, a few charred sticks, the last embers. Abraham held my head in his lap. "Leave me be," I said, moving away from him, feeling again the pain in my chest.

"Sarah. You shouldn't have come."

I rose slowly, leaning upon Isaac. "No? I should have left it to you? You, who would sacrifice my only son? You and your crazy, mixed-up God whose moods turn like the seasons? This August God of yours who suddenly decides it's January?"

"Stop screaming. You're working yourself up."

"How do you know it was God's voice you heard, anyway? What kind of God plays cruel games like this? In my humble opinion it was Terah you heard. Terah you saw. That day he stood by and watched you burn."

"Now who's crazy, huh?" He rose, brushing dirt from his robe. "I knew what I was doing."

"You bound our son to an altar and held a six-inch knife above his neck."

"I had faith, Sarah. I knew God would figure something out."

"God? Do you see God anywhere?" I said, turning to the black hills around us. "If I hadn't called out to my angel . . ."

"Your angel. Your angel. Who do think sent the angel? You think they have nothing to do all day but sit around waiting for your call?"

"Will you two please stop arguing," Isaac said. "I'm tired. I want to go home." I looked at him, suddenly remembering he was the reason we were here. I reached over to brush the hair out of his eyes, but he batted my hand away.

We haltingly made our way down the summit. The sun was setting in a chorus of purples and reds. Halfway down, we met the rest of the herd, paused there as if waiting for something. I sat down on a rock, knees shaking. It seemed like a long way down. There was a rumbling in the lurid sky, the smell of rain. The herd finally roused, scuttling and bumping along. A lamb brushed by my legs. I reached out to grab hold of it, but it darted away. I stared at the yellow-white fleece in my palm. The hope and anguish of one hundred and twenty years settled in my hips, in my calves, in my ankles.

We walked home together but apart, clay beads separated and held by a string. Abraham walked in front, flanked by two animals. He looked slightly defeated, Abraham, and older than the Judean hills. A skein of light, like the freesia-scented light of the angels, clung to the edge of his robe. He was a mystery I would never know. I did admire that thread of light running at the edge of his gown, though.

Glancing back now and again, across the shadowed land, I saw Isaac. A dim figure, melancholy, older somehow. I held the fleece in my closed fist, crushed it into a rough ball. Child of my old age, I had clung too much, and now he was slipping away. Can you blame me for the over-attentiveness, for the constant seeking of his eyes across the breakfast table? His blood, my blood, his home within my flesh. How was I to give that up, to let go?

We never again spoke of what happened. Once, a visitor mentioned Moriah and a silence opened around that word, Moriah—a silence so vast it seemed to swallow us up like three fish in the belly of a whale.

Weeks later, as I sat in the shade of the tamarind, imagining yet again that Hagar would come back, swinging her hips, descending the green-gold hill, I saw a figure approaching. Hagar? I couldn't help feeling she alone would understand. She, too, had been loved and betrayed by him.

There came instead the flash of light and the smell of a sweet odor, like steaming yams. Death came toward me in great glory and beauty.

"Are you Death?"

"I am the bitter name."

"I refuse to go with you. Show me your corruption." And Death revealed her corruption, showing two heads. One had the face of a serpent and the other, a lion. As the looks of Death were not enough to cause my soul to depart, God removed my soul gently, as one would slip an omelet out of a pan and the angel, my favorite, carried it up into Heaven.

After the requisite praise and glory had been given to God by all the angels, after the too-loud blowing of trumpets and much commotion, there came the voice of God, saying, "Take my friend Sarah into Paradise, where are the tabernacles of the righteous ones and the abodes of Rebekah and Rachel and Leah, where there is no trouble nor grief nor sighing, but peace and rejoicing and life unending." I was still holding that rough ball of lamb's wool.

I am holding it now, folding it in my hand over and over again. Mostly it feels shining and golden, like Isaac's hair. But once in a while it is rough and bristled and dark, the hair of Ishmael.

Sometimes I close my eyes and I see Hagar. I wonder about where she and her son went after I sent them away. I remember, sometimes, the look we exchanged that day over the blood-soaked bed of straw, when she placed Isaac in my arms. The way her eyes held mine, an exchange as urgent as the midnight exchange between Abraham's body and my own.

Sometimes I see Abraham. He is wandering into the hills alone and I imagine he is thinking of me and the night we became young again.

Mostly though, I see Isaac, my laughter. He was miserable after that day at Moriah. Never spoke to his father again. Wandered far away, just as his own father once did, and had lots of women. With that golden curl falling over one eye and his brooding silences, silences into which the girls could pour all their imaginings, he was irresistible. I think he was looking for my face in theirs, my constant eyes. One day he brought home Rebekah and she did something none of the others had ever thought to do. She went into what had once been my tent and lit my Sabbath candles. In the dark desert night, the glow of the tent was luminous. Finally, Isaac smiled.

I smiled too, as she sang the blessing. *Baruch ata adonai elohanu melech haolam.* It is an endless song.

Shelly R. Fredman
A Prayer Upon Witnessing Phenomenal Sights

"Do you think this is illegal?" I asked, as we stepped out of Dena's car into the humid July darkness. Forest Park was at our backs, with its zoo and Jewel Box and domed Planetarium, a fat white hourglass set against the sky.

"There are higher laws operating here," Dena said. I rolled my eyes, but said nothing. As we hurried along the city street, the smell of sulphur laced the air. Paused at a stoplight on the way over, we had watched as a trio of yellow-haired boys lit a long line of bottle rockets at the curb and ran to the grass, plunging in head first as the things whizzed and exploded all around them.

In the hospital room, we stared at each other over Anne's head. She was sleeping peacefully, the only hint of disaster a strange clatter in her chest as if her heart had come loose and was bumping around inside.

As Dena and I moved around the room, gathering a blanket, a book, Anne opened her eyes. She began to sit up, but her movements were lethargic, dreamy, a result of the morphine pumping into her. Dena looked at me before she pulled the tube out of Anne's arm. I felt as if we should say a prayer or goodbye or something, as if she would stop breathing the moment we unhooked her. I said a prayer silently, the words coming from someplace outside myself, from some other source.

Three drops of blood spurted onto the white sheet and spread. Maybe we weren't doing the right thing. Maybe we wouldn't bring relief, but only hasten her dying. I wiped quickly at Anne's outstretched arm and placed it at her side.

"Thanks, you two," Anne said, looking from Dena's face to mine. Hoisting her body into the wheelchair was the hardest part.

I wrapped a blanket around Anne's shoulders. She had been staring out vacantly, but now her expression changed and I was almost certain she was taking in all of this. I grabbed a book of Emily Dickinson's poems we'd been reading to her, wedged it at her side, and wheeled her toward the door. Dena scanned the hallway, and motioned to me. I breathed in, gripped the silver bars and pushed Anne forward.

Anne and I met in a baby care class. As our husbands fumbled with tiny washcloths, plastic tubs and golden liquid soap, shiny-pink sexless dolls slipped into the water and drowned again and again. Our eyes met across our swollen bellies, traversing miles of mismatched histories in one leap. It was as if we had simultaneously glimpsed our futures, the bath water a mirror reflecting the coming years, when we would need each other even more than these strangers standing helpless beside us.

While the other women discussed what kind of anesthetic they would have, Anne told me about the midwife she had found. Anne was three years older than me, and she stood a head taller than the rest. Her auburn hair was cut short, framing her strong, angular features. She moved with a confidence that suggested she had attended a dress rehearsal for life none of us had heard about.

We met just after my sister had moved to New York. Anne had come to St. Louis from New York's Upper West Side. In the ensuing years I dwelled on that symmetry—losing my sister, gaining Anne; a trade had taken place.

For nine summers our two families loaded coolers, beach towels and linens into the car and drove up to Lake Michigan to vacation together. We always arrived in Southhaven with the first blueberry harvest in July. Each year, as the children increased, so too the berries. That last July ten of us emerged from the u-pick-em field, arms loaded with silver buckets overflowing with berries, the kids' hands and knees and lips stained blue.

Last April, Anne's cells turned on her and by July the doctors weren't talking weeks anymore, but days. In the hospital room, she was restless, kept wanting to move from chair to bed to chair. "I want to go home," Anne said, again. "I want to get out of here," she said, gnashing at the words. I saw a glimmer of the Anne I knew. In the sharp edge of her voice her strength came through, the steel she could be sometimes. This, at least, was a relief. Not just a shadow, but Anne, here, in this room.

"They can't take care of you at home, Anne," I said. "You know that. That medicine in your arm—you need the medicine." This was absurd. Here I was, advocating medical science to a woman who had insisted on natural childbirth when every obstetrician in town was pushing epidurals. I was pretending I believed hospitals helped people get better.

Dena came in to take over. Her purple skirt was strewn with a batik pattern of birds and elephants. She raked her fingers through a thick tangle of long brown hair. No comb had ever coaxed Dena's hair into place.

"I want to go home," Anne said, looking up. "Now." Dena hurried over to her side. "We'll take you home, Anne. Soon," she said, patting her hand and turning to stare accusingly at me. Days before, we had been discussing taking her home to die. "It's what you would want," Dena had said.

"I know, I know," I had argued, "but how can we overrule Evan? We're only her friends. He's her husband."

"What is this only?" she said. She stared at me then and I knew she was thinking—friends. Like selves. How can a mere husband possibly understand? "I can't believe I'm listening to this." Although she was an insomniac who spent most nights rearranging her life, reworking her travel plans with the TWA operators on the pre-dawn shift, Dena sounded more decisive than ever.

I stared out Anne's tenth-floor window, down upon the park, where stately sycamores were lined up in perfect green rows. They looked like supplicants, their faces turned up, beseeching the sun. To the left of them was a blue-black pond. I had the thought that if I could just take Anne up to Southhaven, if she could just see the waves, feel the fierce Michigan wind, she would get better.

Days in Southhaven began with the sound of Anne's strong legs galloping the stairs, and ended, always, on the beach. When the children had left the beach for good, we shook the sand from our towels one last time. I stared across the water, where the sun lit a path that seemed to reach to the heart of the world. In the twilight, the colors of the land deepened, becoming more than they had been. The grasses on the hill looked to be on fire, the sand had whitened and the once-grey planks of the stairs were bleached to the color of bones. Still, we could not leave the beach, although we knew it would be waiting for us the very next day, again. We sat and watched all the other families gather their brightly-colored beach towels and red coolers, fold their umbrellas and slink off, leaving odd bumps and tracks in the sand.

"This is my favorite time of the day," Anne would say. Although I had heard her say that at least a dozen times before, each year I waited for her to say it again.

Anne's doctor strode into the room without knocking. He was a tall young man with a neatly clipped beard who stood stiffly at Anne's bedside, writing at length on his clipboard before turning to Dena and me.

"Wouldn't it be better for us to take her home?" Dena asked.

"No!" he said, staring down at us, black brows arching. "Do you realize what is happening here? Have you ever witnessed the advanced stages of cancer—the disease overtaking the organs, the closing of the airways, the collapse of bodily functions. Blood, phlegm, urine, lesions . . . We have nurses, highly-trained professionals familiar with these processes. Are you two prepared to deal with this?" he said, dropping his clipboard onto Anne's nightstand, like a gauntlet.

Down the hospital corridor we rushed, Anne's wheelchair moving smoothly across the mottled linoleum. Dena was out in front, scanning, listening. When we reached the end of the hall, we glanced around the corner and saw a nurse coming toward us. We backed up into someone's room, holding our breath in the darkness, watching the nurse's white shoes pass by. Then we began again, slowly. At the last hallway before the elevator, I pushed Anne along, faster and faster. A great feeling of joy, or maybe it was desperation, swept over us. We were closer to Anne's dying and yet closer to the heart of things than we had ever been before. We were infallible, beyond the limitations of the physical world of hallways, doors, walls and glaring emergency exit signals. We raced down the hall, stopping just before we reached a room with all the lights on. We could hear the nurses arguing in hushed whispers. We rushed through the doorway's square of light, all of us lit for an instant, a group x-ray. We plunged toward the dark safety on the other side and rushed down the corridor as if invisible, tugging at the wheelchair, grunting, giggling, swerving past the empty nurses' station and into the elevator where Dena, her hand on the button, whispered, "Hurry, hurry."

She and I collapsed in unison against the cool grey walls as the doors slid shut.

It was a liquid evening, the sky black as India ink, the air finally cool after the weighted heat of the day.

I pushed Anne towards Dena's car, but Dena stood, not moving. She eyed Forest Park across the street, the city park we had been staring down at from Anne's tenth floor window. I stopped, too, recognizing my grove of sycamores. They looked less ceremonious from the ground level, more familiar.

"Let's take Anne to see the pond first," Dena said.

"The pond? Let's get her in the car. We've got to get out of here."

"We're out."

"The pond would be nice," Anne said, surprising me with the clarity of her voice. She propped her elbows on the armrest and sat up taller.

"Don't you think Forest Park is dangerous at night?" I said.

"Danger?" Dena said, "We're going to discuss danger now?"

We made our way along the moonlit path. Near the cattails at the edge of the water, a flock of wild geese was poised. Three of them flew across the water and then, in succession, row after row of them pointed their fat feathered bodies and long black necks toward the far end of the pond and took off.

The first time we invited Anne and Evan up to Southhaven, I had second thoughts even before they arrived. The Midwest was forever failing to live up to Anne's East Coast standards. But when she spotted the Lake's rushing waves, she took off for the shoreline, the wind grabbing her voice as she ran. "It's just like the Cape," she called.

We spent long days in the sun, while the kids excavated tunnels and built castles at the edge of our towels. In the evenings, after barbecued chicken dinners and the dishes and the sunset of a dozen shades of violet that happened just beyond our screen door, we all tried to get the children to bed so we could stay up late drinking wine in the makeshift dining room some aunt had decorated with an orange linoleum floor, mismatched card tables and a picture of a cow at pasture in a gilded frame.

One day, as we sat on the beach, Anne told me about growing up in a house where her mother and father argued constantly, the one thrashing about copper pots and pans in the kitchen, the other yelling back, and then retreating into his wood paneled study, blasting Vivaldi, which was piped throughout the house, at her mother.

The records lilting in the background of my childhood were Rodgers and Hammerstein musicals, I told her. My mother continued to believe in fairy tale endings even after my dad left her, as if she could make her life over simply by persisting in believing.

"Sounds like someone I know," Anne said, giving me a sideways glance.

"I can't help it," I said, "You grow up reading one romantic novel after another and see where it gets you."

"I once heard this poet speak in someone's living room on the Upper West Side. She was describing how she had raised her daughter. She was a big woman and she had this long, flowing gown on and she was sitting in a tremendous chair. She sounded so wise, so loving and yet so separate. So unlike my own mother. Afterward, I had this crazy impulse to climb right into her lap." Anne laughed, a deep, throaty laughter that only half-hid the yearning.

"A better mother. Wouldn't it be great to find one?" I stared out toward the lighthouse, as if she might be waiting there.

"I used to think so. But the more I take in, the more I learn, I'm beginning to think that just might be another form of rescue, the handsome Prince all over again in a different guise. The most important work seems to take place alone."

"Alone? That sounds so . . . lonely."

"Not really. You gather from others, here and there. There'll always be sources."

I anchored Anne's wheelchair into the muddy bank and sat down beneath a street lamp, upon a concrete bench leaning its way toward the water. The bench tilted so far forward it threatened to topple me into the pond. I told them about a book I had just read, the biography of an American physicist who had worked on the atomic bomb. "Like Einstein, he could be told nothing, relied on no one. He claimed that to really understand something, you had to know its beginnings. Scrawled on his office blackboard the day he died were the words, "What I cannot create, I do not understand." I paused, looking out over the water. "I just love that," I said, and then I flung my last bite of baklava toward the murky water at the center of the pond.

"Maybe that explains why men don't have a clue," Dena said. The only one of us whose life was not bound up with a man's, Dena often gave voice to suspicions we would otherwise have kept to ourselves.

"Unless they're raised with sisters," Anne said. We both turned to her, waiting. She began to say something, coughed, began again. "One sister can make all the difference. Evan, he doesn't have any sisters." I thought she might finally give voice to her anger, but she didn't. I worried about a link between those mutant cells and her refusal to confront Evan, wondered about a silence that grows inside in response to copper pots and Vivaldi. Anne's hands rested in her lap. She didn't say anything more.

Dena told us about one of her clients, a long, meandering saga that was hard for me to follow. The night nurse might have discovered Anne was missing by now. She would be calling Evan.

Anne was more alert than she had been in days. "Read to me, Dena," she said. "Read the one about the thunder." As Dena reached for the book, Anne stared across the water, eyes resting on the geese. "The thing I love about Emily Dickinson is her willingness to look at things head on.

She doesn't flinch, not even for a moment." Dena read, the words drifting out across the water, up past the pinched-in dome of the Planetarium.

I looked into the water where the ripples had blurred our shoulders together. I closed my eyes, half-listening to the sound of Dena's voice reading Emily Dickinson to Anne. Her voice was an alchemy of love and devotion and hopefulness.

The next morning we pulled up before Anne's white house, the car idling. We sat there for a moment staring up at the wide, wrap-around porch. The pink and purple impatiens Anne had planted in the spring, just before she got sick, nodded on each side of the walkway.

"I hope Evan is gone," Dena said. He always biked to work, so there was no way to tell if he was there or not. "Do you want me to go?"

"No. You stay here with Anne. I'll go." A gust of hot air hit me when I opened the car door. Newspapers were scattered on the porch. I stepped over a downed tricycle, a yellow bucket and red shovel, and began to unlock Anne's door with the spare key she had given me in the days when we borrowed diapers and formula from each other. Before I could turn the key, though, there was Evan. He held the door open, hand frozen on the knob.

"What do you two think you're doing?" He was chewing on the side of his mouth and I'd never seen that look in his brown eyes before.

"You can see what we're doing, Evan, " I said, voice trembling. "It's what should have been done weeks ago. We've brought her home."

"You can't do this. I can't do it. I can't."

Dena had come up behind me. I looked at her, but she didn't say anything. Her arms were folded over her chest.

"We'll help . . ."

"Don't you understand? I don't want to do it this way. I don't want my kids' last memory of their mother to be . . ."

"It won't be," I interrupted, "It couldn't possibly be. There's so much . . ." I looked down at the yellow bucket. How to explain a child's ability to let go—far better than ours? How to tell him the capacity of their minds to expand like clouds, taking in what's essential?

"She's going back," he said, moving past us.

"You can't do that," I called.

He turned. "You are so naive. You think everything will be fine because she's home. Nothing's changing here, Mariel. She's dying."

He stared past me. A breeze stirred the papers. He walked down the hill to the car, opened the door and kneeled by Anne. After what seemed a long time, he walked to the side of the house, retrieved his bike, and pedaled away.

I wheeled Anne into her room. Shirts and socks and underwear littered the floor. The blue and white paisley comforter was thrown halfway off the double bed, as if some battle had just been won and lost there. The mess was subsumed by the musky smell of Evan, living alone. Dena helped Anne into bed, fluffing pillows at her head and pulling the vanquished comforter up around her. I drew the drapes at the far end of the room, so Anne could look out on the ancient oak whose massive trunk nearly filled her window. I moved around the room, swooping upon the far-flung shirts and underwear.

"Mariel. Enough," Dena said. "She's sleeping. Come on." She gestured from the doorway.

I grabbed a last pile of laundry, glanced back at Anne, and walked into the hall. "I'll stay," I said. Dena said goodbye, and I was left alone with Anne.

Sitting down in a chair by the edge of her bed, I realized I was still holding onto the rough ball of shirts I had scooped up earlier. Anne's eyelids were so translucent a map of blue veins showed beneath them. They fluttered open and fell. Her forearm was bruised where the i.v. had been.

I brushed back a few threads of hair that remained, my hand pausing on her damp forehead. All around us were her things—a big pile of books on the nightstand, along with a collection of herbal remedies she had begun treating herself with weeks before. There was a bottle of almond hand lotion, and her eyeglasses for near-sightedness—the same prescription as mine, so that in a jam we had loaned each other clear vision. These were the things Anne had brought with her to Southhaven year after year. I knew them as well as my own.

As if she had overheard my thoughts, she said, "It wasn't Southhaven, that pond last night, but thanks."

"I thought if we could just be by the water . . ."

"Looking for magic. That's your mother talking." She closed her eyes for a few minutes, and then she opened them. "Alex will be ten next year," she said, "He has moved so far away from me, but I had been thinking in the next few years, when he became interested in girls, I might be able to help him again. Teach him to dance. Something."

"You will," I heard myself say.

Her eyes began wandering around the room, but it was a crazed kind of wandering, as if she wasn't seeing the nightstand things, the bookshelves, the window at all. Finally she closed her eyes. Then she began to cough, uncontrollably. What if she died—now? And I was the only one in the room with her. What should I do? I needed someone who could guide me. Anne was the one I always turned to for strength, for clarity. I looked around the room for something to distract me from my panic, something to read, anything.

I picked up a book from the nightstand. It was one of Evan's. It was brick colored, its pages thin and worn, and it smelled as if it had been held by many hands.

I flipped through it, finding prayers for dew, for the souls of the departed, for rescue and joy. There were prayers said upon arising in the morning, a Travelers' Prayer, a prayer "Upon Witnessing Phenomenal Sights," and a "Prayer Before Retiring at Night." The rabbis were thorough. They had covered it all.

Evan had marked some of the pages with small yellow tabs. I read through some of the passages he had underlined. But there wasn't a prayer to be said when your best friend was dying. Please God, I prayed, help me to find a way to fill the space that will open in my life when she is gone.

I closed the book and held it against my chest and stared out Anne's window. I no longer saw only the giant oak tree. I saw beyond its massive bulk to where a jackrabbit hunkered down beneath a hedge, across the street, its long ears poised to catch a distant wave of sound; saw the crimson leaves of a Japanese maple, saw the thousand water droplets of the sprinkler sweeping over the neighbor's lawn, a tremendous fan of water falling and rising, soaking the grass. I saw scattered images of Anne and me rushing past, borne on a fierce wind, saw them as one is supposed to see her life flash before her, only I was not the one who was dying. I would be left behind here, alone.

She began to breathe the regular breath of the dreaming, and my breathing slowed to match her own. The clock on Evan's nightstand clicked softly, and around it, a silence opened. A strange peacefulness came over me, absent since the day I had first learned she was going to die. I sat there at the side of her bed for a long time, thinking nothing, watching her sleep.

Later, Dena came to take the next shift. I might have stayed in that room with Anne forever, had Dena not pushed me out the door, into the steaming July afternoon.

I was running a bath for Lily the next day when Evan called. I couldn't tell if there was blame lodged between his words or not. He sounded exhausted. I placed the receiver in its cradle and stood there for a long time. Somewhere there was a link between what he had said and what I should do next, but I couldn't find it. The water was running. I ran into the bathroom and turned it off. I sat down upon the bath mat, staring at the water in the half-filled tub. In Southhaven Anne and I always had the hardest time leaving the beach.

"This is my favorite time of the day," Anne says.

The sun narrows its focus on the land, becomes a thin trail of light touching the water in silver glints and flashes. Though the water is far too cold, Anne and I dive in, swimming far out, farther than we ever have before, beyond where it is safe to swim, beyond where we can be seen. We flip and turn as children do, arching our backs, floating with our arms spread wide, squinting up at the sun. When we tire, when our bodies are stung with the cold, when the blood in our ankles feels like blue ice, we swim back to shore. We stretch out on our towels and let the last warmth of the sun dry us. At the top of the stairs our children call. We're hungry, they cry, hungry. It isn't until the water and sky darken to charcoal, and the wind grows fierce, comes rushing through the grasses, that we are finally driven from the shoreline and climb the stairs, again.

Naama Goldstein
A Pillar of a Cloud

The cousin of a third cousin twice removed from the granddaughter of our paternal great-grandmother's niece's nephew's son. The doorbell chimes. American relatives set foot in Zion and they all expect to be put up. They bring us presents, so all right.

But look at this one. Is it the peephole warping her? The doorbell chimes again and no one asks who it is. We can see, the elevator hatch glowing behind her as she stands outside our new Pladelet.

Plada equals steel; *delet*, door. The marriage of the two delivered our *Pladelet*, registered trademark, just a week ago. Slogan: *"Ma aht doh'eget? Yesh Pladelet!"*—"What are you worried? Got *034!*" The door is a hit and deservedly so. This has been a vastly satisfying week of entrances and exits. Either way the sweep of the transition is majestic, heavy, slow. The closing is best. The door is sucked in with a passionate kiss, upon which the bolts pop out, and plug themselves in every side, floor, jambs and top. The owner's manual shows them in X-ray view, a blast-resistant grid. Since the Mavo Dirot attack sales have shot up. Had that mother been this secure, so would have been her kids. There are five of us children here, and twelve bars all told, all controlled by one key. The key has no teeth; it has pocks.

The peephole we hadn't thought much about. We've had those before; it seemed the same as any other. But is not. According to this view the individual outside is built by the example of a dollop of whipped cream, everything settling from a point. Doesn't the object closest to the lens loom largest as a rule, the face? Perhaps the manual addresses this. We would go read up, except that our mother has ears in her head. She has heard the bell, several times. Someone must open. It's a question of who.

"I did last time."

"He should."

"She hasn't opened in a year!"

What's at stake here? We're not timid. But you never know the nature of these greetings, sudden intimacies with residents of unknown cities, strangers, as a rule better to do than us, but in terrible need, big-handed, broad-fingered. Children aren't asked, they're just enfolded.

The dilemma is resolved in a most shocking way. The cousin tries the door handle herself and reveals us where we stand.

"Well, hi! I thought I heard shy little voices. Oh my God."

The peephole lied, it seems for our protection. Though stout, she's normally proportioned, but she is homely in the most offensive way. She has taken our face and mismanaged it.

Behold the family gums. In us they're a touch indiscreet, nothing disciplined smiling can't swathe. But in her! The top lip flares up like a skirt. We study our shoes and the stone chips and shells in the tiles. Some enjoy a funhouse mirror, we do not.

It is a face we trace, in foreign documents, to Vienna. Uncle Isser in Ramot retains a brittle invoice for our name, bought from the Emperor Joseph, no returns or refunds, the initiative the seller's, the purchase mandatory. Klein was what we could afford or we'd have taken Gross. Until then we had been in the eye of fewer folks. We had kept to two circles, first name basis and Titled, the former limited to kin and community, the latter to outside bringers of good or bad, Shayndl with the brilliant son or Gertrude the beggar, the Coalman and the Beast of Prey.

In our possession from an earlier passage are the pages of the Book of Numbers, providing the first-known mention of our first-known forerunner, Calev ben Yefuneh (chapter 13, verse 6), who would have glared upon his weak-kneed fellow scouts to Canaan through our own black-olive irises, beetling our heavy brows and flickering our sooty lashes in high spleen. The fiery red hair, we have surmised, was a Hungarian acquisition, later, from an ardent episode among the Hassids of Satmar. The beautiful Avreml may have passed to us, as well, the milky skin given to sunburn, the dancing crowds of golden freckles. We have been told that our good looks are dramatic. We've been told we stand out.

One hundred and twenty years ago, under fear of erasure, we steeled our expression and parted with the savage nobles of the European woods, seeking the new state of peace and self-dominion.

Here is where the split occurs: On the way to Palestine, certain features stop for a refresher on Ellis Island—and defect. They never rejoin us. Moreover, while in Palestine our complexion yellows with malaria and knots with battle scars, on Coney Island, in Newark, on the East Side, their face begins to alter in the low heat of the melting pot. Witness the cousin, with her double version of our chin.

"Lemme see," she says, agog, as if we are the curious-looking ones. "*You* must be, no. You. I had it down pat on the plane."

Again she displays the private regions of her teeth. The eyes, however, remain guarded.

The eyes.

HaShem above, what has she done to the family eyes? On us they are less than serenely wide-set; we have a naturally focused look. But hers are so little! This makes the face look so wide! A chimp would feel as we do upon encountering her first orangutan. It isn't nice to recognize the kinship in something so patently strange. Oh, those eyes. How easily a look of hyperfocus shrinks to fear, and back again. Too many versions all at once, ours reflecting back at us, transparent, on the glass of her bifocals. What does she have to fear?

"You. No, you," she says. "Uhh, wait. I was expecting girl girl boy, but what I'm seeing is girl boy boy—and boy, yeah, that is definitely it. Either way, the oldest's name I know is—Crud, crud, I give up. We've had a snapshot of you on our fridge since, well, forever. But you all pulled a fast one on me, am I right? You grew up and you're more. I need an update."

They all say this: It's wonderful to know they always have a home here, and family. Our mother welcomes them. Her young ones aren't as receptive, are more dismayed by the disruption of routines, the blurring of turf, and that a guest always gets first dibs on the shower. The presents help warm us.

★ ★ ★

The first guest we remember was a father of another cousin, a child he brought with its mother, the wife. They would not eat our breakfast cereal. The brand name is Boker Tov, which is to say, Good Morning. The units are cylinders, irregularly cut, the color tan, the consistency sturdy. The stuff was too hard on the relatives' jaws and the flavor, they said, was like dust. They bought boxes of imported Frosted Flakes locally at an inflated price. Because of the price they asked that we reserve it for our cousin, Melanie.

They came with gifts! The packs of purple bubble gum lasted us two weeks. The elasticity! The perfume! And a formula that has overcome the bitterness at the end. The wads were reusable. Also they bore long manufactured cakes sealed in plastic, one for each: a perfect uniformity of crumb, an extravagant astringency of cocoa cunningly subverted with a layer of sweet white fat. The whole of it placing no demand at all upon the teeth—a science of contentment. This branch of thought is well developed here, we had all felt, until then. The Devil Dogs dissolved against our palates, our worries bathed in chocolate awe. In appreciation of our uncle's contributions we took only a modest lien of the Frosted

Flakes when the relatives were climbing to the Zealots' suicide fort of Masada in a cable car.

Tension ensued between the mothers. The American aunt, planted in our kitchen, wagged a depleted box of Frosted Flakes at our Imma. Why, said the American, why infringe? When yours are perfectly accustomed to the local stuff. It gratified us that our mother, per the norm one to demand a stoicism on our part, a making do, in this case held her ground on our behalf. They could not hoard stock in our pantry and deny us. Our mother questioned us when they had gone, we hung our little heads. She said no more. She set her teatime sugar bowl beside our Boker Tov the next day's morning. Our hearts ached.

The uncle's family disliked our beds: span too narrow, mattresses too thin, no boxsprings? They moved to a five-star coastal hotel in Tel Aviv. Despite the strained relations they took us out to dinner at a touristy Chinese on the Marina—heavenly, everything deboned, the chairs tall-backed and soft, the music wordless. They let us look out at our sea through their tinted hotel panes and take in lungfuls of the frosted Sheraton air. A couple from a far-flung branch arrived only last month. They were no-tears shampoo and a jar of Fluff.

★ ★ ★

So what will this one be? For one, she's been at least an hour on our sofa sipping orange squash and chatting with our mother while her suitcase remains latched. We mixed the juice. We fetched a plate of lemon wafers, sat, attended to the adult talk without undue disruption. The sun descends. The tiles have left our bottoms numb. The older folks are bent on tracing family lines.

Often the datum doesn't jibe. Our mother will be under the impression someone is long dead, or a convert. The cousin will correct her, no, alive and Jew, just hasn't kept in touch with the Israeli branch. The subject drops its anchor longest by one Cecil Kenneth Lyons, who now lives in Costa Rica with eleven pygmy hens. Our Imma finds the facts hard to digest. In Costa Rica? Operates an air-tram through a cloud forest. The hens he considers his family, humble, he finds, hardworking and generous. The plumage remains downy through all stages of life, and both the males and females feed the chicks.

"Costa Rica?"

"Went with a birding tour, fell in love with the place."

"Well." Our mother holds the plate up once again. "We have birds, too. And you came here."

The cousin accepts a pale wafer, tooths a crispy layer off, and licks the inside filling. "Birds are nice," she says, pursing her lips. "Is there a particular one? Cecil I remember was after the Resplendent Quetzal, originally." She comments that the lemon creme is tarter than she is used to. "Oh God," she says. "Can I just tell you real quick about my plans? I am on *such* a high. I have to see Masada, this I know, the Wailing Wall and David's Tower, Yad VaShem, Tiberias, the Dead Sea. All of those names! I can't believe they're going to come alive. You have to understand. Ever since I was a little girl in Sunday Hebrew school and Mrs. Milstein from the music period got me on this kick, all I could talk about was coming to see Eretz. Had to be her, sure wasn't my parents. She had just been, you see. She couldn't say enough. It was Eretz this and Eretz that and Eretz Eretz Eretz and, next thing that I know, here I am! Making it happen. Am I really? Someone pinch me."

Imma blocks a pincering hand. Our middlemost is prone to acting out on how we feel. We're tired and annoyed and we don't like her manner of speech. The Hebrew studded in the cousin's English is limpened by her accent and misuse of the possessive form. We've noticed this in other relatives, the scant unintegrated stash of Hebrew tossed in like exotic peppercorns in a bland stew. A grammar lesson: Eretz Yisrael equals *The Land of Israel.* Lop off Yisrael, and your remainder? *The Land of.* The lack of resolution makes us jumpy. Six times in one breath makes us upset. To ease our minds, we rest our gazes on the glossy maroon suitcase, a large and handsome piece of luggage of a sturdiness recalling our door's. The outside looks to have been poured of liquid leather, hardened in a loaf-shaped mold, quite a thick loaf, abundant. An inside view would show every sweet pleasure in her world and, most important, a year's supply of Frosted Flakes, box after box festooned with guardian tigers, her personal effects serving as padding.

"If you will it, it's no dream," our eldest says.

"That's beautiful," our cousin says. "Isn't that beautiful? And so true. Look, here I am. But let me not forget my hosts!" She straightens up and snaps out the retracting handle of her case. The loaf follows, rumbling on its wheels. "There is something I would like to offer you," she says, as if we didn't know.

She rests her hand upon a silvery latch. She'll want to tip the suitcase over. We will want to help. We rise. She smiles and addresses us, more or less:

"Is this where I live now?" she says. We grant her the derisive look adults expect at purposefully idiotic quizzes. She puts on an equally broad aspect of bewilderment. "No?" she says. "Okay. You're saying that I'm not always hanging out on your couch?" We shake our heads in concert. "Really? Wow. Then what do I do? Where?" The youngest verbal sibling can take this one. "Great!" the cousin cries. "Okay. Let's get a little more specific. I live where in America?" Our eldest offers up what comes into her mind right after Disneyland. The Big Apple. "Great!" the cousin says. "Okay. Close. Actually Connecticut. South Meadowlark, proud home of Greater Hartford's first and largest Chuck E. Cheese." Most of this we don't get. The playful tone is meant for us, we know, the heightened animation, the little eyes rapidly widening and relaxing as she bobs her head, seeming to near us through the lower half of her bifocals, then retreat above the seams. The esoteric wit is for our mother, who smiles dryly as the visitor plays gentle puppeteer. Not that we mind. We're seasoned hosts. We recognize the prelude to a gift.

"So in conclusion," she says. "Your Cousin Tiffy lives in—" Can't hope to pronounce it, won't attempt. She fills in the blank herself. "And there," she says, "she spends her days camped out on people's couches. Yes?" Correct. "No! Silly Tiffy! Tiffy's ten years out of college. Tiffy holds down a job, a senior position, I might add, since not too long ago. The Lenzomat at Turnstone Mall, a pioneer in bringing one-stop, quarter-hour, exam-to-specs service to the Northeast. Not including frame selection time. I'm an optometrist!" she says. "Couldn't bring the mall, but I have my chief associate's kit." She looks at us. We glance at each other. They don't usually expect thanks at this stage. First we must have a taste. "In other words," she says, "consider yourselves my guests." Strange, but fine. Take it out.

Her finger stirs on the latch. We hold our breaths.

"Thank you," our Imma says. "No."

What! *Why?* No present? *Why* no present? Our youngest crawls over to sit on Tiffy's shoe. She strokes his head, her other hand remaining on the latch.

"There are a lot of you, I know," she says. "But I insist. My pleasure, honestly. The raise paid for my trip so what the heck. It's something I decided I would do. I get the glasses at materials cost. The fifteen-minute promise doesn't travel I should say. I'm going to ask for your indulgence while I wire the prescriptions to the grinders. Shipping will take seven to ten working days."

Our Imma's nostrils flare though she maintains the social smile. "Let's talk about sleeping arrangements."

"Homework time a challenge for the gang? Studies show fifty-three percent of cases, the reason's purely physical! A staggering forty of that's vision."

"In the area of the visual arts my children shine," our Imma says. "The annual school psychometric test proves preternaturally astute spatial perceptions, across the board. And no surprise. Their Great-Great Grandpa Yokhanan of blessed memory cobbled the main street of our city. Samaritan limestone, cut by hand, transported by carriage. Laid them, too, not a gap. Never a set of lenses in the family then or since."

"Had to make do."

"Only thing wrong with his eyes, he sometimes had to close them. Killed in his sleep. Bedouin horse-thieves. He had laid all but the last block."

"No kidding. You'll have to show me where he took that nap."

"Where he was felled there is now a modern quarry, massively mechanized, highly regulated and enormously explosive, closed to the public."

"Not a problem. I'll snap shots of his roadwork. Be great to send back to the crew. We'll take the kids out on location. What's your schedule looking like this week?"

"Asphalt proved better for the shocks, in time."

"Well there you go!" Tiffy says. "Open your door to technological advancement is what I say."

"A well-established point of view," our Imma says, "holds that corrective lenses make for weakened eyes. The eye develops a dependency. The unassisted vision comes to be unbearable. Before you know, you always need them on." She claps her hands against her aproned lap and stands.

The cousin rises, too, our youngest sliding off her foot. We remain seated on the tiles, stunned, as mother, guest, and suitcase move away. Why? Why? The hard wheels roll with an occasional shudder, which the tiles pass to us.

When we recover and catch up, they're in our bedroom, the suitcase gleaming in the shadow of our desk.

Our mother tucks the edges of a sheet under the corner of a mattress. Cousin Tiffy dwarfs one of our chairs, exciting our space with her hands. When she sees us her arms extend in a full stretch, palms soft side up. We fall in her embrace. We press against her thighs and back. We drop our youngest on her yielding lap. Her sweet smell isn't of a soap we know.

"Delicious and delicious and delicious," she says, pinching every cheek. "Priceless. Whose chipped tooth?" Our next to eldest's. But the middlemost curls back his lips, as well, to show a compromised incisor. Him Tiffy proclaims a doll. She grins and her lip flips right up.

And thus we stand, half of our little group and all of her, flashing each other with the coverings of our hard roots. Even the frail connections to the inner-upper lip are shown. Our youngest joins right in, the pacifier falling out. Our eldest is a second mother to him, she melts, and united we grin.

Only our Imma keeps up her reserve. She twists a pillow through the opening of a case. "That's nothing to be proud of."

Tiffy's lenses sparkle with our wounded eyes.

"We broke our teeth because we fell," our Imma says. "We fell because we flouted better judgment. Who was in charge?" Our eldest bows her head. "And who rode who to the point of shared collapse?"

The guilty seal their teeth behind their lips, our eldest sputtering through them: "Who always works till late?"

"Kids!" Tiffy says, spreading her fingers in the air. "Kids will be kids."

Our mother drops the pillow in its place, her fists against her hips.

Tiffy looks down.

"Tiles!" she says. "Even in the bedroom? Wow, stark. Desertlike, barren in the elegant sense of the word. A little hard under the foot. Be hard on a kid's teeth. I was accident-prone as a child myself. My mother had the carpenter put extra cushion in? My choice was salmon plush. Forget it, though," she says. "I understand. If I were you I'd go for this exact look. I mean the specialness of life here is so apparent, even when you stay at home. Look at the stones. Look at the shells. That one's a fossil. Some have to be relics. What a concept. Every individual tile is basically an Eretz bar."

How can we but forgive this loving whimsy with our mother tongue? On the sofa she was happier than at the door and in the bedroom she is happier than there. We're off the topic of our broken teeth. Where this is going is clear. The future is bright. The sun shines through our shutters, tiger-striping Tiffy's mobile face.

If only Imma could be with us in our mirth. Her knitted brow betrays a mounting headache. "Take your cousin to the roof," she says.

Away we go.

And up, along the tiled stairs which rise from the kitchen porch. An ordinary wooden door opens into the high outdoors.

★ ★ ★

Ours is the tallest structure in the area, because the newest, but if a taller one were built here, it would see us like we see the rest: the bulges of utility rooms, prickly with antennae, the blinking solar panels angled at the sun, sending up postcards of the sky. The cousin is spellbound by the horizon.

The craggy hills resemble piles of scrap metal in the coppering light. A column of rich dust rises above the southeast range, nearly inactive in the breezeless evening, pale, whitish-yellow, lumpy, laden as a grandma's hose.

"Fantastic," Tiffy says. "Oh, perfect." She arranges us before this view, steps back and fumbles at her neck. She finds a strap. She draws a compact camera from inside her blouse. She aims, zooms in, out, in, and snaps.

The column slowly swells. The far-off blams of dynamite growl like a belly. Tiffy gasps. "Oh yes." The camera shaking in her hands. Flash flashing, she goes oracular for a moment, not unusual in this kind of guest. The proclamation she recites comes from the third book of the Pentateuch. The scrolls of her flame-colored hair unfurl and stand on end.

" '. . . thou Lord are among this people . . . thou goest before them, by day time in a pillar of a cloud, and in a pillar of fire by night.' " We explain it's from the quarry. She explains it's the effect, and snaps another shot.

A bike with tasseled handles leans against a water vat, a tricycle stands by the generator, and a jump rope is slung on the antenna. She poses us in play. She poses us before our mother's potted cacti, as we holler, Cheese! in our tongue. Gveena! She laughs.

"Forget the word," she says. "Shows too much throat. Let's all just decide to be happy."

Again? All right. But as we organize the team, Tiffy's attention moves on. She is hunting for the source of a near sound.

"What's that?"

The scraping of a trowel.

"By whom?"

By Ibrahim, we tell her, not too loud.

She scrutinizes twilit pools of copper on the tiles, and soon her eye finds the man. He is kneeling, back turned to us. A softening beach ball has rolled down the slope and rests not far from him, beside the PVC lip of the rain-pipe. His shirt is soiled, white-smeared with plaster, suntanned where it clings, and pinstriped where the fabric remains unaffected. He is neither young nor elderly, about the age of our mother. In his hand he holds a trowel, which becomes visible each time he plunges it in a bucket.

"What's he doing?"

Working on our roof, as if it isn't plain. Repairs.

"What was the problem?"

Permeation, what else? Wasn't she just in our room? The results are there. A mottle, greenish-gray, above our beds. In the living room the evidence is older, yellow scaling. The symptoms are averted in one spot, then reappear on the next outfacing wall. Our contractor cut corners, our mother said she'd sue, the laborer became a fixture soon after we took up residence. He shows up every morning.

"Where from?"

The really curious fact is that he always comes in the same shirt. It's plausible he owns six garments of the same design, it's also possible the style is so related, that distinctions blur. Goes for a formal look, buttons and cuffs, slacks, never jeans, never a t-shirt no matter the heat. Always looks ready for a podium, before the dirt.

"He is a natty dresser," Tiffy says. "Let's have him step into our shot."

We let our heads slump to one side in consternation, east. The silly-grown-up act again.

"I mean it," Tiffy says. "Why not?"

Just then our mother's voice carries up from the kitchen porch. It's time to eat, she cries, and we're glad to comply. Tiffy is slower, so her protests have a hard time catching up, though they keep coming. Once she's huffing at our side, downstairs, she gets her answers from our mother.

"He never has. He wouldn't expect or like it. His dinner is waiting at his home."

★ ★ ★

That night we stare at her round form under our sheets and listen to her adenoidal rattle. We can't sleep. How can we let ourselves, beside those eerie powers of mood infection, those strange ideas, and no gift. Still no gift! The next to youngest, and most impulsive, creeps up to the desk.

"Tomorrow," hisses our big sister. She's our conscience. She reminds us of our past: After the Frosted Flakes affair our mother made us swear to wait. How long? Until it's offered.

The suitcase is a black square in the dark. The cousin lugged the whole of it out of our room when she prepared for bed. She changed into a pair of baby-doll pajamas. Through the bathroom door, we heard each spring-latch pop and resonantly thrum in the acoustics of our blue enamel. Later we found this: the soap on the wrong side of the sink, her glasses soap smeared in our dish, a sock hanging from the showerhead, the floor-mat soaked. The toilet has been sanitized, and she's replaced our paper. The new roll doles out a double ply of staggeringly considerate fiber, fleecy, otherworldly, and—could it be?—infused with oils. Such a subservience to parts never so privately entertained. Is this the gift? Somehow it impresses only our eldest. Is this the thing our mother opposed? Could her sense of threat be this overblown?

Late in the night we hear the high emotion carrying into her daily summary, telephoned to our grandmother. "I know whose ass she's thinking of," she says. "I mean the nerve."

★ ★ ★

Our door is locked when we come home from school. It always is. We're latchkey children. But today, before we even fumble with the thick new key, the whole great apparatus shirks its job before our eyes. The bolts retract, the frame gives. The cumbrous door sighs and swings. Our surprise is something like discovering the staircase down has not yet leveled. Within this mind-frame, it's a sort of comfort to find Tiffy on the inside, shouting:

"Guess who!"

The baby is wailing on the floor. The cousin sports our mother's apron, an old one we all remember well. Some stains are ancient but those red ones are brand new.

Who let her use that?

"Mom's gonna be held up," our cousin says. "More work even than usual. And after she has errands, quite a few. She's a procrastinator, like I couldn't guess. Is she a Klein or what? I told her don't you worry, today you've got an extra pair of hands." These we eye, filing past: red stained as well. She closes the door. "I'm making us all sloppy Joe!"

Which is what?

"You'll see. I could only find flat bread. A little more thickness would have been good. Whatever. Once the meat's in the pocket we'll have to eat quick. Listen, I could use a hand in here. I still don't have the hang of where Mom keeps all her supplies. Some of you could set the table. Some of you could run up to the roof and tell Ibrahim it'll be fifteen minutes at the most. He should just come down."

A sour smell wafts from the kitchen. Red flecks the edges of her lenses, red on the toes of her shoes, as they pivot, heading off.

"What do you mean?" our eldest asks.

Tiffy's bifocals sparkle as she turns again. "What do you mean what do I mean?"

Our eldest swallows and repeats our mother's words: "He never has."

"So? Until yesterday, me neither!"

"He wouldn't expect or like it."

"Talked to him. Seems like the first was true. The second, not so sure, there was a language barrier. What I *do* know, when I see it, is a mild but significant squint, what I would call strabismus. I offered him professional attention. Anyone could see the man was moved."

"His dinner is waiting at home."

"I guess today he dines from two cuisines! Look, why the hell not?"

"Our mother doesn't let."

"Your mother has left me in charge."

"To get us killed?"

"Holy crap." Our cousin scrutinizes us through every combination of her lenses. "You guys are genuinely upset!" She squats. She opens wide her arms. "Come here, you."

We hand our wailing youngest over, drop into a half-circle, and look up. Our cousin holds the baby by the underarms. His diaper's wet. He whimpers, and she shakes him once.

"Hmm," she says. "Tiffy needs her hands to tell a story. A Klein or what?"

A story! Our eldest takes the child. He goes to sleep on her thin chest, while we three older ones forget our troubles once again in Tiffy's lively face.

"My Temple Nefesh music teacher," she says, ducking the head seriously, "as you know, Mrs. Milstein. The inspiration for the trip, not just in the past. Actively, now."

They're still in touch?

"I know, I know," she says. She makes her face absurdist now. She plumps her lower lip. "As if *her* teachers would still be alive! Old!" she yelps, then laughs and slumps. "But yes. She is alive. We are in touch. In fact she is now a dear friend, a friend who is slowly slipping away."

How awful. How terrible. Sick?

"The worst kind."

Oh no.

"Of the breasts."

Our eldest nearly drops the baby as she tries to plug our ears.

"What?" Tiffy asks. "Too harsh a topic for your age? The cancer?"

Of course not.

"Then the breasts?"

Shhh! Good G-d.

"Get outta here. I thought this was a largely permissive culture. I thought the majority is secular."

Yes to both. But not us.

"Then I guess I shouldn't tell you she's a dyke."

A what?

Tiffy explains in such a matter-of-fact way, that the idea simply strolls into our head and stays awhile, as ordinary as a sitter on a bench, whom we chase off, eventually, in a fit of giggles.

"What's so funny?" Tiffy says, in such a way that we're inspired to find our composure all at once. "Do you think it's wrong?"

Perhaps not. Truth is we simply never thought about the possibility. We knew about the boy and boy. Leviticus 18, verse 22. But girl and girl? We don't recall a mention. Maybe that's okay.

"The next part should be easier for you," she says. "Ultra traditional. Folks like you would have heard of the practice. Mrs. Milstein, Fiona, sent me here with her dying wish."

To be buried here? HaShem preserve us. She here now? In the case? That kind makes the very worst guest.

"She isn't dead yet," our cousin snaps.

May He bring her full recovery.

"That is no longer an option," Tiffy says. She pushes a hand into an apron pocket, loose and shallow for easy reach, yet she fumbles. She takes a breath and works herself to equilibrium again. Finally she yanks out a small bag. "She sent me for this."

A sandwich bag, darkened, plumped and prickly with crystallized instant coffee, about two-hundred grams.

"No," Tiffy says. "Dirt."

But of course. A sprinkling of the holy soil of Eretz Yisrael. For the eyes in the coffin?

"That's right." She bites her lip and pushes the small parcel back in its storage place. "I got it from your building garden. Just a little. Didn't think you'd mind."

This is just dreadful. Where's our happy Tiffy? We must try to lighten things up.

So what else did she do today? Where else did she go?

"Oh, nowhere. Tour bus not leaving till tomorrow."

Not even a walk down the block? The local grocer offers a particularly fine fizzing sweet. There is the young mothers' clinic, Drop of Milk. The name itself is wonderful, and never has she seen so many infants and their mothers traveling up and down one flight of steps! There are apartment buildings older than ours in design. Different shrubs in different gardens, a deserted house.

"Believe me," Tiffy says. "Terrible sense of direction. I would find a way to get lost."

Did she at least go up to the roof?

"You know I did!" she cries. Because *we* asked.

Somehow, we brought the dreaded subject back upon ourselves. We, us.

"Oh come on!" she says. She punches a few shoulders, lightly, leaves the baby out. "Did I or did I not hear you say the man has worked up there for years?"

He stands for a continuous blight in our lives.

"But do you actually know *him*?"

Yes. He shows up every day in the same shirt. The shirt arrives here clean each morning, but, every night, it goes home stained.

"Not that again. Does he have kids?"

How should we know? And can *she* fault us? She, who did not know our demographics, names, or level of religious practice, her own blood and hosts.

Tiffy shakes her head. "Don't even know where he lives, I'll betcha. Bet you have no idea what kind of a home."

She, who won't set foot on our block. In and out of a taxi.

"He is your *neighbor*!" Tiffy says. "That's closer. You walk the same land. I'm only saying it's a shame, and to imagine what you might be missing, think of the cultural exchange. He probably plays something. I've heard that the musicianship is staggering. That artist sampled it, and I mean, yeah, a little goes a long way, but yeah! Amazing stuff, rides a completely different wave. I'm telling you. Just do it. Climb those stairs,

extend that hand and flash that friendly smile. When you wish upon a star
and so on. Thinking positive is half the game. Live your dream."

The woman is mad.

Her beliefs are inane, we tell her. Can we dream our walls back from
their spreading problem? Can we think away the rot? And when we find
ourselves wall-less, will a wish shorten the fall from a narrow apartment
at the top?

"It's a moot point," she says. "I already invited him. He's coming. Try
to remember we're just talking about a sandwich."

Oh.

How could we have known?

A skillet in the kitchen seethes, dispatching its aroma. Beef? Tomato
sauce. In a sandwich? But that would be sloppy!

Oh.

We stand. We stare down at our mother's apron swaddling the bot-
tom-heavy form. She is ripely shaped, maternally, you might say. We are
young, our minds are flexible. We can imagine her part of the household.
Tiffy leaps up to her feet, agile considering her girth. She has been spared
the usual jet lag. She is full of energy.

"I am!" she says. "I can just feel the air re*storing* me. I also have this
helpful little pill."

She gives us each a coated half. The smile returns.

The barriers have come down. No longer can we look at Tiffy as a
guest. She is our *baby-sitter*, a whole different thing, an outsider who
comes in as the boss. And entertainer! And brings prizes for good listeners, and have we not been that?

The cousin freezes. She regards us squarely through her specs, each
eye divided by the seam. "That you should feel you have to ask!" She
wipes her palms on the lined apron and leaves the pattern sloppied up.
"My little angels. You had doubt?" Tears fill her eyes, then resolve.
"Avanti!" And she leads us to our room.

One by one we plunk down on her bed, which crackles with a mois-
ture-proof sheet Imma didn't think to take out. Tiffy approaches us, and
then steps back, assesses, nears again, and shuffles us, arranges us by height,
closes the gaps. She waits until we're absolutely still. She flips the shutters
and submerges us in dark.

"Now close your eyes."

The first thing we all hear is the metallic clack and spring of clasps.
We anticipate the whisper of cereal settling in its box, the crepitation of

cellophane, perhaps the snick of Cousin's nails against the side of a glass jar. Instead we hear another, fainter clack and spring. We're stumped.

"Every head I tap opens wide," Tiffy says, and taps—each child in turn, oldest to youngest, one by one, and each one pops. The baby needs assistance, because of his age and as he is sleeping. One of us pushes up a lid, one steadies the head, taking care not to compress the pliant fontanel. The cousin bows over, pointing her narrow red ray. Slowly, the baby's pitch black irises uncloak of their own will.

We have already seen what he is seeing, and we see it still. The imagery endures past the removal of the tool:

The eyes are flooded with an edgeless flood of black, which seems to heave, although the heaving isn't seen. How one perceives the heaving one cannot define, and this throws off one's senses from a cliff. Not in a frightening way. The cliffs rise from the stars, it seems, as gravity pulls only faintly. Though the general direction of the fall is down, one floats, and presently the floating pupil fixes on a landscape hitherto unseen, but present all around, a glowing veiny network, like the intricate venation of a leaf, except not green but red, not flat but very deep, the circuitry like never-ending branches of a fragile blood-red tree.

We are suspended in a world of frailty, effulgent, tantalizing, begging to be touched. We keep floating down. While we are at it, we can swim, beneath and over luminescent intersections, our only burden to avoid collision, not to interfere, to leave the glowing system unimpaired. The craft is painstaking, but in this slowness, we can learn. We exercise—we *become*—delicacy, heedfulness, astuteness, fine, fine care.

Until we hear our cousin's happy sigh. The darkness suddenly is ordinary, the daylight sifting, dim, through the thick plastic shutters.

"Wasn't that neat?" Tiffy asks.

The middlemost skips to the window, forces it ajar. Upon our particleboard desk the suitcase lies agape, blooming with clothes. On these a smaller case perches, open as well, the inside lined with velvet cavities, harboring metal tools. One of the cavities is empty. The cousin holds her implement. The handle is black, the head a one-eyed, silver cone, which still emits its concentrated ray, until she clicks it off.

"So?" she says. "Wasn't that mind-blowing?"

We're sure our mind remains largely the same. We've tasted no new flavor, smelled no new smell, masticated no new texture. That was it? Nothing else?

"Sure there's something else!" Tiffy says. "Did I or did I not give you the pitch already yesterday? I saw you sitting there. I saw you listening, or so I thought."

Again she reaches in our mother's apron, this time producing a catalog. Our eldest receives it. The publication is thin, notebook-sized, but densely paged, the pages slick but also powdery, sharp-scented, freshly inked. The language we can't read. The photographs, in rows and rows, page after page, show eyeglasses, framed or not, in metal or plastic. Glass glints over the infinite eyes of numberless stiff-headed models.

"Little girls often like page six," Tiffy says. "The pearly hues. The pink looks amazing on a redhead."

Our eldest casts the catalog aside. She rises as it hits the floor. Gently, she lays the baby on the bed, and smoothes the khaki skirt over her adolescent hips. She steps up to our cousin till her forehead nearly brushes the plump chin, then spins around to face our way. A stain darkens the area where the baby sat.

"She think she's going to make us four-eyed," our big sister says. "Like her."

We know a call to action when we hear one. We arise as one.

We swarm the guest, immobilize her, search her suitcase: skirts and shorts and peasant blouses, baby dolls, bras, panties, fifty rolls of toilet paper. Nothing! What is left to do, except tear our mother's apron off this fraud? The cotton sashes remains tied in a bow while the stitches break on one end.

Our next-to-youngest reaches in the pocket, and removes the parcel of dirt. Then the little monkey jumps up on the windowsill. Perfectly safe; our mother has furnished the window with convex bars. Hanging out, he rips the parcel and shakes it out. He watches as our soil rains down brown and disappears below our myrtles, back in place.

Tiffy never resists. She waits until we loosen our grip and, sneering at her, back away. Our eldest hurries to the baby, whose wild motions have impelled him near the edge. He has been howling with delight at the melee.

Tiffy exacts no vengeance. She does not explode in a burst of temper. She never says a word, after these four: "Seven to ten days." She only leaves.

She tramps, heavy-footed, to her nesting cases, closes the small one and the large over that. Head hanging, she hoists the suitcase off the desk, lowers it, and stands it on its wheels.

A shudder passes through the tiles as she leads the case away. We hear the heavy key turn with the smoothness of ball bearings. Our Pladelet slowly swishes open, yet more slowly swishes closed, and is received.

We gallop through the flat to end the sequence. Our eldest turns the key.

* * *

Our kitchen is filled with smoke. We switch the gas off. Baby on slim hip, our eldest slips her free hand in the oven mitt. Our mission she describes as twofold. We must get the fumes out of our house and change the dinner plans, both before our mother's return.

Taking the skillet to the roof does it all. Ibrahim can see. Whatever ocular deficiency our cousin found in him is indiscernible by us, if one exists. His eyes are very like ours. He watches the smoke rising in between us with a beetled brow, much like our mother would, flickering his lashes much in the same way, over eyes similarly lit, sleek as two oil soaked black olives.

Our mother was once beautiful, and so was he. Although he is stooped and thickened and begins to wrinkle, his hair retains the pigment of his youth, a Nordic blond, some new or ancient history of influx dyed into his locks. The black smoke billows in the wind, tilting aside, unveiling the pillar of the quarry dust, far-off, white, stolid. Black waves in, and again rises.

We have talked to him before, but only as messengers from Imma. These are our first words to him which we ourselves compose:

We would like to go air out the house. Would he mind the skillet?

"I could douse it if you like," he says.

He could do what? We don't know the word.

"Such clever children?" he says. "Your own language?"

They probably teach it in the seventh grade, our eldest says, setting the skillet on the tar.

"Tar burns," Ibrahim says. He reaches through the smoke, his plaster-whitened fingers graying, ungloves our sister of our mother's mitt, and slips it on his own hand. He bends and takes the skillet by the handle.

The column of smoke scatters and regroups as Ibrahim straightens again, then slowly travels west, towards a water tap that curves out of a segment of our building's silver pipes, though every shine in twilight appears copper. As in the same time, yesterday, the solar panels duplicate the sunset. Copper spokes our bikes. A copper droplet quivers from the tap's ridged copper nose. We rise and follow as the column from the skillet, unreflective black, inclines east as though resisting as Ibrahim walks on.

Though the roof is not so sprawling, the journey is long. The sun sinks lower in the sky. On any other day we would be gaining in abandon as we lost the light. Perhaps the mention of the middle-school grade has made us tired, all the hard work still ahead. The eyelids wish to close as if the worker is our teacher.

Is this not one too many radical shifts for children so young as we, in so short a time? We should turn and leave. See the stains on his shirt, see that rigidity in the attire.

But again we hear our mother's words. He might not expect or like it.

He is our partner in mid-conversation. We would not like to leave him wounded. The door connecting our home to where he works is nothing special. He is as locked in here as we by our Pladelet.

So what to say? And where to go from here?

Our next to youngest comes up with a subject. "Do you play an instrument?"

"Why yes," Ibrahim says.

His gloveless hand appears behind him and undoes the button in his slacks' back pocket. He comes up with a pen, and tosses this over his shoulder. In the shadow of the trailing smoke the pen sails in an arc. It is a common pen, a ballpoint cartridge cased in bright blue plastic, which we catch. We hand it to the baby. He puts the barrel in his mouth. Ibrahim throws another, and another. Some we seize out of the air, some we collect from the soft tar. He throws one still enclosed within a pouch of cellophane. His fingers seem to feel this too late.

"No!" he calls out as the thing bumbles towards us. "That one don't take," he says. "I shouldn't have thrown it. The ink has never moistened the tip. A virgin pen knows only to gash the page."

Allen Hoffman
Balancing Acts

I returned to Jerusalem and it wasn't easy. It wasn't easy because time is different here. Time may move as quickly as it does in other places, but it doesn't relinquish its past as it advances. Other cities may be eternal, but only Jerusalem's eternity is an active part of its present. No visitor is a stranger in Jerusalem. With the past so near, his roots are apparent. When I came as a tourist, I, too, felt at home, and an awareness stirred that this, indeed, should be my home because not to be in Jerusalem is to surrender part of yourself. I am an American and we never surrender! So with my family and my paints I came to live in Jerusalem.

I returned to live in Jerusalem, and it wasn't easy, because to live in Jerusalem is to surrender part of yourself. The nearness of generations makes the transient feel permanent and the permanent resident feel transient. All-encompassing Jerusalem. You are in the middle—small, minuscule, and a creation of Jerusalem itself. It is even more complex for you are also, potentially, an essential part of Jerusalem. Surrender is victory! With so much at stake, the tension is dreadful and exhilarating. You can't go home because you are home. You can only run away—or be driven out—and that is hardly new. That's how you got where you came from in the first place. How can you make what is permanent temporary? And how can you make what is temporary permanent? You can only tell the old stories, but can you tell them any better? Or in my case, paint what is already perfect? It's a privilege and a punishment, which is the way it has always been. God had to hold Mount Sinai above the Jews, threatening to crush them with it if they wouldn't accept the Torah, because everyone knew the score: being the Chosen People is a mixed blessing. With the light of Torah under the shade of the mountain, who could postpone the game because of darkness?

At first I thought that I was not painting because of all the aggravations and tedious chores of adjustment in the Holy Land. Of these there was no shortage: the plumbing alone would have defied Neptune. The toilet leaked onto the floor, the bathtub leaked onto the neighbors, the pipes refused the washing machine's pump-driven discharge. And waterworks were once His specialty. He split the Red Sea to bring us into this land! But, after all, I as an American hadn't been chased by Pharaoh. Would I have surrendered?

As these problems diminished, I still did not open my paint box or pick up a sketch pad. Earlier, running errands around the city, I had been struck by Jerusalem's overwhelming beauty. If that didn't inspire me, what would? Later, however, after I had no errands, I continued to walk the streets. The beauty increased. I saw modest, unadorned hills baring themselves in humility and resignation before higher elements of sun, rain, and wind. I saw the gray stone's durable hard edges of eroded harshness, still strong and intolerant, surrendering nothing without prolonged, unrelenting struggle. After a rain I felt the passion of ancient earth's moist hot breath in its cycle of renewal. The rocks remained cool, hard, but infinitesimally less; for each soft drop had made its slight, disintegrating mark.

How I wanted to capture the colors of fertile barrenness! I stared at the ancient olive trees with their hidden roots, gnarled, flinty trunks (surrender!), delicate, curved crowns of small, stiff oval green leaves (victory!). How I longed to capture their gentle, patient life. I watched the faces at a bus stop, reflecting a thousand places; for even the four corners of the earth have four corners, and these people had been to every corner—and to Jerusalem, too. Yes, I was inspired, but I was overwhelmed. The beauty increased, but I was diminished. My steps were merely the most recent echoes. When I arose, the day seemed too long, and when I retired, the day seemed too short. The minutes had different shapes, the hours had different textures. In Jerusalem I stared at my watch in disbelief and wondered where my day had gone. In answer, it ticked; the game had not begun and we were already in overtime! And what was the contest?

I began to wish that I was back where time made sense—in America, where the National Football League played an exciting game in four discrete quarters that anchored a comprehensible Sunday afternoon, with announcers to guide me through every play and replay. On Sundays I found myself wondering how the Jets were doing. I began to wish that I was back where things weren't nearly as complicated nor as beautiful—in Manhattan, where great things were obvious and small things were plain. Where a pigeon was a pigeon. A plain, dirty pigeon on a pebbly, granite-grained sidewalk. No big deal; but if handled right, the stuff of art. Interesting perspective—unsettling, off-angle view from above; good composition—discarded sidewalk refuse; rich subject—the stupid, goggle-eyed bird, weirdly realistic. And eight red toes. What I could do with color and design on those eight toes. Thank heavens, Manhattan is for the birds!

In Manhattan they were ordinary pigeons—scavengers, hangers-on, Broadway bums who parked on grimy cornices, descending to peck Burger King crumbs off warped, half-destroyed benches, but in Jerusalem they were doves, cherished residents of the Western Wall, sole remnant of the destroyed Holy Temple, God's House on His Holy Mountain, in His Holy City. The Western Wall—silent, eroded, abused by millennia—but now its gaps, holes, and harsh fractures are sheltering spaces for harbingers of peace, and the long-silent Wall has a live voice dwelling inside.

The delicate masters of this voice emerge from the Wall and ascend on rhythmic, thrusting wings to circle above the Holy Mountain. Soft, beating wings catching the slanting light, reflecting, shaping, transfiguring the radiant particles streaming from afar onto His Holy Mountain. As they soar, they thrust into the radiance other voices from below. The thick primordial silent voices of the stones of the Wall itself and the earth of the mountain. The joyous wailing melodies of the seed of Abraham, seed of Isaac, seed of Jacob, reciting the psalms of David, purchaser of the holy site. The small fleeting feathered specks wheel and break about in the stream, creating sheltering feather-lined bubbles to convey all the voices and prayers upstream to their Source. Thank *heavens,* Jerusalem is for the birds!

All this seen on Friday evenings when Jerusalem welcomed the Sabbath. The light emanated from the stones too. It was no reflection. Only on the Sabbath did it emerge from its stony, silent vaults. All celebrating sanctity and peace.

Paint that pigeon! How was I to paint any pigeon without painting those doves, stones, Abraham, Isaac, and Jacob, the feathers, the radiant stream of light? The permanent and the temporary, the hard and the soft, the loud and the quiet, the speakers and the speechless, the large and the small, the heavy and the light; the earth, the earthbound and flight-blessed, all chanting in unison to the Indescribable, Eternal Creator, "Why not now? Why not rebuild Your House, Your Holy Temple, now?"

I couldn't untie the rope that I had wound protectively around my box of paints. Confused, I wandered as if I were a small tile floating in a great eternal mosaic. I sat on my roof in the Old City's Jewish Quarter and watched the light change during the various hours of the day. I enjoyed looking across at the Mount of Olives and staring at the gravestones. As my mind was hopping from stone to stone, surprising thoughts intruded: the New York Giants, El Greco, and most surprising of all, my Uncle Maxie. Perplexed, I nevertheless enjoyed the view. It was, after all,

Jerusalem—stone-confusing-beautiful. I had a bleacher seat, but what was the game? Uncle Maxie didn't have a uniform and I didn't have a scorecard!

I walked into town and bought a *Herald Tribune* to find out the results of the Superbowl, a game I understood. I read it avidly, like a letter from a very close friend. The Raiders finally had won. The Vikings had lost again. That was reassuring; I wasn't missing much, but I had a sense of loss. I wished that I had seen it. I put down the sports page and looked across at the timeless cemetery. Did I have a season ticket?

I walked. I met my neighbor. He was pleasant and asked how things were going. Just fine, I replied, wondering what I was doing. I made frequent trips to the post office.

I answered letters. I talked about the weather, the agonies of Israeli bureaucracy, the kids in new schools. What was I doing? "Not much, but it's very beautiful here," I wrote, as if the beauty alone could sustain me when, in fact, with all the loose ends of time, it was strangling me.

My neighbor's father died. The funeral was on a Friday afternoon. a most inconvenient time. There is never enough time on Fridays to prepare for the Sabbath.

Attending a funeral wouldn't improve our chances any. Since I had never met the deceased, I thought I would walk in the funeral procession that left from the hospital and then return home without going to the cemetery.

Another friend and I accompanied my neighbor to the hospital. On the way, I realized from their conversation that my neighbor was not going to the cemetery either but, instead, he planned to go straight home. When I expressed surprise at this, he told me that according to the custom of Jerusalem, children and grandchildren do not go to the cemetery to bury a father. Not wanting to bother or distress him in his grief, I didn't pursue the subject.

Later, however, I sought an explanation among the crowd of mourners waiting for the procession to begin. Most people I approached either didn't know or, if they did, didn't want to discuss it. Embarrassed, staring at their shoes, they would shift their weight, kicking at the ground the way you might at a wedding if a child asked you what the married couple do after the festivities.

I persisted. Finally, a neighbor turned away from the crowd and told me under his breath and out of the side of the mouth—not just from embarrassment, but from fear, too—that, according to the mystical

teachings of Kabbalah, a man's seed that goes to waste results in the creation of demons and other impure spirits. If the children, the legitimate
seed of the dead man, attend the burial, then all that a man has created,
including the spirits and demons, might attend also. The soul rises for final
judgment at burial, and these evil creations might damage his case. The
children therefore do not attend because it is better to have no witnesses
rather than some who would certainly be damaging.

Such an idea struck me as fantastic and cruel. Fantastic because who
could believe such a thing! Cruel because the children should be at a
father's burial. For their sakes—to avoid denial, and for his sake—to show
respect. Although I was shocked, I was also fascinated by the novelty of
the concept.

Still, once the premise is accepted, then the children's returning
straight home makes a certain amount of Superbowl sense. If you can't
rely on execution the way the old Green Bay Packers and Cleveland
Browns did to run straight over the opposition, then you have to employ
a little deception: if your angelic fullback can't destroy the demonic middle linebacker with a crunching head-on block, then you have to get the
accusatory devil to take himself out of the play through a few good fakes.
More your Dallas Cowboy multiple-set offense. Although what happened should be termed a naked reverse; for after the sons had approached the father's body at the mortuary and had placed dirt upon the
closed eyes, they went rambling home around left end with their half-
brother spirits in swift pursuit. While they were heading that way, the real
funeral procession plunged off right tackle and angled for the cemetery
on the Mount of Olives.

Once I understood how the play was shaping up, I had no choice.
Since my neighbor couldn't attend, I had to do it for him, and given the
nature of this Kabbalistic offense, I was all the more important. You can't
tell the players without a scorecard, as they say, which is true enough, but
as I had never met nor seen his father, even if there were a scorecard in
the pressbox of the impure my name and number wouldn't be listed.

So I arrived at the cemetery ready to play. And I did, too. After the
members of the burial society removed the prayer shawl, lowered the
body into the grave (wrapped in a simple muslin cloth—anonymous and
white; no uniforms here!—let the impure spirits guess), placed the thick
concrete tiles above him, and began quickly to shovel the dirt back into
the grave, I, who wasn't in anyone's game plan, stepped forward to shut-
tle in the first play. I grabbed a mattocklike shovel and went to work

pushing the dry, heavy clods over the lip of the narrow grave, reaching and pulling the farther earthen remnants back into place, though this time with Shraga Feivel Tsur ne Glattstein tucked humbly beneath, and finally scraping, broomlike, the loose pebbly soil along the ground into the rapidly diminishing pit. Others wanted the merit of helping bury a man who had been a brother, a friend, a companion, an acquaintance, but to me he was anonymous, and in this Coliseum of Kabbalah I knew I had Shraga Feivel on the road to glory. Let them stare; I kept on: four yards and a cloud of dust.

Finally, I surrendered the shovel and stepped back to watch the second team bury the Devil's chances and end the terrestrial appearance of a man from Jerusalem. If he hadn't made it into the end zone, he was mighty close. I felt confident that our brilliant burst down the sideline had succeeded and there would be no undue criticism in the postgame interview.

Feeling more relaxed as the clock ticked off the final seconds—time had become intelligible!—I looked around, first up at my roof on the hill across the valley. From that distance the stones seemed to blend together and I couldn't quite pick it out of the crowd. I turned to examine the cemetery that I had constantly viewed from afar. It was both very personal and very communal, the stones worn, the ground ungraded, the weeds natural and profuse. The graves lacked that perfect Euclidean geometry that we associate with our average American right-angles-only approach to death. The Mount of Olives offered more freedom of arrangement, a random mumbo-jumbo that followed the lay of the land. All very surrealistic. Almost planned in a dilapidated, slightly chiseled, slightly eternal way. All very comfortable.

And the view! The view was magnificent: the east side of the Temple Mount with olive trees nestled at its base; down to the left the Kidron Valley; directly across the valley—the Jewish Quarter inside the Old City walls.

I'm not saying I was in a rush to join Shraga Feivel, but I did feel a debt of gratitude to him. Tradition has it that the Messiah will first restore the dead to life on the Mount of Olives. Standing by the nearly filled grave, I suddenly realized that the tradition has it right. I resolved to thank the deceased at the first opportunity—after one hundred and twenty years, of course.

That cemetery is just not like other cemeteries. It really is a wonderful place. If you have to die, that's the place to go under, especially with the resurrectional talents of the Messiah. It's dust to dust, but in that earth on that mountain, I sensed that a physical joining occurred simultaneously with the physical departure. I felt sorry for those poor souls whose bodies were lost at sea or left without proper burial. No doubt the Messiah can take care of all his customers, but in the interim they are missing a lot of the fun, if you know what I mean, because the old, decrepit Mount of Olives radiated anticipation. It was three steps above hope. It was high up on the ladder of anticipation. The only question was when? When was the Messiah coming?

I suppose I had always believed that the Messiah was coming sometime or other. His arrival is an article of faith, as they say. I was never one to go out of my way to deny an article of faith. So far as I can remember, when I was growing up in St. Louis, no one worried very much about the Messiah. There were always enough other things to worry about. Personal things like how to make a living, what car to buy, whom to marry. Things that can take up most of your day. Communal worries: synagogues, the St. Louis Cardinals, hospitals, schools, old folks homes, the price of kosher chickens, and the poor Jews of Israel.

No, the Messiah's coming was not a pressing matter. Had it not been an article of faith but, say, an article of clothing, it might have been an old leather aviator's helmet dragged home by someone's father or uncle from World War II and promptly relegated to a dusty attic. The kind of thing no one would ever throw out nor know exactly where it was. So it was with the Messiah.

The Messiah, however, unlike an aviator's helmet, was—is—an unknown quantity. After the Depression, the Second World War, the Holocaust, people everywhere, including the Jews of St. Louis, were fairly burning for known quantities: houses, lawns, automobiles, vacations, security, the good life. It was no mistake that Eisenhower clobbered Stevenson twice. Eisenhower was a known quantity, a successful one. Stevenson was yearning, theorizing, trying to articulate the contradictions and explore the paradoxes. It wasn't a time to articulate; it was a time to consume. The Son of Jesse wasn't in any of the Sunday supplements with garden hoses, seeders, lawn mowers, and other outdoor specials designed to save you time and effort while improving the appearance and value of your property.

You might argue that for the Jews of Missouri, the State of Israel was also an unknown quantity, but it was far away and they tended to view it as left-over business from the Holocaust, a Marshall Plan for the Jews.

They themselves were working hard to move, but not to Israel. They were killing themselves to get to the suburbs west of the city, the real promised land. Lightning out of Zion might have occupied a subtle recess of their consciousness, but it was horsepower out of Detroit that was in their eyes. In all our eyes. As kids we knew every model of every year. Roadmasters, Eighty-eights, and Chiefs. All of them, *oleihem hasholem:* the gracefully low-slung Hudson, the impressive boat-hulled Packard, and the slightly discombobulated Studebaker. And, yes, we too joined Henry Ford's grandson in sitting *shivah* for the Edsel with its weird, vertical grill.

If the establishment of Israel depended upon a Messiah, he was not featured as David, son of Jesse. The men and women who created the state did so precisely because they had given up on divine processes—if they had ever believed in them at all. They had had it with being a light among nations. They wanted to be a nation among nations. If American Jews were looking for cars, the Zionists were looking for a garage in which they could park their wandering nationalism. Who needed another Messiah as long as Ben-Gurion was on center stage? So it was all stacked against the Messiah. Nobody was advertising about him in the classifieds either way—Messiah Wanted or Messianic Position Desired, resume supplied upon request. Given the times, my new situation came as a surprise. It was only the first.

I returned to my roof and began awaiting the Messiah, a position for which I was not trained, but for which I did possess certain virtues. Some people go to pieces if they aren't busy; I'm not one of them. I just happen to like to paint. Everything I see possesses visual interest—a structure or design that can absorb my attention. To what extent the fruit of this aesthetic observation appears in my work has always been a question of interest to me. The connection is not obvious, if, indeed, it exists. It is as if I see with my eyes and paint with my gut or whatever viscera contain those deepest feelings and responses that are not developed but just are there. The artist and sports fan share this gut response that does not permit them to surrender to "obvious" facts and events. So it was I believed in the Messiah's imminent appearance; a people who refuse to surrender Messianic expectations after thousands of disappointing years can only survive on this deeper, gut level. Is it any wonder we make such loyal sports fans?

On my roof, I began to await the Messiah full time with a sense of vocation that had all but disappeared from my life since arriving in Jerusalem. And why not? Forget about your zone defenses and end-zone cameras. There is no instant replay for the great event and I have a seat on the fifty-yard line of the Temple Mount and Mount of Olives!

At half-time I left the roof and descended to the Wall to count the crowd and see whether the Messiah had wandered in without a ticket and was refraining from announcing himself for want of recognition. I would stroll among those present—some prayed, some stared, some just sat and basked in the Wall's presence like old men sitting on wooden benches across the street from the park. Close enough for "being at the park" with its sylvan aromas but far enough away to avoid ants and poison ivy. No Messiah in any of the groups.

I would finish my patrol by touching the Wall, my fingertips gently grazing the scoring of the stone—those random, patterned nicks from the stonemason's hammer. Each one was the work of a single man's single blow: personal and unique. Now the indentations were worn and smooth, but with my touch I felt the hammer's unyielding cacophonous assault when its head met the chisel's tail in screeching metal agony and the stone chips flew like crazed, driven snowflakes. The Creation Moment. It encouraged me; for beginnings imply ends: births, deaths, which are all part of the grand cycle of renewal that means time will have an end when the Messiah comes and everybody lives on the sunny side of the street with doves gently singing.

So I waited. I waited on the rooftop, and I waited by the Wall. I waited in the bus, and I waited in the grocery. I waited at my neighbor's during the week he sat *shivah,* and I waited at the cemetery again thirty days later when we dedicated the gravestone. He continued saying *kaddish* and I continued waiting. In the frenzy of this waiting, I didn't paint. How could I with the Redeemer coming at any moment? Just wait a minute, Mr. Messiah, until I get the green right, then I'll remove the paint from my hands with turpentine and welcome you properly.

Waiting as an act of faith demands expectancy. Expectancy demands attention because without attention, I would just be killing time, a low form of waiting, not the high pinnacle of expectation that places great prodding weights on the Messianic conscience to arrive already and get it over with. I tried to keep my mind on what I was doing. I waited so diligently that inadvertently I developed a new life style.

I realized that I no longer changed underwear very frequently. Only for the Sabbath. In this I was correct. According to the Talmud, the Messiah will not arrive on the eve of Sabbath or the eve of a holiday. When everyone is rushing around trying to get ready for the coming festivities, it would be terribly inconvenient for the Messiah to pop up. The Messiah might be slow, but he's thoughtful. So there was no problem changing underwear for the Sabbath since it was a day off for both of us.

Although I could have spared the time during the rest of the week, it would have been like purchasing a new calendar when the end is approaching. To order one both denies and reduces one's participation in the arrival. You might argue that it never hurts to take out a little insurance—straight-term B.V.D.—in case the Messiah doesn't make his move and it is time that marches on instead, accompanied by its human secretive essences and gatherings of lint.

The answer is simple. Faith is necessary to bring the Messiah, and faith, by definition, precludes looking before leaping, testing the water, and changing underwear. My underwear grew flat, tired, and gray. I itched because the body serves its earthly master as its Heavenly Master ordained. My underwear developed a palpable presence that was interesting, alarming, and unheard of in our family history. Well, not quite unheard of. To my surprise I did recall the odorific uniform. My Uncle Maxie hadn't always changed underwear either and it was to him, a man I had never considered seriously, that my thoughts were drawn as inexorably as an irrepressible itch. An itch of faith.

I don't want to exaggerate; there are differences. It took my uncle, actually my great-uncle, over ninety years to learn not to change his underwear, whereas I progressed to such a sublime spiritual state in approximately one-third the time. In all fairness, I had advantages that he never had: education, an affluent and stable youth, to name two. He, for his part, was rich in talents. He could sing, dance, and juggle with professional skill.

A short, bald man—in his younger years he was powerful, lithe, graceful, and dignified, but then, after seventy years, a rotund plumpness paraded above legs that bowed out under both the weight of the paunch and the weight of the years. He would carefully park a large two-door Plymouth in front of the house. It wasn't so much a parking as an august arrival, an aeronautic landing. If we called to him, interrupting his measured ritual, he would smile and throw us a wave while he finished putting the car in park, engaging the hand brake, turning off the engine, and removing the ignition key. He did this with concentration and concern, as if he were following a mental checklist, the way an astronaut must before emerging from his capsule.

When Uncle Maxie finally stepped out, you knew that Maxie was short for Maxwell. He had great bearing. Arrogant, but polite. A self-assurance and an ease that would have become a great aviator. He might have done better at Orly than Lindbergh. As it was, he had the airs without the achievement. When he entered a synagogue, the responsible dues-paying members detested him; for that little "fourflusher," as they called him, walked the way they only dared to in dreams when the Dow went over a million. Uncle Maxie had at best only an indirect relationship with the stockmarket through his familial benefactors. Still, if we are all self-appointed, Uncle Maxie had a better appointment, and if we are not, then he was an impostor. Either way he wasn't very popular with those who worked hard to earn their place and expected others to waste away in envy.

To appreciate Uncle Maxie in those years (he changed underwear then), it was best to be a kid because Uncle Maxie could juggle eight eggs at once. Seeing is believing. Eight eggs, some white, some brown—count 'em—never fell. For us, this Houdini was entitled to the airs he possessed. And what did he look like while juggling? Distracted merriment. Not the common touch of a buffoon, but not arrogant either. Rather an artistic dignity that is often appreciated in doctors. He enjoyed it all right. What a shame the pillars of the community couldn't have seen him then. It would have made everything easier for everyone.

Well, not everyone. My mother was mildly frantic during these performances, but Uncle Maxie was a great charmer. What woman could get mad at him without feeling that she was persecuting him? This juggling exhibition took place in the living room on the deep, plush gray carpet which we were constantly admonished was not some oversized doormat. On that score we could understand her hysteria. "Don't worry, I won't drop one," he would assure his niece with outrageous confidence.

"It's not you I'm worried about. It's the kids!" she would respond in tones of monumental exasperation. These were the principal, perhaps the only, tones the female line used on Maxie. She probably appreciated her uncle's feat better than we could, for she knew just how old those hands were.

"What's wrong with the kids?" Uncle Maxie would ask, reflecting our feelings at the unjust accusation.

"They'll want to try it too!"

Of course we would, although at the moment, we still tumbled through the air with Uncle Maxie's softly contoured floating eggs. All through the discussion the eggs were in the air. Tumbling, turning, soaring, floating, sailing, climbing, falling. Deftly controlled as if by suggestion from those small, well-proportioned hands. It was too much for the eye to follow. We saw only a pattern. One egg? Like trying to follow a falling leaf on a windy day when the trees seem to be raining them. His hands? Impossible without becoming hypnotized by their precise rhythmic prancings to and fro.

"Don't do it in the living room, kids," he would say by way of appeasement to his niece, but this perfunctory instruction lacked all conviction and interest. What he really meant was—kids, don't do it in the living room while I'm doing it. Uncle Maxie was not a rock-ribbed ally. In a pinch, he was not to be relied upon. We knew that he had deserted two wives, abandoning one with four little children. This predilection for hasty, unannounced departures distressed our parents and grandparents considerably more than it did us. We understood that that was part of the price one had to pay for greatness—the Benedict Arnold of Barnum and Bailey's. Now you see him; now you don't.

"For God's sakes, Maxie, use lemons!" she would implore.

After lunch, our appetites for juggling undiminished, we would be at it with the lemons in the kitchen. In open-mouthed despair: we watched the dull, yellow fruit (how it had sparkled in his hands!) dodge and dart away from our fingers. It seemed an overwhelming task for a mortal with only two hands. In the midst of bruised lemons bonging off the radiator and clunking off the refrigerator, we were struck by the obvious and only reason for our failure: eggs were easier, lighter, more apt to float in minimal breezes, and less slippery than those slick lemons. My brother mustered the courage to open the refrigerator and wrest victory from the egg tray.

"They're lighter," he announced. Success was in his hands. He tossed the first into the air. The second followed, but not quite rapidly enough; for the third had to be launched with extraordinary speed if the first was not to fall onto the floor.

"What was that?" Mom called.

We glanced at the yellow splotch at our feet. The kitchen floor could be cleaned up easily. What fairly fascinated us, however, was the spreading, wretched yellow mass that was descending the wall, its rich, clinging nutrient glue conquering new areas without surrendering old ones. For an embryo it must be the perfect medium, but this golden, rich, nutritious mix was also spreading across our parrot.

This bird, rich in blue-green and red plumage, was really an astonishing creation. Regal, compact, and flamboyant, it cocked its beak in an egotistical smirk; there was no doubt that bird could talk and knew what to say. Most memorable, and fearful to a child, were its sharp grasping claws. If anything inspired me toward art, that bird played its part. Mom had painted it right before our eyes on demand. Although no juggler, she was not without her Uncle Maxian talents—talents that run rich and natural like great seams of high-assay ore that rarely reach the surface, but when they do break through on occasion, they dazzle the eye as only traces of great treasure can.

We never even knew where she kept the palette, oils, and brushes, but once every few years she would bring them out and execute whatever we asked for right on the spot without so much as a preliminary sketch. At first we leaned toward parrots, rabbits, ducks; later it was trains, planes, and other wonders of technology. No matter, she could do it all. Then she would step back, admire it for a moment, and forget about it until some years later some mysterious impulse sent her for her oils again.

We were expecting some form of retribution to explode on our hindsides. To our surprise more than our delight—unrealized expectations among primitives always present a problem—we merely received a reprimand or two. "God dammit, can't you kids ever listen?" A little "Why did God curse me with children like you," but nothing with any emotion. She had expected it. "Damnation," she muttered, angry and sad, with the timeworn frustration of the sedentary civilized against the destructive unrestrained joy of the nomadic primitive. For all his genteel charm, Uncle Maxie was a socioeconomic barbarian—a Hun of family life, an economic Vandal. She had known that once the latter-day Visigoth had been permitted to perform in Rome, it was only a matter of time until the Sistine Chapel was sacked, if you will, for that parrot was a very rich bird.

Then, too, Uncle Maxie was her uncle. Maybe she remembered her childhood pleasure in having an uncle who could juggle like that. Or again, maybe with her palette and paints, she had some of the same chromosomal splendor and knew that it couldn't be totally suppressed. Those Litvaks didn't worry so much about skeletons in the closet; such calcareous residents bespoke permanence and predictable behavior from their dull, dark dwellings. What spooked Litvaks were the mysterious twists of the essential, living genetic material. Tay-Sachs disease, Houdini juggling, and Raphael oils aren't in the blood; they're in the stuff that makes the blood and everything else. Little Litvak chromosomes that suddenly override the deep sustaining rhythms of life and break into a little tango all their own while the deep inner sustaining rhythms go to hell. Whatever else you say, it's worth the price of admission and it promises to be a show stopper.

There's some of the Litvak in me, too, although it's watered down by a Russian influence, less brilliant, more melancholy, but not without its own charm: deep obsessive perversions that alter the very basic rhythms. For the Russian, a minor fleeting theme lasts not seconds or minutes, but decades and in some cases generations. Potatoes versus daisies. Still, that Litvak chromosome or part of it is somewhere inside of me, undiscovered, but I fully expect it to burst forth some time. Whenever audience participation is called for, I cling to my seat for fear that some deep, mad force will propel me onto the stage where I shall perform a perfect *kazatzke,* skip marvelously along a tightrope, or recite from memory the epic poem of Peru. (Anything but juggle.) And I'm enough of a Litvak to feel disappointed in spite of all my Russian fears if it doesn't happen someday.

Being a bit of a Litvak doesn't mean I'm like my Uncle Maxie. No one was thought to be like Uncle Maxie. It was a great mystery and an even greater scandal that Uncle Maxie was like Uncle Maxie. His lack of apparent followers was cause for a collective familial sigh of relief. He was not the hero of the family, but rather the black sheep, although a very fair, blond, blue-eyed one. By the time he was my great-uncle, the hair had departed and the light complexion had garnered its fair share of those dark mottling marks which we called liver spots. But the eyes were something else—forever roving and forever blue—a rare, light, clear blue, the blue of a soft winter's afternoon sky when the cool light has just begun to recede. From appearance alone, one would hardly guess that we were relatives. Until I came to Jerusalem to await the Messiah, I was rather thankful for the lack of similarity. Now, however, I was here, and I found myself thinking about him with mixed emotions. And why not? Why should my emotions be any different from His mixed holy blessing of the Torah? After all, if pigeons and doves, why not a talking parrot with ruthless grasping toes? A kosher dove would never speak, but in America silence doesn't articulate and you need words for heaven's sake. Is it any wonder my emotions were mixed?

I found myself thinking that neither of us changed underwear toward the end. Whatever else you say about the rest of the family, they change their underwear daily, socks too. And there's a lot of toothbrushing as well. I used to change underwear religiously although the brushing of teeth was never my thing. Uncle Maxie, however, was a superclean man. I have no doubts that he brushed at least twice a day and showered at least once, probably twice. That whole family, my grandmother included, were hygiene nuts. The word "dirty" was pronounced with a grimace for fear that the powers of dirt might be so great as to permeate the word itself and contaminate the speaker. Even among the men in the family, the word "filthy" was used only in anger and wasn't even permitted in polite conversation. On this I differed from them. Insofar as they kept kosher, the motivation was cleanliness. On the Day of Judgment, none of them would have been surprised if the first thing the angels did was check behind their ears.

My Uncle Gabe, Uncle Maxie's younger brother, who had the honor of being Uncle Maxie's primary patron, warned me against all commercial hamburgers because he had been told that they were made from kangaroo meat and would give you a jumpy stomach. In addition, Uncle Gabe always demanded from hotels at least fifty extra towels to "sanitize" every exposed surface. His toothbrush lay above and below so many embossed, bleached white towels that the princess herself could have fallen asleep on the whole pile without so much as imagining a pea lay beneath, much less a bristly plastic toothbrush.

I tell all this for several reasons. For one, things that sound screwy—people, too—can often be on the level. The level, in a manner of speaking, has its ups and downs like everything else. Who knows for sure that there isn't a little frozen kangaroo meat in a Big Mac, and who knows for sure that the Messiah won't come today, or better yet, who knows for sure he isn't downstairs waiting for us now.

I have another reason, too—I wish to demonstrate that Uncle Maxie was a very clean person. As black a sheep as he was in a family that valued stability, loyalty, hard work, and decency, he could not violate the real taboo, cleanliness. Once when I pressed Uncle Gabe for any reason that could possibly justify Uncle Maxie's double desertions, he loyally defended his older brother: "His first wife was a very dirty person. After a day's work, he used to have to come home and clean the house. She once cooked a chicken without gutting it. Can you imagine that?"

Frankly, I could.

"What was wrong with the second one? The mother of his four kids?" I asked.

"She wasn't very clean either. Not like the first, but she was dirty, too," he said sadly.

If Uncle Maxie stopped changing his underwear, there had to have been an unusual reason. He was still lucid and in good spirits, unless his sisters insisted that he change his underwear. Then a chase ensued around his small apartment. What the results of this steeplechase featuring two octogenarians and a nonagenarian were I never knew, although I do confess a great curiosity. For all of Maxie's former fleetness of foot, at that time I think my money would have been on my grandmother and great-aunt. My grandmother had great staying power. I do remember her distress. "It's so unlike Maxie; he was always such a clean person."

My mother claimed that his behavior was typical of old men. "They can't part with anything near them. It's related to impotence and death." I reject this analytic thesis for two reasons: Maxie was the least typical person I ever met, and his impotence was far from proven. A year later, in his final weeks, when he was well into his nineties, he was charming hospital nurses with all his old verve. "He's such a wonderful old man. We all love him," and it wasn't clear from what distance.

Uncle Maxie wasn't changing his underwear because he was waiting for something, something redemptive, and Uncle Maxie awaited it eagerly. His not changing underwear was an act of faith, an unarticulated faith that the Messiah would come. If there are closet homosexuals, perhaps my rascally old great-uncle was an underwear-drawer Messianist.

Uncle Maxie's juggling was intimately connected with his awaiting the Messiah. The Messiah will usher in a new era: strife will vanish, peace will reign. Historical time will be ruptured. Time will stop. We will be men but as in the Garden of Eden before sin. What a market there will be then for Messiah, Son of David's garden specials! It will be life of a very different consciousness. What in our world can now be glimpsed only in rare moments will in that world be the ongoing reality.

Uncle Maxie was a master of illusion, truly alive only in those moments when he directed the eight eggs into the air simultaneously. How tragic the world was for him when those eggs were not in the air. In those rapturous moments, however, when the tedious days, months, and years of clumsy gravity gave way to dexterity and flight, then Uncle Maxie knew there was hope. If the Holy Sabbath is said to be one-sixtieth of the World to Come, maybe a seventy-year-old's keeping all the potential chickens off the griddle is some small percentage of the Messianic Era.

I'm not claiming that he articulated all this. Let's face it, toward the end his memory was none too keen and the old man might have had moments when, if he weren't slipping toward senility, he wasn't keeping his distance all that well either. When his fingers lost dexterity, his eyes lost focus, and his body lost graceful coordination, and the day came when he spilled drinking water from his cup, he whose hands had once been so sure then strived to recover those days when he could juggle eight eggs while dancing a jig and singing Verdi. In those moments when he fought to recapture his past and focused on subjects swirling in memory, they did not have the scent of fresh eggs or the fragrance of Sunkist lemons, but they did have the whiff of redemption. He caught the scent of the Messiah or at least one-sixtieth of it.

Not that he was too good for this world. Quite the contrary. I suppose I shouldn't criticize someone whom I am beginning to resemble, but I didn't come to Jerusalem not to call them as I see them. Uncle Maxie had marvelous God-given talents that couldn't buy him a cup of coffee, be supportive of another human being through love, or afford himself any measure of stability. When it came to unrealized potential, Uncle Maxie was a superstar. If he didn't need the Messiah, I don't know who did, because what is the Messiah going to do if not permit us to realize our divine potential?

In the world of Truth there must be a little book where people are listed according to talent. Who knows if Einstein, Moses, and Babe Ruth will lead the list? Or if Maxwell Wein, Warren G. Harding, and Don Larsen (the only perfect World Series game to his credit and his career status shows more losses than wins) might not be given a Messianic resurrectional instant replay and rewrite the divine record books. When envy has died, those eclipsed will cheer louder than the rest; for they will be the most appreciative. Uncle Maxie couldn't manage anything on his own. His brother supported him, his sisters fed him, and the whole family clothed him. He had more different initials on shirt pockets than most commercial laundries ever cleaned. And to top it off, he was a deserter. He left those kids with his last name, I suppose, because he couldn't take it with him.

Uncle Maxie was only for Uncle Maxie. The eternal child. In some ways the perfect child: bright, beautiful, talented, charming, and totally dependent. When his parents died, his younger siblings assumed the nurturing role with generosity, love, and compassion. He grew old, but he never grew up. His brother supported him. His sisters changed his linen, did his wash, brought him food, and, yes, they sprinted after him with clean underwear. And in filial piety he promised never to reject their support nor to share the spotlight with anyone else. It was a great performance.

The whole world participated in his monumental commitments to self. Lyndon Johnson developed a Great Society just for him and his beautiful baritone. Or so it seemed when federal monies became available for the aged. Uncle Maxie rode the Golden Age Club boom the way IBM commandeered the space age. He joined and performed at every club for miles around.

Uncle Maxie was musical, but for him the bugle only blew retreat. Well, almost "only." He surrendered his children, his pride, his livelihood, any and all responsibilities (who said Americans don't surrender?) but he never surrendered center stage. That he wasn't about to surrender to anyone (who said Americans don't have principles?), including his great-niece who had been invited to perform Yiddish and Hebrew folk songs for the Jewish Golden Age Club. In the middle of "Aufn Pripatchik," as she strummed on her guitar, the attentive audience broke into raucous laughter. She looked up to discover her great-uncle had snuck up behind her and was making faces. Later, when the fourth generation of the female line that had indulged him shamelessly asked him to justify his behavior, he, not buying women's lib—or anyone's lib for that matter—answered, "We had 'em standing on their heads." Maxie was Shirley Temple's big brother, world's oldest performing child star. And it wasn't easy.

A child, his attitude towards death must have been a fear that fueled his rejection of anything so unpleasant. Young children believe that death is an exclusive province of the adult realm. At Uncle Maxie's advanced age, immortality must have been a difficult proposition to maintain. All his friends had died, and he could no longer juggle. Yet he himself wasn't prepared to give up his golden-age status, which represented such a rich investment in years.

What options were there? As things stand, there is no way to tell the Angel of Death to get lost, but there is the chance to change the rules. If you're losing in the fourth and final period, announce that the game has five periods. But games have rules. Only children don't understand that—and Maxie was the perfect child. He never accepted anyone else's rules his whole life. Maxie expected the Messiah to bail him out. Why should he have expected less? People had been bailing Maxie out for four generations. Let's be fair, the Messiah had been promised; it wasn't Maxie's idea. Why shouldn't the Messiah save him from dying? His ears were clean, weren't they?

If I sound too quick to judge, it is not without reason. To put it in perspective, the doves of the Wall are not the pigeons of Broadway. I don't care what the Litvak parrot says; birds of a feather flock together. The two of us don't molt our skivvies with the rest of the family. We let them wear out and leave them *in situ*. If I sound confused by all this, I am. When I came to Jerusalem, of all the people I expected to see balanced on top of the Western Wall, the last one was my Uncle Maxie—and juggling eggs in his underwear yet! And now I discover that I am scaling that holiest of walls to join him. I remember him not without affection. Without illusion, too. I remember him with fear. He deserted wives and children. This I didn't do yet, but I deserted everyone else by coming here to Jerusalem. We share a common economic attitude toward family and government called dependence. He was a superchild. And what artist isn't childish? Creation is an egocentric act. Every artist knows full well that when the evil tongue is said to kill, these words refer to criticism. No, if artists aren't children, then politicians aren't liars, and lawyers aren't thieves. In its proper context, each vice has its social rewards.

Since arriving in Jerusalem, I've been in virtual retirement. Uncle Maxie was one of the great retirees of all time. When I look up there and see him sitting on the Wall, I have reason to fear.

I have more than a sneaking suspicion who waits for the Messiah. The Messiah is for losers. The big cop-out. Yes, the Awaiters of the Messiah gridiron eleven have perfected one play and one play only—punt formation. Let's be honest, faith has its seamier side. You can root for the right team for the wrong reason and that team can still win, too.

I was frightened. I was frightened because I had surrendered enough of myself already. The thought of running around the rest of my life in shirts emblazoned with everyone's initials except my own filled me with dread. I was frightened because my brothers were too far away. I was frightened because Maxie's life was so unhappy when the eggs and lemons weren't in the air and I didn't even know how to juggle. I was most frightened to wait in a land where time was so strange. I was so frightened that I went to work.

I took everything up to the roof. Without hesitating, I cut the rope. Before I had everything set up, I had already started blocking out the basic areas. Barely looking up, because I knew what it looked like, I worked with almost fevered swiftness. Possessed, I stayed with it until the darkness descended. A contact drill Vince Lombardi would have loved! Then, grabbing everything together at once like a mad refugee, I hauled it downstairs into the house and continued until the early morning. After a few hours' rest—I'm not sure that I slept—I returned to my painting. By midmorning, I had dragged everything up to the roof. I wouldn't answer the door. I told my wife not to call me to the phone. I didn't change any clothes at all, and I hardly ate. Finally, on Friday afternoon, an hour before the Sabbath, I finished. I brought the painting and all my equipment into the house and in continued frenzy I put everything away.

"I'm finished!" I yelled in triumph, seized with a great burning desire to prepare for the Sabbath.

"What can I do to help?" I asked my wife.

"Take a shower," she suggested.

"No, I must help," I said.

I collected the garbage from under the sink, the old newspapers, the bottles. I ran out the door, down the steps, and all the way to the garbage container. On the way back, I met my neighbor. It was the first time in three days I had left the house. He stared at me uneasily for he had not been permitted to visit while I was working.

"I'm finished," I said.

"You're not going to shower?" he asked.

"The picture," I explained. "I finished the painting. Please come and see it," I invited.

He looked at the pail of garbage in his hand.

"All right," he said, "when I'm finished with everything. Right before Sabbath," he added enthusiastically.

"Fine."

I ran upstairs to shower.

I was dressed except for my shoes when he knocked. He, too, was freshly scrubbed.

"I never had a private showing before," he said with a laugh. He entered with the sly, hampered step of the very curious and the very involved. He was my neighbor and he wanted my painting to be good so that he would mean all the kind things that he would want to say.

As I led him into the room that was my studio, my wife gathered the girls to light candles.

He looked at the painting once and his eyes widened. A man who is in very precise control of his emotions and his appearance, he quickly reined himself into a neutral mask of observation. Even then, his eyes moved too quickly, darting back and forth as if to confirm what he thought he had seen. Then he realized that he had to say something. In embarrassment, he looked down at his feet and hesitantly shifted his weight. He cleared his throat.

"It's late. We'd better go to pray. We can talk later," and then he quickly added, "It's very interesting, of course."

The poor man, his eyes always betrayed him. They were filled with disappointment and a twinge of disgust—for *this* you came to Jerusalem?

"It's based on the verse in Daniel," I explained. "The one about the Messiah: 'I saw in the night visions, and behold, one like the son of man came with clouds of heaven and he came even unto the ancient of days.'"

"Yes, I see," he said, seeing very little. "I'll be late," he added and he left.

I stayed and carefully examined my creation. It was the view from the roof: I had captured a beautiful Mount of Olives. The clarity, poetry, and decay of the cemetery. The tombstones of mere stone, but so deeply rooted in faith that from those roots amid the bodies returning to eternity they draw nurture that suggests that they themselves are the congregation of the faithful. And what faithful! Exuberant, boisterous, but disciplined—no straight lines, no right angles, but grouped together in a zone defense to block out every spirit and demon in creation. The mountain itself has the solidity of a mountain sitting on center stage of the earth and the soft, delicate magical potency and assurance of a hill as fragrant as an almond blossom. The cemetery, too, is part of this procreative paradox of passionately gentle deathly renewal.

And above the mountain, the cloud-acclaimed herald is arriving. Uncle Maxie sails in airy majesty. He is not alone. Blissfully silent and no longer grasping, the brilliantly plumed parrot sits on his shoulder like a dove, for this is the age of peace when silence articulates and beauty is shared. Uncle Maxie is not ascending as an El Greco would have him. Nor is he floating in aimless memory like some aged Chagall figure. Rather, Uncle Maxie is purposeful and masterful, a cross between Charles Lindbergh and Tom Corbett, space cadet. He is arrival. Arrogant—deservedly so, that's a good number flying along with the clouds—but polite. His jaw is set. His eye is firm. His stance is dramatic and aggressive, as well it should be. His flesh isn't youthful but it has good tone. This is the Uncle Maxie of seventy years. He has his bald head, his paunch, and his bandy legs, but he's a son of a gun, all right! There's life in those thighs. The lean pluck of an old rooster, flexing his comb before crowing the dawn of the new day, The Day. And you can see part of his thigh, too, because Uncle Maxie is wearing the purest ribbed white underwear you can imagine. But these are not modern B.V.D.'s. These are long, form-fitting underwear, appropriate for an elder, for a herald, and for the discretion of Jerusalem. The pants descend gracefully to mid-thigh the way they do in the old silent movies when disrobing did not imply indiscretion. The T-shirt sleeves are halfway to his elbows. The flamboyant initials on his chest are at long last truly his: M. V. P. (When the dead live again, it goes without saying who gets that award!) His hands are held low in stately arrival. These are the hands that juggled eight eggs, but there are no eggs, nor lemons, for Uncle Maxie doesn't need them now. He himself is in the air. This is the age of the Messiah! All in the radiant stream of light.

I look up to find my wife by my side.

"For *this* I came to Jerusalem," I whisper.

Andrea Jackson
Istahar
A reinterpretation of an old Jewish story.

After the flurry and confusion of flirtation and temptation came the colossal misunderstanding. How could I tell God I was not as good as He thought I was?

Shemhazai: so tall, so handsome, and wreathed in light. I had had many suitors but was unprepared for a literal angel in human form. I was tempted, oh yes, to give in immediately, to experience that whirling completeness with one who could give it the seasoning of Heaven. But I aspired to marriage and lost myself in daydreams. Our children would be heroes, and I would be honored like a queen. When I died, angels would grieve over my bed and my own husband would carry me to Heaven.

I was skilled at using my wit as well as my beauty to keep a man's interest without surrendering. Angel or no, Shemhazai was dazzled like the rest. One day, I asked him to tell me the Secret Name of God. I thought he would laugh and saunter away, to meet me as usual, later, at the marketplace. Instead, so besotted was he that he shared with me the greatest secret of Heaven! I was at a loss what to do. I spoke the Name just once to see what would happen, and suddenly, there I was in Heaven, in the midst of a crowd of seraphim and right in front of the Heavenly Throne. I recognized at once that I was not dressed properly. But even if I had been, I would have stood out with my earthly vividness, the calluses on my hands from carrying buckets, and my broken toenails. God, the old man with hair like lamb's wool, looked at me with an old man's eye toward precedent and example. He declared in His voice of thunder that I had flown to Heaven to escape Shemhazai and rewarded me, He said, by transforming me into a star.

If He did not want me to anticipate the act with pleasure, why did He create me with that eagerness between my legs? Now my virginity must be preserved forever. Stargazers say I am the brightest in the sky. Lovers admire me as they consummate their passions. None of them knows what makes me burn so fiercely.

Continuity; or, The Clone

When Irving Block was 50 he admitted to himself that his son and only child, a pale sculptor, would neither take over the business Irving had built up nor, probably, produce any children. Obsessed with the urge to perpetuate himself somehow, and wealthy enough to be able to throw away money on a whim, Irving paid an extravagantly large fee to the Capital Clone Center in return for their undertaking to produce an exact clone of himself. They agreed to raise it in a carefully monitored environment somewhere in Utah, provide it with a first-rate education through the college level, and deliver it, completed, to Irving when it reached age 25. Invited to select a name for the baby, he chose Ike, the long-abandoned nickname of his youth. He completed a medical questionnaire, submitted to a series of physical and psychological tests, left the requisite tissue sample, and returned home to St. Louis. As was Irving's habit once any purchase was completed, whether a car or a corporation, he thought no more about the matter.

One sunny October afternoon, approximately twenty-five years and nine months later, Ike rang the doorbell of the suburban house where Irving lived with his wife, Esther. Irving was out, but Esther hobbled to the door. At age seventy-five, she was still slim, although rather stooped, and wore her long gray hair tied haphazardly at the back of her neck.

In recent months, Esther had become increasingly forgetful. When she opened the door and saw the young man, she recognized her husband. She felt a little confused and disoriented, but the feeling was familiar, so she disregarded it. "Ike," she said. "I've been waiting for you."

The young man looked uncertain. "Is this the Block residence?"

"For ever and ever," she laughed gaily, and kissed him on the mouth, and took his hand, and led him toward the bedroom.

Two hours later, Irving returned from his Men's Club and found no one in the house. Walking through empty rooms he came at last to the back door, opened it and stood at the top of the steps. In the back yard, playing in the autumn leaves, wandering among his son's sculptures, and pausing every few moments to embrace, was a young couple. The woman—her face unwrinkled, her back erect, her brown hair blowing in the breeze—resembled his beloved Esther as she had been when he and she were newly married; the man was the image of his own youthful self. Arms about each other's waists, they looked up at him and laughed as if it were their house, their statues, their autumn leaves, as if Irving had become suddenly the one who did not belong.

Pressure

Everyone died young in your mother's family. An inherited predisposition perhaps, but you suspect it's all that enthusiasm and performance: always "on," and then a stroke at 58. You're 58. You read an article about blood pressure and feel nauseated and faint, thinking how your blood fights you from inside your own body. When you become animated, you feel it pushing against your temples, trying to burst the fragile vessels. You believe pills would signal failure. Exploring alternative methods, you discover the mood-shifting power of meditation. You sit quietly repeating the word "One" over and over, then open your eyes and feel you have been in another world. You try to practice this while driving and almost hit a bus; you accept that there are limitations. Nevertheless, you resolve to cultivate mindfulness, to be peacefully aware of your body at all times.

To please your husband, you have gone with him to see *Titanic*. In the theatre, you wonder which hospital is nearest, in case your un-medicated blood pressure spikes during the movie and causes a stroke, but this thought makes you feel as if a band is tightening about your forehead so you direct your attention instead toward the screen. The characters are enjoying their voyage, falling in love, but everybody in the audience knows what's coming. Sure enough, there is trouble. People are trapped in the body of the ship. They run down a long hall. Their exit is blocked by cascades of water. They run to the other end. That exit also is blocked by cascades of water. They run down a different hall. The way is blocked by iron bars. You couldn't even run as far as these people; you'd be out of breath in the middle of the hallway. You are out of breath now. You recall the need for mindfulness and sit absolutely still except for the elemental rhythm of your breath. Air enters and exits your nose, cool in and warm out, stirring the tiny hairs. Your diaphragm expands with every breath, tightens against your waistband, contracts again. Your back, buttocks and thighs press against the padded chair. There is a point of strain at your unsupported lower back. Your boots are flat on the sticky floor and inside them your feet perspire gently. The screen is far away, separated from you by a hundred shadowy heads. The thought comes to you that this movie is boring. All that running back and forth.

Cheryl Maayan
The Hole in the Pantry

"Molly, dear, are you there!?! Can I borrow an egg?" Aunt Rose hollered through the hole in the pantry.

"Of course you can, Rose, darling. I'll pass it through. I always have an egg for my sister. I had an egg for you yesterday. I had an egg for you last week, a tablespoon of butter the day before that. But let me ask you this, if you're borrowing an egg, should you not give back an egg?"

"You want an egg? I'll give you an egg tomorrow. I'll send Arlene to the grocer. Never mind that she hurt her ankle. She'll get you your egg if you're in such a hurry."

That's how it went every day, Grandma and Aunt Rose yipping and yapping through the hole as they prepared dinner. The house we lived in shared a common wall with Aunt Rose's house next door. My Grandpa, a carpenter, chiseled an oval-shaped hole to open the pantry on our side with the pantry on my cousins' side. The hole looked like a cave-opening and was just big enough to pass a plate, or a pot, or a piece of gossip.

"Psst, Phyllis! Come in the pantry," I called through the hole. "I think that boy Jeffrey likes me. He kept turning up between classes today and smiling at me."

"Is he the one you met at the pool? I think he's swell."

"Let's swipe your mom's lipstick again and wear it to school tomorrow."

★ ★ ★

"Aunt Molly! Are you home? It's me, Eileen!!!" My four year-old cousin dragged a chair twice her size into the pantry so she could peer through the hole. "Aunt Molly? Tell me a story."

"Always a story, you want, my little one? How about a cookie?"

"A cookie and a story. Pleeeease, Aunt Molly? Tell me about the old country. About your ten sisters and brothers and the chickens you kept."

"Ten sisters and brothers. Yes, we had a family! You think this Brooklyn house is noisy with cousins, aunts, uncles and grandparents in every flat? You don't know from crowded! At night we sisters cuddled up on one mat, the brothers on the other. Doing the laundry took all day when

we were your age, precious one. And the only thing we always had
enough to eat were eggs—fresh and warm from underneath a chicken."

★ ★ ★

"Margie, I'm sending through some clothing Arlene's outgrown. It'll
fit your skinny little Phyllis. She could use a little meat on her bones like
her cousin, you know."

★ ★ ★

"Rose, dear! I baked some cookies for the kids. It was no trouble at
all. I'll pass them through. And here's your egg."

"Aha! A miracle! I lend an egg, and here . . . an egg in return. Such
things I thought were not possible. Perhaps you could lend me an extra
egg? I'm fixing gefilte fish."

"Of course, dear. But if you're making gefilte fish, I'll send an onion
through the hole. Your gefilte fish needs more onion and more salt."

"If you're such an expert at gefilte fish, why don't you make your
own?"

★ ★ ★

"Margie, the boys are driving me bananas. Tell me what to do with
Allan and your Michael. Yesterday they put Vaseline all over the toilet seat
and Arlene's date, Jeffrey, slipped right in."

"I heard the two of them working up a few tricks as well. They're
planning to get their hands wet, then sneeze, splashing everyone in the
room. I say we pretend we don't know what they're up to, and then do it
to them first."

"Shame on you, Margie! With your attitude we'll never teach them
to behave. No wonder they're such rascals."

★ ★ ★

"Aunt Molly, are you there? Sing me that tune that your mama used
to sing you in the old country!"

★ ★ ★

"Phyllis, Jeffrey asked me to the movies this week. I'm making a new dress, can you help me pin it?"

"Yea!!!! Did you use the fabric I sent through the hole? I'll be over in a jiffy, Arlene."

★ ★ ★

"Molly, my famous gefilte fish, coming through the hole. Eat and be healthy!"

★ ★ ★

"Molly, dear, you know the boat that your husband, the expert carpenter, has been building in the basement all these months? Well, they went to take it outside while you were at the market and—Molly, this you won't believe—it won't fit out the door. Be careful, his mood is foul."

★ ★ ★

"Margie, the boys are at it again. Allan and Michael stayed up and waited until Arlene and Jeffrey got home from the picture show. They waited behind the tree outside, and just as he was about to kiss her goodnight, they started whooping like cowboys and Indians. Every dog in the neighborhood started barking."

★ ★ ★

"Aunt Molly, are you there? Tell me about the time Uncle Max carved this hole."

★ ★ ★

The day finally came when we had to move out of the Brooklyn house. As I was watching the movers pack up, I heard little Eileen call my grandma through the hole, like she always did. "Aunt Molly, are you there?" Grandma climbed into the pantry, leaned her gray head down so that Eileen could glimpse her wet eyes. "Aunt Molly, Grandma says we're going to have to close the hole when you all leave. Why do you have to go?"

"I will miss you, little one. This hole, dear, brought our family together for many years. When your grandma and I left the old country we were ten and twelve years old. Losing our parents and our sisters and brothers left a hole in our hearts. This little hole in the pantry spackled my heart, where it had a hole of its own. Just remember our pantry, Eileen, and tell stories about it to your grandchildren."

"I love you, Aunt Molly. Do you have any cookies?"

"A cookie, you want? Today I saved a sweet just for you. Here, your last gift from the hole in the pantry. Eat and be healthy, little one."

I watched as Grandma reached her arm through the hole, passing that last sweet to little Eileen.

Miriam Raskin
Not Every Blemish Is Leprosy
And Miriam was shut up without the camp seven days; and the
people journeyed not till Miriam was brought in again
                                          Numbers 12:15

Listen to me, darlings, Miriam said. "I love you with all my heart. Loved you before, but now that you have risked your liberty by visiting me here, I love you even more."

"We wanted to see you, Ima," the tall girl with the flowing hair said, "to make sure that your needs were attended to, that you have food to eat, and that you are not too lonely." The young women, seated on the ground in front of her, legs crossed under them, looked at her with tenderness. The old woman sat on a bench next to the solitary tent to which she had been exiled. It was the rule: lepers were ostracized for a week, for the sake of purification, and she had been officially tagged with the marks of the disease.

"I am fine, as you can see," she said. "You need not fret. I have been around for a long time and know the games men play. They know I do not have leprosy; my skin is sensitive to the sun and dry and scaly with age but leprosy is an altogether different matter. Leprosy is dangerous and frightening and an overt sign of the disfavor of our God in Heaven. Although I know in my heart of hearts I have done nothing that would earn me the disfavor of God, I understand that Moses felt it was important to teach me a lesson. It's the lesson I never want to learn," she laughed as she said this, "that I should keep my mouth shut and not speak what men do not want to hear. So I must spend my week alone, outside the camp, and try to learn it. But I won't, of course."

"Ima, I don't understand." It was her granddaughter speaking. "Moses and you have long relied on one another for companionship. Why would he do this to you? You are friends, are you not? if not more? Some say you are his sister."

Miriam had been leaning towards the girls but now she straightened her body, allowing the shawl that covered her head to fall to her shoulders. Her thick gray hair, still streaked with black, fell in a long braid down her back. Her eyes shone like stars in the desert night as she looked off into distance and smiled, nodding her head slowly in agreement.

"It's true," she said then. "True that that is what people say. Although it is not true that I am his sister. I love Moses like a brother but it is not true. Still, nothing grows like a rumor once started. Trying to squelch one that has no basis in fact is like chasing a bird that has flown off into the heavens. Run, run, try as you will, that bird is gone, that rumor is free to fly into the minds and beliefs of anyone in its path. So the tale of the Miriam who pulled Moses out of the bulrushes has attached itself to my life story as firmly as the linen bindings cling to an Egyptian mummy.

"But I am not his sister, and I did not pull him out of the bulrushes, if anyone did. I am his friend and trusted confidante. Except when I tell him things he does not want to hear, when I suggest that the wise and perfect Moses may have made a small misjudgment of some sort. Then it is another story. Then he has to tweak me a bit to assure himself that he can.

"Because he knows that I know he is not perfect. I know his weakness. He is an exceptional human being who is gifted with unusual intelligence and extra-ordinary vision and imagination, not to mention considerable good looks and charm of the sort that inspire followers, but he is not perfect. Who is?"

The girls chimed in at once to answer the rhetorical question. "You are, Ima. You are perfect. You are wise and honorable and bring happiness wherever you go. The way you dance and lead the women in song gives courage to those who might otherwise be overcome by fear. And your counsel to the widows and the forlorn is always perfect."

"I wish it were so," the old woman countered. "But being perfect is not even among my aspirations. For Moses it is. He thinks so much, studies so much, as if he must know everything there is to know. And then do everything right, in that intellectual approach he has in which everything must be done according to a predetermined plan. He has plans for everything, rules for everything. If he never saw God, he would be a holy person. It is not seeing God that makes Moses holy; it is his view of God, his intuitive understanding of the holy life, his vision for all of us, living in connection with one another.

"He tortures himself, gives himself head-sundering pains, trying to make life right for us. Come, dance with me, I say, and he retreats into the mountain. And that is his weakness, precisely that. He cannot dance, cannot allow himself to dance. Everything is dead serious, and in his cleverness he knows that this is a weakness, that this is not the way life is to be lived. Not in this wilderness. Not in Egypt. And not in the land he believes is promised us. He has my sympathy."

She stood up. "Enough of this. It is best you go back to camp, and don't worry about me," she continued. "I know how to make myself happy. Even when I am mistreated. Come, let us dance." And she picked up the hem of her long skirt, twisted it into her sash, and clapped her hands above her head in a slow and steady rhythm. She moved as gracefully and as energetically as the young women that followed her, as they made their own music, followed their own beat, to the edge of the encampment.

Miriam Schwartz
The Story Tree

In a land far away, in the edges of a deep and magical forest, there existed a very tall tree that reached to the sky. Not only was this tree the very tallest tree in the deep and magical forest, but also in its branches were held glistening magical gems of all kinds. There were luminescent diamonds, sparkling emeralds, glistening rubies, shining crystals, and many more gems of every color of the rainbow, and every shape known. There were gems shaped like circles, triangles, diamonds, stars, and even pentagons! Yet it was not the appearance of the magical gems contained in this tree that made the tree so special. It was the magic contained within the gems that made them so priceless. For within each gem, there was a story, and the stories could only be revealed when placed in the palm of a sleeping child.

You wonder what kind of stories were held within these gems? Why, there were stories of heros, and princesses, croaking frogs, fiery dragons, and magical potions. There were tales of screeching witches, talking animals, and flying children. Yet these stories were locked tight in the gems, and the gems were locked tight in the branches, which were grasped by the tall tree, which existed at the edge of the deep and magical forest. And these dream gems could only be released by a very special kind of angel.

You wonder what kind of angel could release these stories? Well the angels of dreams and stories of course! Each child has an angel of dreams, and each night, as a child lays its head upon their pillow, their dream angel brings a special kind of invisible dream dust made from the leaves of the story tree, leaves which are crushed by the hooves of a special giraffe with who has the longest neck in the world. The angel of dreams places this magical dream dust gently into the eyes of the yawning child as they lay in their bed. This dust puts the child asleep immediately, and once alseep, the angel can retrieve a dream gem for the sleeping child.

You wonder how the angels attain the magical dream gems? Well, at the moment when the eyes of the child close, the angel of dreams departs from the bedroom window of the sleeping child, flying at the speed of light to the edges of the magical forest, where the story tree stands very tall. As the angels arrive, the gems sing out melodious songs to attract the angels, and the dream angels know from the song exactly which gem to choose for the sleeping child. They then say a special blessing that sets the gem free from its branch, and the angel hides it in a secret pocket in its wing. The sgem may be an emerald or diamond, star shaped, or square, yet no matter what type it is, it is sure to contain a beautiful story for the child who will receive it.

Once retirieved, the dream angel holds it in the special secret wing pocket, where it is safe and snug for the journey back to the child. The angel flies once again with the speed of light out of the deep and magical forest, away from the tall tall dream tree, and back to the bedroom of the sweet child. And the angel places the dream gem into the hands of the sleeping child, where the gem glows and shines bright. This is the moment that dreaming begins, and once holding the glowing gem, the child is placed into the story contained within the gem. In the dream the child can become a special princess who kisses a frog, or a brave prince who fights a flaring dragon, or a child who flies way high in the sky, or any other character whose story exists in the dream gem.

Yet the moment that the child wakes, the dream gem disappears from the child's hands, and returns to its place in the branches that are grasped by the tall tall story tree. And the gem will shine and shimmer as it waits to be plucked by another special dream angel, who will hear its sweet song, and then choose it to be place palm of another sweet sleeping child.

Adina Talve-Goodman
Swirling Souls
*Parents tell their children that one day they will find love. But some
need not search. Some have had love since birth and they need only wait.*

I

Penina was a beautiful girl. Dark, burning eyes. A mysterious spirit.
The town's pride, a most wonderful beauty. God gave her life in heaven
and set her down to the earth. Her father was the rabbi and her mother
the former town beauty. Penina's sister's name was Buna, wisdom.

The family walked through town with smiles, except Buna, who covered her slightly crooked teeth and otherwise ordinary features. The rabbi
was a kind man. He took walks at night without his wife and daughters.
Some say, without God, as well. Others say he did not walk at night, his
wife was too beautiful. She was beautiful, but not like her daughter. Some
mothers are comfortable giving their looks to their children, but not her.
She tried to find ways to snatch it back, "If you become too pretty, like me,
people will hate you. Don't worry, I don't think that will happen to you."

The mother loved Buna most. Far from lovely, Buna posed no threat.
The mother bought Buna books, poetry, told her stories of women who
studied and left town. She taught Buna to love poetry, music, science, and
independence. Buna feared men, they rarely even spoke to her. Her father,
the rabbi, afraid of her intelligence, ignored Buna. He loved the beauty, the
one from God, Penina. She gave him reason to come home at night. For
him, she was a comfort. At times he wished Penina had been born a man
so she might have a future more than her mother's. He liked giving her
what her mother didn't have. Penina studied religion, art, and grooming.

The beautiful Penina always loved Buna, but her jealousy often inter-
fered with the relationship sisters can have. Buna loved Penina, it was hard
not to. Buna could see the beauty, in Penina's eyes: full, mysterious. She
was drawn to her sister, it was hard not to be. And they laughed together,
but they could not cry. Their minds were linked but their souls were too
afraid for them to melt into each other.

"Good night, Buna Buna. Love you."

"Love you, beautiful Penina. Sleep well."

Down the narrow hall crowded with photos of beautiful Penina, slept
the rabbi and his wife. Neither craved the other, but they made love for
their children.

The family spent summers in town, rarely going away. The mother drank red wine and fanned the hot air while the rabbi studied and taught. The girls loved summer. Every day after breakfast, they carried fruit for lunch in a small picnic basket and ran to the river. The running was never a race.

By the river, Buna would sit against a tree with a book while beautiful Penina sunbathed naked. She was content in her body, proud to show it to the sun. Penina had a spirit which she hid, possibly from herself. But Buna knew it was there.

"Buna, baby, what are you reading?"

"The Guide of the Perplexed."

Penina stood up, naked, beautiful. Bits of dirt and wood chippings held onto her skin as she reached with her soft arms and pulled her long hair into a knot. Alone and with Buna, she really didn't care about beauty. But it wrapped around her always. She stared at Buna and her book until Buna looked up. Then she began to run to the river. Her long legs seemed to glide. She stopped at the edge, sinking her feet into the bank. Letting the mud swallow her toes, she exhaled. Breathing in, she pushed off from the mud and dove into the river.

Buna loved to watch her sister's release at the river. She waited for the exhale and smiled as she imagined her sister's beauty leaving her body. Buna could never stop herself from taking a breath of air at that same moment.

"Come swim with me. I'll teach you to dive."

"I'm reading."

"You're always reading! Come, swim with me."

"You're always swimming, come read with me."

Penina smiled at Buna. Buna smiled back, it was hard not to return gifts from beautiful Penina. As she climbed out of the water into the mud, Penina realized this summer might be the last that the two of them would share. She was getting ripe.

Her parents had begun talk of marriage, a natural occurrence. Marriage would work fine for beautiful Penina. But she would miss her quiet Buna. She felt a need for Buna, even if Buna didn't need her.

Without drying her naked body, Penina sat down across from Buna. She studied Buna's ordinary features, finding beauty in the way her sister held a book: close to her, like a sister. Penina longed to be held like a book.

"Why are you staring?"

"Buna, do you love that book?"

Buna tilted the book down to her knees, still holding it between her fingers. In a soft voice she asked, "What?"

"Do you love that book?"

"It's good so far. I'm not very far yet. I keep getting interrupted with strange questions."

"I'm sorry. It's just, well, the way you hold a book is so wonderful. As if you're in love with each one you read. You're the only girl I know who reads like that."

"I'm the only girl you know who reads." They both laughed. Buna looked at Penina: naked, free, and beautiful. Buna loved Penina not because of her beauty; she loved how Penina loved her. A natural love, sister love.

"Buna, my Buna, do you realize this may be our last river summer?"

"Yes. You'll marry soon and buy your own river with his money."

"Would you come to my river if I bought one? Would you come to my river and swim naked with me and let the sun kiss our bodies?"

"No. The sun kisses you, Penina, it does not kiss me." Buna looked up from her book into Penina's eyes. She couldn't stop herself from thinking of all that was good when she looked into Penina.

Penina turned her face to the sun. Closed her eyes and imagined a bridegroom. He must be kind like her father, challenging like her mother, wise like Buna, and handsome. She would not settle for less than Buna. After a few minutes, she turned back to her sister.

"Buna, if I don't love him, if I can't love him—"

"We'll leave. Fly away at night, ride the air like swirling souls." Buna continued reading as she spoke, "But if you can love him, if you do love him, I'll go alone. I don't need you to come with me, but you can if you want."

Lie. Buna wanted her sister with her, she wanted to find the world with Penina by her side. She wanted Penina to find the world differently, so they could compare and love both.

Penina ran to Buna's bag and took out a notebook and pencil. She sat down across from Buna and began to draw her sister's eyes. Buna looked up from her book, shutting her eyes.

"Don't draw me! Don't draw me! You draw me with your eyes." They laughed. Penina did draw Buna more beautiful than she would ever be. She also drew her sister older than she was. Penina drew Buna as she felt her.

When the sun began to set, beautiful Penina dressed herself and Buna finished her book. Penina took the lead on the uphill walk home. Buna walked slower. At home they ate a late supper. The mother and Buna discussed the book. The rabbi and Penina talked about his students. The mother and the rabbi did not talk to each other. Buna and Penina laughed.

That night, Penina and Buna talked about weddings, not about love. They spoke of cakes, food, men, dresses. Love was the subject they didn't touch that night. All other nights they talked only of love, but not tonight. Tonight they spoke only of a wedding, one wedding, the wedding.

Now, in another town, lived a rabbi whom everybody loved and the time had come for that rabbi to marry. Through the townspeople and Penina's parents, a marriage was arranged between the foreign rabbi and the town beauty. In one month, only one, Penina would be married to that rabbi.

On the days before the wedding, Penina spent her time naked by the river with Buna. Penina swam in the river mud and they laughed. They did not cry. Each one held a confession, a secret for the other. And yet, they stayed apart, in awe of each other. Both waiting, fearful, and a little angry that this would be their last week as connected souls, as only sisters.

The day before the wedding, their last day, Buna spoke.

"Pini, I love you—and I forgive you for being beautiful. I forgive you for not knowing I'm not."

Penina stared at her sister, "Buna, baby, I love you—and I forgive you for seeing only my beauty. I forgive you for thinking I want it." Buna gripped her book, Penina dug her fists into the dirt.

"Penina, I'm sorry I can't swim with you the way you need me to. I'm sorry if I get in our way." Buna's eyes finally began to tear, and her throat became tight with words.

"Buna, I'm sorry for not staying with you here, by our river. I'm sorry if you felt you needed to swim for me. I'm sorry I've left you here alone."

Penina stood and walked to her smaller sister. Buna was now shaking with tears. Penina sat next to Buna as she wept.

"I'm not alone. I'm sorry you felt it was you." Buna began spitting words, "I'm sorry this is the first time I've told you how good you are because I know you know that, but I'm sorry that I was never the one to tell you."

Penina wrapped Buna in her arms and they wept into each other, fixing each other. They held and yelled at each other, crying together. Then Buna apologized again, "I'm sorry that I stop myself from loving you." Penina rocked her sister and kissed her head.

They stayed that way, entwined, until both could feel a steady breath. Penina spoke to the peak of Buna's head, "Tomorrow," Buna's throat began to tighten again, "I marry."

Buna responded into Penina's chest, "I know."

Buna looked up into Penina's eyes and saw her own reflection. The wise Buna saw her sister for what she was, a soul. Her soul.

II

Penina sat drained on her fluffy cream-colored bed and stared at her future. Across the blue room hung an honest white dress. Embroidered with small pearl beads, it swayed lightly to the rhythm of the wind from the open window. The scent of a jasmine bush, planted below her window when she was born, hung in the room. Penina dragged herself from her bed and submitted to the pull of the dress. As she passed her sleeping sister Buna's bed, she ran her hand over the wooden edge. At the edge of the bed, she stopped. One hand remained on the bed as she reached out to touch the dress with her other.

The dress hugged, held, and perked her nicely. Penina stroked the seams and tapped the beads, but they sent no shiver through her body. So she tried harder. She let go of her sister's bed and held the dress in both hands. She tried dancing with it, swaying to the wind, but the rhythm felt wrong. She sniffed the dress, but the scent of jasmine was too strong tonight. Disappointed and exhausted, she smiled at the dress and hugged the waist. Pressing her cheek to the bodice, she whispered, "Tomorrow."

"Don't expect the dress to respond."

Penina let go of the dress and turned to her hazy-eyed sister. Buna sat up in her bed, "Why are you awake? Aren't you tired?"

Penina ran her fingers over her dress once more, then gave up and sat down with her sister. "Yes," Penina said, "I'm beyond tired."

"Then go to sleep." Buna fell back into her bed.

"I can't."

Buna raised her body again. She stared at Penina who looked at her dress as if she expected something from it.

"Are you still drunk?" Buna asked.

"No. I never really was, just shaky from all the dancing."

"Well, I am." Buna said.

Penina laughed and turned to her sister, putting the dress aside in her mind.

"I still can't feel my toes."

"Could you ever feel your toes?"

"I—" Buna paused to grab her forehead, "—can't really remember."

Penina climbed under Buna's covers, they stared across the room out the open window, remembering the night and the racy songs they sang with the aunts, great aunts, grandmothers, and cousins. Songs about the wedding night, guides and instructions. Surrounded by their women, Buna and Penina had danced in the center. Dancing, twirling, drinking. The grandmother taught the girls how to open their throats to red wine and the aunts showed them how to belly dance. The women sang out about men and danced with each other to a female rhythm, a similar breath. The mother, with her six sisters, danced in the circle around the girls.

Their faces turned the color of the wine as they twirled and beat the floor. The aunts commented on the mother's resistance to the wine, saying it could only come from experience. And they drank on. They left the house and ran down to the river where they continued to dance but now under the moon. All sisters howled and wailed at the moon while their feet turned up the old dirt and river mud. Penina began to remove her skirt while she ran toward her river, but her mother grabbed her arm and shook her head "no." Penina felt happy with her family, she was not thinking about tomorrow.

"Aunt Miri offered to let me stay with her in Firenze," Buna said.

Penina looked over at her wedding dress, "That's wonderful," she said. "Will you go?"

"I don't know, I can't decide. I don't speak the language—"

"You'd learn."

"She and I aren't very close—"

"You'd become close."

"I've never been away from home—"

"You'd be fine. Happy, even."

"What about you?"

Penina paused. She looked from the dress to her sister, "Me? Well, I'm getting married."

"True. Tomorrow."

"Today."

Buna soon fell asleep again, with her mouth half open. But something held Penina back from sleep. She lay next to her sister staring at the moon. Painted in the sky, the moon's swirled surface shone on Penina's beautiful, tired face. She hadn't studied at the moon so since she was a little girl. Trying to see, almost to taste. Eventually the moon moved higher up in the sky and Penina could not see it through the window. She closed her eyes, not to sleep, but to smell the jasmine bush. The jasmine blanketed her face and she remembered hiding in the bush with Buna, making flower chains and crushing the jasmine buds to make perfume with her small sister. Her breathing slowed to the same pace as her sleeping sister's but her mind ran on. A slideshow of memories played in her mind guided by jasmine and moonlight. She found treasures: building mud cities, playing in the street, and napping with Buna. Small memories, specifics. As she watched her life, she began to sleep.

"Drink this."

Buna and Penina awoke to their mother forcing two glasses into their hands.

"What is it?" Buna asked.

"It'll get rid of those black circles under your eyes and bring some color back to your cheeks."

Buna drank the strange mix with her eyes closed while Penina took short sips, gagging after each one. When they finished, the mother addressed Penina, "The rabbi and his guests will be here at noon, we have until then to get you ready. Go and bathe, wash your hair."

"But I'm hungry, I haven't eaten yet."

"No time. You'll eat tonight." Then she turned her attention to Buna, who jumped at the surprise focus. "You get dressed and come help us with the food. Leave the bride, she has work to do."

The mother took back the glasses and swept out of the room. The smell of onions had already invaded their room, pushing back the jasmine. Penina stood and made the side of the bed she had slept on. Without speaking, she crossed to the door and entered the room where her mother had drawn her a gardenia scented bath.

Buna watched her sister walk to her bath, a weighted, heavy walk. Buna stood and finished making the bed. She dressed and went down into the kitchen with the rest of the women. Aunt Miri winked at her as she entered and took a swig of wine. Her mother set her to work slicing onions.

Penina sat in the bath with the gardenia scented oils her grandmother brought her. She absently washed with tired motions. After a while, her fingers began to prune and she stood to get out of the bath. She saw herself in the mirror and felt no excitement. She wanted to think of the dress, the wedding, the dancing, but something pushed her back. Her thoughts went to jasmine, and sitting safely under the bush, to her room, her bed, her sister.

In the kitchen, Buna stood over a counter slicing onions. She wiped the stinging tears from her face and listened to her aunts.

"She's so lucky: a rabbi!"

"I agree. She'll make an excellent wife."

"I've never seen such beautiful eyes in all my life. They shine. They actually shine!"

"Keep chopping," Buna's mother poked her ribs. Tears began to stream down Buna's face as she thought of the formality between her mother and her sisters. Too much space between the sisters had created casual agreements and breaks in conversations. Was that her future with her sister? Could years of sleeping next to each other, running to feel the wind, hiding in the jasmine bush, and the river all fade? Buna's tears flowed freely and everyone thought they were from onions. But Aunt Miri wrapped her arms around Buna's shoulders and whispered, "Good. Cry it out, my love. But don't worry, she was yours first."

The mother climbed the stairs, rubbing her lower back as she walked. She knocked and opened the door without an answer. Penina sat sobbing on the floor just as she did as a little girl when her mother would yell at her for singing too loudly. She sat in a puddle of gardenia-scented water, her wet hair sticking to her shoulders and forehead. She looked up at her mother and began to leak sobbing noises along with the tears. They stared at each other for a moment before Penina hugged herself tighter. The mother stared down at her weeping daughter and waited. After a minute, Penina's crying slowed but did not stop.

"Now," began the mother, "wash your face with cold water, put a damp towel over your eyes, and brush your hair. I'll be in your room when you're ready to put on the dress."

Penina shook her head with little girl intensity and drew up more tears. The mother started for the door.

"Mother," gasped Penina between sobs, "I don't love my dress."

The mother stared at her beautiful daughter, opened her mouth to speak but instead swept out of the bathroom into the hall. She wiped her tired eyes and crossed to the bedroom her daughters shared. Light streaked the blue room as she opened the door. A smell tickled her nose as she stepped inside and she began to look around the room for its source. When she reached the window near Penina's unmade bed she remembered the jasmine bush she had planted while pregnant. Praying over a seed that its life be sweet and healthy. Overwhelmed by an old scent, she sat on Penina's bed.

"What are you doing?" asked Miri.

The mother turned her face to her younger sister and replied, "I don't know."

Miri sat down beside her seated sister and scratched her back as she scanned the room. She had helped her sister paint this room blue. The color of truth, wisdom, self-expression, and independence. Perhaps they should only have painted half the room blue.

"I remember when we painted this room, you and I. Before you had children. You wanted sons—how many? Four?" The mother didn't answer. Miri continued, "Anyway, you got daughters. Beautiful daughters. But we painted this room for sons."

"Do you remember my wedding day?" asked the mother.

"Yes."

"Was I happy that day?"

Miri was surprised by the question, "No—well, not at first. Don't you remember? You cried, I held you. I guess you were frightened or something, but you got over it. Actually you got drunk. Remember? We snuck wine from the kitchen and drank in our pink room." Miri laughed.

"Penina is in the bathroom and she is crying," confessed the mother.

"Marriage. I remember each wedding of my sisters, all six. All different, beautiful, happy. Spring, and summer, just one in fall. Each one off on an adventure equipped with cooking skills and a womb." The sisters laughed. Miri continued, "But you, you and I, we were having adventures already. Your wedding cut short our discoveries. I thought your wedding meant you were leaving me." She paused to remember how her sister always found treasures wherever they went exploring, and how she never wanted to look. "We were so young, so little—"

"So beautiful," said the mother.

Penina entered the room with her hair brushed and her face dried. Aunt Miri stood up and left. The mother swept up the white dress and slid it over Penina's body. Penina stood obediently, like a mannequin being dressed for a holiday sale. The mother fastened each clasp and tapped every bead. When she finished dressing her doll of a daughter, they walked to the mirror. Penina stared at the dress stoically with no desire to twirl or sway.

Around noon, the aunts began to shriek with anticipation. Buna sat quietly in her green dress as she watched her aunts draw over her sister's beauty with heavy cake make-up. Buna reached into her bag and pulled out a book.

A stiff, formal knock at the door marked the anticipated arrival of the groom. Penina shot out of her seat and looked to Buna, who rose slowly. The mother opened the door and greeted her husband. Penina tried to see the groom through the window but there were too many people to tell who he was. She stepped up to the door, Buna followed close behind.

Penina's mother took her arm and presented her to the rabbi. Penina took one look at the foreign rabbi and said, "I can't marry him. I'm sorry." She ran to her room, with Buna following. Chaotic mumbles and murmurs waved through the crowd. The rabbis stood stunned and confused.

Safe in the blue room, Penina collapsed onto the floor. Buna arrived seconds later with her eyes wide. She closed the door and sat beside her sister. Penina stared at the floor and hugged her body. Buna looked from Penina to the window where the sounds from the crowd below were coming in. She heard her mother saying she'd take care of everything. Knowing her mother would be coming, Buna turned to her sister. "Penina, what happened?"

Penina shot her eyes at Buna: no longer full and mysterious but swollen and frightened. She spoke softly, "Did you see him?"

Buna shook her head "no" and furrowed her brow. What could she know from seeing him? Penina's breathing became heavy and she began to rock herself back and forth. Buna placed her arms around her sister's shoulders to stop her.

"He's," Penina began, "he's—" She stopped and shut her eyes.

"What? What is he?" Buna asked.

"Ugly!"

The mother swung open the door. Her graying hair came out of her bun in wisps. She bore down at Penina and said, "Buna, come here." Buna, so intent on understanding the refusal of her sister, didn't recognize her own name. The mother repeated her demand, Buna rose quickly while her mother pushed her into the hallway.

Penina crawled to her window, raised her head slightly and looked over the crowd. She saw her father confused and frozen with his arms outstretched at the door and his mouth open in awe. Behind him, people pushed and questioned each other with rapid motions. A baby was shrieking, the sound vibrated in Penina's ears, but she could not find the child. Her aunts were pushing through the crowd, attempting to restore order. Aunt Miri had her arms around Penina's father. She held him like a mother holds a screaming child, but the rabbi wasn't screaming. He wasn't even moving, really. Just standing, reaching, with his mouth open. His eyes were melancholy. Aunt Miri was trying to help him lower his arms, but he would not. The sight of Miri pushing down on the rabbi's arms and watching them float up again created a rumble in Penina's stomach. Something began to build in her stomach until her body shook—and she quaked with laughter.

In the hallway, Buna waited for her mother to address her. The mother took Buna's wrist and tugged her away from the door.

"Go on, Rabbi."

A man shorter than Buna walked to Penina's door and entered without knocking. Buna narrowed her eyes as he passed. The rabbi wasn't short, she realized, he was slope-backed. A curved spine caused a seedy, predatory stance in him. His face was fine but because of the thrust in his neck, the lighting made him appear pale with dark circles under his eyes. The rabbi reminded Buna of the monsters in childhood bedtime stories that her father told. Most of the monsters were misunderstood heroes, but monsters just the same. Monsters don't marry beauties except in stories, Buna thought. She turned to her mother with a secret smile spinning on her face waiting to nest.

"Buna, this day will not end with a smile for you."

"He's ugly, Mother."

"Yes. But today he goes into that room armed with much more than beauty."

The mother saw the smile drop from Buna's face. She looked at her daughter and offered her something to replace the lost smile.

"When I was young, my father opened the world to me. He taught me how to read, not just how to look at words, but how to enter them. We studied together, parsed texts. As I grew, my father and I stopped learning together. I continued on my own and eventually surpassed him. When you were born, your father looked at you and knew, as we all did, you were not the one to watch. Penina would be watched. You would be different. He became frightened of you. No older than ten and you could bring out ideas like the old rebbes who lived with texts. He couldn't teach you, I did. I gave you what your sister will never have. You will leave, alone, but free. She will marry, accept that. This day is bigger than you. You will leave. Live a life I know you dream of."

Buna digested the words but one sat in her mind: alone. A provocative word, evoking fear, excitement, serenity all at once. Alone.

Meanwhile, in Penina's room, the rabbi stood staring at the laughing bride. Penina's body quivered without emitting sound. Hair fell over her face as she turned her body as if being tickled by some friendly hand. The rabbi wanted to watch her move like that all day, but he began to feel awkward, standing unnoticed.

"Hello."

Penina stopped laughing and scurried over to the corner where she sat looking at everything in the room except the rabbi.

"I didn't mean to frighten you. I'm sorry."

He began to slowly walk towards the bride. She jumped onto the bed. The rabbi strained his neck to look up at her. Penina finally looked into his face. Different from his body, his face carried a gentility and calm that Penina had never seen before.

"Before you choose to break my heart and our wedding day is ruined, may I tell you a story?"

Penina looked confused. She was beginning to think that besides being ugly, this rabbi was mad. But, she had already refused him, he deserved a chance. She stepped off the bed and stood across from him, all the while thinking: monster.

The rabbi looked around the room. He looked from the bed to Penina and asked, "May we sit on the floor?"

Penina sat, the rabbi followed. He stared at Penina's eyes. Her gaze was not upon him, but he still felt lucky to have seen it. Penina felt the rabbi looking at her and quickly turned her head away.

"Tell your story."

"Yes," the rabbi laughed. "Sorry."

A surprising laugh, Penina thought.

"Penina, Penina; you forgot, you forgot."

Penina perked a bit, the rabbi smiled.

"Swirling souls."

She turned to the rabbi and looked into his eyes. Surprising eyes.

"We've been together before everything. We went to God, you and I, and asked to be placed in bodies so that we might hold each other."

He touched her face and she did not move away. Again, he smiled. Surprising.

"God said yes, but that one of us would be imperfect. And before you could speak, I said, 'Let it be me.'"

He held out his hand to Penina and she rose without taking it. The rabbi rose, too, defeated. Penina turned to the rabbi and lowered her head to kiss his mouth. Surprising kiss.

And so the wedding took place but guests held their breath as the bride signed the *ketubah*. Only Buna breathed deeply. The ceremony went on without disruption. Penina's father's hands returned to him. The aunts grinned and wiped tears from their eyes. Only the mother and Buna kept dry. Buna stared at the groom in disbelief. The mother was not proud nor content. She sat hardened, looking at her husband's hands performing the ceremony. His gestures are slow and weak, he's so unkempt, his voice has never lost that nasal twinge, she thought. But there he was, her husband, her life.

After the ceremony, no one asked the groom how he had persuaded his bride. They were all too afraid. The bride appeared happy. She danced with her monster groom and they fit together nicely. Buna did not dance. She sat with Aunt Miri and made plans to go to Firenze.

The groom noticed his new mother-in-law sitting alone with a glass of wine.

"Hello."

The mother looked out of her wine and into the groom. She noticed a wild boyishness behind his hunched exterior.

"Hello to you, rabbi."

"May I ask you a question?"

"Yes. But I'm afraid I may be drained of wisdom for the day."

"'Why 'swirling souls?' How did you know the story would work?"

The mother looked at her husband. She saw him dancing with his beautiful Penina. The rabbi twirled his daughter the way he never could his wife. As she stared at them she said, "Life is a circle, rabbi. I have been here before."

III
Life
Stories

Minnie Appel
Life in St. Louis

I was about five and a half years old and my dad was in America already without us six months. I don't know what it was—whether the soldiers threw over the Tsar or if he gave them their rights to do things. There was a big gate in the front of our building, a long gate. All the men from the yard got sticks. They thought they could overcome the soldiers. All of a sudden the soldiers got on horses with whips and they started to frighten everybody. The soldiers opened the gate and went in. They came in the apartments and started throwing everything down from the windows.

My mother and my two sisters and I went and hid in the cellar. My brother hid in the garrett. All of a sudden I hear a man going by talking in Russian. What he said means "No Jews in here." One of my sisters wanted to open the door. I pulled her back. I was five and a half years old. If she would have opened the door and gone out, we would all be gone.

In Odessa, Russia, my dad was a Russian teacher. He decided that he didn't want to teach no more, so he started out for America. He had a sister here, a brother-in-law and a nephew.

When I came to America they stopped me at Ellis Island because of my eyes. My brother and my sisters went to my father in Springfield, Illinois. Luck happened they did pass me and let me through, so then I came to Springfield.

My mother didn't like it there. She was afraid we would marry out of our faith, so we came to St. Louis. I came to St. Louis when I was six years old. My dad couldn't teach no more. He had to go to school first. His brother-in-law was a junk dealer so he taught my father how to deal with junk, but he didn't like it. He had to make a living.

Someone took him in to the Famous and Barr in the linen department. My sister and I started to go to school. Then another girl came from Europe. We got to be friends. We all went to a one room school. The girl decided she didn't want to go no more. She wanted to go to work. So she quit school. My sister went right after her. She quit school, too. I said to myself what am I going to do here all by myself? I quit school, too.

My dad didn't know what to do with us. He took us to the Famous and Barr as cash girls. We both worked up to cashier. They paid $7.00 a week. We worked and decided that we didn't make enough money. My sister and I started to work in a skirt factory.

It was a Saturday afternoon. One of the bosses said to me, "Minnie, I want you to work this afternoon." I said, "No, I can't work this afternoon."

So he says, "If you don't work this afternoon don't come in Monday."

I said, "O. K." I tried to get all my things together. So the other boss came. His name was Goldberg. He says, "Minnie, what are you doing?"

I says, "I'm taking all my things together because what's-his-name told me I can't come in Monday if I don't stay this afternoon." I was independent.

Mr. Goldberg says, "Don't listen to him. Put everything back in place where it was before." I did. I was about seventeen years old.

My sister liked the skirt factory alright, but I didn't care for it. I quit. Somebody recommended me to a cap factory. The man who I married was a cap-maker and we worked in the same place. I made buttons. I worked there for a week. I didn't like it so I quit. I went another place to work.

I guess my husband noticed me. One afternoon my sister calls me. "Minnie, I want you to come by. Somebody wants to see you."

I said, "If she wants to see me let her come to me."

"It's not a she," she said, "It's a he."

I said, "Well, I don't know."

She says, "You better dress and come now."

So I dressed and I came up there. I saw a gentleman sitting there. I thought, "Who's that?"

We started to talk. He gave me some gum. I thanked him for it. We were sitting til about 11:30. Then I said, "I think I'll go home." He said to me, "Miss Perlmutter, can I take you home?"

"Well, you can take me home, but I haven't got far to go, just one house to the other."

He said, "That's not far enough for me, but it will have to do." So he took me home. I was going to say good-night. He says, "Miss Perlmutter, can I take you to a dance?"

I said, "A dance? O. K."

He said, "Can I take you to a show after?" I said, "One at a time!" I went to the dance with him. Next time I went to the show and we started to go together. It was Passover so I invited him for supper. It got time to go home so I took him down to the door. He wanted to kiss me good-night. I said, "Nothing doing."

He says, "Why?"

I says, "Because I only know you for about two months. We're not engaged and we're not married yet. We got plenty of time for that."

He got sore. Next time he didn't come. So my brother in-law said, "Minnie, what did you do to him that he didn't come?"

I said, "I didn't do nothing. I just didn't want to kiss him good-night."

My brother-in-law went over to where he lived. He talked to him. Next day he came running. It was a little too quick to get engaged. He takes out a little box.

I said, "What is that?"

He said, "Open it and you'll see."

I opened it. It was this ring that I'm wearing. I said, "I think it's too quick, too quick to get engaged. I don't know you so much. Too quick." He felt so bad about it. I said, "O.K." So we were engaged.

He said, "Can I have my kiss now?"

About two or three months later he says, "Minnie, I've got something to tell you. I don't want to tell a lie. I was engaged to another girl that was my uncle's sister." He didn't tell me that before. He says, "I didn't even like her, not love her. They made me get engaged to her. I changed my mind. I told her it was off!"

I says to him, "Why didn't you tell me that before you gave me the ring?"

He says, "Because I was afraid you wouldn't accept."

So alright, he was out of the engagement. I didn't even know him before. So he had another girl, that's all. I would have accepted him anyway. Things like that happened. After six months we were married and we lived together for fifty-eight years.

★ ★ ★

In 1927 when I went out of the house the tornado started. I didn't get to the store. Everything was stopped. The horses all over were dead.

My husband didn't know what became of me. He closed the store and started to go around looking for me and crying.

I was trying to get somebody to pick me up and take me home. They wouldn't do it. It took a long time till a lady drove past. I says, "Please take me home. I haven't got my own car." I didn't know her, but she took me home.

Then my husband came home. I don't know how he got home. My dad was missing and he fell almost down in a sewer. They brought him home real late at night. We all survived. It was a terrible tornado.

I remember I had the basket with food. I thought to myself what do I need that for? I threw it away.

You couldn't even pass by because of the horses, all the dead horses.

My father when he was eighty-six was up and around, walking, going. He was so eager to go. On Easton Avenue he used to stay with my sister. He liked grapefruit. He used to like to go get grapefruit from the store. So when he was coming back he had a stroke right by the grocery store. My sister came there and there was a man in a car. He says, "Come on, I'll take him to the hospital."

When my father was there I came to see him.

My sister came there and said, "Look how nice and red his face is."

So I told her he's not red natural, it's a bad thing. And he passed away.

My mother died when she was seventy-six, but she was a very sick woman. She had asthma. She couldn't walk. First she lived with me for eighteen years, not because I couldn't get a home for ourselves, but because I took care of her.

I was going to learn how to ride a car. We had a Ford at that time. When we were in business we had to have one. My dad started to teach me how and I started to drive. All of a sudden on the other side of the street came a car. I got scared to death. He took over. I never drove any more.

I used to come to the store around one o'clock. I came one day to the door. It was locked. It was dark inside. I said to myself something happened. All of a sudden a policeman came from the inside. "Are you Mrs. Appel?"

I said, "Yeah, what happened?"

"They took him to the hospital to give him a shot."

I said, "What for?"

"He was held up and hit over the head."

When the robber got inside he started on him. He put a bandage in his mouth, tied him up, started to beat him. "I can kill you if I want, but I'm not gonna kill you."

I was standing by the store and waiting for him. The police brought him and he looked like a tramp. Everything was torn up on him.

I says, "Well, now we're gonna sell the place," and we did.

Minnie Appel, July 15, 1898–September 28, 1992

Nancy E. Berg
Location, Location, Location

1. Camp Ellis Beach

Trying to prepare for the next semester's courses, I'm auditioning potential texts. I am drawn to memoirs, fascinated by them, at times repelled. The luminosity of the language freezing deliquescent memories into coherence. My New England discomfort with too much self revelation. Self exposure masquerading as introspection makes me queasy. The best of them make me envious.

I envy them their memories, their abilities to recover them and their talents in conveying them.

The most compelling of these memoirs are narratives that are beautifully shaped by invisible hands into a subtle weave of interconnected motifs, moments of recognition, and felicities of language. Any fragmentary quality is a calculated strategy. My memories are elusive like my dreams, momentary sensations, glimpses of color and motion, wisps of scent. Anything more concrete is a reconstruction imposed after waking in vain attempts to assert logic and even order on the fading vanishing images. I mull over the difference between my memories and theirs as I clean up my desk—a stalling tactic whose benefits last only a bit longer than my dreams. I come across an old postcard I don't remember.

The postcard shows a typical nineteen sixties beach scene—small figures on the sand, blue water, blue skies and fair weather clouds. The ocean line curves into the shore, two white spots are either delinquent waves or small boats. The figures closest to the camera are two men, one in a white tee shirt and dark shorts sitting on his heels, hand to mouth, probably smoking, looking toward the water, the other propped up on an elbow. Looking more carefully I see that he too is wearing a shirt although at first it looks like skin. He sports a bulky watchband on his left wrist. The cluster to their right is more familiar: one woman in a two piece bathing suit, another basking in a low chair, a kerchief keeping her hair from blowing in the breeze, a man crouched over the blanket, another beach chair to his back. Small items littered around them. The beach is strewn with bathers and their possessions, also tufts of weeds, big black trash cans as punctuation. A mother and child lean over at the shore's edge, looking for seashells. The masts of a sailboat far off. I tell myself I recognize the exact spot; we are just off-camera past the bottom right hand corner.

I look at it and am flooded by remembering. Eating overripe fruit on dark scratchy woolen blankets, the color of the peaches' flesh improbably vivid, the sticky juice dribbling down to my bent elbow, the gritty sand mixed in no matter how carefully I hold the fruit. My sister and I are brown as berries, splashing in the cold salty water, between the estuary of the Saco River and the fishing pier.

Every morning we wake when the sun lights up the dark green window shades. The beds here are higher than those at home, iron frames, flat feather pillows and thin woven cotton bedspreads in faded pink. Our feet run across the bare floor, some of yesterday's sand between our toes. We are quick to put on a dry bathing suit and get to the beach.

The cottage is on a choice lot—in the morning one gets the breeze off the ocean on the back porch, in the afternoon it's time to move to the front porch for the river breeze. It is on the corner, all crab grass in the sandy yards, the front yard big enough to park a car and home-made trailer. The local fire station, maintained by an all-volunteer force, is on the other side. One night we hear the alarm and run out with everyone else. Either we got there too late, or the fire wasn't much to begin with, a pathetic flame on the sand. For years it is what I imagine when someone talks about house fires. My sister says I'm lucky, my pajamas have feet and I won't have to wash my feet again when we get back.

My grandmother is the rarest of creatures here, a summer person who has become part of the landscape. She spent nearly every summer of her adult life at the cottage once she owned it. Yet we never saw her on the beach. She would stand on the back porch in her sleeveless house-dress and call us in for lunch. Bessie is famous for her lobster sauce and potato pancakes, always cooking full meals even in the heat of the summer. Lunch comes with a side of salad: iceberg lettuce, thickly sliced cucumbers and tomatoes with her favorite Catalina dressing, sweet, glutinous and orange. We sit in the kitchen, still in bathing suits and sand-covered, sticking to the dark red vinyl of the booth. After lunch we are free to return to splashing in the waves and lounging on the blanket. My sister chases me with wide ribbons of seaweed. At low tide we wander the sandbanks for starfish and other treasures, bringing them back to the cottage to save. We rarely get to keep them; they start to stink as they dry out. When the tide comes in we move our blanket back up toward the rocks just in case. We run into the water with an inner tube hauled up from Boston and take turns floating in the waves.

Dinner is more of a production. Clutching a few dollars we walk down the street toward the pier to Huot's, the place that set the standard for onion rings for all time to come. The menu was typical seaside take-out; clam cakes were their best selling item. My sister and I would fight over who got to keep the wooden fork that anchored the onion rings. The soda machine on the side of the clamshack dispensed small bottles of grape and orange soda. There may have been other flavors, but none I would have chosen.

There was a sit down restaurant around the corner. I don't remember ever eating there until years later, when I was in college, visiting my grandmother on my own. The rhythm was different then. Every morning I would walk a block or so in the opposite direction from the pier to the corner store for Bessie's daily ration of newspapers. I think my mother was friendly with the woman who owns it when they were both teenagers. Huot's was now shabby. The soda machine was gone, and they didn't even put the wooden fork in an order of onion rings which now looked much smaller. But the rings were still perfect—golden and crispy batter, sweet juicy onions inside. Few people know I am Bessie's grand-daughter; I masquerade as one of the summer renters, or even a day tripper.

The house that partially blocked the ocean view is gone, taken out in a winter storm a few years back; the road between the cottage and the beach is no longer there.

The firehouse is blocked up; any emergencies are attended to by the larger Saco station. There is a gift shop near the restaurant selling souvenirs and such. The woman who owns it is too friendly, tries too hard. I try to avoid getting caught there. It's next to the new ice cream parlor.

The water is cold, too cold to swim. Some years later—my last trip to the beach—I wade into the water only so as not to be embarrassed in front of my brother-in-law and niece.

The cottage has two floors. When we were little, the second floor was usually rented out. A woman who looked and laughed like Phyllis Diller brought her Boston terrier Queenie with her. I don't know if she rented the place because she was friends with my grandmother, or whether they became friends once she began renting. Upstairs had a second kitchen, a bathroom with a claw foot tub and a shower that leaked, two bedrooms and a sitting room. When there were no renters we could stay upstairs. Otherwise we stayed in one of the two bedrooms downstairs, the one with the staircase to the second floor, or the one with the wood stove and improvised shower.

The cottage was white, with trim painted in a dark shade I came to think of as Camp Ellis green. Latticework hung from the bottom of the house, stapled to the stilts. Sand, cats and more crabgrass fill the space where we thought a basement should be.

The one-way road that ran by the back and the side was all that separated the yard from the beach. At night the constant crashing of the waves was punctuated by the whoosh of an occasional car driving by, from the pier or the restaurant. Sometimes we heard snatches of music or laughter from the car with its windows rolled-down.

My grandfather came up for the summer once he was retired. All those years he had rarely spent even a weekend, too quick to return to his tire shop in the city once he drove up his wife. Often she would just take the bus.

In no time at all Dave became a fixture at the pier. Hanging with the fishermen and their families, he was warmly welcomed in this most insular village. He bought a motor scooter and would zip around, offering rides to some of the children. Bessie would stand at the porch door, worried that he would hurt himself, concerned that he was making a spectacle, perhaps even wishing to join in. She was famous in her own way. I spent a day accompanying her early in her widowhood from the social security office to the fish store in Roslindale, everywhere she was greeted and offered condolences by from the fishmonger to the government clerk. "Bessie for mayor" said one, in tribute to her political insight and her sharp tongue.

Of all the visitors to our dead-end street back home, my grandfather was the most popular. While my grandmother would hasten to the front door, he would just be opening the door of his very old black Cadillac, and would sit half way out offering big bunches of grapes to the neighborhood kids.

Years after he died, Bessie continued to spend her summers up at the cottage. She would stretch out the season, staying through the Jewish holidays if they came early enough, praying at the modest synagogue the next town over. She would have arranged for someone to drive her there and back weeks before.

At least a month before her annual migration she would be packing for the summer, and for at least a month after her return she would still be moving back in. She tried to do the same thing with her winters, purchasing an inexpensive condominium in Florida, and spending several months packing in anticipation. It never took. Too many old people, too many snowbirds, too few memories.

After she died we sold the cottage. Too often one of us would have to drive up to check on it after a bout of severe weather. One year we were sure we saw its gray roof floating out to sea on the television news. The burden of ownership seemed to outweigh the pleasures. Now in memory, I can forget the long rainy days, the inevitable family squabbles, the certain boredom, and instead bask in the memory of the warm sun, tasting the dried ocean salt on my skin.

2. Haifa

"Jerusalem prays, Tel Aviv plays,
Haifa works."
      Popular saying

"I fell in love with Haifa . . . at first
sight . . . Above the sea a city, pure
and white, lay at the foot of a green
mountain washed in spring rain."
      Sami Michael

On my first trip to Israel, we were greeted at the airport by a group of Israelis holding limp bouquets of half dead flowers. (Our flight had been delayed by several hours.) We were immediately whisked by bus heading north to the port city of Haifa. I think it was night by the time we got to the city; I have no recollection of my first view. We stayed in rather spartan lodgings tantalizingly close to the opulent Dan Carmel, the flagship hotel of a small luxury chain.

We were on a summer-long study program where we would take classes in the morning ("Hebrew" and "Knowledge of the Land"—a mix of geography, history, geology, botany and touring) and usually in the afternoon we were joined by the same group of Israelis who met us at the airport. Most of them were students of our "Knowledge of the Land" teacher during the year at the prestigious Reali School. We were their summer camp and often their pet projects. (Two girls known as "the twins" decided to take me and my friend under wing. They worked on our accents for weeks before we discovered that their strong Romanian accents weren't considered much of an improvement over our American ones.) Together we'd take short trips to places of interest in and around

Haifa, and occasionally longer trips: three days to the Upper Galilee, four to the Negev, eight days in Jerusalem. Each weekend we'd be invited to stay with our Israeli counterparts. On the way to their homes we would each buy a bouquet for our hosts, carefully carrying the flowers upside down so that the water would drip back up the stems.

Friday nights were always times for major gatherings of the larger groups—Americans guest and Israeli hosts—at one of the Israelis' homes. Saturday we would sometimes join the host family for a hike, but most of the time we would go to the beach. The skies were always clear and blue and the water warm. Most days the lifeguard's flag was white, signaling calm seas and safe swimming. The red flag urged caution and the black effectively closed the sea, either because the waves were too high or the undertow too strong for safe wading. The sun was much stronger than any of us visitors were used to. People played *matkot* in pairs by the water's edge. Little kids ran around naked. Extended families armed with huge coolers would stake out their turf and spend the whole day eating. The grown ups would alternately be chasing their children and avoiding the sun, sand and sea. Wiry men with leathery skin permanently tanned would walk the beach hawking *artikim* (popsicles) and ice cream novelties.

Saturday nights we'd meet in *Merkaz HaCarmel*—the upper city center—and either go to a movie or wander about grazing on terrible pizza from Riminis and wonderful ice cream.

Sunday mornings were back to the regular weekday: struggling to get up for classes, occasionally foregoing the midmorning break (chocolate spread on slices of coarse white bread) to sneak in a ten minute nap, valiantly trying to stay awake through lectures on the Crusaders or flowers of Israel. One of my favorite destinations was *Shvitzaria K'tana* (little Switzerland), a lovely woodsy area great for picnics and walks that locals thought looked like a Swiss forest. In our Knowledge of the Land classes we dedicated much time to studying the city of Haifa, and its three sections: the lower city, *Hadar* in the middle, and then *Merkaz HaCarmel* on the top. I imagined the city as a tiered wedding cake. With its winding streets that occasionally dipped during ascensions, or switched back on themselves, it was often hard to figure out exactly which layer one was on.

The food was fairly basic. Best were the breakfasts of tomatoes, cucumbers, cheeses and breads. Lunches were almost always schnitzel, a breaded and fried cutlet of poultry. Surprising that none of us grew feathers by the end of the summer; I know that I have not eaten another schnitzel since. Over the years the culinary situation in Israel has vastly improved. Even the fads that sweep the country—from baguette sand-wich shops on every corner to stir-fry and ciabatta in every café—are an improvement, and supplement the local Yemeni *jahnun* takeaways, Indian restaurants and truly gourmet establishments.

Haifa was labeled the "city of the future" by none other than Theodore Herzl, founder of political Zionism, and indeed it is known for its progressive politics and high tech business ventures. Barely more than a small fishing village in the mid-19th century, Haifa had a population of approximately 4000 when the German Templars built their own com-munity near the port. Baha`u'llah, the founder of the Baha'i faith, followed on their heels and chose Haifa to be the site for the world head-quarters. The Baha'i shrine amid the gardens, the most recognizable symbol of Haifa, contains his tomb. Haifa served as a major point of dis-embarkment for Jewish refugees—both legal and illegal—from Europe, before, during and after World War II. (The Af `Al-Pi Ken Museum, a monument to the illegal immigration, is there near coast, displayed in a beached ship, marked by a sculpture of oversized chains.) A tradition of tolerance took root, and even in today's troubled times, the city is a model of integration and Jewish-Arab co-existence.

While Jerusalem is immortalized in literary works from time immemorial, and Tel Aviv has earned its prominence in Hebrew letters due to its Bauhaus sensibility, Bohemian past, and Sheinkin trendiness, Haifa holds its own. The very first novels I read in Hebrew are set in Haifa and to this day remain among my favorites: A. B. Yehoshua's *HaMeahev* (The Lover) and *Hasut* (Refuge) by Sami Michael. Both authors live in Haifa; Yehoshua has recently retired from teaching world literature at the University of Haifa whose faculty also includes poets Meir Wieseltier and Nathan Zach as well as novelists Shimon Ballas and Ronit Matalon. Michael lives in an apartment in the new neighborhood of Emek HaShemesh, valley of the sun, strangely named as it is high in the hills overlooking the bay. In these paradoxes lies the beauty of Haifa: the Val-ley of the Sun set on a hill; a mostly Jewish city settled by Christian Tem-plars and symbolized by a Baha'i shrine; a swatch of Switzerland—peace amid the turmoil of the Middle East.

3. Osage Ave.

Philadelphia's Osage Avenue became known internationally May 13, 1985 when the police dropped a small bomb on a house in the 6200 block and the resulting fire was allowed to burn. There were eleven fatalities, and numerous investigations. The city had a long history of trying to deal with the Move, a back to nature movement that included raw foodism, very casual hygiene, and public address harangues. I was overseas at the time and remember being pulled over to the television to watch the news—look, isn't that your city burning?

But for me, Osage Avenue is the site of my first real apartment. Not one of a series of temporary rentals I shared with other students. Already planning to get married, Stan and I put a great deal of effort into finding just the right place. As we were both graduate students, we needed something affordable. Public transportation was a plus. I wanted a sunny kitchen and Stan insisted on a fenced in yard for his dog that would, in time, become mine as well. We saw a lovely—if impractical—carriage house in a park, a storefront bedroom, a walk up on a street that the landlord warned us "got dark at night." At the time I didn't understand what he meant but I heard the wink in his voice.

We found an inexpensive one-bedroom apartment in West Philadelphia (alt. 80 ft. above sea level). The neighborhood was easy walking distance to my school, near a park, and a healthy hike from the center of the city. The area itself was in a period of transition, and we were advised to take care to lock our doors. After our car was broken into and the radio stolen, we too put the sign "no radio, no money" in the back window. When we drove out of town people laughed at the sign, but it kept us from having to replace the glass again. One of our friends was not so lucky. He found his "no radio" labeled window smashed in, a note amid the shattered glass: "just checking."

Many of the houses on our side of the street were three-story two family homes called twins, as each side presented a mirror image of the other when first built almost 100 years ago. Most of them had been heavily divided and lightly renovated into apartments. Ours was on the first floor and went from the front to the back of the house. It opened out to a moderate-size yard with a tall chain link fence. The kitchen's best feature was its exposed brick wall, but alas, its small bay window faced our neighbor's back door and was frugal with the sunlight. In addition to the small bedroom, eat-in kitchen, bathroom, and living room there was a bonus room in the back—a closed in porch that ran the width of our side of the twin. Maybe 12 ft by 5 ft, we somehow managed to squeeze in 3 desks (what today would be termed "work stations"), a futon for guests and all of our books. The place was remarkable in its seeming ability to expand and house our lucky finds. Residents on the block disposed of unwanted—but still serviceable, and sometimes quite lovely—items of furniture by placing them on the sidewalk. We still have the small china cabinet that only needed a fresh coat of paint, and a matching set of dining room chairs; the loveseat has been passed on to others, as has the sofa. We also had access to the basement that became the storehouse of my box collection the last year we lived there. Friends mocked my enthusiasm for cardboard until they faced moving and then they were only too happy for me to share.

There were three other apartments on our half of the twin. An anthropologist lived in the back of the third floor. She was always interesting and I admired her sense of style. We lost touch once she moved back to Jamaica to finish her fieldwork. She sent us a postcard from her site with pictures of baskets. I still have the peacock feathers she left behind, and the black cotton sweater we had each bought independently.

A young married couple with cats lived on the second floor. She was a German literature graduate student from California, and he a German getting his doctorate in economics, and I remember that they told us the story of their courtship and hasty marriage. His visa was about to expire. We used to take care of their cats when they traveled, commiserate over graduate student travails, and occasionally get together for pasta dinners. A few years ago she called to see if we were still married (we are) in the wake of their own divorce.

The third floor front apartment was a mystery. No one else seemed to enter or leave the building with any regularity. We lived downstairs for months before the landlord mentioned the "love nest." The apartment was almost empty, furnished with only a bed and two chairs; the refrigerator, he reported, cooled only champagne. The couple would meet once a month, one of them coming up from Delaware. There were a few times that I saw an attractive woman with her careful lipstick, and once a rather nondescript older man entering the building.

On the other side of the building in the mirror image twin lived Pat and Mike, an old hippie couple. She actually went by the name Patricia, but the cinematic reference served as a mnemonic. She co-wrote cookbooks with authors famous enough for me to recognize. I don't know what he did. We mostly nodded to them until one day she came over and shared with me intimate details of their relationship, which at the moment was undergoing a rocky stage. Nonplussed, I tried to murmur neutral phrases of comfort and encouragement, hoping to stem the tide.

Just imagining late middle age sex was more than I could handle or wanted to. After that she always avoided me, and I learned to be very careful regarding confidences, realizing that sometimes the regret after sharing confidence leads to retreat.

Next door lived Sam, a cook at one of the hospitals in the area, who was nearly always dressed in his white coat and black and white checked pants. Before we got to know him we once called the police on him. Casting furtive glances all around, he was trying to enter his own apartment through a window. We found out later that he often forgot his key. He once brought us an institutional sized box of powdered cake mix (just add water). Before we had a chance to donate the five-pound box of flour, leavening agents, and flavoring to a food pantry, our dog Livy managed to get to it, and gorged herself on what could have been yellow cake for several dozen people. Gasping from thirst she lapped up the water we set out for her when we discovered the mess. The mix seemed to rise in her stomach and she was in agony until the next morning. This was a dog who also helped herself to a bag of dried chickpeas, a complete dinner of homemade gnocchi, sauce and fresh grated parmesan cheese, and a large block of Mexican baking chocolate. Knowing chocolate can be dangerous to dogs, I called poison control. "Is she lethargic?" the voice on the other end of the line asked calmly. "Um, she's a Great Pyrenese, she's always lethargic." We watched her overnight and she seemed none the worse for the encounter with the great gift of the Incas.

She did, however, need a surgical procedure another time on an entirely unrelated matter and had to wear a cone collar to keep her from being able to scratch her ears. I checked on her from time to time and happened to notice that she no longer had the cone on. I flew out the back door and down the steps, crashing through the old boards. Stumbling over to Livy, I grabbed her by the collar and brought her in, quickly calling the landlord on my way out. "The back stairs just collapsed," I said after identifying myself. "Are you okay?" asked Herb's wife. "I don't know," I replied distractedly, "I have to get to the vet." Shiny new stairs replaced the splintering boards by the time Livy and I got back from the vet. She was fine, but I entered the pantheon of tenant legends.

In the neighborhood were also Lars, the long time resident who had painted his corner house pink; the eternal student one door past Pat and Mike who was still trying to decide if, after 20 years, she should try to finish or abandon her degree; the travel guide for quadriplegics who kept trying—in vain—to keep his plants from getting stolen; and the family of scammers across the street. Every so often we'd get a knock on the door and find desperation on the doorstep. The baby needed medicine, the girlfriend was at choir practice, and the ATM ate his card. Could he please borrow a few dollars. Just until the girlfriend got out of choir practice. Variations included running out of diapers, gas for the car, formula for the baby (who was never seen), but the choir practice was consistent. We would sometimes keep track of his progress with other friends on his route. It wasn't until we moved that we found out he lived across the street. The width of the street, and the density of apartments on our side, meant that we were much less likely to know people on the other side.

Yet we knew everyone else who had dogs within several blocks, even if we only knew them by their dogs. Livy and I would walk the blocks around our house, sometimes starting to the north or the west, sometimes to the south or the east. When it came time to move and we were debating among several choices, it was Livy who heard the lists of pros and cons of each option, elaborately detailed, as we walked along the crisscross of streets, numbered or named after common trees. Spruce, walnut, chestnut, pine were all obvious; it was Osage that stuck out. It wasn't until we moved to Missouri, the option Livy herself seemed to favor, that I first saw—heard of—the Osage orange.

And it was in Missouri that someone, upon finding out where we moved from, mangled the city motto, asking: "Philadelphia, isn't that the land of friendly people?"

Well, yes. I miss the very walkability of the neighborhood, the many ethnic restaurants nearby (a choice of Ethiopian places, of Thai and of Indian), the green grocer at the end of the street. I miss our friends, our evenings at each others' homes, or enjoying the restaurant renaissance downtown. But most of all I miss the cozy apartment surrounded by quirky and likeable neighbors, and the promise inherent in beginning a life together.

Freda Berns
Coming to America

A family was going to Baltimore, so my mother gave me to them to go as their child. I was twelve years. Papa talked to me before I left Russia. "You should know you're twelve years, you're a kid, you're a baby yet. You'll get with older people. You'll grow up. Mamma wants you to go and I don't want to hurt her. I'm gonna let you go. But I'll send you money any time you decide to come back. Write me and I'll send you money and you'll come back.

"You should know you're no more than a kid. You don't know anything. You'll get older. When you get together with other people you'll learn that everybody is raised different. Everybody acts different. Everybody talks different. Everything is different. You are not like everybody; everybody is not like you. It's a different world altogether. I went through it and I know what it is like. You like the nurses and the maid at home. Everything will be a different life for you. You should watch yourself. Don't go out with anybody that you don't know. See who they are and what they are. When you don't know you should see what is. Look around. Look how everybody talks, how everybody acts."

So I go in to the maid's room. I says, "Did you hear what my papa says? He says I'm a baby."

She says, "He's right."

"I'm twelve years. I'm a big girl!"

The way he says "You're a baby"—oy, I felt terrible. My mother came home. I tell her what daddy says and I tell her I went in and told the maid. My mother said, "He's right!"

Now I know. Many times I think of it. I lay awake. I think what my father used to say.

I remember many times, I think he was sitting here. I think of my father, how he knew everything.

That's how I came to America. My sister was here already and two brothers were here. I came with another sister of mine some years older than me. She said she was my mother.

★ ★ ★

My mamma told me that if anybody comes to the boat and wants to take me off I should be careful, I shouldn't go with a man. I remembered my sister; my brothers I didn't know. I was too young when they went away. I should say, "I want Altke." Ida was my sister's name here but in Jewish she was called Altke because my mother wanted she should get old, she lost so many children.

My brother came and asked if they seen a girl from Poneviej from Mufsha Simonovich. "A girl is here, her name is Fegel. Is she here on this boat?"

They said, "Yes."

I hollered, "Don't tell him! Don't tell him ! I should only go when I see my sister."

So he says to me, "If you see Altke, will you go with her? She is here."

I said, "Yes, with her I would go. But I don't know you. I wouldn't go with you."

And she came and I went with her. My brother went with us. I stayed in his house. He said, "She was so afraid of me!"

My other brother, Sam, lived in Newark, New Jersey. Him I didn't know either. He came to see me. I looked at him. I said, "I would never know you are my brother. With Dave I wouldn't go and I wouldn't go with you."

★ ★ ★

When I was in America a short time I didn't like it. Oh, it was terrible. At home I went to Hebrew school and I went to the Russian school. I was good in everything. My mother wrote my brothers and sisters that when I'll come here the first thing I should go to school what I'm very good at. Instead, my sister-in-law made me stay home. Taking care of the children was no life. I wrote my mother a letter saying, "Send me money. I can't be here. I don't like it. Everything is different here from what it was at home. I want to go home." I wrote the letter in Jewish and the address in Russian.

I said to my brother, "Show me where is a mailbox and I'm gonna mail the letter myself."

He said, "It's too far from here."

I put it in his shirt to hide it. Let mamma read it. I said I wouldn't close it but I put a stamp on the envelope. I was young and I didn't have enough sense to think that my brother will read the letter. After all, I was only twelve years old.

They read the letter and tore it up and I wouldn't get no money. I kept on saying, "Mamma don't like me no more. She sent me away because she don't like me no more." It was a terrible thing.

When my mother came to America twelve years later I said to her, "I wanted to come home and I wrote you a letter, but you never answered and you had so much money."

She said, "What letter?"

My brother was standing there. I said to him, "Where did you put the letter?"

"In the garbage."

I thought my mother didn't want me.

★ ★ ★

My father wouldn't come to America for anything. He said, "I don't need America. I'm a rich man and I got a big name." He was a doctor and the court gave him his rights, the way he talks and he knows all the languages, so he could be a lawyer. Poor people who didn't have money to pay, he used to take their trial and help them. The government would find boys who would try to run away to America not to be a soldier and put them in jail. The people used to come at midnight to ring my father's bell and they used to say, "I want to see Moishe." The Jewish people used to call him Reb Moishe, but the sign on the door said Movsha, Movsha Simonovich.

Then the Russians chased all the Jews out from where they lived and sent them away to Siberia.

My father was sent there. He was in a house where fifteen men were reading the Torah. He seen that the rest of the Jews should learn.

My mother was fifteen miles away from him. She didn't want to live where he lived. She used to come to him every day.

★ ★ ★

From Siberia my mother came here. She had so much gold and so much silver and so much money, people told her if other people found out about her money, she's going to get killed. A young man told her the gold and silver was too heavy for her to carry and he'll give her paper money that she could hide easier. So she took the paper money.

When she came to America she found out it wasn't worth anything. My son still has some of it.

★ ★ ★

People go through so much that I don't even want to talk about it. See, at home when people told stories it made you feel so bad you used to cry.

★ ★ ★

Listen, even if it's not right and it's my fault, I'll tell you the truth. I don't like lies. My papa used to say, "If a person says lies his name goes down, it doesn't go up." The best thing is everything the truth. If you tell so many lies at the end you'll find out that everything is a made-up story. My children used to say, "Just say nice and be nice is my mother's way."

★ ★ ★

My husband wouldn't know me. With the arthritis I got I couldn't keep a needle in my hand. I can't touch the fingers. How I got this arthritis I don't know. I never thought there was anything like this. I didn't know it gets that you can't do anything.

My nephew, Dr. Simon, is a big surgeon. He would do anything to make my arthritis better. He wrote to different doctors about it. My father was a doctor, too. Finally, Dr. Simon says," I'll wake up your father. Maybe he hears of something that will cure your arthritis."

I says, "Jerry, don't wake my father. We need you here with the living."

★ ★ ★

There are good times here, nice parties. I never say I don't like it. I say everything is just wonderful.

You should never know from it. I wish you that with all my heart. The men talk: they talk. They don't know what they're talking about. The women don't know what they're talking about, too. A woman says to me, "When I was sitting by this table you wasn't born yet."

I said, "I wasn't born yet!" When they talk things like this. . . .

★ ★ ★

While I was making a lemon chiffon cake I hear my son say to his wife, "You call up the people that know you. They'll send for you. And

I'll stay here with Karen and Mamma." A woman at my daughter-in-law's office made a surprise party for her daughter. "Karen will be able to do her school work and I'll talk to Mamma. When Mamma wants to go home, I'll take her home."

I was in the kitchen but I heard the way he talks to her—quiet, quiet. My daughter-in-law came in the kitchen. I said, "Anita, you're almost dressed and your husband is sitting and looking. Let him get dressed."

She says, "He's tired." She went in the other room to put her jewelry on.

So I says, "Sandy, I didn't even talk to you tonight. Come on in the kitchen. I want to tell you something." So he comes in the kitchen. I says, "Sandy, I'll tell you something. You're going with Anita to the party, you'll take me home and then I'll tell you good night and have a good time. I'll be home and you won't have to worry that I'm alone with Karen. She's got to do her school work."

He looks at me. "Mom, I'm tired and I want to be home tonight." I say, "Anita's a young woman and you're a young man. Now's the time for you to live. You should always have a good time. If you don't get dressed and go to the party and take me home, I'll never come here for supper. You know your mother. I tell you I mean it."

He says, "Mom, if I'm tired and I can't get dressed and I want to stay home, why are you against it?"

"Because I don't like it. I liked to go with your father and I want you to go with your wife. I like to see you dressed. Get dressed right now and you go with her to the party and take me home."

He got dressed and took me home and went with his wife to the party. I told them, "Thank you for bringing me and I hope you have a good time. You both look nice. For me it's a pleasure to see you. That's the best thing."

★ ★ ★

I was in the beauty parlor by the hairdresser. A woman asked me, "Can I speak to you and would you answer me a few words?"

I said, "If I'll be able to answer you."

She says, "Mrs. Berns, do you believe you're gonna live five more years or ten more years?"

I says, "That ain't up to me. When they say that's your day when you're born or when you die you haven't got time to say goodbye and you don't know what you want to say. To lay in the dirt you got time whenever the time comes, but when the time comes you can't say yes or no. That's your time and you're going."

The lady said, "You know, that's a good answer. You gave me such beautiful answers, I don't know what to say."

Freda Berns (Nee Fegel Simonovich, Poneviej, Lithuania, March 15, 1902–March 23, 1979)

Stan Braude
Endings

Part I: Last Gasps
Uganda 1986

In the summer of 1986 the latest civil war in Uganda was just wrapping up. Museveni had swept out Okello's forces and had taken back Kampala. Meanwhile I was stuck in Nairobi waiting for my first research permit from the government of Kenya. A few months earlier two researchers had been caught running a tourist operation out of their camp. They were thrown out of the country and all pending permits were indefinitely on hold. I paid my room and board by painting houses and was desperate for a job more befitting a future field biologist.

Luckily a project officer at WWF (World Wildlife Fund as it was then called) heard of my situation and offered me a job that nobody else would take. He needed me to deliver a Suzuki jeep to The Impenetrable Forest on the southern border of Uganda. Dr. Tom Butynski had just moved there to develop a program to protect the gorillas and chimpanzees in the forest. I was given an envelope of cash, car keys and the name of a professor at the University in Kampala where I could stay along the way. I was told to buy some jerry cans for petrol and to fill the vehicle with supplies. But I was so eager to get out of Nairobi I ignored these instructions, filled the tank and headed out the next morning.

It is possible that the paint fumes had gone to my brain and clouded my thinking, but in reality I was just naïve and foolish. In Nairobi you could go to a grocery store 6 days a week and there was even a Woolworth's downtown. I planned to get supplies at one of the towns along the way. I knew nothing about the real Africa outside of cosmopolitan Nairobi.

I made good time from Nairobi to the Uganda border at Juja. It helped that the current president came from nearby Eldoret and he made sure that those roads were well maintained. The Uganda side of the border was very different. The potholes in the road were actually big enough to swallow a VW beetle, but the jeep just drove down into them and up the other side. This made driving slow and it took all afternoon to get from the border into Kampala. I asked directions to the University and to Dr. Pomerance's home. I was relieved to finally arrive there just as the sun was going down. Pomerance was coolly cordial: "You made it all the way from Nairobi today? You are quite lucky you arrived before dark.

Museveni hasn't quite consolidated his gains in the capitol and there is still fighting some evenings."

He even offered me a cold drink before announcing, "Oh, you can't stay *here* tonight. I leave on a field trip with my students early tomorrow morning and things are just too chaotic. Look at all these boxes strewn about willy nilly. You can stay at the hotel over on Tank hill. No doubt they have a high fence and good security. You should be quite safe there."

I was too tired to argue and amazingly found the hotel before they locked the gate for the night. I cursed Pomerance as I lay in bed listening to the shelling and shooting in town. But more than 14 hours of driving had totally sapped me and I fell asleep before too long.

The following morning I woke early and got on the road again. I was determined to make it to the forest by nightfall. I did not want to sleep in another "hotel." About an hour south of Kampala I realized I needed gas but every gas station I passed was burned out and abandoned. Museveni's forces had swept north through here only weeks earlier and they took anything they needed, especially gas, along the way.

At one of the military checkpoints a kid (who couldn't have been older than15) carrying an AK47 asked me for a ride south. Not wanting to piss him off, I cheerfully agreed. He wasn't much for company but we got waved through the other checkpoints quite easily. When I mentioned that we were running low on gas he told me to pull over at an abandoned, burnt out garage. Another adolescent with a machine gun waved me into the office and told me to crawl through a hole in the wall behind the desk.

What an idiot I had been. Of course these kids were going to kill me and take the jeep which was worth more than they could steal in ten years of common banditry.

Scorpions Scorpions are typically depicted as deadly inhabitants of exotic deserts, but they can be found globally from Switzerland to southeastern Missouri. Despite their evil image in James Bond films, scorpions can be caring mothers and valuable predators of pests that destroy crops or stored grain. Knowing this doesn't relieve the creeps that go up your spine when you find one in your sleeping bag at bedtime or in your shoe in the morning. Nonetheless, when you live in scorpion territory it is easy to get careless and forget to check.

After a long drive from Nairobi to northern Kenya I was exhausted and thirsty. Rather than drive another 5 km to headquarters to pick up a bed, I decided to unpack the vehicle, have a few warm cokes, and grab some sleep on a blanket on the floor. In the morning I even wrote home that I wasn't worried because the house had been abandoned and there wouldn't be any small animal prey to attract snakes or scorpions. A few hours later I found a huge scorpion in the corner, and I checked my sheets and shoes for weeks after.

But I never expected the one that got me several weeks later. We had changed a flat tire the day before and sent the flat to headquarters to get repaired. A friendly ranger delivered the patched tire to camp while we were out working and it sat next to the cabin through the afternoon. When we returned that evening I put away the equipment and loaded up for work the next day. Then I wrapped my arms around the patched tire to hoist it up on the hood of the Land Rover where the spare is stored. My forearm must have startled a tiny little scorpion hiding in the tread. She struck me right on the soft inside of my forearm.

Bagged Cobra   I drove up to Nathan's house at first light to collect him for work. This was part of our routine. We had worked together since I began trapping mole-rats in Kenya in 1987. We knew one another, and the job, well enough that we could work a whole day without saying a word between "good morning" and "see you tomorrow." Over the years this job had paid for his dowry, his house with a real tin roof, two plots of land, a small store in his village, and years of school fees, uniforms and books for his six children.

We were usually on our way to set our animal traps before the sun was completely up. We had both had coffee already but Nathan had not slept much the night before and was still washing up. In addition to the usual sounds of mosquitoes buzzing around the net, geckos dashing across the walls, and mice scurrying in the thatch roof, Nathan was sure he heard the periodic woosh of a snake somewhere in the house. But every time he swept the room with his flashlight he saw only geckos and mosquitoes.

I paced a bit impatiently, declined the offer of more coffee, and finally went to the back of the Land Rover to get our traps ready for the days work. I noticed that we were low on sweet potatoes which we used as bait. Nathan had a big gunny sack of them in his house so I went to grab some before we were off for work. I reached into the bag just as Nathan came in from washing up. He looked over at me and yelled "Nyoka!"

Malaria   In East Africa every headache and fever is diagnosed as "malaria." After living there for a while it is easy to become skeptical of such claims, and lax about taking prophylactic medications such as chloroquine. But having already had malaria twice and having a new baby at home I was more careful than usual about sleeping under a mosquito net and taking a weekly dose of fanzidar (a new anti-malarial sulfa drug).

After 8 weeks in the bush I felt pretty smug about how careful I had been and how much data I had collected in such a short time. I was also getting some international recognition for my work and was invited to give a guest seminar about my work in Germany on the way home. My Swissair flight was on time, I had a seat with extra leg room, the airline even remembered my vegetarian meal. Everything seemed to be going my way.

But when the meal came I wasn't hungry. A few hours later, during the movie, I began to sweat and feel achy in all my joints. Twenty minutes later I was feeling cold and asked the flight attendant for another blanket. I was slumped in my seat sweating and moaning. The film *Outbreak* was the blockbuster hit that summer and the poor guy next to me couldn't get ebola out of his mind.

Leopard Release Today seemed to be my lucky day. I had been invited to lunch at the Senior Warden's house where I could look forward to fresh salad, real cheese and cold beer. I finished my work early, packed away my equipment and headed for the park headquarters. As I pulled up at the old stone and log building the warden was packing his family into his Toyota safari pickup (with a bench seat mounted in the bed and a roof hatch over the cab). They were off to watch a leopard release and I arrived just in time to join them. Leopards are shy and nocturnal. After 20 years working in Kenya I had still never seen one in the wild. I hopped into the back with the warden's five year old son and Erik, a visiting French wildlife film maker.

We drove a few kilometers up river to a bare patch of broken lava on the shore of the Bwatherongi river. The wildlife capture unit was unloading the steel cage from the back of their old Isuzu Trooper. The leopard had been raiding livestock and was trapped earlier that week. He was hot, hungry and pissed off about being bounced over bad roads in the back of that trooper. He lunged at the rangers who were positioning the cage and tying the release rope on the door.

The cage was aimed at the dense bush along the river so that the leopard would have a safe place to run and hide. The warden warned

everyone to get into a vehicle and at the last minute told his 5 year old
to get into the cab of his Toyota along with his wife and younger son. I
hopped in back with Erik and leaned around the side of the cab to watch
the release.

Suddenly, the leopard was dashing towards us and the vehicle was
lurching in reverse.

Sleeping on the Job   Even though the sun was on its way back down
below the horizon, the temperature kept rising past 100 degrees. Luckily, there was zero humidity in the scrub desert of Kenya's Northern
Frontier District (the NFD). Even though we weren't as uncomfortable
as we would be on an August day in St. Louis, the heat eventually wore
us out and we settled down to an afternoon siesta.

For most of the inhabitants of the NFD the afternoon siesta is a natural part of the daily routine. But we were working out in the bush trapping rodents and we usually kept busy from dawn until dusk. Work always
ended before 7 pm. Park rules prohibit driving after dark to keep people
safe from the lions, leopards and hyenas who hunt at night. But of course
everyone walks around the camp and headquarters at night and the dusty
paths are covered with paw prints every morning.

On this afternoon we were working near Joy Adamson's old campsite where she had trained the cheetah, Pippa, to hunt and live in the
wild. Joy wrote about how this area frequently flooded in the rainy season. She was stuck in her camp where she sketched and wrote about her
tame felids. We were stuck sitting in the middle of a dirt road where we
tried to pass the time reading books we would never have the patience
for at home: *War and Peace, The History of Philosophy,* or Darwin's
biography.

The luxury of rain was months away but the bush was dense and the
grass was still tall. We were watching our traps and waiting to catch the
last animals in yet another burrow system. After removing more than 100
animals from this colony the day before, we hadn't caught anyone all day
and gave up checking the traps by lunchtime. Between the heat and the
700th page of some 19th century Russian novel, sleep was unavoidable.

It is unclear how long we had been dozing when we were gently
roused by the sound of a motorcycle approaching from down the road.
This was surprising since motorcycles were currently banned in the park.
One of the old rangers, Ayub, had told us about the bicycles which were
issued by the park service in the 1960s. Ayub and a friend were cycling

to headquarters when his friend suddenly came speeding back around a corner yelling something about lions. Ayub, saw the lions sleeping in the road just as he came around the corner. When he tried to make a sharp U turn on the gravel road he skidded right into the lions. They were so startled that they ran off into the bush. Not long after that, bicycles and motorcycles were banned inside the park.

A moment later we finally heard the cicada-like buzz of a trap and jumped up to get the animal we had been waiting for all day.

Part II: Last Words
Uganda 1986

A bullet to the back of the head would be quick. But I didn't know Uganda. Before I had a chance to wet my pants, the old man hidden in the hole in the wall offered me a cold drink and asked about my journey. The many civil wars and the Idi Amin years couldn't erode the hospitality and generosity of the older generation of Ugandans.

Later that afternoon I topped off the tank again at Kabale and bought all the fruits and vegetables I could fit in the back of the jeep. The dirt road into the Impenetrable Forest was barely wide enough for the jeep to pass. Seeing the burnt out remains of vehicles that had rolled over the side of the mountain sobered me up and slowed me down. Arriving before dark was suddenly less pressing. Arriving in one piece was my immediate concern.

I pulled the jeep up to a small log cabin shortly after dark. Tom was surprised to see me. There wasn't much communication with the Nairobi office. He was delighted to have his jeep and all the fresh food but then he found out that I ignored the instructions to buy staple supplies or jerry cans for fuel.

"What good is a vehicle if you have no fuel?"

After dinner he announced that he was off the following morning to survey the condition of the other parks in southern Uganda now under Museveni's control. I decided not to take it personally that everyone seemed to be leaving as soon as I showed up. If I had brought jerry cans and fuel there might have been room for me on that trip. Instead, we made plans to meet on the Zaire border in a week and hopefully I could get a lift back to Nairobi in a small plane meeting Tom there. Meanwhile, I could help Tom's rangers remove poacher's snares in the forest and help work on widening the road.

The next morning Tom left and I hiked into the forest with his deputy. We collected dozens of wire snares that week. We also heard the hoots of chimpanzees and saw their abandoned nests but most of the wildlife in that forest was wary of human sounds and smells and kept well clear of us. We walked through the forest every day. With all the illegal logging and encroachment it didn't feel so "impenetrable" any more.

On schedule we met Tom on the Zaire border. Early that evening a small single-engine fixed-wing plane bounced to a landing next to our campsite. The pilot, former game warden Hugh Lamprey, was there to conduct some preliminary aerial surveys of the Uganda parks. The veteran bush pilot was unfazed by the termite mounds that littered his landing strip. He was happy to take me along. His only concern was weight but I guess I looked thin enough after a week of rice and peanut sauce.

We cleared customs at Entebbe, which still displayed the damage of the Israeli raid to free the hostages in 1976. That evening we arrived back in Nairobi, and I returned to painting houses. Two months later Lamprey flipped his overloaded plane during takeoff when it hit an aardvark hole on a rough landing strip in Serengetti.

Scorpion To my surprise, I didn't even feel the sting until I had finished bolting the spare tire down. It felt a bit like a bee sting; I only found the little scorpion while looking for a squashed bee on the tire. The pain comes from a toxin which is sufficient to immobilize small prey so that they can be dragged into a burrow and eaten by the scorpions little offspring. The throbbing pain that can be felt for another hour is mostly the result of the swelling. Nonetheless, all those years of fearing scorpion stings were far worse than the actual sting.

I was reminded of two Norwegian tourists who came to our cabin in the middle of the night years before. They wanted to know how far it was to the nearest hospital because one of them had been stung by a scorpion while he was collecting firewood after dark. They shared the popular belief that the sting was deadly and wanted to know if they could make it to the hospital before it was too late. Without electricity or a fridge, we had no ice to offer to reduce the swelling. So we advised cooling the affected limb with a damp washcloth and offered scotch as an analgesic.

At best, the damp cloth served as a placebo. Nonetheless, the Norwegians returned in the morning to thank us for the expert medical advice.

Bagged Cobra   I jumped up because of the commanding sound of Nathan's voice. A moment later my brain registered the translation of nyoka = snake. Nathan had seen the gunny sack move just as I reached for it and realized where the snake was that he had heard all night. It probably followed a gecko or mouse into the sack and couldn't find its way out. Now that I had opened the sack the snake, an Egyptian spitting cobra (*Naja haje*), was on its way out.

Nathan's reflex was to strike. He grabbed a broom and wacked the cobra on the head. That only served to piss it off and it quickly moved its 6 foot long body out of the bag. But Nathan hit it again and again, eventually crushing its skull before it had a chance to spit or strike back. He was horrified when I suggested that he hold the corpse up for a triumphant photo. This was driven more by the gut level repulsion for snakes than the prudent knowledge that many snake bites are delivered by the presumed dead. In the end he agreed to hold it up by the tail end to show its length. And for years he showed off that photo with great pride.

Malaria   No matter how careful you are, you still have to leave the protection of the mosquito net to empty your bladder at night. On top of this, rampant underdosing with fanzidar and other anti-malarials has led to resistant strains of malaria in East Africa. One of these must have been injected into me during a rare unprotected moment during the prior two months.

I used to think that living out in the bush, away from people, I was at lower risk of infection because the mosquitoes wouldn't have anyone to pick up the malaria from. But any other mammal, and even birds and lizards, can carry malaria. The only real protection is avoiding getting bitten. Since it was too late for that, the next step was trying to kill the plasmodium when it was vulnerable.

When the plane landed in Zurich I went to the airport clinic and received a heavy dose of fanzidar. I continued on to Germany where I slept for two days before I was finally admitted to a hospital. The local med students were delighted to see a case of malaria. Those who spoke English woke me frequently to interview me, draw blood, and hook me up for an EKG. I still feel guilty for my awkward unease as a Jew laid out on a gurney, connected to a half dozen electrodes, and surrounded by doctors discussing me in German.

The lab confirmed that the fanzidar had cleared the plasmodium from my blood, but the ultrasound confirmed that my spleen was ready to burst as it worked overtime to remove damaged blood cells from circulation. I checked myself out in time for my guest lecture and received the biggest shock of the week: the bill. The receptionist tried to argue that I was covered by the national health plan because I was temporarily employed in Germany (for my one hour lecture). But this didn't fly with her superior, I would have to pay. The total bill for the ward bed, medication, rehydration iv, blood tests, ekg, ultrasound, and countless consultations came to only $273. In Germany the parasites are also kept out of the health care system.

Leopard release

Even as we were rushing backwards, the leopard jumped up on the hood of the Toyota and then onto the roof. I turned my head and glimpsed Erik next to me as the leopard was biting the top of his head. A second later we backed over the bank of the river and I was thrown from the vehicle. When I surfaced the rangers were shooting, children were screaming, the seat I had just fallen out of was shredded, and the leopard was gone.

The warden's wife was afraid the vehicle would sink so she lifted the children out of the open roof hatch and handed them to me to put them ashore. Then I slogged back through the mucky bank to help carry Erik out of the vehicle and lay him down under a nearby acacia. He was conscious.

A few minutes later Erik was loaded in the back of a vehicle and driven to headquarters where he was met by a retired British Army medic and three Kenyan surgeons who were training more park personnel in emergency first aid! They gave Erik a saline IV to increase blood volume before he was evacuated by air. Once Erik was at the hospital the wounds were cleaned but not stitched because the mouths and claws of predators are covered with anaerobic bacteria that would fester if trapped in a sutured wound. Erik's wounds healed quickly and all of his scars would be covered by his hair and clothes.

A week later Erik flew home to Paris and I returned to the warden's house for drinks after his boys were put to bed. It was then that I discovered how lucky we had really been that day. When the warden saw the leopard turn away from the bush and sprint at the Toyota he put it into reverse and tried to back away. But the leopard had caught Erik's eye and followed us. When it jumped onto the cab of the vehicle Erik quickly bent down so the leopard only got the top of his head rather than his face and its front claws went into the trapezius of Erik's back rather than the soft abdominals that leopards typically claw to eviscerate their prey.

But our luck was far more amazing. When the warden saw the leopard standing over him through the roof hatch he reached up and grabbed its testicles. At the next moment we hit the water and the leopard jumped to get away rather than turning on the warden or me. The adrenaline that surged into the warden's blood fortunately sharpened his senses and reaction time. Fortunately he is the kind of man for whom adrenaline triggers fight over flight.

Sleeping on the job As we jumped up out of our chairs a pair of scruffy adolescent lions jumped up in the grass just meters away. They had been creeping up on us while we dozed and we had mistaken their rough, heavy breathing for motorcycles. We must have startled them with our sud-

den movement. All the books tell you that lions sleep during the heat of the day, but I guess these young lions hadn't read any of those books. I was torn between the desire to get that rodent out of the trap and the need to get to the imagined safety of the Land Rover. Nathan had a healthier respect for the danger, if not for the animals. We got into the Land Rover and proceeded to chase them away with the even throatier growl of the Land Rover's badly tuned engine and a few short lunges.

This happened 15 years before my close brush with the leopard and I still thought wild animals would respect the invisible boundaries around a vehicle, or the porch of a house, or the edge of the campsite. Many years later we were trapping in the campsite and decided to check on our traps before bed. En route we saw two pair of big red eyes sink down at the edge of the campsite and we cautiously returned to the hut without turning our backs. Over the years a number of park rangers have been attacked by lions within the boundaries of headquarters. But it was always someone stumbling home drunk.

Sadly, after keeping me safe for so many years Nathan was killed in 2004 by a truck. He was walking along a dirt road near his home and it came around a corner too fast for him to jump out of the way. He hadn't been drinking but the driver probably had.

Robert A. Cohn
My Past Life Experience

In the early 1950s, in the secure childhood in University City, Mo. a virtual Paradise on Earth for a Jewish kid, concerns about the hereafter or past lives were not uppermost in my hormone-driven, teenage mind. Then, suddenly, my father died of cancer when I was only 15, and he had just reached his 54th birthday. The unfairness of losing such a young Dad when my brother and I were so young, shook my childhood, naïve faith from my early Sunday school days at Congregation Shaare Emeth, that "God was in His Holy Temple."

As a young skeptic, who fancied himself somewhat of an intellectual, I found myself drawn to the scientific method I had learned in the excellent U. City school system. When the central nervous system was no longer functioning, one's earthly existence was over, once and for all. Stories and beliefs about the immortality of the soul, reincarnation or heaven and hell just seemed like so much superstition.

Then in 1956, a bombshell best-selling book, *The Search for Bridey Murphy* was published by Morey Bernstein, a Colorado business executive. Bernstein, a self-trained hypnotist, had six hypnotic sessions with a housewife called Ruth Simmons, a pseudonym for Virginia Tighe, whose identity was revealed years later. In her hypnotic trances, Tighe was able to "recall" events from a previous life as Bridey Murphy, in Cork, Ireland, 100 years earlier. Bernstein later attempted to get Tighe to recall another past life in Amsterdam

In *Yesterday and Today: A Dictionary of Recent American History*, Stanley Hochman reports that after the initial excitement over the Bridey Murphy case, scientists weighed in with alternative explanations. "It was later discovered that both her (Simmons-Tighe's) parents and foster parents had Irish backgrounds," and that "skeptics suggested that in this way she might have unconsciously imbibed the details of Irish local color that made her trance sessions so convincing."

Hochman quotes Yale University psychologist John Dollard as saying of the Bridey Murphy case, "We may be reasonably sure. . . . that a searching psychological study of the subject would take all the 'mystery' out of this case. It would also reveal the remarkable power of the unconscious mental life to bilk not only a naïve hypnotist, but also the subject."

So, the Bridey Murphy case, which created more than a mild sensation during the era of Hula Hoops and early rock 'n' roll, soon faded into a distant memory. Mostly, I held on to my adolescent skepticism, but part of me remained open to the possibility that there just might be something "real" about the case and others like it reported through the years.

My interest in the possibility of past life experiences was rekindled back in 1972, when Irving Litvag, a good friend, former editor of the *Jewish Light* and longtime publicist and essayist/author, published *Singer in the Shadows*, the definitive study of a famous case right here in St. Louis, which seemed to suggest that there is reality to past-life experiences.

Singer in the Shadows, which was praised by Isaac Bashevis Singer, details the story of the well-documented case of St. Louis housewife Pearl Curran (Mrs. John H.), who seemed to have been frequently "visited" by the spirit of Patience Worth, a 17th century English woman. Ms. Curran, who had a limited education and who had never left the Midwest region, from 1913–1937, claimed to have had 24 "visits" from Patience Worth. She began receiving "communications" from Patience Worth in 1913 through a Ouija Board, a popular 19th and 20th century game which purported to put people in touch with the spirits of the dead.

During the next 24 years of "contact" with Patience Worth, Curran dictated seven full-length books, thousands of poems and other materials which received critical acclaim from critics and skeptical researchers. In an interview with the *St. Louis Jewish Light* at the time of his book's publication, Litvag said there were three possible explanations for the Patience Worth case: "Perhaps it was a hoax, although there seems to be no evidence to support this theory. Perhaps Patience Worth was a subconscious personality of Mrs. Curran, but this could not fully explain the great literary skill and the knowledge of 17th century England. Finally, it just could be that Patience Worth was in fact a spirit—A Singer in the Shadows—who emerged for 24 years in St. Louis."

In any event, Litvag's book was praised by the Nobel Prize-winning Isaac Bashevis Singer as "one of the best biographies I have ever read. . . . a masterpiece of research and presentation."

More recently came the reports about Jenny Cockell, a native of rural England who had a series of dreams about a long-dead Irish woman. Under hypnosis, Cockell seemingly "became" Mary, later identified as Mary Sutton, who died in childbirth early in the 20th century. "I cried as she cried. I knew her pain as my own," writes Cockell in her 1993 book *Across Time and Death: A Mother's Search for Her Past Life Children*. Working with others, Cockell was able to locate the probable town in Ireland in which her past life person lived and gave birth to children early in the 20th century. On a visit to the Frish town, Cockell claims to have discovered some of her "own" children she had given birth to as Mary Sutton and when she met them knew details about her life that only their "real" mother could have known. Her case is described among others in the book *Investigating the Paranormal*, by Joe Nickell.

Also of interest are the works of the noted self-described psychic Sylvia Browne, author of *Past Lives, Future Healing*. In addition, the series of "occult" books by Jane Roberts, especially *Seth Speaks: the Eternal Validity of the Soul*, as well as Deepak Chopra's *Ageless Body, Timeless Mind*, explore past lives and related topics.

Among those who would probably have greeted the Bridey Murphy, Patience Worth and Mary Sutton cases and their like as false or wishful thinking, was Brian Weiss, M.D., a prominent, highly educated Florida psychiatrist. Weiss, a Phi Beta Kappa, *magna cum laude* graduate of Columbia University, and of the Yale University School of Medicine, became a highly regarded traditional psychiatrist of the "old school." After graduation, Weiss accepted a faculty position at the University of Pittsburgh, and two years later joined the faculty of the University of Miami, heading its psychopharmacology division. Later he was named associate professor of psychiatry at the medical school, and was named Chief of Psychiatry at a large, university-affiliated Florida hospital.

And yet, despite his commitment to rigorous, empirical evidence, Dr. Weiss has become one of the most prominent believers in and advocates for the reality of past lives, and their efficacy in finding the source and cures for many emotional and even physical symptoms among his and other patients and followers.

Weiss details his journey from skepticism to belief in past-life experiences in his best-selling book, *Many Lives, Many Masters*, in which he writes, "Years of disciplined study had trained my mind to think as a scientist and physician, molding me along the narrow paths of conservatism in my profession. I distrusted anything that could not be proved by the traditional scientific method. I was aware of some studies in parapsychology that were being conducted at major universities across the country, but they did not hold my attention. It all seemed too farfetched to me."

Then Dr. Weiss treated a patient he calls "Catherine" to protect her anonymity, and his life was altered forever by the experience. "For 18 months I used conventional methods of therapy to help (Catherine) overcome her symptoms," writes Dr. Weiss. "When nothing seemed to work, I tried hypnosis. In a series of trance states, Catherine recalled 'past-life' memories that proved to be the causative factor of her symptoms. She was able to act as a conduit for information from highly evolved 'spirit entities,' and through them she revealed many of the secrets of life and death. In just a few short months, her symptoms disappeared, and she resumed her life, happier and more at peace than ever before."

In a later book, *Mirrors of Time: Using Regression for Physical, Emotional and Spiritual Healing*, Dr. Weiss describes Catherine, "a woman in her late 20s, who was suffering from depression, phobias and panic attacks. A year of conventional psychotherapy had produced no results, which prompted me to try hypnosis—I felt that recalling her repressed childhood traumas might explain her current symptoms. . . ."

When the above efforts failed, Dr. Weiss, using hypnosis, "instructed her to go back to the time and the events that caused her phobias. To my complete amazement, she went back approximately 4,000 years to a former life in the Middle East." Dr. Weiss reports that Catherine described her experiences and surroundings in her past life "with an extraordinary wealth of detail." At first he thought that her memories were mere fantasies, "but Catherine began to improve after that session, and all of her symptoms eventually vanished as she recalled more past lives while under hypnosis. Within a few months, she was completely cured—without the use of any medications."

Weiss, who described himself as a "right-brain" skeptic before he treated Catherine, found the experience to be astounding. "Nothing in my background prepared me for this. I was absolutely amazed when these events unfolded." He adds that he does "not have a scientific explanation for what happened. There is far too much about the human mind that is beyond our comprehension."

As Weiss and Catherine continued their journey, and as he expanded the techniques to other patients with similar results, Weiss's initial skepticism gave way to stunned belief. He found that Catherine's past-life experiences seemed to hold the key to her recurring nightmares and anxiety attacks. Weiss was also astounded when Catherine seemed to "channel" messages from the "space between lives," which contained revelations about Dr. Weiss, his family and his dead son. "Using past-life therapy, Dr. Weiss was able to cure the patient and embark on a new, more meaningful phase of his own career," states an introduction to another Weiss book, *Through Time Into Healing*.

Weiss found that by bringing patients back to their past lives, he could help cure their present problems, by identifying the source of the trauma in a previous life. For example, one patient with a chronic pain in the back, was found to have been a Roman soldier in a previous life who had been struck with a spear or a sword during battle. Once the source of the "original" trauma was found, the seemingly intractable symptom went away for good.

Weiss published numerous additional books on his past-life work, including *Messages From the Masters; Only Love is Real; Same Soul, Many Bodies,* and *Mirrors of Time.* He has also become an extremely popular speaker, leading intense workshops on his techniques to appreciative audiences around the county.

Dr. Weiss has been a very popular featured speaker at the Greater St. Louis Jewish Book Festival, always drawing several hundred people to his presentations. Dr. Brian Weiss's brother, Peter Weiss, M.D. practices medicine and resides in St. Louis. Brian Weiss has many "true believers" in the St. Louis Jewish and general communities, including two friends of mine, Leslie Waldbaum and Michelle Rubin, who urged me to attend his most recent Jewish Book Festival appearance in November 2004 at the Jewish Community Center.

An overflow audience filled the Pasternak Auditorium at the JCC's Wohl Building in St. Louis for Dr. Weiss's talk and demonstration of his techniques. He invited the large audience to take part, voluntarily, in a trial run of his hypnotic techniques to bring them back to past-life experiences, and to describe them to one another after coming out of the trance.

Weiss began by strongly reassuring the audience that their participation was purely voluntary and that no one could be hypnotized against his or her will. He also stressed that he would not make people "quack like ducks or bark like dogs," or otherwise make fools of themselves.

I had become less skeptical about paranormal possibilities ever since the Israeli psychic Uri Geller bent my office key by merely stroking it and demonstrating apparent telepathy to a room full of doubting journalists while on a St. Louis visit. Now in my 60s, and engaged in the serious study of the Torah, Talmud and other sacred texts, I am now much more open to spiritual realities than I was in my adolescent, scientific method period.

Weiss put on some soothing background music and spoke in a calming, dreamlike voice. He began to gently encourage the participants in the audience to fully relax every part of their body from the top of their heads down to the tips of their fingers and toes. Some within the audience went "under" almost immediately; others remained wide-eyed and in the here and now throughout the session. I was among those who went into a kind of "Twilight Zone" of drowsy nodding off while my mind followed Dr. Weiss's words, producing vivid images as he spoke.

Weiss asked us to envision a time in a childhood that was especially blissful and happy and free of worry. My mind happily wandered back to those "lazy, hazy crazy days of summer" of my childhood. School was just out at Delmar Harvard grade school. My best friend Lester Goldman and I had a seemingly endless summer ahead of us to have "solid fun," as he put it—setting up Kool-Aid stands; reading comic books; falling asleep to the soothing breeze and hum of old-fashioned electric fans. . . .

Weiss then asked us to imagine being in a beautiful, serene garden, walking along a quiet, safe path, which led to a Golden Door. He urged us to walk through, then told us we could keep going farther back in our present life into a past life, going through the birth canal, into the womb, and then "back out" into a previous life, where we could safely come to rest and "re-experience" how our past selves felt on a given day.

For me, my past life experience was a total surprise. When I felt myself sufficiently "under" the hypnotic trance, I heard Dr. Weiss encourage us to look at our hands and feet and be prepared for them to look different from our "present" hands and feet. He was right, I looked down and my modern Johnston and Murphy dress shoes were replaced by black military boots of the kind I remember from movies or my ROTC experience at Washington U. My modern sport jacket morphed into a blue military coat, complete with brass buttons engraved with eagles. The freshly pressed, clean uniform appeared to be that of the Union Army during the Civil War, or perhaps some time between the Revolutionary War and the Mexican War.

I surmised that the year must be 1853, and somehow that seemed "right." My hands were much larger than my modern editor's hands. In fact they were huge and very strong, and they were grasping a blacksmith's tool to easily bend a molten horse shoe at will. I thought of the Henry Wadsworth Longfellow poem "The Village Blacksmith" who stood "under the spreading chestnut tree" with his "large and sinewy hands." I bent the horse shoes easily and it felt like I knew what I was doing. It was a cool, crisp, bright autumn day. I was standing in an immaculate stable with beautiful, highly groomed horses, mostly chestnut or shiny dark black in color. I assumed that my past life was that of a blacksmith attached an elite, well-trained unit of the U.S. Army Cavalry in 1853. I was also aware of the presence of the image of a fresh-faced, all-American country girl, with corn-silk blonde hair and blue eyes, wearing a gingham dress. Was she my wife or girl friend back home visiting my past life in a day dream, which gave her image a golden "shimmering" glow?

The entire experience described above and which only lasted a few "actual" minutes seemed and felt incredibly, vividly "real." Not only could I sense being in the large, clean, well-ventilated stable, but I could smell the hay in the clean facility, feel the cool outside air, see the almost polished looking well-groomed horses and enjoy bending the horse shoes—not to show off, but because that was what I "do" in my former life, just as writing is in my present life.

Of course the entire experience could have been the result of my own fertile imagination running away with itself. Perhaps I was influenced by the images of clean stables and beautiful horses in the film *Seabiscuit* which I had recently enjoyed. And yet, and yet, just maybe, it was indeed *real*.

If the experiences as an army blacksmith, as well as the Bridey Murphy, Patience Worth, Mary Sutton and Catherine cases were indeed real, how can I square this with Jewish concepts of the soul and the hereafter? The answer to this question has become much more important in recent years to me and other adults who have been devoting time to the serious study of the Torah, Talmud and other sacred Jewish texts

Dr. Weiss himself positively identifies as Jewish, and wrote a foreword to an interesting book by Rabbi Elie Kaplan Spitz, *Does the Soul Survive: A Jewish Journey to Belief in Afterlife, Past Lives and Living With Purpose.* (Jewish Lights Publishing). Dr. Spitz, spiritual leader of Congregation B'nai Israel in Tustin, Calif., and a graduate of the Jewish Theological Seminary (Conservative) and Boston University School of Law, like Dr. Weiss, is a serious traditional scholar.

In his foreword to Rabbi Spitz's book, Brian Weiss writes, "I am on the one hand, a well-known psychiatrist who has studied more than 2,000 patients in the past 20 years, patients who have remembered details of prior lifetimes and whose clinical symptoms have often dramatically resolved because of these memories. . . . I am, on the other hand, a Jew, taught in a Conservative synagogue in New Jersey. In my Jewish training, I was never introduced to the doctrines of reincarnation and soul survival after physical death. The vast majority of Jews in the United States knows nothing about the existence of these doctrines in mystical Jewish literature, or they are just now beginning to suspect that there is far more to Judaism than meets the eye."

Weiss recalls his participation in a live video conference via satellite that linked him up to a large audience in Jewish community centers in Detroit and Philadelphia, in which two Orthodox rabbis hosted the event, and "we engaged in a spiritual dialogue about reincarnation in Judaism, the clinical and religious perspective."

From his studio in Miami, Dr. Weiss concluded, "the rabbis and I agreed. We were on the same page. The rich tradition of *gilgul*, or reincarnation in Judaism was presented and was in general harmony with my detailed clinical investigations. Many Jews in the two audiences had their private beliefs in soul survival and reincarnation validated."

For his part, Rabbi Spitz, in his book, discusses Jewish concepts of the soul, writing, "Although there are a variety of understandings of the soul in the Jewish tradition, the common starting point is that the soul is no less than an extension of God. In the creating of Adam, the Torah says, 'God formed Adam out of the dust of the ground, and breathed into his nostrils the *neshamah* of life; and Adam became a living creature." (Genesis 2:7).

"In Hebrew," Rabbi Spitz continues, "there are three terms used for breath—*nefesh, ruach* and *neshamah*—words that in the Jewish mystical tradition are also used to describe facets of the soul. The image of breath conveys the idea that soul is intangible, animates life, and links us to the source of creation." He adds that the rabbis of the period of the Babylonian Talmud, largely completed in the fifth century C.E., elaborated on the link between the soul and its source as follows:

"As God fills the whole world, so also the soul fills the whole body. As God sees, but cannot be seen, so also the soul sees, but cannot be seen. As God nourishes the whole world, so also the soul nourishes the whole body. As God is pure, so also the soul is pure. As God dwells in the innermost parts of the Universe, so also the soul dwells in the innermost parts of the body."

In its 4,000-year history, Judaism has developed numerous concepts of the soul, the hereafter and the resurrection of the dead. The Sadducees, or priestly class denied the concept of the resurrection of the dead. The rival Pharisees, founders of Rabbinic Judaism, did believe in the resurrection of the dead and immortality of the soul. Rabbi Moses Maimonides, the giant among rabbinic sages, included a belief in the resurrection of the dead as one of the 13 principles of the Jewish religion, to be "believed with a perfect faith." There are theories about "the World to Come," including *Gan Eden,* or Paradises and *Gehennim,* a place of banishment, roughly similar to heaven and hell. Other sources are more ambivalent about the hereafter. The Talmud instructs us that the World to Come is like the banquet hall, and this world is like the vestibule or reception area outside the banquet hall. We must conduct ourselves in the vestibule in such a way as to deserve entry into the positive realms of the World to Come.

In the increasingly popular Kaballah, the Jewish mystical tradition, Isaac Luria's *Zohar* defines five principal elements of which the soul is composed—*nefesh, ruach, neshamah, hayyah,* and *yehidah,* according to the *Encyclopedia Judaica.* Life, spirit and soul are the three lower souls; the two higher elements can be attained only by elects. . . . There is no one vision of what will happen to the different parts of the soul after their separation from the body, because each one undergoes individual refinements and purifications and each ascends to different places in the supernal worlds. Only with the resurrection of the dead, the Kabbalists profess, do all the parts return and become unified, and from that time they remain connected to the total spiritual unity (God).

Thus it is possible that the various elements of the soul have different journeys. The *nefesh,* bound up with the body could have one path. Aspects of the *ruach,* or spirit, or the *neshamah* could perhaps split off from the original body and come to rest in another body in another time—a possible Jewishly valid way of explaining the apparent results of Dr. Weiss's work.

If all of the above speculations cause one's head to spin, no wonder. More and more, the Jewish mystical tradition, including Kaballah, is finding a receptive audience among scientists, especially advocates of what is called the "new physics" or "New Age Physics." The ultimate mysteries of mathematics, philosophy, science and religion overlap and loop around themselves. Is determinism or free will the way of the Universe? Is there a Unified Field Theory that could "explain everything"?

In the recently published book *Judaism, Physics and God,* Rabbi David W. Nelson provides a provocative fusion of religion and science, in which he "examines the great theories of modern physics to find new ways for contemporary people to express their spiritual beliefs and thoughts." Nelson discusses cosmology, qunatum mechanics, chaos theory, relativity and string theory, "attempting to "re-frame Judaism so that it is in harmony with the concepts of modern scientific thinking."

Another recent book by yet another rabbi, *DNA and Tradition: the Genetic Link to the Ancient Hebrews,* by Rabbi Yaakov Kleiman, details the exciting research that finds a remarkable consistency in the DNA structures among the Kohens, or *Kohaynim,* who according to tradition are descendants of Aaron, the brother of Moses and the first High Priest of the Jewish people. Cohens or Kohens all of the world, from remote outposts in Africa to the former Soviet Republic of Georgia to Alabama were found to have virtually identical DNA.

The above DNA connection validates the famous quote by Benjamin Disraeli, the British Jew who became prime minister. When a member of the Parliament made a snide remark about Disraeli's Jewish origins, he replied, "Yes, I am a Jew, and when the ancestors of the right honourable gentleman were savages on an unknown island, mine were priests in the Temple of Solomon."

Reading all of the above sources, along with the works of Dr. Weiss, leaves me open to the possibility that it is possible not only religiously, but metaphysically and scientifically, that there a "soul-stuff," a multi-faceted life force that can be passed down spiritually from one human vessel to another. After my own sojourn back to the days when I was apparently a blacksmith in 1853, wearing a dark beard and feeling right at home bending horse shoes in an elegant, cool stable, I am more open to the possibility. Paraphrasing Shakespeare, there indeed "many things on heaven and earth" which are not "dreamt of" in the philosophies of most people, but which are no less real because of that fact.

Whatever the truth of these matters might be, I am grateful to Dr. Weiss for the excitement of my thrill ride back to 1853. By the way, I let myself "see" how my blacksmith past life ended—with a gunshot wound to the chest in combat a few years after 1853—perhaps during the Civil War. I felt the intense burning in my chest, which mirrored the chronic acid reflux heartburn which had tormented me for years. Once I learned the source of my past-life trauma, the symptoms almost completely disappeared, and with the help of a little faith and prescription Prilosec or Nexium, both my body and soul are doing just fine, thank you very much.

I close with a passage from the Talmud *(B'rachot 60B),* which praises God for our soul, which the Holy One breathed into creation and breathes into us, which jumped out at me at services last Shabbat:

The soul that you have given me, O God is pure! You created it and formed it, breathed it into me, and within me, You sustain it. So long as I have breath, therefore, I will give thanks to You, my God and the God of all Ages, Source of all Being, loving Guide of every human spirit.

May it be God's will!

Sophie Dricker
Escape From Russia

I used to be a good swimmer in a lake. I loved it. Who had a bathing suit? You had to live in a big city like Odessa or Kiev. The people there had bathing suits. Where I lived nobody knew from bathing suits. You just had to wear a nightgown or go naked. So I used to sit under the water all the time, nobody should see me.

★ ★ ★

My father left Russia when the Revolution started. The Russians caught him and Frank Fershter when they tried to cross the border. They escaped from the guards. My father brought Frank to St. Louis. They came to St. Louis because Frank's father and my father were old friends. I remember Frank from when I was six years old.

Everything was censored. The government didn't let any of my father's letters go to the family or our letters go to him.

The Revolution was terrible. Kerensky was the one that really started it. He wasn't bad, but then different people was taking over. Every day there was a different government. The people was killing one another. In a little town called Choshinev the Cossacks killed six hundred Jews. They made a big grave and they were chopping up the people. One man was alive. The Cossacks went so fast they didn't hit him enough to kill him and he came out of that grave and was telling how horrible it was. We all knew him. He used to come to our town buying chickens and eggs. In that town my uncle and my cousins were killed.

A lot of people in our town got killed and a lot of them ran away to different towns where it was quieter. Right across from our house, three of our neighbors, I heard them scream and the Cossacks chopped off their heads. The Cossacks were passing our house and I took up a prayer book and I was saying *Shema Yisrael* and kissing the *mezzuza*.

Three times we had a chance to be killed. Three times Cossacks came in and asked my mother if my father was sending her money. That's what they wanted. How could you have money when every day was a different government? My mother said, "My husband left me. I don't hear from him. I don't know if he's alive or dead. "

The Cossacks said, "Are you telling the truth?"

Some of the Catholics got killed, too. Right next door, our neighbors—they were good neighbors—the Cossacks killed the father and four sons. To hear them scream—I was deaf for a month. The bells of the church were ringing. Oh my God. It was terrible. The next morning we were afraid to open up the door and look.

The corpses of our neighbors were laying outside by their house.

The *Kibbutzim* came to help us. After that everybody knew when the Cossacks were gonna come in and make a pogrom. Then we would sleep on the floor. The people from the *Kibbutz* were guarding everybody.

★ ★ ★

When I was sixteen I made up my mind that I was gonna leave Russia and go to Kishinev, Bessorabia. We had relatives in a small Russian town just across the river that was the border between the two countries. So my mother sent me to stay with them.

I didn't have no money, but the agent who was going to take me across knew that my father was in America and would pay. We were a lot of people, maybe twenty-five, who the agent was taking across the border. I couldn't go right to Kishinev because I had to pass a lot of little towns.

We crossed the river at night in row boats. It was dark so we didn't know where we were. When we woke up in the morning everybody started screaming. We were lying on graves behind headstones in a cemetery. The agent made us be quiet.

Bessorabia is a big country and not everybody was going to the same place. The agent took everyone else before he took me. I was the only one going to Kishinev. He took me in a forest. I didn't trust him. I said, "What are you doing?"

He said, "I can't help it."

I said, "MY God! How long will I be here by myself?"

He had a list of where each person was going. He said, "I have to take these people first. I will not leave you here. I promise you I'll come back."

I said, "I hardly know you. How do I know you'll do what you say?"

I watched him, which way he was going, but even if I would try to follow him I didn't know where he went when he got out of sight. Then I heard dogs barking and people talking a language I didn't understand. Waiting until I saw him—that's what you call brave.

* * *

I came to St. Louis in 1922 and got married in 1925. And in 1929 I was a widow already with a little girl. So you see, my husband left me something.

I gave up the apartment and I went to live with my father and mother. My father said, "Sophie, you're over twenty-one. You know what to do. "

I says, "I can't leave the baby."

He says, "Don't worry about the baby. Do you want to work?"

I knew what he meant: "You better go to work to make a living."

I says, "O.K. I'm going to look for a job."

My father and my mother raised my daughter. They lived until my daughter married.

* * *

When I worked I was the only Jewish girl. The rest of them were gentile and colored. When anybody got sick they didn't send nobody but me for a collection. I would collect. When I got sick with my detached retina they were praying, they were sending cards. When I came back to work they had a big sign,

"WELCOME BACK."

I didn't care whether people were colored or white or anything.

I worked in that place for twenty-eight years. I always liked to work on men's clothing. You know why? It's not so particular. They wanted to teach me to be an operator because an operator made more money. They set me down to show me how to do it. I didn't even know how to stop the machine. I said, "No. I don't want it." That's why I never learned to drive a car either.

* * *

I got a will with my daughter what to do when I die, what I want to wear. I want to be laid down and people should come to see me. I got the dress ready. I want a white orchid. I told my daughter to put that down in the will. I just don't want to be thrown in right away. I believe in God and everything, but I'm not fanatic about being buried.

My daughter's gonna do what I asked her to do. It is like a promise.

★ ★ ★

You know what the Rabbi says to me? If everyone will feel the same way and do the things like I do, then the world would be beautiful.

Sophie Dricker (Nee Sonja Pollack, Bersheck, Ukraine, December 18, 1903–May 4, 1993)

Frank Fershter
Life in Russia

I remember in Russia in 1911 there was a typhoid epidemic. My mother was sick, my brother and I. All of us were sick. I had three cases of typhoid at the same time. I had stomach typhoid, head typhoid and one that broke out on my body. I couldn't eat anything. They told me not to eat a thing.

In about three weeks they gave me half a biscuit. I was hungry. I noticed there was a piece of a slice of bread laying on the floor. I couldn't tell them that I wanted the piece of bread so I told them that I don't feel like lying in bed, I was kind of hot. I asked them to put me down on the floor. As sick as I was I reached for that piece of bread and I ate it. Boy, that done the job. Did I get sick!

We lived in a small town so the people was always friends. They were in the house and standing in a crowd and talking. When you come in it was just like coming into a hospital room. I remember there was a *schoket,* a kosher butcher there. He was the main clergyman in the town.

My mother wanted to know what everybody is talking about.

He says, "We're just talking quiet because we don't want to bother you people. You're sick and we don't want to make noise."

After we got better and started going out, this *schoket* came up to my mother and said, "Do you know what we were talking about that day? First of all, Frank's life was hanging on a silk thread. Every time he breathed out we expected him to expire. We knew that if you'd find out, as sick as you were, we'd have two corpses instead of one." Naturally they attributed that to God. They ignored the contribution of the doctor and the medicine.

★ ★ ★

It was a Sunday in 1912. An automobile passed by. It was the first time the people had ever seen an automobile. I had already seen one because I had been to different places.

The peasants were smart people, they were intelligent people, but they weren't educated. They didn't know what to make of it. It was the time of Haley's Comet. Some said it must be a part of the comet. Someone said it must be something that brings the end of the world and someone said a devil sits in there and operates the machine. I don't know how the peasants knew about Haley's Comet. The town where I lived had about fifteen blocks and I don't think amongst all of those people there were ten people that could read or write, but everybody knew that something was coming; they just didn't know what it was.

I had a book that described Haley's Comet. Somehow the peasants knew that I had it. So they came up to me and said, "Froika, we want the book that tells about the comet that will come and destroy the earth." So I told them it's not as bad as that. It won't destroy anything. I couldn't tell them that nature provides the comet. If I told them that, I'd have to explain all these things and I didn't know anything about them myself. So I told them it's God's doing and that's all.

When they spoke in our town about the comet everyone thought, "Who knows what will happen?" But after I read about it a couple of times I knew that it just comes naturally. The comet comes every so often.

★ ★ ★

I remember just like today. There was a bunch of Russian boys and girls visiting at our house. That evening we were sitting around the table and drinking tea and talking. One of the fellows said goodnight. He was going home. All of a sudden he comes back and he knocked at the window. He said, "Come on out, ladies and gentlemen and you'll see something."

We went outside and looked around. The comet was there. It was almost as big as the moon. The comet and its tail covered up almost the whole horizon. It made the night like a street now looks when the street lights are on. It was beautiful.

I still remember as I walked out of the house it looked to me like the fiery tail was all on me. I wasn't scared, I was stupefied. I didn't think of God, I didn't think of angels, I didn't even think of nature. I thought just of that thing. It looked like gold. The comet didn't have any certain quality. It just looked like something the imagination would make. It was a dream. It was like being in space. It was such an experience, I'll never forget it.

(Froika Fershter, Bonderova, Ukraine, April 24, 1896–November 13, 1992)

Barbara L. Finch
One Journey to Judaism

People who become Jews by choice have many different stories about the paths that led them to embrace this religious tradition. For me, the journey began over a tuna salad sandwich.

It was a hot summer day in 1993, and I was eating lunch in my mother's kitchen in Charleston, West Virginia. At that time my mother was 86 years old. She was frail, and although her memory was certainly intact, she was becoming increasingly withdrawn. She preferred to talk about the past rather than think about the present or discuss the future.

On this particular day, I attempted to engage her with questions about her girlhood and the early years of her marriage. Swallowing a bite of my sandwich, I casually inquired, "So, how did Grandmother react when you and Daddy got engaged?"

"She was fine with it," Mother replied, "after she determined that Daddy wasn't Jewish."

For several seconds, I couldn't breathe. A glob of tuna oozed out of my sandwich and plopped onto my plate. I stared at it, and then at Mother.

"Jewish?" I said. "Whatever made Grandmother think that Daddy might be *Jewish?"*

"Oh, several things," Mother said. "You know he looked Jewish. And his father owned a furniture store, and he absolutely refused to go to church."

She went on to describe how my grandmother had hired a lawyer to investigate my father's background. When no Jewish relatives were discovered, she had given her blessing to the marriage.

The rest of my lunch sat on my plate as I pondered this new information about my family history. It didn't really surprise me that my grandmother, a straight-laced Victorian who flaunted her membership in the Daughters of the American Revolution, would not have wanted her oldest daughter to marry a Jew. After all, this was in the late 1920s, in a small city in southern West Virginia. Anti-Semitism would not have been uncommon at that time and in that place. As far as "looking Jewish," whatever that means, my father was tall, with dark hair and a dark complexion (and I always thought he was handsome). It's true that his father owned a furniture store, and many of the prominent merchants in town at that time were Jewish. It was also true that he never darkened the door of a church, except to attend weddings and funerals. And I, who had always struggled with my religious faith, even as a child, always considered this an admirable trait.

But wait a minute! What if the lawyer hired by my grandmother had been wrong? Or what if he told her what she wanted to hear? Or what if my father, who was a lawyer himself, and the only child of an only child, had managed, for whatever reason, to cover up his past? What if Daddy really was a Jew?

"Do you think Daddy might have been Jewish?" I asked Mother.

"I have no idea," she replied. "It was a long time ago."

And it was a long time ago. My father died in 1970, and, to my knowledge, I am his only living relative. The people who might have known him when he was a child or a young man are all dead. And my efforts to trace his ancestors, although perfunctory, have yielded few results (not surprising, since his mother listed her father's name as "John Smith").

That summer afternoon in 1993, as I put the remains of lunch away in the refrigerator and washed the dishes, I realized that I was tremendously excited by this talk with my mother. And although I was certainly curious about whether my father might have been Jewish, I really didn't care. In some obscure way, that conversation with my mother gave *me* the permission I needed to be Jewish.

At the time I was 55 years old. I had spent the first 30 years of my life as an unbelieving Presbyterian, the next 15 as an unconvinced agnostic, and the remainder as an unsatisfied Unitarian. I remember saying to a Jewish friend one time, "If I could choose my religion, I'd choose Jewish." She had given me a strange look and replied, "So, why can't you?"

Still, it wasn't until two years later, after my mother had died, that I took the first step. I enrolled in an Introduction to Judaism Course, sponsored by the organization that was then called the Union of American Hebrew Congregations. "I'm not interested in converting," I remember telling my sponsoring rabbi. "I just want to learn something."

Apparently, I learned a lot. Several months later, I found myself in an unlikely pursuit: temple-shopping. One Friday night, sitting in a suburban synagogue waiting for services to begin, I started leafing through "The Gates of Prayer" and came to page 705. This is what I read:

I am a Jew because the faith of Israel demands of me no abdication of the mind.

I am a Jew because the faith of Israel requires of me all the devotion of my heart.

I am a Jew because in every place where suffering weeps, the Jew weeps.

I am a Jew because at every time when despair cries out, the Jew hopes.

I am a Jew because the word of Israel is the oldest and the newest.

I am a Jew because the promise of Israel is the universal promise.

I am a Jew because, for Israel, the world is not completed; we are completing it.

I am a Jew because, for Israel, humanity is not created; we are creating it.

I am a Jew because Israel places humanity and its unity above the nations and above Israel itself.

I am a Jew because, above humanity, image of divine Unity; Israel places the unity which is divine.

It was then that I knew, without a doubt, that I wanted to be able to say the words, "I am a Jew."

On the first day of November, 1996, I officially became a Jew by choice. As I stepped from the *mikveh* and wrapped myself in a warm white robe, I somehow felt close to my father. Was he really a Jew? I don't know. It doesn't matter. Today, I am, and that is all that does matter.

Shelly R. Fredman
Samuel's Coat

The grass is a dull shade of brown and the little flags at the edge of the subdivision walls are limp and tired-looking. The crack of fireworks no longer interrupts the sky and the morning silence in the house has a heaviness to it, as if it is laden with sounds that are not there. Zach's guitar. Micah's piano. The soft and not-so-soft patter of feet in the morning—children waking, running water, brushing their teeth, getting ready for school.

I told myself I wouldn't do what my mother had done—live for her children. As if theirs, ours, was the real life and hers only a counter life, insubstantial, circus-like, the rungs and rods on which the sparkling life hangs. Driving the carpools, setting the plates at the table, taking a secretarial job so the dance lessons can be paid for, the kids sent off to earn the degree.

And yet, it's what I, we, have done. My younger son cooked for weeks before he went off to camp—he loves food and couldn't imagine eight weeks on a strictly camp food diet. So he froze and packed banana breads and carrot cakes in little silver foil packages, stacked them one atop another in the freezer, stockpiling for days before he left. The kitchen's sigh of relief when he finally finished baking was almost audible—as if I could hear the mixmaster crying—I'm tired of these dizzy circles. Let me be.

The amp my eldest bought for music camp and set up in my living room—"These are the best acoustics here, mom," is gone, just a dusty space on the floor and some music sheets scattered around.

My daughter hasn't left yet, but hers is a different energy, a different kind of noise. She keeps writing and rewriting her camp list, crossing off the items we've managed to find, making a clean copy to bring with us to the next store.

We parents walk around, listless, comparing notes. "Who's left at your house?"

"Rachel gets back Sunday. Karen's gone for four weeks; Susan eight. Michael won't be home until August."

One father I know has a slump in his shoulders I recognize. He's just sent the light of his life off to eight weeks of camp. She will return for a brief time before going to college in the Fall. When they mailed his daughter's roommate questionnaire out, instead of sending it off to her, he filled it in. "Do you prefer someone quiet?" they asked. "No," he wrote, hearing his own loneliness. "Are you generally a neat person?" they queried. "Of course," he responded, picturing his daughter's room, clothes strewn over the chair, high heels snaking a trail to the closet.

How did they expect us to remain separate, when the training involved a hungry mouth at the breast, cries of hunger, thirst, pain. How was I to retain a Buddhist's sense of calm, of non-attachment, when your nightmare cries woke me at 1 a.m.? When a thunderstorm's crack sent you running into my bed? And what of the basketball games, when, in the final seconds, you approached the free-throw line to take the final shot.

Who was to say whether that was your heart beating or mine?

When my father left, I was twelve years old, but I didn't cry. I'd been instructed by my mother to "catch all of life's blades by the handle," as a plaque she'd once hung in our living room—yes—our living room! put it. Is this ache in my throat the only way to make up for lost time? Get a life, I tell myself. Go shopping. Find a job.

But I was trained by an anarchist in college who taught me about how we Americans have been hoodwinked by the American dream, trading our muscles for mascara, useless products that clutter our houses and usurp our revolutionary impulses. So shopping is out, and conventional notions of success don't "float my boat," as the saying goes. So I go to yoga—daily—and try to see the negative thoughts as clouds drifting across a brilliant blue sky.

I'd like to find my brilliance, that shiny thing that once called to me, but there's a bug in the circuits and I'm wondering if it's possible, if I just keep this pen moving, for someone to write their way out of despair. The parameters of this loss are so wide, so unyielding. If I could paint it, it would be a blue and black field with nary a golden flower in it. The rabbis suggest I sing my pain away, as David, the psalmist once did.

But I don't have the notes, the lyrics, the key.

August we spend on Cape Cod and it is easier here. The loss is a farther away thing, as if I've left pieces of it behind, like the shirts and shoes that didn't make it into the suitcase. The house we rent doesn't seem so empty—it is filled with books on Chinese water coloring painting, nautical-themed posters, the biography of Thomas Paine. These are the detritus of other lives. They don't set me off the way it did when I wandered into Zach's empty room and rummaged through the things that didn't make it into his duffle in his frantic 1 a.m. packing the night before he left for camp: a love note scribbled on a sheet of blue-lined notebook paper, an essay for Honors Lit III, replete with red-inked markings, a CD case stripped of its disc, the latest from the Dave Mathews Band.

It is easier, too, because the ocean, which I have always loved, seems to speak to me without words—the best communication of all. Its waves go in and out and in again, they spill and die and are reborn every few minutes and tell me that nothing matters so much and everything, every single thing, is at stake.

This year, we have unwittingly rented a house on the bay side of the sea. I say unwittingly because these same owners whose interests extend from Chinese watercolors to Thomas Paine have neglected to advertise their bayside location on the realtor's printout sheet. Have they grown so accustomed to that expanse of blue oneness resting outside their door that they hardly notice it is there? Does the setting sun's stripe of shadow and light playing on marsh and grass and water fail to move them, fail to do what it does to me—set the horizons within in realignment, shift the boundaries and put them to right? Or is it simply that the rental figure, the price tag, one of the heftier ones we've paid—says it all?

Either way, when I return to St. Louis at August's end, and the children have disembarked from planes and cars—all three—and the thirty odd loads of laundry are all washed and dried and folded and put away— the camp sheets in a special box in the basement I will try to avoid—it is those changing bands of light and color I cannot forget. The blues and browns and greens of grasses, marshes, sea.

The wise woman I vacationed with in Cape Cod (I choose vacation partners carefully) did yoga every morning, in the great room, on a yoga mat laid over the Oriental carpet. A yoga mat she had thought to bring along. I, a yoga dilettante, had left mine at home.

Laya pointed out to me, "You're thinking about it wrong. You have to welcome change. Change is the way of the world. It's a constant becoming."

Ahhh. My mistake was in believing anything would be forever. There was the childhood before my parents' divorce that had a lilting, everlasting feel to it. And the adolescence after. And somewhere in between my world split in two. So here I am, suspended perpetually in the gap so that when my daughter did finally finish her camp list and was packing a pbj to take with her on the plane, I had to repeat out loud to myself, like a mantra, she is not leaving forever. She is not going to die. She's just going to camp for four weeks and then surprise surprise you get her back. It's not like your father leaving and your world being destroyed and pretending it's not happening, having to pretend it's not happening—because you're all running around catching knives by the handle, when it's the blade you're feeling, the dagger inside.

Constantly becoming, Laya said, and change is good and a welcome thing like the cool, minted wind and the green leaves turning red on the trees, outside.

It is September and though I am trying to cling to what Laya said, still, like a fool, I am counting the Lasts. Because next year Zach will be at college and I'm the one who has to put him on that plane. The last Rosh Hashanah. The last middle of the night drive home from Chicago, where we've spent nine of the last Jewish New Years. My husband is asleep in the back seat, the two youngest are overlapped in the seat behind, snoring, and Zach and I are driving past Funk's Grove and Litchfield. He asks what I am thinking as I stare out at a star-filled sky. I am thinking we don't get out and look at the stars enough. I am thinking when my mom loaded me on a plane for college, it was the first time I discovered I had separation anxiety and went to see a therapist because it was impossible for me to fly.

"What are you thinking, Mom?" Zach asked, a question I am famous for asking him. Delighted—some seed has been planted—and yet, what should I say? Should I tell him my New Year's vow is to work on embracing change, a grasp of the ever-advancing leap from season to season to season, a cycle of birth and death and rebirth, Nature's call? Or should I tell him the truth, that I am counting "Lasts," the last high school open house, the last building of the sukkah, hoping somehow that at the end of this year of Lasts, I'll come up—out—with my bucket "full"?

Instead, I tell him about a workshop I'm preparing and after we talk for a while, I stare out at the darkened fields and think of what the Jewish tradition teaches us—what its stories of loss are. There are lots of them, beginning with Adam and Eve, their fall and exile, but I'm more interested in the women. Long line of those, too, from Sarah to Rachel to Leah. All of them loved and lost. But two in particular stand out, at this time.

First, there is Lot's wife, who looked back. You know the story—urged to run from Sodom, because our God in heaven was going to destroy it, Lot and his family are told they can leave, are free to go, on the condition that they scoot and don't look back. A wise decree, in fact. A less painful way to say goodbye to your loved ones, people you've lived alongside of all your life—broken bread with, birthed each other's babies with, watched the fire die down with as evening's blue clouds set in. Head out across the desert and don't turn around. Keep moving forward. It is sage advice and something a man, like Lot, seemed to have no trouble obeying.

But oh that foolish nameless wife. Did she hear the cry of her best friend's child? Did she forget something—a letter, a postcard, a key? Did she pause before she turned, knowing she was risking everything? Did she choose to do it anyway, because she needed that last goodbye, because one last look was all she needed to will her feet forward, toward whatever lay ahead? We'll never know. She remains there, frozen in salt, a pillar of tears, punished for her losses, her inability to let go and move on, a monument to backward glancing, at the desert's edge.

And then, there is Hannah. Hannah is first taught on Rosh Hashanah and in our congregation, in Chicago, they chanted the Haftorah about her and how she had to watch as others gave birth to son after son and she was childless. But then she went to the temple at Shiloh and prayed so fervently and with such passion that the priest who led the service thought that she was drunk. But God, who is a wee bit wiser and more discerning, heard her prayer and soon she gave birth to Samuel. The catch is, as in all good fairy tales, she had promised the child to God and so at four, she delivered him to Eli, gave up this child she had wanted so badly and loved and nursed and taught—to God.

After the Haftorah, at our shul, a woman sang a beautiful Hebrew song about a mother bird releasing her young from the nest, a song an Israeli friend of mine happened to sing to her daughter, Nili, on her bat mitzvah day. I guess the song and Hannah herself stayed with me, on that drive from Chicago with Zach at the wheel.

And then, during Neilah, there she was again. Hannah. Heart opened by the day of fasting, hearing the gorgeous voices of my best friends in the choir telling me, "Nothing is more precious than life," knowing that one of those friends, Susan Weissman, truly did already give her precious son, Nathan, four, back to God and miracle of miracles, continues to live her life and get up for work each day and brush her teeth and put on her shoes and sing! Yes! sing, at *Neilah* services to all of us. There was Hannah and, as if she was bending down to tell me, I knew it would be all right. Because like Samuel, I have raised him, Zach, for a purpose, a purpose greater than myself. He is the best I have to offer the world. I have nursed and loved and taught him—and now, like Hannah, I will release him to

God's world. I will look back, like Lot's wife, many times, but perhaps, because of her, not too much. I will go forward.

Besides, Hannah never really finished her work on Samuel. Every year, the midrash says, she made him a coat, a little coat. Every single year. As he grew. Did she tear out the old stitches or begin anew each time, selecting fabrics to match the changing seasons? We'll never know. We do know, as Laya says, it was ever changing, a constant becoming, a mother-son-mother love story that goes on and on.

Rabbi James Stone Goodman
Dark Moss

I was present, once, for the repair of the past. It was unexpected, but it was Jerusalem—the common the miraculous, the ordinary the extraordinary, bound up with each other, everywhere, daily.

Todd introduced me to Thomas. Thomas had come to Jerusalem from Germany to say the *Kaddish* (memorial prayer), on behalf of his father, for his grandfather. His grandfather had come to Israel from Berlin in 1932, lost track of his family left behind in Germany, and Thomas's father and grandfather never found each other again. Thomas's father had spent eleven years in Buchenwald, arrested as a Communist and kept as a Jew. He survived the War and became an official in the East German Communist Party. He married a German woman and raised three sons, the youngest Thomas. After Thomas's grandfather and father both died, Thomas recovered his identity as a Jew living in Berlin about the time the Berlin Wall came down. He taught himself a little Hebrew and came to Israel in search of the Israeli remnant of his family, his grandfather had married a second wife there, on a journey of secret destinations. I met him the day he came to Jerusalem.

Would you like to meet Thomas? Todd asked me. He wants to go to the Wall (the western wall of the Temple). Todd set up a meeting in the Old City, inside the Jaffa Gate.

We met Thomas early in the afternoon, just inside the Jaffa Gate. He was thin, fair-skinned, carrying a camera around his neck, his fatigue jacket full of film and other camera paraphernalia. We sat in a café, introduced each other, drank a dark sweet coffee, then we walked through the Armenian Quarter to the Wall.

The three of us arrived at the Wall mid-afternoon, three o'clock. There were only a few supplicants working the Wall that day, so we had most of the space on the men's side to ourselves.

We stood in a huddle, Thomas, Todd, and I, our arms around each other, three men from half a world apart drawn together probably for the only time in our lives to perform a ritual that emerged spontaneously. Todd pulled out of his pocket a piece of barbed wire that he had picked up off the ground at Auschwitz and carried with him for a purpose that had clarified only that moment. He gave it to Thomas.

We talked about holiness and broken hearts. Thomas asked quietly,

"Is there something that cannot be lifted to holiness? Can anything be raised to holiness?"

"Almost everything," I imagined.

He was holding the piece of barbed wire in his hands as if he were asking permission to place it, among the other messages, in the Wall. Visitors to the Wall place messages in its ancient crevices, messages to God, called *kvittelech*. Thomas placed the piece of barbed wire in the Wall.

He then placed his hands and his forehead against the Wall and we said the *Kaddish* (memorial) prayer together. I watched him speaking the words of the *Kaddish* and as I watched this is what I saw:

Birds. There are two kinds of birds that I saw flying around the Wall, swifts (Hebrew: *sisim*) and palm doves. When Thomas put his forehead against the Wall and began to speak the *Kaddish,* the swifts whipped around wildly. I noticed no difference in the doves, they were nesting quietly in the Wall, but the swifts went screeching and careening madly for the minute or so it took Thomas to slowly pronounce the words of the memorial prayer, which he had taught himself for just this occasion.

Something in Thomas's prayer disturbed the atmosphere on that day, and the swifts, who have accompanied two millenia of *Kaddish* prayers at the Western Wall, sensed the interruption. Since the destruction of the Temple of which this was the Western Wall of the outer barrier, since the year 70 the swifts have accompanied generations of *Kaddish* prayers at that very spot, or so I thought, until I told the story to Miri who lives in Jerusalem.

When I told her about the swifts, she said to me, "The swifts are very special, but they were not always here. They returned to the Wall when the Jews returned. I know an Arab in the Old City who told me that before the Jews came back in '67, there were no swifts here. The swifts returned to the Wall with the Jews."

We are taught that the soul of the *Shekhinah,* the indwelling spirit of God, rests in a bird at the Western Wall. I quoted that teaching to Miri. "Would that it were so simple," sighed Miri. "Whose God? Which wall?"

In the *Zohar,* the classical text of Jewish mysticism, there is a notion that the ultimate test of Abraham is a test both of Abraham and his son, both his sons, Isaac and Ishmael, to teach Abraham something that was missing in his own generation that could be reconciled only through his sons, and the descendants of his sons. There was something disturbed, broken in Abraham's generation that would only be repaired in the future, through his children, through Isaac and Ishmael, and the descendants of Isaac and Ishmael. All peacemaking has profound implications not only for the present, and the future, but for the past.

I looked at Thomas and I witnessed a healing moving through him into the past, healing something broken in his father, and healing something broken in his grandfather, something that could only be repaired by Thomas. I felt Thomas's prayer healing something in his past that the personalities themselves could not heal, closing the circles.

I understood how history could be healed, how a person's act of sacred intent in the present could transform past deeds. I saw it. I saw it through Thomas's act of healing, moving back through his family to repair something that had been broken generations ago.

We spent some time in silence at the Wall, the three of us, then we each wandered our way out, Thomas returning to Tel Aviv, then Germany, Todd back to where he was staying in Jerusalem, myself to our apartment in an old Arab neighborhood near the industrial part of South Jerusalem.

I hadn't forgotten about the swifts, but this was Jerusalem, the extraordinary sometimes so ordinary, the land, the birds, the stones full of significance and deep story.

On the way home, I walked through the Armenian Quarter and through the passageway by the outer wall of the Bishop Gobat School, down the side of Mt. Zion, through the Valley of Hinnom, and up Emek Refaim, the Valley of Healing, towards our apartment. On the way down the side of Mt. Zion, I looked at the rocks along the path that I have walked hundreds of times. Many of these rocks have been unearthed and are the same rocks that boundaried the Mount of Zion in Second Temple times. We have been going up to Zion this way for three thousand years.

At first, it seemed as if a dark stain had spread over the face of the rocks, like the leprous house in Leviticus, a dark stain that appeared on the rocks. I looked closer and saw that the dark stain was actually a moss, a dark moss, I looked closely, it wasn't easy to recognize but that's what it was, moss. There were also flowers in the crevices of the rocks, and wild grass, and this growth I had never noticed before, dark moss.

I wondered if my ancestors, pilgrims going up to Zion, had stopped at that same place to look at the dark moss. I wondered whether the dark moss had grown along with the rocks, for these thousands of years, or whether it was recent, since the destruction of the Second Temple, two thousand years ago, or since medieval times, or since the sixteenth century when we came down from the north to visit Jerusalem, or whether it was modern, since the founding of the state, since the air has been clouded by the exhaust of machines, or whether it was a spiritual sign, like the leprosy that grew on the walls of houses, a sign of something that is growing, something that can be tended, something changing into something else, the moss darkened by uncertainty, fear, anger, something unrepaired, or perhaps the blood that has been spilled all around had dried on the natural green, dried dark, so dark that you didn't notice it, you hardly knew that there was something growing there, but there is, there is something growing there.

   I saw it.

*Resh Lakish said, great is teshuvah (repentance), because it reduces one's deliberate sins to mere errors. But did not Resh Lakish say at another time, great is teshuvah, because it transforms one's deliberate sins into merits?   —Babylonian Talmud, Yoma 86b

Felicia Graber
The Pearl Earrings

Whenever I open this drawer, I see them, the earrings. I see them framing her small delicate fine chiseled face, highlighting her dark complexion and enhancing her refined air. Her black eyes and hair and her simple hairstyle completed her almost Hispanic appearance. Those beautiful eyes never seemed to smile however and the slightly drooping corners of her lips added to the poignancy and sadness to her face. I seldom heard her laugh or saw the corner of her lips turn up in a genuine smile, but when she did her eyes glowed with a brilliant light. There was something elegant, noble in her bearing. During the last years of her life, her black hair was speckled with gray yet her almost wrinkle free complexion belied her age. Lipstick and a light dusting of face powder were the only touches she used to enhance her features. She dressed simply and pleasingly, preferring classic, ageless styles to current fads. But she always wore her jewelry, nothing showy, mind you—tastefully small and elegant. And she always wore her pearl earrings.

She did not have a happy life. Brought up in a strictly traditional Jewish household in a small town in Poland, she rebelled early against the obligatory orthodox restrictions. Her dream was to go to Palestine, to learn farming and join a collective community, a *kibbutz*. She got a brief taste of her dream when in 1933 she joined a group of young men and women and enrolled in an agricultural school in the land of her ancestors. I think that that year was probably the happiest in her life; she would often talk about it, describing the dirty, strenuous work with love and nostalgia. She would describe her friends, her teachers, the summer heat, the dreams she had had for her future.

But then, the telegram came. Her mother who she adored was gravely ill, her days were numbered, so Tania packed a few things and made the difficult trip back home. She fully intended to return to Palestine—she knew that pioneer existence was her destiny.

However life had other plans for her. She never did returned. Her mother died, her sister followed a few months later. She and her brother felt the double blow intensely. How could she leave him all alone when he needed her support and help? So she got a job and remained in Poland.

In March of 1939 she married, her future seemed to look up, but again, fate intervened: a few months after her wedding, on September 1,

Hitler invaded her country and life would never again be the same. By the time her daughter was born, the following March, living had become a struggle. Daily new restrictions were imposed on the Jewish inhabitants. She had to leave her beautiful apartment, the new linens, the furniture barely 2 years old, she could only take whatever she could carry. And this was just the beginning of a long and dangerous journey that would propel her into a new and perilous, treacherous world where a wrong word or a wrong gesture could mean the end of her and her daughter's life.

An Inadvertent Hero

Tarnov, Poland, end of June 1942. The Germans have been occupying Poland for almost 2 years. Restrictions on the town Jewish inhabitants have progressed from harassment, imprisonment, confiscation of property, beatings, and intimidations to expulsion and deportation to death camps. The ghetto has been established and a curfew is in force.

Israel Leder has been lucky to find a room within the ghetto walls for himself, his wife and his 18-month-old daughter, which they share with another couple and their two children. His large five-room apartment with all its content has been confiscated, as has the watchmaker store he owned with his father. His parents and his father-in-law have been "resettled" together with other older citizens of the town a few weeks ago. Resettled? Israel has no illusions; he has heard the eyewitness accounts of mass shootings in near-by forests and strongly suspects that he will never see them again. The last letter he received from his sister a few months ago indicated that she too expected the worst.

Some of his friends, young men and women, have fled to Russia but he and his wife had not been able to do so—his wife was five months pregnant at the time, could not make the dangerous and exhausting journey—later it was too late and besides who could take an infant on such an adventure into the unknown?

Earlier that year he had endured severe beatings, had barely escaped death when an German officer caught him with a two-pound sack of illegal white flour bought from an acquaintance. It was a precious gift for his mother who was not well and could not tolerate the coarse flour available to Jews. Jews you see were not allowed to have such luxuries such as fined white flour. The Nazi had broken a chair on Israel's back, had beaten him with an iron pipe and held a pistol to his head trying to extract from him the name of the dealer of that contraband. But Israel kept insisting that he did not have that information. He knew it would be a death sentence to reveal his source. Finally, the officer had given up, convinced.

Now, while getting settled and exploring his new home in the ghetto, Israel happened to come across an opening which led to a large empty space under the roof—a perfect hiding place for whoever needed to disappear when rumors of a new roundup flared up as they often did. Eventually this space would provide shelter and temporary safety to over a hundred people who had not been able to keep up with the ever-changing rules and demands handed down by the German authorities. Israel and his wife would feed and care for these people at the peril of their and their daughter's lives.

That fall, he would claim a blond, blue-eyed baby boy as his own to the questioning soldiers. A desperate parent, afraid of taking the infant into the hiding place lest his cries alert the Germans, had placed him in the crib together with Israel's black haired black-eyed daughter. Even though neither he nor his wife had any traces of this child's coloring, their gutsy replies and assertions to the inquiries put the authorities off.

Later that same year when, with incredible luck the Leder family was pulled out of a transport to a concentration camp, Israel again claimed a little blond girl, the daughter of a friend, as his own and managed to sneak her off the transport with them. A few weeks later, seeing that their situation was precarious, he managed to get hold of false papers and engineered a successful escape for his wife and child to the Aryan section of Warsaw.

During these perilous years, this man, again and again came to the rescue of his fellow captives in the ghetto: he surrendered the prized name of a driver who was to help him in his own escape to another man desperate to rejoin his wife living in hiding. He also arranged for the escape of two young women using his connections, resources and putting his own life in jeopardy. Finally, after a successful flight to Warsaw to join his family, his room became a place of refuge for any escapee who needed an emergency night's stay. That at a time when most people, in the same situation, never revealed their address to anyone for fear of being caught.

He always said: "I just did whatever I could to help someone in need."

In the Talmud, it is written: "He who saves one life, saves the world." What should be said of someone who saved dozens?

If It Weren't Impossible, I'd . . .

How I wish I could find someone to hypnotize me and send me back in time to recall the first two years of my life. How I wish I could tear out of the deep recesses of my brain images, pictures of grandparents who, so I have been told, adored me. How I wish to remember these very special people long gone.

I was their first and only grandchild, adored, fussed over, spoiled. According to my parents, they came by daily, as long as it was safe, in order to hold me, to play with me. My paternal grandfather's greatest joy, I am told, was to be given the opportunity to take me for a walk, to have him all to himself. He did not expect any other grandchildren, one of his two sons had died in his teens, his daughter could not conceive and his other son had married quite late in life. So—I was " IT "—the eagerly expected and yearned for descendant, the one to carry on the family traditions if not the name. What would I not give were it possible see him and maybe even be able to talk to him for just a few minutes.

According to all accounts, the man was a tower of goodness, patience, tolerance and devotion to his children, to his wife, to his neighbors and to his God. His son, my father as well as his daughter-in-law, my mother could not sing his praises enough: the way he behaved in business, the way he cared for his family, his generosity to all in need, his gentleness, and the way he would be able to sooth the most heated argument.

I have only one picture of him, one that had been salvaged by a cousin who had fled burning Germany and settled in the New World. He stands there with his wife and daughter, erect, head high, the picture of a grand old gentleman. He has a short, black beard, neatly trimmed, is wearing a black coat over a black suit, a black hat, and black tie and is holding a black umbrella. However, there is nothing sinister about him, maybe I am just imagining it, but his face seems to radiate the gentleness of his soul.

How I wish I could hold him, hug him, see his soft smile. How I would love to feel his hand on my head, look up into his eyes and tell him all about the wonderful grandson that would be borne after the war and who is named in his honor. I would tell him about his wonderful four great-grand children and his eight great-great grandchildren. How proud he would be of them, not only of their accomplishments but also of the wonderful people they have become. He would radiate with joy at the business sense they inherited from him, at their straight, decent character, their commitment to the traditions he cherished so.

But he was not even granted a normal death or a grave to rest in peace, a place where we could visit and find some solace. He was brutally shot while being loaded like cattle on a German army truck, shot because his rheumatism did not allow him to move fast enough to please his captors. His crimes? He was a Jew, an "old" man of 60 who was useless as a productive slave and of no use to the occupiers.

Julie Heifetz
Why Write a Patient's Life as a Short Story

As a 57-year-old Jewish woman, the daughter of a physician from the days when medicine was practiced as both an art and a calling, I am appalled by the predicament in which we, patients and healthcare professionals alike, now find ourselves.

"Time to get to know each patient?" a young resident laughed sardonically. "That would be so nice. But it's just not possible with the number of people we have to see in a day." In addition to the time constraints mandated by managed care, developments in pharmacology and technology are so impressive that talking with patients has become passe. Yet the greatest increase in scores that measure patients' satisfaction in their interactions with their physicians occurs when a physician puts down her pen, indicating she is there to listen.

Determined to do what I can to humanize the healthcare experience for patients, I teach hospital staff and skilled volunteers how to write the short stories of incoming patients.

This program relies on volunteers working alongside staff. Writing the stories requires additional skills for the volunteers, which they learn and practice in training sessions. (For the women, it has taken longer to find their voices as writers than it has to feel authentic as listeners.)

The use of stories in hospitals to help people heal seems to me not only inherently Jewish but also so female, and I came to it via my work with Holocaust survivors.

As a Jewish child I knew the power of the story. My only positive memories of religious school were those times when our teacher read Sholom Aleichem, Isaac Bashevis Singer, or other Jewish writers, though none of them were women. The stories redeemed the entire religious school experience for me, and I looked forward each year to re—reading the story of the Exodus at Passover, when we repeated out loud with family and friends who we were and where we came from.

My childhood interest in listening to stories led me to study psychology. I was trained to elicit and reframe the stories people told in order to help them heal. But it was my participation in the Oral History Project of the St. Louis Center for Holocaust Studies that led me to discover the therapeutic benefit of *writing* people's stories for them. Writing had always been my way of dealing with emotions, sorting things out, thinking deeply about a subject. Listening to survivors' stories, I had no other way of coping than to write. I wrote first-person narrative poems in the survivors' voices, and shaped their stories.

Wanting to thank the people I interviewed for participating in the oral history project, I gave the survivors copies of their taped interviews. They were less enthusiastic about the tapes than I had anticipated. They didn't like their voices, felt critical of the way they told the stories—the silences, the crying, the length of the unedited interviews. Since many went on for five or more hours, they believed that no one in their families would listen to the tapes in their entirety.

And so in addition, I gave them copies of what I had written based on the interviews: narratives in their own voices, condensed and crafted as I understood them. I was amazed by the results. The survivors loved them. Many who had not wept as they told their stories cried when they read them. They said I had captured their essence on the page, telling their story as they wished it to be told. As audience, reading their own stories, they were able to hear themselves as I had heard them and feel for themselves what I felt, tremendous sadness and rage about all that they had experienced, respect for their ability and the courage to speak about the horror. I had entered their stories in a way that demonstrated I was with them in their pain and in their resilience, and that I cared.

From that experience, some survivors were able to begin their own writing. Others felt freed from the omnipresence of their Holocaust experiences. And though I will never forget the time I spent interviewing and writing about the Holocaust, I too have moved on professionally, taking what I learned from that experience and working for 25 years with other disempowered people with stories to tell: students at risk, women who have been sexually abused, prisoners, people with cancer, geriatric patients and those suffering from traumatic brain damage, strokes and other life-altering conditions or illnesses.

The Vital Patient Story that developed from my work in the Holocaust Oral History Project reflects Jewish ethics: treat every individual with kindness, compassion and humanity.

Here's how it works: The one- or two-page stories are placed in the front of the patient's medical charts so that physicians and nurses who read them can quickly come to know their patients better. The stories create a connection between the professional and the patient, one human being to another. It doesn't take an hour of the physician's time to gather and write the story, only a moment to read it. Employing the techniques of good fiction writing, the stories are compelling and moving, told in the patients' voices. The better the interview and the quality of the writing, the more power the story has, and the more beneficial, revealing what matters most to the person who's ill. It is a way to fulfill our mission as Jews not only to save individual lives, but to help repair the world. This project honors the individual by listening to her story and writing it, using it to inform and connect others with the experience. One patient with aphasia, a language disorder that resulted from a stroke, summed up the program, saying, "You write our stories. You understand. You make everyone feel like a mensch."

As I witness the early results of the program, with patients who suffer less depression and anxiety for having their stories known, and staff more committed to the field of healing for being more deeply involved with their patients, I can feel my father smile. .

Ethel Kessler
Mother's Gift of Music

I placed the record on the turntable and wondered if the 50-cent thrift shop relic of Yiddish folk tune would remind me of mother and songs she used to sing. At the first strains of the ethnic melody sung by Molly Picon and Menashe Skulnik, Jewish theater artists of Rudy Vallee's time, I closed my eyes and felt myself drifting back to childhood.

I saw my mother bent over her mending, repairing other people's clothes. I heard her beautiful voice singing while her feet pumped the peddle of the old treadle sewing machine which sounded like a bass fiddle accompaniment. Her hands fed the cloth into the needle with swift sure strokes. Those strong hands, although filled with lines and wrinkles from years of using a hot pressing machine, were gentle whenever they touched me. When she spoke, her large, dark brown eyes looked directly at me, giving me her undivided attention. She listened.

Widowed with four children to support, she managed to provide a happy home for her family with those agile hands. Her cheerful, sparkling clean, cotton dress accented olive-colored skin and naturally curly, black shining hair. She smelled of fresh Ivory soap.

People, old and young, children, friends and customers left her presence in a happy mood after a few of her "old world" witticisms on why it was great to be alive.

"Even an old mended dress will look lovely if it's washed, starched and ironed just so," mother used to say, if I objected to one remade from an adult's. I recollect she possessed golden hands. She could make a stylish copy from just looking at a dress in a picture.

"It's raining," I would grumble.

"Rain brings good luck. The flowers and grass need a drink," she'd respond.

Or, unhappy with a pimple on my face, I'd whine, "Look at my face."

"Forget about your face, smile and let the beauty inside of you shine out. That's what the world sees," she'd console me.

Unable to make a decision, I'd fret, "What shall I do?"

"Be honest with yourself and you'll have the right answer," she'd calm me.

Exhausted from doing chores like pulling weeds or raking leaves in our large backyard, "All this work will kill me," I'd complain.

"Hard work doesn't kill, it strengthens," mother laughed as she'd reward me with milk and cookies for a job she considered well done.

I recall her stories of when she came to America. William Howard Taft had just become president. She had left Kiev, Russia, during a pogrom. Because she was a Jew, she had not been free to worship as she pleased; she had not been free to own land or business.

Mother escaped with her parents, brothers and sisters (just like Tevya in the play, *Fiddler On The Roof*). In America, the "streets paved with gold" meant to her that she could own and operate a small tailor shop; she could close her store on religious holidays and she could encourage her children in the rewards of honest effort.

Her shop nestled among other "mom and pop" stores in an older section of St. Louis on Market Street where streetcars "cling-clanged" continuously on iron rails down the middle of the cobblestone road.

Jerked back to reality by the scratching of the record announcing the end of side one, I quickly turned it on side two.

Molly Picon was singing a song about a mother. I got a lump in my throat when it reminded me of one my own mother had sung.

"*Mominu, Mominu, Mominu, Vas a Meidala Velt?*" (meaning, "Mommy, Mommy, Mommy, what does a littler girl want?").

The lilting refrain brought back the year I was 8 and mother said, "I've been having a hard time making ends meet. It's been noticed by others—like bill collectors. Your aunt and uncle, who haven't been lucky enough to have children of their own, want your older brother to go live with them. They feel they can give him a better home."

"You won't do that, will you mother? You always say we have each other so we are all blessed. You give us the best home anybody could want. We always have fun. Anyway, we'd miss Samuel too much."

"Of course, I wouldn't give up one of my children or separate him from the rest of you. Brothers and sisters belong together, no matter what. I'll think of a way to get by," mother promised as she stood up straight, five feet of fierce independence.

She solved the problem by moving from our pretty "flat" (that's what an abode covering the whole floor of a building was called in those days). She shrunk the size of the store and set up our living quarter in the back. Saving the rent money helped her manage.

I remember mother intently listening to her favorite radio program, *A Doorway to Life Is a Happy Childhood*. She digested the daily seminars that poured forth from that dome-shaped, wooden talking box as she sewed. She tailored many theories that doctors and teachers expounded upon to benefit her own family, stretching herself to the fullest to help her children grow.

"Give a child music lessons, the benefits will last all that child's life," the radio voice advised.

"I bought you a piano," mother happily informed me as I rushed in from school soon afterward.

"It's beautiful. But, how did you get the money?" I questioned, knowing well at 9 years old that money didn't grow in the backyard.

"I bartered. I'm going to make the former owner, who runs a storage and moving company, the best hand-tailored suit in the world and I will keep his clothes cleaned, pressed and repaired for the next five years. I've got the suit material so there's no cost except my labor."

My fingers wandered over the keyboard producing inharmonious noise.

"I'll find you a teacher. You'll learn to play beautiful songs and we'll all sing. You children showed such good sportsmanship in giving up your rooms that you deserved a grand reward. Maybe music will make living in back of the store easier."

True to her word, mother found a music teacher who consented to come to our section of the city. (I received piano lessons during the worst depression this country every endured.) Even though not naturally musical, I practiced diligently.

"You're making fine progress. The scales and Strauss waltzes sound better today," she told me almost every day. "Mother, I try so hard. Yet it sounds terrible."

"Keep trying. Hard work brings good results," she'd encourage me. With mother working in the small store and my playing just a partition away, we became almost constant companions. She willed her natural musicality into me because years of playing turned my noise into harmony.

"Guess what, mother. I'm going to accompany the annual songfest this year at school," (now 15 years old) I reported. "Because of excitement, I forgot to be nervous or shy. It's a big honor," I proclaimed, gasping for breath. "You were right. All the works was worth it."

That winter mother bought her first new coat and I knew the worst of the depression had ended. All during the financial low period, she had paid for my piano lessons by skimping on herself.

Chanukah that year found the family once again living in a pretty "flat." Opened gifts lay all over the room and lighted menorah candles cast a soft glow on the faces gathered around the piano. "Play 'I Have a Little Dreidel,'" mother requested. Her voice led us in the traditional Chanukah song.

As I listened to my old thrift shop record, I remembered those earlier Chanukahs. I was 8 again. Mother was lighting the Chanukah candles and chanting the blessings as we gathered around the table.

"All I can give you this holiday is a song and prayer," she had whispered then. We repeated this ceremony for eight nights with her voice leading us in melody. Could she have known what an everlasting gift the memory of that unique celebration would be?

The rasping sound announcing the end of the recording of Yiddish songs broke the spell. I smiled, feeling good. The 50-cent record had given me a priceless trip back to mother.

Linda Kram
Chicken Soup

When I think about my grandma Eva, I think about her independence, her love for her family, and her sense of humor, but mostly, I think about her chicken soup. I've always loved chicken soup and Grandma's was the best. She started with a kosher chicken and added carrots, celery, onions, and spice. The soup simmered in a big pot all day so the smell filled the entire house. She made rice in a separate pot and let it cool. Just before serving she took the chicken and vegetables out. They were served separately so we could add as much or as little as we wanted. I always added chicken, carrots, and rice. The cool rice and the hot soup mixed so they each ended up the right temperature. I usually had three or four bowls at a sitting.

Our relationship often focused on the chicken soup. One day at Ladue Junior High, I was having a particularly bad day and suddenly I began to smell chicken soup. I went to the cafeteria thinking they were making it for lunch but they weren't. I tried the home ec rooms and even the chemistry classroom thinking maybe they were using chemicals that smelled like soup but no luck. When I arrived home, I told my mother I had smelled soup at school all day. At that very moment, the phone rang. It was my grandmother. She said, "I made you soup. Have your Dad stop by and pick it up on the way home."

Years later, after I was married, I invited Grandma Eva over for dinner and decided to make chicken and matzo ball soup. I didn't know how so I bought a chicken and matzo ball soup mix. Grandma told me how much she liked it. She commented on the soft fluffy matzo balls and I confessed it was a mix. She smiled and told me she knew. "But it took me many years to learn how to make soup just right. Be patient and you'll learn," she advised me.

Eventually, my husband and I moved into our first home. We invited the family to celebrate as we dedicated our home and put up the *mezuzot*. Grandma came with a small grocery bag. "I brought you soup for your new home," she explained. I was really excited and could hardly wait for everyone to leave so I could have my soup. As soon as the last guest left, I rushed to the refrigerator and opened the bag. Inside were the soup and a carton of cottage cheese. Knowing that my grandmother would often have people stop at the store with her as they drove her places, I guessed she had stopped at the store and left the cottage cheese at my house. I decided to surprise her and return it without calling. When I got to her door, I knocked and proudly handed her the cottage cheese. "Grandma, you left your cottage cheese at my house!" She started to laugh. "Did you open it?" she asked. "No, I don't like cottage cheese," I said. Then she really started to laugh as she opened the container and showed me what was inside. It was rice for the soup. We both laughed then and I finally went home and had my chicken soup and rice.

Not long after that, my grandmother passed away. My parents, aunts, and uncles, and cousins gathered at her home a few days later to go through her things. Each one of us took things to remind us of her. When it was my turn, I took the sweater she always wore and I took Grandma's soup pot. Now when I feel worried or upset, I put on her sweater and use the pot to make my own chicken soup, from scratch not a mix, and it always turns out just right.

Cissy Lacks
White Pants

My mother is 93, a little low on energy but, admirably, still ready for an adventure, which is why my sister wasn't surprised when an opportunity to eat lunch at the Chicago Yacht Club piqued my mother's interest.

"I'm sure glad my white pants are clean," was her first reaction.

My sister didn't understand the importance of white pants, but she didn't question our mother who is always thinking about being properly attired.

"We want you to go, but it will be a long day, you know," my sister told her.

"I can always lie down if I get tired," my mother answered. "I really want to go. I've wanted to ever since I was a teenager."

My sister was not following my mother at all.

My mother grew up in Jewish immigrant north St. Louis. She had just moved to Chicago a few months earlier and couldn't have known anything about the Chicago Yacht Club. How could she have wanted to go ever since she was a teenager?

"Where would you lie down?" my sister asked her.

"On one of those wooden recliners," my mother answered, perfectly confident in her solution.

"Mom, why would they have recliners?"

My sister continued to be puzzled by my mother's side of the conversation.

"Well, I've seen them in all the movies."

"In the movies?" My sister had no idea what my mother was talking about.

"Yes, all those movies I saw when I was young. Everyone is wearing white, and the yachts have decks lined with wooden recliners. Women are always sitting on them with their feet stretched out. I'll rest in one on the upper deck, not like my mother who came over from Europe in the steerage of one of those big boats. Going on a yacht would be a fantasy come true. And as long as I can lie down when I get tired, I can do it."

At last, my sister understood.

"Mom, the Yacht Club is a restaurant."

"A restaurant?"

"It's not a ship; it's just a club, a club and a restaurant, for people who moor their boats on Lake Michigan."

My mother is nothing if not practical. Once she gets it, she gets it.

"Nothing special about a restaurant on a lake," she said. "I'll save my white pants for the 4th of July picnic at your house."

Marcia Moskowitz
Sarah and Leah

Like the matriarchs whose names they bore, my grandmothers seemed to be from another world. They were old, their English heavily accented; they wore old lady clothes, shapeless dresses and laced shoes and we always addressed them with respect and reverence. One bubbe was a part of my life for my first ten years. The other was a part of my life for my second decade. One died when I was ten, the other when I was twenty. Although they have been gone for over 45 years, their presence can still be felt in a multitude of ways.

My memories are shaped first by a child's perception of life and later by a teenager's. Over the years I tried to fill in the spaces with stories from my parents and from other relatives but ultimately these two women live in my mind's eye. Their life stories were similar but their personalities and characters were completely different. They both came to this country at the start of the 20th century. Both came from the Ukraine (they called it Russia) with their husbands and a brood of young children seeking a new life in America. They were young women in their thirties and were part of the wave of Russian immigrants that settled in New York.

Bubbe Greenberg, my maternal grandmother, never referred to by her first name of Sarah, ran the house where I lived those first seven years. We lived together in the downstairs apartment of a two-story semi-detached house on a quiet street in Brooklyn. Bubbe and Zeyde (he died when I was four) had bought the house with their hard earned money. Somehow from his meager earnings as a brick layer and carpenter Bubbe with her scrupulous attention to pennies had saved enough to purchase a house with a backyard and an apartment upstairs that was rented to tenants. With them lived my parents and I, my aunt Fanny (Bubbe's oldest daughter), her husband Harry, their son Larry five years my senior. So there we were, six adults (five after Zeyde died) and two children—three family groups sharing one kitchen, one bathroom, two bedrooms, one living room, one dining room that became the bedroom my parents and I shared. The key to understanding the dynamics of the family was that it was Bubbe's house. She ran the kitchen. She cooked all the meals, did all the marketing. In the fragmented memories of my childhood, images of her come to my mind that verify her presence in my life every day of those early years.

I remember going down into the basement with her in the morning to the coal furnace. She would shovel out the ashes, sifting through for the unburned pieces of coal that she would carefully place in a bucket to be used again for the next day's fire. I remember trotting after her as she went to the bakery so that I could get my favorite cookie. I remember baking *challah* with her. She would give me a small piece of dough to shape—she would never risk my childish hands messing up her loaves of sacred bread. I loved her raisin babka baked in a large rectangular pan. I remember her placing brown paper over the clean kitchen floor in preparation for *Shabbos*. I remember her dismay when I started to dry a "meat" plate with a "dairy" dish towel. I remember the tiny yellow eggs that she would save for me when she cooked her soup chicken for *Shabbos*. I remember all adult conversation in Yiddish and no one knowing I understood the language. Bubbe insisted that she speak only English to me because I was an American child. Her English was "broken" heavily accented, grammatically incorrect but it was the language of America and she had to make sure I spoke it.

She read the Yiddish daily paper and her prayer book every day. She was always busy. She was either cooking, cleaning, sewing, washing, reading or praying. I knew even then that her children were not as religious as she was. She too accepted this as part of the price of living in America. She never ate in a restaurant but when my parents and I moved to our own apartment when I was seven, we kept a set of glass dishes for her. She would eat her hard boiled egg on those dishes because our kitchen was not kosher. Wouldn't she be pleased that one of her great grandchildren named for her, now keeps a kosher home?

I remember going to *shul* with her, sitting in the women's section (behind the curtain) trying to figure out why she was so wrapped in prayer. I remember the blue and white Jewish National Fund box on the table that she always put pennies into when she returned from marketing. I remember her lighting *Shabbos* candles at a small table in the hall, her hands over her eyes, chanting her prayers. I remember the pickle barrel on the stairs to the basement. I remember the preparations for *Pesach* and the sensation I was always underfoot. I remember the way Bubbe could add numbers in her head. I remember how she cried on the day Israel was declared a nation and she kept saying her life was blessed that she had lived to see it.

But what are the pieces of Bubbe's life that I learned from others? She had six children but only four lived to adulthood. In that far off shtetle she lived in poverty. Her first child, a boy, was favored because someday he would say *kaddish* for her. In one of those incredible family stories my mother told, Bubbe took her two sick little girls to a physician a few towns away. She drove the horse and cart herself. The children became gravely ill and died. She arranged for their burial, oversaw it and came home with an empty wagon a day later. There was never anymore to the story as it was told. When her husband went to America to earn money to bring his family to the new world, she took care of everything at home herself.

The family that set out for America in 1911 consisted of Bubbe, her husband Abraham, their four children—Lou, Fanny, Lee (my mother) and Mollie—and Bubbe's mother. They made the journey across the Ukraine in a wagon to a port city and then in steerage across the Atlantic. At Ellis Island, her mother was turned away because of problems with her eyesight and my Bubbe never saw her mother again. Years later when news of her mother's death reached her, she took off her shoes and sat down to begin *shiva*.

Two of her children brought her grief in their marriages. Her youngest daughter Mollie ran off with an Italian Catholic man when she was sixteen. He was in his thirties, divorced and had children. Although my grandparents never sat shiva for Mollie, her husband was never allowed in the house and only in Bubbe's later years was Mollie again a welcome visitor. Bubbe's oldest daughter Fanny went to Cuba to find a Jewish husband who was looking for a way into America. My mother was the smartest of her sisters and when my grandfather would not let her attend high school (he felt that girls did not need an education) it was Bubbe who argued for her to attend a business school for a year. She made sure my mother had Hebrew lessons and some music lessons.

My parent's first child, a boy, died at the age of four months. I was born nine years later. It's no wonder I was Bubbe's favorite, the child who could do no wrong. Although she didn't laugh or try to amuse me, I always knew she loved me and favored me. I was the good girl who as her youngest grandchild would realize the dream of America.

When I think of her, I realize I am nothing like her in temperament and personality but everything like her in what I value in life. From her I learned my love for Judaism, my devotion to family, my passion for working hard, my respect for education, and no doubt my love for the English language.

Bubbe died when I was ten and I remember crying and trying to understand the ache in my heart.

Bubbe Monashkin, my paternal grandmother, didn't enter my life until I was four years old. A bitter fight had occurred in the family and she had nothing to do with my parents. When a beloved uncle called to wish her *mazel tov* because I had been born, she answered that it meant nothing to her. There was reconciliation sometime in my fifth year and we began to visit Bubbe in her small apartment at the other end of New York—an hour's ride for us from Brooklyn.

Once Bubbe Greenberg died we saw more of Bubbe Monashkin since she was the only grandparent left. She had a beautiful voice and loved to sing and would delight me with songs in Yiddish and Russian. Often she would speak in Yiddish to me, and I would answer in English. Like all the Monashkins, she was a storyteller and enchanted me with tales of sneaking out to go to the theater when she was a young girl in Russia. She had a personality that loved laughter and mischievousness. From early on I was aware of my striking resemblance to her. Even now when I see pictures of her, I see my own face looking back at me. This bubbe cooked and baked but as my mother observed about her mother-in-law "she was no *balabusta*." Her house wasn't clean and nothing was organized nor ran on time—major sins in my mother's eyes.

I loved listening to Bubbe Monashkin's tales of life in Katrinislav. When I was sixteen, I asked her how she felt leaving Russia. I said "Weren't you a bit sad?" She looked at me and said "I turned around and spit." Another time when I wore jeans, she questioned my need for pants with a zipper in the front. "You don't have anything to take out." In 1954 the image of an old world bubbe saying this to an American teenager was more than a little incongruous. I remember I couldn't stop laughing. It was from this Bubbe that I learned the stories of Russians and their attacks on the Jewish ghetto, of hiding in the house and blocking the door, of grabbing Jewish children off the street so they would not be used for target practice by sword wielding Cossacks on horseback.

Bubbe Monashkin had six children, five boys and one girl. The girl Hannah was deformed by an injury in childhood and never grew to normal height. She also was left with a bent spine that didn't allow her to stand erect. Bubbe favored, protected Hannah and Hannah manipulated the world and her mother to get what she wanted. My grandfather and his two eldest sons came first to America where they worked to earn money to bring the rest of the family here. Grandpa returned to Russia and brought his wife Leah, his daughter Hannah and the other two boys Harry and William (my father) to America.

My mother never forgave her in-laws for allowing my father to leave high school to work in the business—a family-owned candy store.

Unlike my mother's family, my father's family did not seem to value education. All the children worked in the store. No one saved any money or planned for the future. My bubbe adored her sons, thinking one more handsome than the next. And to a great degree she was right.

My father never spoke of the rift with his mother and my mother always believed that had her father-in-law been alive, it never would have occurred. The story, like one of the ghosts in the family closet, I sensed throughout my childhood. It was when bonds had sundered and hatred filled the void. I knew Hannah was involved. The story finally came from my mother's lips when I was well into adulthood, long after Bubbe died. Hannah had convinced her mother that my father had stolen money from the store and Hannah and Bubbe came to accuse my parents who were living at the time with my mother's parents. My father could barely respond to his mother's accusation, rage choked his words. He tried to argue. My mother supported him but it was Bubbe Greenberg who stepped forward, put her hands between the battling mother and son and said in Yiddish "Leah, you are mistaken. Your son is not a thief. Your son is a good man. I vouch for him."

My mother's expression showed her admiration for her mother. She said, "Can you imagine a mother-in-law defends a son against his own mother." I heard the story only once. The incident had occurred long before I was born but I can picture it as if I were there and what spilled forth from that moment helped shape who I am.

I am a grandmother now and I marvel at how I am a combination of my two grandmothers. My physical self, my love of story telling and my laughter are one bubbe but my soul is surely the other. What will I give my granddaughters for their memories? For now it is the wool outfit Bubbe Greenberg knitted for my beloved doll—a jacket, pants, hat, mittens and booties—that my granddaughters put on their American girl dolls when they come to visit.

Rabbi Steven Heneson Moskowitz
An Orphaned Kaddish

The biblical book of Kohelet opens with the words: *"Havel, havelim."* Most have translated these words as vanity of vanities. Or futility, utter futility. I prefer vapor of vapors. This seems more in keeping with the melancholy spirit of the book. Nothing endures. Nothing can be grabbed. The sun rises. The sun sets. We are born. We die. So too with the vapors. It is remarkable that a book about the fleeting character of our years would even make it into the Bible. "It is better to go to a house of mourning than to a house of feasting; for that is the end of every man . . ." (Kohelet 7:2) How did the book of faith come to hold a book that contradicts its very spirit? Nothing matters Kohelet declares. Nothing is lasting. All is vapor. But if not for this book I might not have met my friend, Marsha. But now she too is gone and her breath is but a vapor.

It was not so long ago, during the bitter month of Heshvan, on a bright but cool Sunday, I buried my friend. Marsha had been a student and friend from my years at the 92nd Street Y. At the young age of 63 she succumbed to cancer.

I have officiated at many funerals during my years as a rabbi. All are sad. Some are tragic. At times there is a large gathering of family and friends. At other times there is a small gathering. But Marsha's funeral was unlike others. At her funeral there were only a few friends. We were nine in all, one short of a minyan. There was no family save a cousin. There was no husband, no brother or sister, no son, no daughter. There was no one to tear the kriah ribbon. And no one destined to say kaddish.

The Mourner's Kaddish is called *"Kaddish Yatom*—the Orphan's Kaddish." It is called this because the obligation to recite kaddish is most pronounced for a son or daughter. On the day that a son or daughter begins mourning for a parent they become like orphans. It is the child's' mitzvah more than anyone else's to remember a parent. It is only when mourning for a parent that the kriah ribbon is worn over the heart. For other relations it is worn on the right side. This mitzvah is not a statement about feelings. It is not a statement about whether or not the children loved their parents. It is a statement about what is required of each of us when a parent dies.

For Marsha there was no one to assume the sacred obligation. It is not that she was not loved. Her friends loved her. And she had known love. In fact in the months before her death I learned that her fiancée had died in a plane crash before they were able to sanctify their commitment. Soon after his death she lost both of her parents. She never found another love. She did however love life. I was surprised to learn of her tragedies for she always struck me as vibrant and ebullient, caring and loving. (She probably would have chastised me for my melancholy regarding her death.) She never stopped living—until her last days when her breath became fleeting.

We met in a class I taught on Song of Songs and Kohelet. She imbibed the lyrical love poetry of Solomon's youth. To hear her read his words was to understand the spirit of love that had once touched her life. "Oh give me the kisses of your mouth/ For your love is more delightful than wine." (Song of Songs 1:2) The class occasionally blushed when she breathed a heaving sigh at Solomon's words. Over the years we talked about poetry. We relished the words of Yehudah Amichai and A.B Yehoshua. We found enchantment in the philosophy of Moses Maimonides and Abraham Joshua Heschel. We debated politics, she holding on to her liberal sensibilities as I grew increasingly conservative. We talked about fear. We talked about death. We talked about faith. We talked about God.

I discovered that she had an appreciation for life's finer details. She traveled the streets of New York and the avenues of Europe and Asia in search of delicacies, whether it was the best coffees, teas, spices or cheeses. She loved lobster and kobe steaks. She raised orchids in her Manhattan apartment. By the time we gathered at her apartment on the afternoon of her funeral, the orchids had withered. There was no child to tend to her passions.

I longed for the child who had not come to be. I have officiated at funerals where there were children like Isaac and Ishmael barely able to contain their venom and rage for each other, but who managed to speak the kaddish together. And I have officiated at funerals where there were family members like Ruth and Naomi who would not allow the title of "in-law" to divide them. They held each other and comforted each other so well that one would have thought they shared the mitzvah of kaddish.

On that lonely day last year, I would have chosen even an Isaac and an Ishmael. There was no one to call an orphan. Instead it was the kaddish who was orphaned. I have promised myself that I would not let her kaddish be cast aside. But I am not sure I can rescue it. It is not that I lack the strength or even the courage. It is instead that her kaddish does not really belong to me. I am not sure I can wrest it from the vapors and take ownership over it simply because I want to. Nonetheless I will say kaddish for Marsha. I will light a candle for Marsha. I will remember her. I will tell Marsha's story. She merits it.

On the yahrtzeits of her death, it will not be her memory or her life that is fleeting, but the kaddish she so deserves. It will be the kaddish that appears *"Havel, havelim*—A vapor of vapors! Thinnest of vapors!"* (Kohelet 1:2) I pray I can hold on to her orphaned kaddish.

Miriam Raskin
The Funeral

When my maternal great-grandfather died in 1936, I was five years old and already impressed for life. He was a tiny man, perhaps five foot two or three, and he lived, with a wife I remember not at all, on the third floor of the apartment building in Hamburg that also housed their daughter, my Oma Josephi.

Of course, I don't really remember him, anymore than I remember anything, anybody. But we liked each other, that I know. And a few ancient photographs with scalloped edges testify to our occasional outings to the city's lush botanical gardens during our family visits to Hamburg. The old photos show him dressed in a dark three-piece suit for his appointment with me, his face crinkling to what must have been my constant delight, as we walked through the park, inhaling the fragrant aromas of untold numbers of uncommon flora. I see him holding my hand as I balanced on the cast iron rails that surrounded the geometrically precise plantings. I imagine him listening gravely to my questions about the universe, never tiring of my childish prattle. I loved him, I suppose, although I did not know much about love.

He dressed formally as a matter of course and, as a matter of principle, wore a skullcap in the house. Rare as it was in our proudly assimilated family, he wore it as an emblem of his individuality, of his faith, and of his hopes for his family. Usually, it was plain and black but on Friday nights, when the dining table was adorned with the finest silver and the most elegant linens, a beautifully embroidered white *Kaeppelchen* covered his head when he took his place at the head of the table. I can still feel the hush settling around the table when he lifted the kiddush cup and held it high, and still marvel how from his undersized body there could emanate such a grandeur of spirit that the entire familial assemblage was drawn, almost against its will, into passionate Shabbat blessings and lusty renditions of *Ose Shalom Bim Ramov*, so that for those inspired moments this slight, unimposing little man mysteriously became a coalescing force, a model of noble character and a tower of strength. My mother fills me in on the facts.

"Do you know what he did for a living, this hero of yours?" asks my mother. "He did this and that. The most important thing he ever did in his life was nothing more impressive than delivering bread door to door for a local bakery. He was never very lucky in life."

No? But he was lucky in death. He had the good fortune to die in bed of an ordinary illness at a reasonable age, never knowing, never guessing, how unfounded his faith was to prove, lucky enough to die before the gates of hell opened to bring grisly unimaginable deaths to his children. Thank God for that, my mother would say, but I, less generous, more unforgiving, do not bring those words to my lips. He was lucky, that was all. As were we, I suppose, in not knowing when he died, and we grieved, that his interment in the Jewish graveyard of Hamburg with the customary blessings would be the last such family burial for decades to come.

I was not there to witness the somber occasion. My parents deferred to the prevailing views on child development and judged me to be too young to attend the funeral. Let's protect the child from the sadness, they thought, and left me in the care of a neighbor. Let's protect the child from the grief, they thought, and kept their own locked inside themselves. So it was that, doubly protected and doubly bereft, I missed what turned out to be the last family funeral for forty-five years, the Nazis having assumed responsibility for dispensing with the remains of all the family members who died in the intervening years as a matter of neatness and public health when they did the killings that caused the deaths.

What they told me then I don't know. What I felt then I do not know but I suspect it was grief, real grief of the sort our family deemed somehow *declassé*, for even now, when I am myself an old woman, the strains of *Ose Shalom Bim Ramov* sometimes overwhelm me with such sweet sorrow that tears flow from my eyes in the most harmonious of circumstances and I imagine I can see, through the embarrassing inexplicable tears, my great-grandfather's delicate-as-Dresden-china face at the head of that long ago Shabbat table leading us all in song. And then I am grateful for the memory, thankful to be reminded that once, long ago, before death on a cosmic scale intruded into our family history, it included this exceptional specimen, this ordinary man who was my great-grandfather.

Marylou Ruhe
The First Day of Freedom

When the war was over, I worked as an interpreter for UNNRA (United Nations Relief and Rehabilitation). I lived and worked in a Displaced Persons Camp near Hanover, Germany. The D.P. camp was a showcase for visiting dignitaries and British and American journalists. One day we had a very special visitor: Mrs. Eleanor Roosevelt, wife of the President of the United States of America.

I remember her well: tall, impressive, slightly bent forward and she had a loping gait as she walked. One could not call her pretty by any stretch of the imagination but one was impressed by her forthright manner. Goodness and strength of character were clearly visible in her face and behavior.

After the camp inspection was over, one of the journalists in Mrs. Roosevelt's entourage asked me if I would agree to an interview. Reluctantly I agreed. After some questions covering my past and present circumstances, the interviewer surprised me by asking what had been my most memorable experience of the war. This is what I told him.

As the days grew longer the sun rose earlier and had some warmth to it. We slowly thawed out and almost stopped shivering after the long, cold winter of 1944–45. April 14, 1945 was the day it happened for me and my "sister-inhabitants" of the barracks in Salzwedel Labor camp. Something was in the air; we could feel it and breathe it. We were almost too scared to believe it, but the end was near. A new beginning was dawning and we held our breath. All of us, the women prisoners, forced-laborers of the cruelest war in the world, were outside in the open roll-call area, standing and waiting. It was quiet. The bombs had ceased falling. The cannons were silent. No planes droned overhead. The world stood still.

A woman held a bouquet of flowers (where she found them I could not imagine). And then it happened. Dark green heavily armored tanks with white stars burst through the double barb-wired gates of the camp. An enormous cry rose from our throats as we welcomed our American liberators.

The friendly faces of the GIs grinned at us in wonder as we climbed all over the tanks and lorries, screaming, crying, laughing and dumbstruck at this momentous event.

Nothing in the world could equal the feeling we had at that moment. The years of oppression were over and the heavy loads of suffering, pain, fear and despair lifted from our hearts as if by magic, replaced with hope.

We could dream again and the future was ours. It was almost too much for us to comprehend . . . this awesome feeling of elation. This tremendous change in our lives happened in one single instant. "Yes," I told my interviewer, "The first day of freedom was the most memorable day in my life."

Marc Saperstein
Eulogy for Rabbi Harold I. Saperstein

How many times did he do this: stand in front of a group of mourners and their friends, and articulate in his eulogy the meaning of a person's life for us. How often I remember him urging us not to focus on the grief of loss, but rather to appreciate and celebrate the richness of a person's talents and achievements. Now it is our turn to shoulder this awesome responsibility—and we feel so inadequate to the task. Rather than my reviewing the extraordinary experiences of his life and his service to this congregation and the Jewish people, therefore, let us, through the miracles of modern technology (with a technical assistance from my sister-in-law Ellen and NPR) listen to his own voice once again, on June 27, 1980, his last sermon as Rabbi of this Temple:

(recorded voice of Rabbi Harold Saperstein:)

It was in October, 1933, that I first rose to preach from the pulpit of Temple Emanuel of Lynbrook. I was not yet twenty-three years old. I had no idea that my life and destiny would from that hour be bound up with this congregation. But life works in mysterious ways, and here I am, 47 years later.

It is reported that when the Abbé Sieyès was asked what he had done during the French Revolution, he answered, "I survived." I suppose if I were asked what I've done during these 47 years, I could say, "I survived." But I'm glad I can say so much more than that. It has been an exciting era in which to live and work. It has seen the depths of depression and periods of feverish prosperity.

It has seen me directly involved in two wars: the painful but rich experience of World War II in Europe and the proud and exhilarating experience of the Six Day War in Israel.

It has given me the opportunity of serving American ideals and the Civil Rights struggle in the South, and the agony of feeling compelled to criticize my own country regarding the ill-fated war in Vietnam.

I have seen the hell of concentration camps immediately after their liberation and the glory of Israel reborn. I have visited Jewish communities all over the world, and—most important—I have had the privilege of serving God, of ministering to this congregation, of participating in peak moments of your lives, of sharing with you my thoughts, Sabbath after Sabbath and festival after festival. Looking back I can say, "I've not only survived, I've had a wonderful time."

Yes, he was a participant in the turbulent events of our century that many of us experienced only vicariously, by listening to him. But his heart and soul were not only with the survivors of the concentration camps, and Soviet Jewry, and Israel—they were more than anything else with the members of this congregation. It is from this experience that he spoke in the Ordination sermon he gave to my class of new rabbis in 1972, from which I quote:

"To the young, groping and searching in the darkness of a world they never made; to those of mature years, so engrossed in their problems they have lost sight of their purpose; to the aged, whose eyes are dulled more by loneliness than by the years; to all of them you will have the opportunity of bringing the message that life is meaningful.

In a world thirsting for identity, you will have the exciting task of sounding the summons to your people to be Jews—strong and proud of their Jewishness, custodians of a heritage deep in its understanding of the human heart and lofty in its vision of humanity's goals.

In a time of moral confusion, you will have the privilege of drawing sustenance from the bottomless well of Torah, dealing with problems of the hour but deriving your strength from timeless sources." (full text of the sermon in Harold I. Saperstein, *Witness from the Pulpit: Topical Sermons 1933–1980* (Lanham: Lexington Books, 2000), pp. 292–98).

Here he was sharing with a new generation of rabbis what he found not just so challenging but so uplifting and fulfilling about his own rabbinate.

And what about the last period of his life? The period of decline? Rabbi Norman Lamm, the President of Yeshiva University, in a eulogy for Rav Soloveitchik, who like Dad died of complications from Alzheimers after a period of severe decline, pointed out that in Jewish law, the pattern of respect for a scholar is similar to that for a Torah scroll. He then noted that there may be a *sefer Torah she-nisraf*, a Torah scroll that remains in perfect condition and then is suddenly consumed in a conflagration—and some rabbis who die suddenly at the peak of their powers. But there is also a *sefer Torah she-balah*, in which one letter after another becomes faded and disappears, until there is nothing left. But even though that Torah scroll can no longer be used for reading in the synagogue, it must be treated with dignity, and buried with respect. That was the fate of *avi, morenu ve-rabbenu*, our own *sefer Torah,* our rabbi and teacher, as one memory after another faded, and one skill after another was lost, through the ravages of Alzheimers disease—to the point where the only source of joy he had left was being together with his beloved wife of 60 years, reaching over to hold her hand, leaning over to kiss her. Yet he continued to be treated with the utmost dignity and love and respect by everyone around him, to the very end. And we continue this honor today.

There is in our tradition, however, a very different image, which emphasizes not what is lost, but what is permanently acquired in a lifetime. One of his favorite sermons, which I included in *Witness from the Pulpit*, he called "The Days of Our Years," echoing the phrase from the Psalms. In the Zohar, the classic text of medieval Jewish mysticism, there is a wonderful image: when the soul leaves behind the earthly body, each day on which a person has performed a *mitzvah,* appears and becomes a part of a multi-colored, radiant garment in which the soul appears before its Maker.

Think back over the days of his years from 1933—how many *mitzvot,* how many acts of religious devotion, of kindness and compassion he performed. He may indeed have forgotten them, but these acts endure in some real and powerful sense. Think what a magnificent, radiant garment, composed of the days of his years, adorns his soul in our memory, and in eternity.

Milton Steinberg was a brilliant Conservative Rabbi at the Park Avenue Synagogue, whom Dad greatly admired, and who died tragically in 1950 at the age of 46 (a *sefer Torah she-nisraf*). One of Steinberg's sermons to which he frequently referred had the paradoxical title, "To Hold With Open Arms." It was about the nature of true love in our most meaningful relationships. You want to hold another, to comfort and protect, but you have to give the other space, you have to know how to let go. I remember when Dad taught me to ride a bike, running along side and holding onto the back of the seat in case I began to wobble. And then at one point he let go, and I was riding by myself. That was to hold with open arms.

In the final months and weeks of his life, we have tried to show our love by letting go as well, recognizing that he was on some level withdrawing from this world of ours, connecting (we trust) with another, more permanent one, completing a process that is the inevitable circle of life. And today as well: we hold him, in our memory, in our love, as with open arms we bid farewell.

And now, as this congregation prepares to bid a final farewell to him, let us listen for one last brief moment as he said farewell to you:

(recorded voice of Rabbi Harold Saperstein:)

> *Shalom, Shalom u-verakha.* Peace, peace and blessing to you all. The memory of your love will warm the hearts of Marcia and myself to the last breath that we shall draw. And this Temple will be our spiritual home as long as we shall live. Amen.

November 19, 2001
Temple Emanuel of Lynbrook, New York

Amy Scharf
Power in the Word

The person who taught Mary Dalton the alphabet was "a little Jewish woman." Mary, now 39, told me this tonight on the tail end of a conversation about Judaism. "She taught me my ABCs about five or six years ago."

"*I'm* a little Jewish woman," I offered, wondering how coincidental she thought it was.

She laughed, "No, I mean *little*. In her eighties." I pictured a kind, shriveled crone pointing to each word with her finger like a *yad*. Selfishly glad that whatever had stopped Mary from learning to read at the time had delivered her, through the Literacy Council, into my life now.

First in tonight's tutoring session, I had Mary read a poem I'd cut out from a direct mail piece from the Laubach Society. The poem was by a man who used to be illiterate: he wrote about telling a book that he would conquer it someday. Mary read most of it without any trouble. Understood it, even leaving out the bigger words she couldn't quite tackle. Good retention. She reads more than either of us know. I'm confident she does because she is too smart not to read when she's not feeling self-conscious. She freezes up a little bit with me, the knowledge of being watched making her stumble. But on some level, she knows she can read. She is learning to tell herself she can, slowly, unconsciously. I remind her now and then. "You're doing it," I tell her, like I'm running next to her and just let go of her bicycle seat, and she didn't realize it for a few seconds. There she goes, off on her own and she didn't even know she was doing it.

Next she spoke, long and inspirational. Sometimes we have these little sermons that keep me there, enthralled and uninterested in anything outside of our tutoring dyad. After her monologue and a little discussion, we got to the writing segment of the evening's session. Mary wrote, "Live thankful every day." Didn't want to get more philosophical than that, or heavier. She had said enough heavy things and just wanted to write down the hopeful part.

I intend now, in my writing, to lean back and let her words pour out my fingers. I want to give her voice—I mean I want to honor and expose the voice that she has. I always wish I had brought a tape-recorder, hidden it under the table as she spoke—profound and strong and insightful and half-literate—and then played it back for her. That's a little unrealistic; but she has no idea of her power.

And I don't think anyone else really does, either. So I listened, hoping that some-
day she would be heard by more than just me. It's hard to do her justice in my
retelling, but it's the best justice I know how to bring her.

"I remembers," she started in, "the night I was in the hospital having
Franklin. Lee weren't around, and they had served us a lombster dinner.
A lombster dinner!" Her dusky voice rose with excitement. "I was there,
at Jewish Hospital. And they do that for the new parents, serve a nice dinner. But Lee was gone. I was so mad, I didn't want to eat. And I was
watching t.v., and on it they said that the company I was working for was
moving. I thought, 'Now, that person standing there on that dock look
familiar. Wait a minute! I *know* that person standing there! That's where I
work!' And shore 'nough, they had got their lawyers and made their decision and they made a public pronouncement right there on the news.
And that was the end of my job. I swear, Amy, looking back, I shoulda
eaten that lombster dinner, I shoulda eaten both mine and Lee's—
because I didn't know it, but I was never gonna' be able to afford a lombster dinner after that!"

Gleeful laughter, now thirteen years later. She rocked in her chair and
shooed her hand in my direction, as though I had cracked a funny joke.
I think I smiled. Imagining her under her damp sheets in the hospital
room, alone, watching her employment fold up like a cloth napkin while
she recovered, without appetite, from giving birth.

"I shoulda knowed, Amy, right then and there. I was startin to figure
out I was gonna have to leave him. But it was years before I knew what
Lee was up to. He couldn't hold a job, could never hold a job. But I didn't
know what was really goin on until I had to go find him myself, finally.
My sister was babysittin at that time; I had got another job that was going
absolutely nowhere, I couldn't even make rent. Had to stand there and
face the Rent Man and tell him, 'I'm sorry, I can only give you half this
time.' It was so humiliatin, Amy. He said, 'Where your husband? Where he
at?' but I didn't know myself. 'I don know,' I told him. 'He ain't been here.'

"I went out to find him, went out in the street, Amy." Mary's eyes
grew. She backed up, seeing a squalid picture in her head. But still she
looked directly at me. "I visited crack houses, I saw things I never even
knew *existed*. Finally I finds him. Amy, you never seen such a place. Those
terrible ways they show people living on t.v., in crack houses," leaning
forward, "*it's all true.* There he was, lying there, all messed up. And these
people around him, they's some ladies, all whorin and strung out. I tell
you, Amy, I don't know what he brought home with him, but I lost my

appetite for him. Right there and then. We'd been used to each other, you know. But after that, I couldn't even think of it. I didn't know anything about AIDS then; but sometime I still wonder if I picked anything up . . ."

"I think you'd know by now," I said quietly. "You've had plenty of check-ups since then, right? You've been checked for it? Been to your doctor a bunch of times in—how long has it been? Eight, ten years?"

She counted in her head. "Seven, bout seven. Yes, you're right. I guess I'd know by now." Sighed, shook her head. "He didn't even see me at first. I made myself known, there in the crack house, standing there, watching Lee. Just watching him. He didn't see me, though. Not until I tapped him on the shoulder."

She acted out his leap of surprise and sideways glance. Low, brusque voice, " 'What're you doin here, Mary?!' " She giggled. I think because I giggled, because she imitated him so well. Or at least, when she told her story, I could imagine it so keenly that her imitation of him inflated him with dimension, no longer the flaccid form supine in the corner of the room in my head.

" 'Just came to see you, Lee. Just came to see you.' Those days he was into telling me I ain't seen anything. 'You don't see me,' he told me, 'You ain't seein nothing!' I just stood there and watched him. And then I left. I just wanted to go in there and let him know I knew where he was. I knew now. No more lies."

I thought of Indian tales about warriors who galloped long distances to sidle up next to their enemies and touch them, a higher and more noble insult than doing them any harm.

"I knew I had to leave him," Mary continued. "Cause when he'd come home on drugs he'd be *so mean*. One Saturday I was going off to my new job and he comes home in the morning before I left and says to me, 'I'm gonna' beat the hell outta you.' I just wanted to go to work, it was Saturday and I was getting some overtime, and I just wanted to leave. I didn't have time to fight, I had to go to work. But there he is, 'I'm gonna' beat the hell outta you, you runnin your lip like that all the time.' "

I can't repeat her words describing a scene with a cold iron and a bloody mouth and her teeth in her hand. But I can see the smile surrounding her golden laugh and take strength from her ability to persevere. I don't understand the source of my own spirituality but I know when it has been tapped.

"I went to a battered women's shelter. Me, Franklin, and Bonita." She smiled inwardly at her children. "Ooh, Bonita hated me then. Said I took her away from her daddy. She'd had her daddy around all her life at that point. She was about eight. Ooh, she was mad. Lee treated her fine. But I had to get us outta' there. I didn't have no other choice. Now, she says 'Momma, you were right to do that.' But boy, was she mad at the time. She hated me for it.

"So we stayed in the battered women's shelter a little while, and I got onto Welfare. I wasn't making hardly nothing at my job, it was a dead-end job; I couldn't even afford daycare. So I took Welfare for the first time. The case-worker said it'd make more sense than staying at this job that was going nowhere, couldn't pay my bills. I went back and took a lot of things that was mine, things I'd paid for. Stored them at my father's. I couldn't tell no-one, though; this was my thing. I felt so embarrassed. It was mine to work out, alone.

"Amy, I was so naïve when I met Lee, I had no idea what he would turn into. You never can tell, though. It wasn't women that took him, it was drugs. He was on drugs. And you get a man on drugs, you in trouble. Cause he ain't no good, then. He get all tangled up into all this bad stuff, you know, and it's a miracle if you yourself don't get on 'em too. Just to cope.

"But now I know. I read this—" she patted her red-leather Bible, "and I know I didn't get here myself. That's why I want to read. Because I'm a valuable person, and I deserve to make my own choices. I don't know what happened when I met Lee, but I was crazy, so excited. He played the flute, you know, was a musician. I have a thing for musicians, Amy. I don't know what come over me, I just went into it and forgot how important I was."

I found it hard to believe how universal her soliloquy had become. She directly addressed the pull of love and the loss of self, the shrouding over of the sense you had before the other person walked into your life and fooled you into believing he was righter than you. Addiction, drug abuse, mistaken relationships, all the blindness she summarized in her story.

"It took me years," she repeated, "to figure out what was going on with Lee. Years. *I just didn't see it.* Now I don't know how I could have missed it. But I'm done being stupid. Now I know I'm valuable, and I'm thankful for that. I don't care about no Thanksgiving; I'm thankful anyway. I live thankful every day."

I've told Mary in the past that she ought to consider becoming a preacher, and she has said, "Really? Yes, other peoples have told me that, too. I guess it's just in my commiction, you know, my passion. And I talk a lot." She has laughed then, her shoulders nearly enveloping her neck, her cheeks eclipsing her eyes. She's so cute when she laughs, and beautiful when she smiles. And her unwavering brown eyes when she tells me her beliefs are potent enough to make me believe. In something, even if only her: it isn't "only" her. It's Mary Dalton and all her power; it's Mary who has moved me to inspiration and laughter and close to tears. Regardless of me and my movement, though. She's Mary Dalton, and she's learning to read.

Yetta Schneider
A True Story

I'm going to tell you a story, a true story.

My father knew right away when he came for maneuvers Russia was going to have a war, so he left Russia and came to the United States and then the 1918 war broke out.

Then, America was closed to Europe. My father and my sister were here. My father didn't hear from us. He didn't know if we were living or dead, my mother, my four brothers and me.

I was in the 1918 war. A bunch of soldiers used to come in the house. We had to give them beds and we had to lay on the floor.

My mother had to make a living. So she used to have to take pins and needles and go in the little bitsy towns to sell. Once it was late at night. I was tired; I was only ten years old. I locked the door. She came home and she couldn't get in. So she said, "Yettela, Yettela, open up dolly, open up honey." Then she started to curse me.

The end of it was she had to go next door and to sleep over night. I didn't let her in. I was a sound sleeper. I was ten years old. Who cares who comes in?

We had a very good landlord during the war. The government wouldn't let nobody out from Russia. Then one night the landlord took the hay from his wagon and took the hay out and put my mother down, my four brothers and me and put the hay on us. He was smuggling us out. The soldiers stopped him. They said, "What have you got there?"

He said, "I got hay for the stable for my horses."

One soldier took out a spear and wanted to put it in the hay to see if it's true. But another soldier, our luck with God's help, said, "Oh, let him go."

That's the way we struggled. Then we came to the border. My mother and my three oldest brothers ran in water. It was in March. The ice was melting. They went in water up to their chests. Me and my little brother was on the Russian side until they smuggled us out. We was in a little house that was always like a synagogue. There was always chanting. But that little house was not a synagogue, it was a hiding place. We slept on a big bench. To turn over we had to get off the bench and lay down again.

Finally from Warsaw my aunt was there. She thought my father left money, which he did. She went to a man, an agent. He came to us to take us to Warsaw.

There is an organization over one hundred years old. It's still working. It's called HIAS. The HIAS took care of refugees. For seven years my father didn't know if his family was alive or dead.

This organization found out where people belonged. All the money my father sent for seven years to Russia had been confiscated. The family never got the money. This charitable organization—all over the world, no matter what religion or what nationality—found out where my father lived. They wired my father a telegram telling him that his family is alive, and if he'll send the money. Finally we had to wait eight months to get passports and get on a ship.

This organization that I'm talking about not only brought the families but it also provided jobs in the United States. There were listings of jobs in every town. My father landed in Galveston, Texas. They found out there was someone in Springfield, Missouri who needed shoemakers. So that's where my father went.

The ship we came on had second class and first class. Well, we were on the deck. From the first class they used to throw chocolate and pennies. We kids used to rush over to get it. It was really funny. You start to think of it, think back, it's really funny and so odd, it's really something.

It wasn't wonderful then, but, thank God, to think of it and see how silly we were and how inexperienced we were, it is wonderful.

We came to Ellis Island. When you get on the ship they examine you if there is no boils, no nothing. Well, we went through. We got off the ship and went to Ellis Island. They examine you again. They find a boil by my mother under the arm. I'm ten and the kids are all younger than I am. We're screaming and hollering and its terrible. They took my mother away to the hospital. I was afraid they should send me to America without any mother.

Now my mother was a smart woman. She went to the bathroom and she took hot water and squeezed out the pus. The doctor comes the next day and says, "You're OK. You can go out."

She came out. We were there about seven days. Then we're ready to go. The gates is open to go to America. I was a child; I wanted everything. So my mother saw the chewing gum, five pieces. We ate it and ate it up, all of us.

Everything I saw I wanted. I wanted bananas. So like a monkey I ate it with the peeling. I didn't have sense enough to take the peeling off.

Then they put us on a train to Springfield, Missouri. They put on tickets with our names.

Some fella, an American boy, came up to me and says, "Now, I see you don't know English. But I'm interested when you'll get to learn English. I'll give you my address. I just want to see the progress what you're going to make."

He bought me chocolates and everything on the train. He got a liking to me.

My mother kept the address in a bundle that we had when we came to America. We forgot all about it. We didn't know what the bundle is. I look for the address after I understood English and had learned English. I looked for the address and I looked I couldn't find it. To this day I'm sorry that I didn't get to correspond with that fellow.

When we saw my father and sister it felt like somebody was born all over again.

★ ★ ★

We came to Springfield, Missouri. In a big city you can get away with speaking Yiddish, but in Springfield there was no Jewish grocery store or anything. Everybody spoke English. My mother had to learn in order to go to the market. She went to night school. Her head was at home with four kids and the house and everything. She said the heck with school.

She learned a few words. She took out citizen papers. The first papers you took out when you were here five years, the second papers when you were here three more years. My mother said, "I'll tell you one thing, Judge. That's all I know who the President is."

The judge says, "That's enough. Here is the papers."

We came to Springfield in September right before school. I was green. I spoke Yiddish. There was a Jewish girl in the school. She was American. The teachers thought because she's Jewish she can speak the language. So they brought her in the class. The teacher asked her to translate. She said, "I can't understand Jewish."

The children used to teach us English. One girl picked up a handkerchief and she said, "Yetta, you see this? This is called a handkerchief." I learned fast.

We had spelling. I learned spelling by heart. I didn't know what the words mean.

In arithmetic the teacher writes 100. 1 thought she's showing me how to make 100, so I make 1000 and show her that I know how to do it.

The boys at school learned my brothers bad language, bad words and told them to go tell the teacher. And they did. The teacher was smart. She knew that there was something wrong. My sister came to America many years before us. So the teacher wrote her a letter, she should come to school. The teacher explained to her what's going on.

★ ★ ★

I got to be eighteen years old. My father was very religious. He wouldn't let me go with gentiles and he didn't let me go with girls, because if I'll go with girls, I'll go with boys. So I stayed home all the time. Well, I got sick of it. I said, "Dad, you'll either let me go, or send me to St. Louis to my sister." So he sent me here to my sister.

(Yetta Schneider, nee Lotven, Ronov, Lithuania, June 6, 1906–November 15, 1980)

Charles Schwartz
My House in Crete

I had hardly slept the night before, after coming home at three in the morning drunk on wine and Retsina. Somehow, I made it back, driving my old Peugeot with the bald tires and the weak brakes up the one-lane gravel mountain road, past the spot with the white stucco shrine where people lit the candles for those who drove off the cliff. After I parked the car and started the walk up the path to my house, an old woman appeared when I turned a corner. She was holding a candle lantern and the light on her grizzled face scared the crap out of me, even if I didn't show it at the time. She kept saying something in her local dialect that I didn't understand, except I knew she was talking about my house, because she kept pointing to it with her bony finger and saying the word *spiti* which I knew was the word for house.

I waited until I got inside and closed the door, fumbled for some matches to light a candle, before I let myself panic. I tried to sleep, but couldn't, even with all that alcohol coursing through my veins, because I kept seeing her face in my window, holding her lantern, even though I knew that wasn't possible because there was a sheer 100 foot drop from my back window down to the foot of the cliff.

I had glimpsed the old woman on the day I arrived in Kritsa. I had walked up the stony path to the uppermost house, the vacant house that I had rented from Maria, the young Greek woman I had first met while standing on line at a bank in Athens. When I walked around one of the houses on the path, I heard a noise and turned around. I saw the old woman by her window and when I looked at her, she closed the shutter. I hadn't thought about it at the time.

I had told Maria that I wanted to live in a remote village, away from other tourists, in order to learn about the real Crete. I told her I was obsessed with archaeology and that is why I dropped out of college and came to live in Greece. Maria told me about the house; it belonged to her family who had moved to Athens from Crete years before and how it had stood empty. She also said the village, named Kritsa, was a very remote and beautiful place, with about a hundred homes, and that the village was hundreds and hundreds of years old. But the clincher was the price: 720 drachmas, about twenty dollars rent per month—but I had to fix it up myself.

Maria wrote me a letter, to bring to the owner of the village café. I was to pay him the rent each month, and he was to give me what I needed to set up house: linens and blankets, some pots and pans, dishes and utensils, and cleaning supplies. So I took a ferry from Athens to Crete and drove my white '66 Peugeot 504 up the mountain switchbacks for thirty kilometers, until I came to the place I was to call my home.

I found the café, but the owner, Mr. Hatziyannis wasn't around. Another man was there, whom I took to be his son and who looked at me suspiciously. He read the letter and immediately asked for the 720 drachmas. He then tried to brush me off with some directions to the house but I wouldn't leave because I couldn't understand. After some effort on my part, he shook his head in disgust and left the café and walked me there himself.

The village houses were built into the mountainside like a giant staircase, with each house's front balcony acting as part of the roof of the house below it. To get to my house, I first had to walk up a long flight of cement and stone stairs above the main road. At the top of those stairs, the path went in opposite directions, but it met again on the other side of each house and continued uphill with more stairs and more houses and also walking paths going horizontally to the next staircase over on the hill. As I climbed the stairs, I could see onto the front balconies of each of the homes, and beyond that, to the front doors. I could see furniture on the balconies and laundry hung out on clotheslines.

We finally came to the house. It was the last one in the village, at the very top, and located to the side of the other houses. From the balcony, there was a view down the mountain past the houses below and into a barren gulley and then up to a ridge where a walking trail was barely visible. To the right was a sheer drop to the hillside. The man from the cafe felt along the top of the doorframe and took down an old key. He opened the door and it seemed as if no one had been inside the house in years. There were spider webs hanging from the ceiling and a layer of dust covered everything. I perceived a snicker as he walked to the window and opened it up. He picked up an old broom that was leaning against the wall and handed it to me. I told him that I needed cleaning supplies. He lifted his hand as if to say I shouldn't worry, smiled and left.

The house was dusty and smelled like an old suitcase, but it appeared dry and intact. On the ground floor, where the kitchen was, there was a sturdy wooden table with four chairs, a huge sink in a cement counter with a few seashells imbedded into the surface. The bumpy stucco on the walls was peeling and in places, I could see some chicken wire and stones underneath. The floor was made of thick grey wooden planks. A large metal skillet and a soup pot hung rusting from hooks on the wall. I turned on the faucet over the sink; it clunked, coughed, and then ran with at first black but then clear water.

There was a back door, which led across an uncovered breezeway for about ten feet, to another door, which was the bathroom. The bathroom was a small, dark room with a tiny window and a cement floor with a hole in it. Nearby the hole was a huge ceramic covered jar of water with an old copper ladle. In order to flush the toilet, you had to take some water and pour it down the hole. Another door from the kitchen led to a circular staircase surrounded by stucco walls with embedded wooden steps. I went up the staircase and peered out a small window on the way up. It was a view of the back of the village. I could see some other houses and below, rocky crags and outcropped boulders rising to the top of another, higher barren cliff. There were a number of white wooden bee-hives by the foot of the hill.

At the top of the stairs was the bedroom. The closed shutters made the room dark and stale. There was an old brass double bed, and, at first, I became afraid because it looked as if someone was lying there. I opened the shutters and could see the bed was empty. The only other furniture in the room was a wooden table and a chair. Another door from the bed-room led to a smaller room that went up against the pitch of the roof. This could have been a storage room or it could have been for a baby. A small window faced the side of the house.

About an hour later, the café owner's son returned with some clean-ing supplies: He brought a bucket with some rags and a bottle of soap. I spent the rest of the day cleaning. Around seven, just as I was feeling hun-gry, I heard a knock on my door. I went to answer it and there was a young woman about fifteen who introduced herself as Crysanthie and who handed me a warm plate of food. She spoke a little broken English and told me it was from her parents. I looked down from the balcony and saw a middle-aged couple waving from a balcony down and across. I waved back. I didn't invite Chrysanthie into my home because I wasn't sure if it was proper. Instead, I ate the food right there on the balcony, with her and her parents watching.

It was delicious. There were green peppers stuffed with rice and meat, some cut up roasted potatoes, and some green beans. There was a thick slice of rough wheat bread, and a glass of red wine. It was a great meal.

Within a few weeks time, I had everything I needed. I knew where to buy fresh food and staples such as olive oil, wine, tea, bread, eggs, sugar and pasta. I spent my days taking photographs and looking for out-of-way archaeological sites within hiking distance of the village. It was on one of these walks that I started to question whether I wanted to stay in Kritsa.

I had discovered an old book in a second-hand bookstore in Athens that described some of the lesser known and relatively unexplored archaeological sites in Crete. One of these sites was from the Byzantine era, and I was actually able to find it on a highly detailed geological survey map I had also bought in Athens. In order to get to the site, I had to follow a path going west out of the village and that appeared to continue on the other side of a river. I followed the path until I came to the river, and then I noticed that there were a series of large boulders that served as stepping stones all the way across. I crossed and picked up the path and, finally, found the site, which turned out to be the ruins of a beautiful house or palace with mosaic floors, intact staircases and discernable rooms. I visited this site several times, but one day, on my way home, someone had left the severed head of a dog on one of the stepping-stones in the middle of the river. In order to avoid stepping on the dog's head, I stepped into the river. Since the current was heavy, I lost my balance and fell into the freezing water. I climbed back onto the stone with the dog's head in order to get out, but first I knocked the head into the water. I felt this was some kind of warning aimed at me, since I had never seen anyone else from the village on the trail to the site. I walked back to my house and felt like leaving.

I drove down to the port, intending to get drunk. I had been feeling lonely anyway. My so-called girlfriend back at home never responded to any of my letters, and I had made only one friend in the village—a doctor from Athens, named Dimitri, who came there to fulfill some requirement to work in an underserved rural area. I didn't care that much for him, because he made fun of the people who lived in the village, and I felt he was a snob.

So there I sat, on the cement floor of the balcony, leaned up against the wall. I basked in the winter sunlight. I blew into the hot mint tea in my glass and tried to cool it off. The thick glass was perfectly warm in my hands. I let the steam spiral into my face; up my nose and into my eyes like some homeless ghost searching for a new body to inhabit. The amber tea shimmered hypnotically in the glass. I knew in my mind that I had to find out what the old woman wanted.

My Greek was better now, after hours of listening and practicing with language tapes in my cassette recorder, but, I wasn't ready to speak to her directly. In addition, I never saw her outside of her house. Whenever I walked by, her shutters were closed. Therefore, I decided to ask Dimitri to come with me and speak with her.

When she answered her door, Dimitri began talking but she looked at him as if she didn't understand anything he said. He tried speaking louder and slower but to no avail. After we excused ourselves, he told me that the woman must be over a hundred and stone deaf.

After the experience with the dog's head, I never went back to the archaeological site. Nearly every day I drove down to the town where I had made some new friends. One of them owned a small boat, which we sometimes used to explore the coastline and as a platform to swim. Usually, I would drink all night and hang around with my friends until daylight before driving home. I was afraid to run into the old woman.

A few weeks after the incident with the old woman, Maria, the young woman who rented the house to me, came to visit. She was impressed with how well I was settled in and with my progress learning Greek. She asked me how things were going. I told her the story about the dog's head. Maria said it didn't mean anything. She said she was sure it had nothing to do with me and was probably a just a feud between some other people or a prank pulled by teenagers. Then I told her about the old woman waiting for me on the path.

At first, Maria seemed surprised but then she refused to believe that the old woman tried to speak to me. She told me that in all the years she had lived there growing up, she never heard the old woman say a word to anyone. Maria said everyone in the village knew that the old woman hadn't spoken since her husband and her son died in a car accident on the road from the village. She said they died by the shrine.

A few days later, I decided to pack up and leave Kritsa. I moved to the opposite side of the island. My new village was closer to the seashore. It was a bright and happy place with friendly people. But even after I finally settled in, I still became uneasy whenever I thought about the place I left.

Maury Schwartz
My Father's Hands

My father was a master in the use of his hands. He used his hands to teach lessons, to express love, and to express his joy in living. When I was older, I asked how he learned to use his hands so expressively . He explained that he had learned this from his Rabbi in the Yeshivah in Odessa. He explained how.

In one class the students were studying the portion that deals with the renewal of the covenant between God and the Jewish people (Exodus 33:1). Moses had descended from Mount Sinai with the tablets of the Law. A student, a senior to my father and the most brilliant student in the class, asked if Moses had really spoken with God, and if God had given him the Torah. The Rabbi responded: "Either God gave the Torah to Moses at Sinai or he didn't. On the one hand (the Rabbi opened the palm of his hand and lifted it) if God gave the Torah to Moses we are all obligated and commanded to revere the Torah to follow its precepts. On the other hand (the Rabbi opened his other hand with the palm up and lifted) if God didn't give the Torah at Mount Sinai, what difference does it make?"

The Rabbi continued, using his hands to assert his views. Finally the Rabbi lifted his thumb high over his head and concluded the discussion showing how only one possible conclusion could be reached. I saw my father use his hands and thumb on numerous occasions over the years. I find myself doing the same when I am reasoning a problem.

My father's hands could also be very tender. He would stroke his children on the face and arms when they were sick. He would cover our heads with his hands and kiss us.

When he danced at family weddings, my father danced with deep feelings, his legs moving rapidly and his hands clapping, moving and rotating and his fingers moving this way and that.

I remember when my mother went into a diabetic coma, my father sat beside her and said, "Laya, my hands will make you well." He stroked her until she came out of the coma (the orange juice also helped).

When my father shook your hand, he took your hand and imprisoned it in his two hands and passionately moved them up and down. When I received my B.A. at Washington University, among several hundred other graduates, my father behaved as though I had won the Nobel Prize. He had heard me speak about the Chancellor of the university,

Arthur Holly Compton, an authentic Nobel Prize winner. After the graduation ceremony, the family gathered around me under a tree. My father left the group and returned with Dr. Compton. He brought the Chancellor to our family gathering and took Dr. Compton's hands in his and spoke to him about my great achievement. Dr. Compton was impressed, and when he was able to free his hands from my father's grasp, he proceeded to congratulate my mother, my brother, my sister and the other family members. And then he turned to me and told me how proud I should be of my father.

Today, many years after my father's death, I find myself wanting to be touched by his hands. In synagogue services, when the Torah is being read, a *yad* (a pointer) is used to read the holy words. The *yad* is a symbol reminding me of my father who used his hands to soothe, to stroke, to teach, and to comfort.

Pop, I miss your touch.

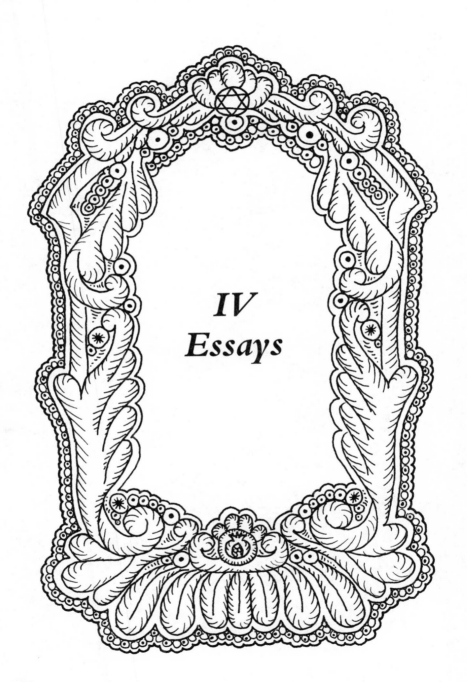

IV
Essays

Marc Bregman
Serah Bat Asher*
Biblical Origins, Ancient Aggadah
and Contemporary Folklore

If there ever was a legend that is the product of the collective Jewish imagination, it certainly must be the legend of the remarkable woman known as Serah bat Asher.

Serah in the Bible

The Hebrew Bible mentions her only three times, revealing little more than her name and family lineage. She makes her first brief appearance in one of those long and rather tedious sounding geneological lists (Genesis 46:17):

> The sons of Asher: Imnah, Ishvah, Ishvi, and
> Beriah, and their sister Serah.

From here we learn that Serah was the daughter of Asher (bat Asher in Hebrew) who was the son of the Patriarch Jacob. From the larger context of this passage we learn that Serah was one of those seventy souls who made up the household of her grandfather Jacob when they went down to Egypt to join Joseph who had risen to power there. Nahum Sarna, in his Jewish Publication Society Torah Commentary on Genesis (Philadelphia, 1989, page 315, to Genesis 46:17), makes the following perceptive comment on this verse:

> It is inconceivable that Jacob's twelve sons, who themselves had fifty-three sons in all, should have had only one daughter. In light of the general tendency to omit women from the geneologies, there must be some extraordinary reason for mentioning her in this particular one, although no hint of it is given in the text.

Significantly, Serah is mentioned again in the much more extensive geneological list based on the census of the Israelites who left Egypt at

*Reprinted from: Marc Bregman, Serah bat Asher: Biblical Origins, Ancient Aggadah and Contemporary Folklore, The Albert T. Bilgray Lecture, March, 1996, The University of Arizona, Tuscon, Arizona.

the time of the Exodus in Numbers Chapter 26 (44–47, 51, compare I
Chronicles 7:30):

> Descendants of Asher by their clans: Of Imnah, the clan of the Imnites; of
> Ishvi, the clan of the Ishvites; of Beriah, the clan of the Beriites. Of the
> descentdants of Beriah: Of Heber, the clan of the Heberites; of Malchiel, the
> clan of the Malchielites . . .

And then among all this painstaking geneological detail, the biblical text
suddenly seems to have a flash of recollection, and interjects:

> The name of Asher's daughter was Serah

And then the census roles on with mathematical precision:

> These are the clans of Asher's descendants; persons enrolled: 53,400 . . . This
> is the enrollment of the Israelites: 601,730.

Note that by this time the household of Jacob had grown from an
extended family of 70 to the Israelite nation numbering over 600,000—
and yet Serah, Jacob's granddaugher, is mentioned by name and it would
seem with some emphasis. Jacob Milgrom, in his Jewish Publication Society Torah Commentary to Numbers (Philadelphia, 1990, p. 226 to Numbers 26:46), notes that Serah is one of the only females in the geneological lists and adds suggestively: ". . . her presence remains a mystery."

Serah of the Sages

The mystery of this unique female figure increases exponentially
when she captured the imagination of the Rabbis of the talmudic period.
For they seem to have reasoned that if Serah was mentioned by name in
the census list of those who made the Exodus, she must have still been
alive at that time. And thus, according to the sages, this same woman who
came down from Canaan to Egypt in the time of Joseph was still alive and
well several hundred years later when Moses led the Israelites out of
Egyptian enslavement on their way through the desert to the Promised
Land. This seemingly insignificant interpretive innovation takes on great
importance whem we note that after Joseph dies at the close of the book
of Genesis, the book of Exodus (1:8) opens with the following rather
ominous note:

. . . And Joseph died, and all his brothers and all
that generation . . . And there arose a new king over
Egypt who knew not Joseph . . .

Thus the Rabbinic Serah seems to provide a link between the death
of Joseph and the birth of the next great Israelite leader, Moses. Indeed one
Rabbinic text (Pesiqta de Rav Kahana, Be-shalah, ed. Mandelbaum, p. 189)
specifically puts the following allusive statement in the mouth of Serah:

ani hishlamti minyanan shel yisrael, ani hishlamti ne'eman le-ne'eman

Which might be expansively translated:

I completed the number of seventy Children of Israel who accompanied
Jacob to Egypt (see further below). I linked one faithful leader of Israel,
Joseph (who is called "*ne'eman* faithful" in Genesis 39:4), with the next faith-
ful leader of Israel, Moses (who is called "*ne'eman* faithful" in Numbers 12:7).

Once it was determined that Serah "spanned the generations"
between Joseph and Moses, and having granted her such remarkable
longevity, it is perhaps only natural that the Sages included this
extraordinary woman among those few immortals who "never tasted the
taste of death" and "entered Paradise alive" (Yalqut Shimoni II, remez
367, Derekh Eretz 1:18). No wonder that this female figure from the
beginning of Israelite history—about whom so little is said in the Bible,
but who remained alive throughout subsequent generations—provided
an irresistible stimulus for those who crafted Jewish legend throughout
the ages.

Unfortunately what has come down to us about the legend of Serah
in the classical texts of Talmud and Midrash is painfully fragmentary. All
that seems to survive are snippets of traditions in which Serah seems to
suddenly appear, and then disappear, only to reappear at critical moments
in Jewish history. One of my personal dreams is to try to reweave these
separate strands into what must have once been a contiguous and richly
woven tapestry of legend about Serah—one flowing narrative telling her
epic story from the days of Jacob until the final redemption. Let me show
you the some of the threads I have so far managed to gather. The following discussion has no pretense of being an "exhaustive" recitation of the
many Serah legends.

Jacob's Blessing of Immortality

One of the earliest episodes in Serah's life explains how it was that she was granted immortality. Ironically, this legend is found, in its fullest form, in one of our latest midrashic sources (compare Targum Pseudo-Jonathan to Genesis 46:17). Sefer Ha-Yashar (Va-Yigash) which was apparently written in Italy in the 16th century, tells the following story:

> Jacob's sons, who had sold their brother Joseph into slavery and told their father he was dead, later discovered Joseph was second only to Pharaoh in Egypt. And the brothers now had to somehow tell Jacob that Joseph his son and their brother was still alive. Afraid of breaking this news to their elderly father too suddenly, they decided to employ Asher's daughter, Serah, since she knew how to play the harp in a soothing manner. At their instigation, she sat near Jacob—according to one parallel (Midrash Ha-Gadol to Gen. 45:26) while he was deep in daily prayer—and sang repeatedly: "Joseph my uncle is alive and rules over the land of Egypt." Not only was Jacob understandably delighted with this lyric revelation. But, "the spirit of God came upon him and he knew that all she said was true." And so Jacob blessed Serah . . . and said to her: "My child, may death never rule over you for you brought my spirit back to life."

Notice how this rabbinic retelling differs daringly from the biblical narrative (Genesis 45:25–28) while creatively reworking biblical materials. For in the biblical text it is simply Jacob's sons who tell him: "Joseph is still alive and he rules over the land of Egypt." However, the biblical narrative goes on to relate that Jacob's "heart fainted and he believed them not", until he saw the wagons which Joseph had sent to carry him back to Egypt. Only then "the spirit of Jacob their father revived."

Serah Receives and Reveals the Secret of Redemption

Serah received via Jacob and her father Asher yet another redemptive secret. According to another legend (Pirqe de-Rabbi Eliezer 48, Exodus Rabbah 5:13), there was a secret password that would be known by one who was to redeem Israel from Egyptian enslavement. This verbal sign was given to Abraham, apparently at the time of the Covenant of the Pieces in Genesis Chapter 15, which predicts this enslavement and its eventual end. Abraham handed this secret of redemption on to Isaac and Isaac to Jacob. Jacob passed it on to Joseph and Joseph shared it with his brothers at the time of his death in Egypt (Genesis 50:24–25).

"And Joseph said to his brothers, I die, but God will surely visit you *(ve-elo-him peqod yifqod etkhem)* and bring you up out of this land to the land of which he swore to Avraham, to Isaac and to Jacob. And Joseph made the children of Israel take an oath, saying, God will surely visit you *(peqod yifqod elohim etkhem)* and you shall carry up my bones from here.

The legend goes on that Asher handed on this secret password *(peqod yifqod elohim etkhem)* "God will surely redeem you," not to any of his sons but to his daughter Serah. And wisely too, for as we have learned it was Serah who survived into the generation of Moses. When Moses came to the Elders of Israel and performed miracles before them to prove that he had been sent by God to lead Israel out of Egyptian enslavement, the people immediately believed—according to the biblical narrative (Exodus 4: 2931a). But according to the rabbinic legend, the Elders first went and consulted with Serah. She told them: These miracles are worthless! But when they then told her: Moses has also brought what he says is the word of God, "*(peqod peqadeti etkhem)* surely I have redeemed you" (compare Exod. 3:16, 4:31b) immediately Serah said: This is the man who will redeem Israel from Egypt for this is the secret password that I learned from my father.

The Whereabouts of Joseph's Bones (Exod. 13:19)

Perhaps the most famous Serah legend is about how she helps Moses discover where Joseph's bones lay hidden in Egypt. The rich variety of traditions about the whereabouts of Joseph's bones are based on Exodus (13:17–20), which relates how the Israelites actually left Egypt, after Pharaoh relented from his previous refusal.

Now when Pharaoh let the people go, God did not lead them by way of the land of the Philistines, although it was nearer; for God said, "The people may have a change of heart when they see war, and return to Egypt. So God led the people roundabout, by way of the wilderness at the Sea of Reeds. Now the Israelites went up armed out of the land of Egypt. And Moses took with him the bones of Joseph, who had exacted an oath of the Children of Israel, saying, "God will be sure to take notice of you: then shall you carry up my bones from here with you." They set out from Succoth and encamped at Etham, at the edge of the wilderness.

Sensitive readers of the biblical text perceived what seems to be a disturbance in the smooth flow of the biblical narrative. The statement "Moses took with him the bones of Joseph . . ." seems to have been inserted, almost as an afterthought, into a more general description of how the entire people of Israel left Egypt, and particularly by what route. To further complicate matters, the continuation of this curious verse suggests that Joseph had made the oath concerning his bones incumbent, not upon any single Israelite leader, but upon all the Children of Israel. Modern biblical scholarship is quick to point out that the this somewhat elliptical passage in Exodus simply serves to recall and resolve the fuller story related at the end of the book of Genesis (50:22–26, partly quoted above). We have already noted the break in the continuity of generations suggested by the beginning of the book of Exodus (1:6–8). This discontinuity explains why most Israelites living in Egypt at the time of the Exodus did not know about Joseph's oath to take up his bones with them when they left. Clearly only someone possessed with a very special kind of wisdom, such as Moses, could know to fullfill such a long forgotten command. But the question remained: How did Moses know where to find Joseph's earthly remains which had been buried by the Egyptian embalmers? The Sages answered this question by again summoning Serah to aid Moses, as exemplified in a snippet of what seems to have been an early rabbinic sermon preserved in Mekhilta de-Rabbi Yishmael (Be-Shalah, ed. Lauterbach, Vol. I, pp. 176–177):

> And Moses took the bones of Joseph with him (Exod. 13:19). This proclaims the wisdom and the piety of Moses. For all Israel were busy with the booty while Moses busied himself with the duty of looking after the bones of Joseph. Of him Scripture says: The wise in heart takes on duties (Prov. 10:8). But how did Moses know where Joseph was buried? It is told that Serah, the daughter of Asher, survived from that generation and she showed Moses the grave of Joseph. She said to him: The Egyptians put him into a metal coffin which they sunk in the Nile.

The Wise Woman in Avel of Bet–Ma'akhah (2 Sam. 20:16)

Serah makes another appearance in the time of King David. Here again, thanks only to the rabbinic retelling of another biblical narrative. In Second Samuel chapter 20, Yoav, David's captain, has pursued the rebel Israelite, Sheva ben Bikri, to the fortified town of Avel Bet Ha-Ma'akhah. Just as Yoav is about to breach the wall and destroy the town, according to the biblical narrative (verse 16 ff), a "wise woman" (ishah hakhamah) suddenly cries out from the city and convinces Yoav to let the town hand over the rebel rather than be completely destroyed. Significantly the "wise woman" identifies herself by saying (verse 19): *anokhi shlumey emuney yisrael*. In the biblical context this is usually translated: "I am from among the peaceable and faithful of Israel." As pointed out by Isaak Heinenann in his influential book Darkhey Ha-Aggadah, the rabbinic sages tend to identify unnamed characters in the Bible with named ones. Heinemann called this tendency *ha-berihah min ha-anonymiyut* "flight from anonimity." In this case, the sages identify the "wise woman" who saved the city of Avel with none other than Serah. And this led to a reinterpretation of her statement, *anokhi shlumey emuney yisrael*, which was now understood to mean: "I completed the faithful of Israel", alluding to her role in completing the number of seventy "faithful" souls who accompanied Jacob to Egypt (see above)(Genesis Rabbah 94:9, Midrash Samuel 32). In this way, by means of midrashic method, Serah became the archetypal (or more properly, the "oicotypal") "Wise Old Woman" of Jewish legend.

In the Study House of Rabbi Yohanan

The Sages not only wrote Serah into the days of Moses and David, but they even gave her an honored role in at least one episode from their own times. According to one midrashic text (Pesiqta de-Rav Kahana, Beshalah, ed. Mandelbaum, p. 188):

> Rabbi Yohanan was once sitting and expounding about how the waters became like a wall for Israel [at the time they miraculously passed through the Sea which had split open before them to permit their exodus from Egypt [see Exodus 14:29 —*ve-ha-mayim lahem homach mi-minam u-mi-smolam* "and the waters were a wall for them on their right and on their left"]. Rabbi Yohanan explained [in the Aramaic dialect of Roman Palestine] that the waters looked "like a lattice" *ke-ileyn qanqilayya*. However, just at that moment, Serah bat Asher looked in *adiqat serah bat asher ve-amrah* and said: I was there and they (the waters) were not like that but rather like lighted windows *ke-ileyn emfumata*.

Now at first glance this may seem like a rather minor point of biblical interpretation. But what is remarkable here is that we have a woman— who is not even to be invited into the all-male preserve of study house or synagogue—contradicting the teaching of one of the most famous Talmudic sages. Note that Serah is able to correct the rabbinic teaching not by bringing an alternative interpretive tradition from the Oral Torah, but on the basis of her own personal experience and eyewitness account of the biblical event being expounded. It seems we have here a relatively rare rabbinic acknowlegement that women, who are generally excluded from being the bearers of the "learned" tradition, may possess "experiential" knowlege that may be superior.

Serah in Paradise

In medieval Jewish mysticism, Serah is granted an honored place in Paradise. According to the Zohar (III, 167b):

> Serah bat Asher presides over one of the palaces reserved for righteous women. Here, three times a day, a voice rings out announcing the visit of Joseph, the righteous one. Joyfully, Serah retires behind a curtain to gaze upon the light of his face and show him honor. And here, each day, she proclaims: "O happy day, that I brought the good tidings to my grandfather Jacob that you were still alive." Then Serah returns to her women companions to teach them Torah and to join with them in praise and thanks to the Master of the Universe.

Several of the traditions we have seen so far share a common theme. Serah possesses and transmits special wisdom. Perhaps the rabbis, by granting such a role to one woman who "spanned the generations" and lives on in Paradise, are in some way admitting that women in general may bear secret knowlege. And this feminine wisdom deserves to find expression—even if it has to be shouted into the Study House from outside or even it is Torah learning to be shared primarily with other righteous women in heaven!

Serah in Later Jewish Folklore

In Jewish imagination, Serah the granddaughter of Jacob survived not only into the days of Moses, David and Rabbi Yohanan. According to one very interesting line of tradition, she followed her people from the Land of Israel into the Babylonian Exile and continued her legendary existence there. Despite the Talmudic tradition that Serah was granted immortality, the Persian Jews of the city of Isfahan believed that Serah bat Asher actually lived among them, until she died in a great synagogue fire in the 12th century CE. This synagogue and its successors were subsequently known as the Synagogue of Serah Bat Asher. In the Jewish cemetary of Isfahan, there was to be found, at least until the end of the 19th century, a gravestone marking the final resting place of "Serah the daughter of Asher the son of our Patriarch Jacob" who died in the the year equivalent to 1133 CE. The gravesite of Serah bat Asher marked by a small mausoleum known as heder Serah Serah's Room" remained for centuries one of the most well known pilgrimage sites for the Jews of Persia.

It is perhaps fitting that Serah not only continues to live on, but even managed to return to the the Holy Land in the folktales of contemporary Jewish storytellers living in the modern state of Israel. I think it best to conclude this modest investigation of the legend of Serah with paraphase translations of two previously unpublished examples.

Let the storytellers take over again from here!

Israel Folktale Archives (IFA) number 11999 recorded by Moshe Sarshalom in 1978 as told by the Darshan ("Preacher") Mulah Shmuel Shammai from Yazd, Persia:

> Once there was in Isfahan a boy name named Hayyim who lost his sight. When the physicians gave up hope of curing him, Hayyim was told by his neighbors to go and prostrate himself at the gravestone of Serah bat Asher and there to lift up his hands in supplication to the Heavenly Healer.

Here the storyteller explains as follows:

> In the Iranian Exile the Jews are accustomed to prostrate themselves at the gravestone of Serah, as the custom here in Israel is to prostrate oneself at the tomb of our Matriarch Rachel in Bet Lehem. Like the tomb of Rachel, so too the tomb of Serah is located in a "room" (i.e. mausoleum). This room has wonderous doorposts. It is well-known that only people who are of good character and deeds may enter; but anyone else—the entrance to the room shrinks before him and prevents him from entering.

> Young Hayyim prayed and fasted so that he would be found worthy to enter the room and in the evening he went to the room of Serah in Isfahan and the doorposts of the entrance open wide before him. He entered and spread out his hands before the Heavenly Healer. He cried with a broken heart and offered his petition: O Heavenly Healer, return to me by the merit of this righteous woman the light of my eyes. But if you say: I have promulgated an irrevocable decision and I cannot repeal it, then be it known to you that my soul longs for Torah. Give me, then, my father and my king, the light of

Torah. Give me wisdom to understand Your teaching. When Hayyim had finished his prayer, he fell asleep. At midnight, while dreaming, there appeared to him a woman, whose face was like the face of an angel of God. She said to him: I am Serah bat Asher. I have joined in your prayer. Behold I bring you good tidings that God has had mercy on you and has granted your second petition. Hayyim was happy that his prayer had been answered and awoke from his dream much encouraged.

As time went on, Hayyim learned Torah. He knew it and the Siddur and the Mahzor by heart. As Hayyim grew, his dream was fulfilled. He immersed himself in the depths of Torah. He became a much sought after Hazan ("Cantor"), a well-known preacher and a famous Mulah. Behold, he is none other than the Mulah, Hayyim Rushan ("the Blind" in Iranian) from Isfahan. May his merit protect us!

IFA 9524 (Story 28) recorded by Tamar Agmon as told by the Hakham Eliahu Mudgukshvili (from the village of Kolashi in Gerusinia, at the time 40 years old living in Ashkelon):

Once there was a king who made laws against the Jews so that people would laugh at them. He made them wear funny hats and strange clothes and odd shoes, one red and one black. So the Jews were embarrased to go out of their homes.

One day the king was hunting in the forest with his soldiers. He saw a doe and chased after it but was unable to catch her. Suddenly the doe stopped, turned, looked straight at the king and charging at him, jumped right on his head. But still the king couldn't catch her. And he was very embarrased in front of his soldiers. So the king chased after the doe until he had left his soldiers far behind. The doe entered a cave and the king followed. This cave had a door and the door closed behind the king and he was caught there in the dark. Several days passed while the king was caught in the dark. Then the king suddenly saw emerging out of the dark a beautiful maiden, a woman warrior with her female soldiers. She called the king to come to her. She asked the king: Do you recognize me. He said: No. She said: I am the doe that you were chasing who jumped on your head and you were unable to catch. I want to know—Why have you made laws against the Jews?

The king then asked her: Who are you? She answered: I am Serah bat Asher. Joseph was my uncle and my other uncles went down to Egypt and found him alive. When they came back home they told me to play my harp and to sing that Joseph is still alive and rules over the whole of the land of Egypt. The Holy Spirit possessed Jacob our father and he blessed me with immortality. Angels took me to Gan Eden (Paradise).

The king promised her that he would revoke the laws against the Jews and she released him from the dark cave. The king kept his word and gave the Jews beautiful clothes so they could celebrate all their holidays. The king told the Jews what had happened to him and asked them if there was in their books someone called Serah bat Asher. They answered: Yes, sure, (*ken, betah*—colloquial idiom) she was blessed by our father Jacob with immortality.

Now this king had a certain priest whom he called and told to remove his cermonial hat and robe. He said to him: You are no longer my priest for what you tell me is lies. The name of the God of the Jews is truth. Then the king ordered all the shopkeepers to sell to the Jews for less than they had been charging. And then the king built a big synagogue where he had entered the cave so that the Jews could pray on all their holidays as a memorial to Serah bat Asher.

And here the storyteller comments, again in rather colloquial style:

And even today there is a place like this still standing—I donno know exactly—it's written in the Torah that there's a place like this.

In the wonderful world of the Jewish imagination, everything—even the synagogue memorializing Serah bat Asher—is somehow "written in the Torah." What could be a more apt actualization of the statement in Mishnah Avot (5:22): "Search through the Torah and search through it again—for everything is in it."

As we have seen, Serah bat Asher, who "spanned the generations" from biblical times until today, can still be glimpsed between the lines of Torah. The separate strands of tradition about this immortal lady of legend still beckon to be retold and reunited.

Bibliographical Postscript

The legends of Serah bat Asher were surveyed briefly in entries in The Jewish Encyclopedia (New York, 1905) s.v. Serah, Ispahan, and in Otzar Yisrael, s.v. Serah. Surprisingly, there is no separate entry on Serah in the Encylopaedia Judaica (Jerusalem, 1971); only her tomb is mentioned in the entries on Isfahan and Persia. Serah is mentioned, but—to my mind at least—gets rather short shrift, in Louis Ginzberg's usually more complete Legends of the Jews (Philadelphia, 1938); see Vol. 7 (Index), pp. 424. For the etymology of the name Serah, see The Interpreter's Dictionary of the Bible (New York Nashville, 1962), s.v. Serah and Entzyqlopedia Miqra'it [Encyclopedia Biblica] (Jerusalem, 1982), s.v. *Serah*.

My teacher, Professor Joseph Heinemann z"l, of The Hebrew University in Jerusalem, was I believe the first to bring together and discuss in a more extensive way many of the traditions about Serah; see Aggadot ve-Toledotehen [Aggadah and its Development] (Jerusalem, 1974), pp. 56–63. More recently, Leila Leah Bronner has devoted a chapter to Serah in her book, From Eve to Esther: Rabbinic Reconstructions of Biblical Women (Louisville, 1994), pp. 42–60. Regrettably, after noting the paucity of previous studies of Serah (p. 42), she acknowledges Heinemann only for having described Serah's role in the episodes about Joseph's bones (p. 58, note 18). James Kugel, In Potiphar's House (San Francisco, 1990), Chapter 5 deals with those aspects of the Serah legend that relate to Joseph. Howard Schwartz has briefly retold "The Chronicle of Serah Bat Asher" in Gabriel's Palace: Jewish Mystical Tales (New York-Oxford, 1993), pp. 47–50, with sources and commentary on pp. 279–280; a revised version is due to appear in his Reimagining the Bible: The Story-Telling of the Rabbis (Oxford, 1997). See also the presentation of Serah for children in Sandy E. Sasso's But God Remembered: Stories of Women from Creation to the Promised Land (Woodstock, 1995).

Professor Eric Rabkin, of the University of Michigan, kindly participated in a stimulating dialogue on some of the Serah traditions cited above which we hope to edit for publication in the not too distant future. And finally, I wish to thank Professor Lou Silberman, of the University of Arizona, for calling my attention to Serah's appearance in Thomas Mann's Joseph and His Brothers—Part IV Joseph the Provider (New York, 1944), pp. 323–344.

My dream of trying to reweave the separate strands of Serah traditions into a larger whole has so far yeilded one experiemental episode, "The Whereabouts of Joseph's Bones." A public reading of this inventive retelling of one of the most famous Serah legends provided the basis for a presentation in honor of Rabbi Bilgray on March 27, 1996.* My thanks

---

*Subsequently published in abridged form: Marc Bregman, "Serach: The Recovery of Joseph's Bones", Living Texts—A Journal of Contemporary Midrash 4 (Winter 1998), pp. 12–17.

to the members of the congregation at Temple Emanu-El of Tucson for their helpful and encouraging comments. This chapter is part of what I hope will become a complete "scholarly novel," imaginatively retelling the entire epic of Serah bat Asher. The complete work, Serah bat Asher: Lady of Legend, will include a thorough introduction to the evolution of the Serah legend and extensive thematic commentary discussing the traditional sources for each of about thirteen episodes. A description of the project with a copy of the experimental retelling of the Joseph's Bones episode is available from the author on request: *mbregman@uncg.edu*.

Walter Ehrlich
Coming to St. Louis

In the fall of 1907, a thirty-two-year-old traveling salesman for a Russian textile firm found himself in a remote and dreary Siberian railroad station. For four months he had trudged from town to town, eking out his meager living. Now the days were growing shorter, and he approached the ticket agent in that desolate station, seeking to get back to Kiev to join his wife and two small children in time for the High Holy Days. But the agent put him off, insinuating that he was an anarchist plotting to wreck the train. Having been instructed to report any questionable persons to the colonel commanding the local military garrison, the ticket agent did just that. Imagine the salesman's astonishment when that Russian officer turned out to be a close college friend whom he had not seen since the two had graduated from the University of Kiev. One had entered the business world and was selling textiles; the other had risen to the rank of colonel in the Russian army. Some strange fate now brought them together again, ten years after their graduation, in the colonel's dank office near that small Siberian train station.

"If you were a stranger, Gus," the colonel said, addressing his old friend by his long-familiar first name, "I would have to deny you passage on the train, maybe even imprison you—just because you are a Jew. But we're old friends, Gus, and I want to help you—so long as no one else knows about it. But when you get to Kiev, don't stop there. Get out of Russia. Bad times are ahead for you Jews."

The colonel not only saw that his longtime friend Gus got a train ticket to Kiev but also gave him one of his uniforms to wear, along with necessary credentials and papers. Surely no one would challenge a high-ranking Russian officer on a train! And so across Siberia, into Russia, and on to Kiev, a strangely silent and sober Russian "colonel" wearing an ill-fitting uniform made his perilous way home—thanks to the fateful coincidence finding an old college friend in a position of authority in a drab and isolated Siberian train station.

When he reached Kiev, Gus found that his family was safe only through another miracle. Marauding bands of antisemites had viciously attacked Jews living there. A Gentile friend—who later lost his own life at the hands of terrorist Russian police—had spirited Gus's wife and two small children out of the city away from roving plunderers, hiding them in a hay wagon and then secreting them in the relative safety of a nearby farm. (Years later, they recalled their utterly paralyzing fear, huddled in that load of hay, with drunken and ravaging saber-wielding Cossacks only inches away.)

Those experiences convinced Gus and his wife, Anna, that they must leave everything behind and emigrate to America. As with so many others, the husband went first and the others followed. Anna had an uncle who lived in St. Louis, "somewhere in America"—Dr. Moses I. DeVorkin, a well-reputed physician prominent within the city's Jewish population. And so it was, then, that in 1908 Gus arrived in St. Louis, and with Dr. DeVorkin's help he found employment as a lowly stock clerk. When he died almost fifty years later, Professor Gustave K. Klausner of St. Louis University's School of Commerce and Finance was hailed as one of the city's most beloved and respected teachers and humanitarians. Driven from his native land by Russian barbarism, he became one of many who contributed significantly not only to the St. Louis Jewish community but also to the larger non-Jewish community—thanks to that chance meeting with an old college chum in an isolated and barren Siberian way-station.[1]

Among the Jews who fled eastern Europe in the early 1900s and settled in St. Louis was one large family group from the *shtetl* of Glukhow, not far from Kiev in the Ukraine. In contrast with most other Jews in that area, Naphtali and Zelda were relatively well-to-do, thanks to successful business associations with several graf-owned hardware and lumber enterprises.[2] But that did not shield them from anti-Jewish persecution. At the same time, they kept reading about the St. Louis World's Fair and the many innovations showcased there. And so, like many other Jews, Naphtali and Zelda abandoned what they had in Russia and emigrated with their children to America—in this case, as much to seek better opportunities as to escape from antisemitic oppression. The youngest child, only three at the time, unfortunately came down with an untimely case of the measles while they were crossing the ocean. Fearing that immigration officials would refuse the child entry, Zelda disguised her ailing youngster as part of her baggage. She bundled him up in a large tablecloth, inter-mingled with items of clothing and bedding, the ends pulled together and tied as a large knapsack, all the time trying to keep the uncomfortable tot quiet so as not to disclose the ruse. Miraculously, it worked, and the family made it through safely. On to St. Louis they went, to join Glukhow *landsleit* who had settled there earlier.

And so it was, then, that Naphtali and Zelda DeWoskin came to St. Louis. Baby Nolan DeWoskin got over his measles all right, but ninety years later, long after he had become a naturalized citizen and had voted countless times, he still was not certain whether he had ever entered the United States legally! Nevertheless, possessing a golden voice and trained in traditional cantorial chanting, he served diligently for many years as the *chazzan* for Brith Sholom Knesseth Israel Congregation. Older brother Philip DeWoskin, who as a child had been barred from attending art school in Russia, became one of the city's preeminent and innovative photographers, recognized nationally for his pioneering work. Much of his artistry was exhibited periodically by the Missouri Historical Society in its stately Jefferson Memorial museum in Forest Park. Like so many others, the DeWoskins and their progeny, unwanted in oppressive Czarist Russia, found a haven in St. Louis and contributed positively to many phases of the city's growth and development.[3]

Leon Koilich was born in Kishinev, in Bessarabia, Russia, on the seventh day of Chanukah in 1892. The name "Koilich" had only recently become the family name; his father Abraham Saltzman had acquired it to avoid being conscripted into the Russian armed forces. Russia's Jews, especially those who were observant, were well aware that once in the military, they would no longer be able to observe the traditions of their ancestral faith, notably *kashrut* and other prayer and holiday ritual observances. So the family bribed a Russian official and purchased the passport of one Itzik Koilich, a young man who had been rejected for military service because of his debilitated health. Thus Abraham Saltzman became Itzik Koilich. He had six children, three boys and three girls. One son apprenticed as a tinner, another as a bookbinder. The youngest, Leon, displayed such a strong propensity for learning that his upbringing concentrated on encouraging him to become a scholar and perhaps even a rabbi. At the tender age of eight, for instance, school authorities awarded him a new pair of shoes for his academic excellence in *cheder*.

Leon was only ten years old when the bloody Kishinev pogrom erupted during Passover of 1903. Years later he recalled in his autobiography that for several days antisemitic newspapers had been publishing scurrilous calumnies against Jews, demanding action against the "Christ killers" and "drinkers of Christian children's blood." Then, one evening,

> . . . while sitting at the *Pesach* table we heard terrible cries and yelling and looked out the windows. We saw a terrible scene of men, women and children running in panic, and the air was filled with feathers of pillows, and the mob of murderers chasing them, and we realized the pogrom had started.

The mob of chooligans [*sic*], under the protection of the police, went from house to house with axes, hammers, knives, and sticks and killed, maimed, and raped in the Jewish homes. . . . They also broke into synagogues and destroyed everything. They took out the holy scrolls, threw them on the floor, danced on them, and committed ugly acts on them to shame the holy scrolls. Some of the Jewish attendants who stood up and protested against their action were killed in cold blood. After three days and nights of killings, the Jewish leaders raised a large sum of money and bribed the chief of police, who thought that there was enough damage done to Jews to make an attempt to stop the mob from more bloody action. Over 100 innocent men, women and children were slaughtered during the three days of the pogrom. Many hundreds were maimed, and much of the poor's possessions destroyed and taken away by the mob.

Ongoing depredations and pogroms convinced four of Leon's older siblings to emigrate to America, but he, his parents, and one sister remained in Kishinev. As with so many other Jewish families, some went to America and some stayed behind, either permanently or to join them later. Leon continued with his studies in several yeshivas, quite certain that he could never acquire such a proper Judaic education in America. But incessant Russian antisemitism and repeated appeals from the relatives in America finally persuaded the four who had remained behind that they, too, should emigrate to America.

Once the necessary arrangements were made, it still took almost three anxiety-filled months to get from Kishinev just to the Austrian border. Travel by rail was inevitably in lowest-class dark and dirty trains, sometimes even in filthy cattle cars. At Dubno, they were removed from the train and languished in the local police station for four days, not knowing why they were detained or what their fate might be. Local Jewish leaders finally came to their rescue by bribing police officials. A similar experience occurred near the Austrian border at Pochaev, their status made ever more frightening and precarious because the police temporarily confiscated their passports. Suddenly word spread of an imminent pogrom. The terrifying news stampeded Pochaev's Jews into frantic flight; the Koilich family was fortunate enough to join up with a driver and wagon and thus escape from the town. Once the situation settled down, they finally reached the border, where it still took two attempts to get through. The first resulted in another arrest and imprisonment for several days in a squalid and filthy stable, after which they were sent back to Pochaev. A few days later they tried again, hiding in a wagon train of farmers traveling at night to get their produce to market in an Austrian town across the border. Of course, they had to bribe the farmers. This time they succeeded, but not without several anxious and terrifying moments when guards searched the wagons and almost discovered the concealed passengers.

Once out of Russia, they proceeded by wagon and by rail across the continent to the Belgian seaport of Antwerp. There they had to be on constant alert for sharpies, swindlers, and thieves incessantly looking for easy pickings among the throngs of weary and unsuspecting itinerants, until they finally boarded ship for America. After twelve days of a miserably crowded steerage crossing, at last they reached their destination. Filthy and steamy conditions in the bowels of the ship were compounded by the lack of kosher food; all they ate was stale bread and bits of potatoes washed down with foul-smelling water. Then, to top off what already had been a most trying and arduous experience, they landed not in New York as they had anticipated, but in Toronto. That change, made by the ticket agent in Antwerp, may have been most fortuitous, for Leon's mother had become quite ill and probably would not have been admitted by Ellis Island medical examiners, whereas they all made it through in Toronto. With assistance from Hebrew Immigrant Aid Society people in Canada, they finally completed the rest of their journey and joined anxiously waiting relatives in St. Louis.

One bright spot amid all their travails, Leon later noted, was that the move gave the family the opportunity to discard the name Koilich, which they had never liked, despite how it had contributed to their very being. However, instead of reassuming the father's original name—Saltzman— they came to America under the name of Leon's American brother-in-law, Lander.

And so it was, then, that Leon Lander settled in St. Louis. Like Gustav Klausner and the DeWoskins, Lander became another prominent member of the St. Louis Jewish community, an ardent and active Zionist, and perhaps most important, superintendent of the very important Associated Hebrew Schools. And like them, what he did as a St. Louis Jew made a significant contribution to the growth and development of the overall St. Louis community.[4]

These three incredibly dramatic adventures were replicated over and over by most of the eastern European Jews who eventually settled in St. Louis in the early 1900s. In fact, they vividly illustrate the general "push" factors which impelled large numbers to leave what had been hearth and home for perhaps generations and to risk a new life in a strange and distant land.[5]

At the root of these "push" forces were many outright anti-Jewish government policies that prevailed in eastern Europe in the late 1800s and early 1900s. At first aimed at "Russianizing" and "amalgamating" Jews into the general population, czarist policies increasingly identified them as "alien" people responsible for virtually all of Russia's increasing degeneration. Most abhorrent were the bloody riots and pogroms in which thousands of innocent Jewish men, women, and children were mercilessly murdered or maimed. Such depredations were by no means new to eastern Europe, but they were intensified in the late 1800s, beginning with the infamous May Laws of 1882. Histories of this period tend to single out the bloody massacres in Kishinev and Kiev, but several hundred more communities were subjected to these unconscionable atrocities, often more than once. Sometimes government officials actually ordered the violence; often during "spontaneous demonstrations" they simply turned the other way as drunken and rapacious gangs brutalized Jewish residents. Fear and apprehension spread throughout the Jewish population, as age-old accusations of "blood libel" and "ritual murder" spread widely and wildly, abetted by an antisemitic press and a Russian Orthodox Church that repeatedly denounced Jews as "bloodsuckers" and "a criminal race," the source of virtually every malaise in Russian society. Fearful Jews never when or where the next bloodletting might occur. For those living under such a cloud, unquestionably it was a frightful environment from which they sought to escape.

St. Louisan Israel Cohen described his experiences during one of those pogroms in Odessa in the winter of 1905:

> . . . I lost there my father and my little sister. I saw them butchered before my eyes, by fiends in human form. I tried to save them, but was knocked down senseless and left for dead in our own home. When I became conscious again I found myself in a pool of blood, with their dead bodies lying about, their hands and feet chopped off. Slowly I began to look around, fearing there might be another attack, and began to search for my mother. I found her crouching in a cellar, half dead with fright, and well-nigh famished. I managed to find some food and water, and we remained in hiding for two more days, until the murderers had become drunk with blood and vodka and it was safe to go out. . . .[6]

An anonymous St. Louis Jew gave this description of a pogrom in Siedlecz, a small town not far from Warsaw:

> Soldiers hacked Jews to pieces with their knives or swords. A nose or an ear would be cut off, then fingers and toes, to be followed by the feet and hands of victims. Finally the arms and legs would be cut away. . . . This form of torture was varied at times to the opening of arteries, leaving the victims to bleed to death while the brutal soldiers stood about and jeered at their sufferings. . . . Women became especial victims of the fiends. After being brutally assaulted by soldiers often in the streets, in many instances their clothes were torn off and lighted candles passed across their bare bodies, inflicting agonizing burns. . . . Jew baiters set fire to a house in which eight luckless Jews had taken refuge, intending to shoot down their victims as they rushed from the burning structure. The Jews chose to be burned alive in the house rather than entrust themselves to the merciless soldiers. This form of murdering Jews was several times resorted to, and at least forty Jews were burned alive in their homes by their own choice in preference to rushing outside to face worse torture . . .[7]

Still another St. Louisan, Dr. Morris D. Marcus, recorded his mother's vivid recollections:

> . . . Yes, *Moishe liebe,* it was terrible, those Cossacks. They rode into our *shtetl* with long spears in their hands, and they ran them through men, women, and children, made no difference, and I remember one Cossack spearing a baby in its mother's arms and riding with the little on twisting up in the air. Such cruelty, may they linger in hell.[8]

Physical violence, however, was only one manifestation of eastern European antisemitism. Although pogroms were widespread, many communities mercifully were spared that particular form of depredation. But they did experience other forms of social and economic repression that made life for Jews both miserable and precarious—especially considering the ever-present fear of the dreaded pogrom. For example, Jews could reside in only limited areas. Travel was restricted. Jewish quotas in universities were stringently established and enforced. (Ironically, as historian Howard Morley Sachar has noted, thousands of young Jewish men and women were forced to go to western European universities for their education, only to return later with strongly nurtured Zionist and revolutionary philosophies.) Many Jewish doctors and lawyers were expelled from their professions. Large numbers of Jewish artisans (such as cooks or watchmakers) were deprived of the right to practice their crafts. The Yiddish theater was outlawed. Use of the famous Moscow Synagogue was forbidden; in fact, Jews were expelled on separate occasions and in a variety of ways from such large urban centers as Moscow, St. Petersburg, and Kharkov. It did not help Jews that the Russian Orthodox Church, which exercised such a strong influence over the Russian people, both preached and practiced virulent and pernicious antisemitism. These represented official repressions. Equally insidious were deep-seated prejudices and hatreds ever present in ordinary day-to-day relations between Jews and non-Jews. By any standards, the "zhyd" was a second-class member of Russian society, viewed as a hated and alien race. Jews were being driven inexorably toward pauperism, and making a decent living or providing for even basic family needs became increasingly difficult for many whose very existence was cruelly dominated by abject poverty and societal discrimination. As their lives became unrelentingly more miserable, then, more and more Jews—even if they were fortunate enough to escape the horrors of a pogrom—longed for an environment in which better social and economic opportunities existed.[9]

Another "push" factor, especially for young Jewish males, was the direful prospect of military conscription. Jewish boys could be drafted as young as at age twelve. They then had to spend at least six years of "preliminary" training, followed by twenty-five years of regular service. Considering life and conditions within the Russian armed forces, being conscripted was at best a life sentence at hard labor; if war came, conscripts inevitably became expendable cannon fodder. For Jews, too, it was perfectly clear that being in the Russian armed forces meant an end to traditional religious observance. In fact, drafting Jews into the army, where their religious activities could be rigidly and ruthlessly controlled, was a deliberate czarist policy to convert Jews to Christianity. No wonder, then, that so many Jewish men emigrated to America to escape military service. (It should be noted, by the way, that many of those same men, as well as their offspring, later served bravely and loyally in the American armed forces.)[10]

In addition to the specter of a life wasted by military conscription, an increasing number of Jews fell into the category of political enemies of the state. Enlightenment ideologies of the French Revolution had spread throughout western Europe during the early decades of the nineteenth century, but only in areas conquered by Napoleonic armies. That, of course, did not include Russia, where centuries-old czarist despotism not only prevailed, but actually increased in autocratic tendencies. By the middle of the nineteenth century, however, western democratic doctrines began to penetrate appreciably into eastern Europe, in various forms of Hegelian and Marxist radicalism as solutions to the many socioeconomic problems increasingly facing Russia's masses. The disastrous Russo-Japanese War of 1904–1905 fueled the dissonance enough to trigger unprecedented revolutionary outbreaks. Jewish intellectuals, victims anyway of government antisemitism, saw a viable salvation in the broadening revolutionary movements, and many became associated with a variety of socialist dissidents. Many of those intellectuals had acquired their revolutionary ideas in western European universities after being excluded from the Russian educational system. The uprisings of 1905 resulted in some temporary reforms, but reaction soon set in. Jews became subject to potential arrest and exile not only for their religion but also for their status as revolutionaries. Many Jewish intellectuals saw escape to America as more than desirable; it became, indeed, a necessity for survival.[11]

Just as many eastern European Jews experienced comparable "push" forces which impelled them to leave their longtime Old World homes, so did they share another common hardship: the actual move to America. There was nothing simple or mundane about that undertaking. In his classic study of the immigrant experience, historian Oscar Handlin vividly detailed its several distinct phases.[12]

The first was making the painful and often irreversible decision to leave. Many thought about it and talked about it at length, but inevitably a time for decision finally arrived. Few of their descendants who later grew up in St. Louis—regardless of neighborhood or environment, regardless of economic or social status—have had to make as traumatic a decision. Moving to another locality to go to school or for an occupational change, or even to go to war, cannot compare with tearing up deep-seated familial roots and leaving behind the sources of lifelong nourishment. Even those who fled pogroms did more than just escape to physical safety, as urgent as that was. They also undertook a long and dangerous journey, not just to a haven from violent persecution, but to a distant place, with little or no real knowledge of the perils that lay ahead to reach that destination or of what they would find if and when they finally got there. Sure, there were letters from relatives and friends, but how much could letters really convey? And how accurately? Equally influential were the many legends of a "Goldeneh Medinah," a land of riches and freedom. What could be a more persuasive "pull" factor? And what could be more uncertain?

Once the determination was made to leave, the next step was to implement that decision. Sometimes obtaining exit papers, visas, and passports and making travel arrangements proved surprisingly uncomplicated. Some received money and tickets from friends and family members already in St. Louis. American and European immigrant aid societies provided considerable financial and travel assistance. Nevertheless, just getting the necessary papers quite frequently entailed greasing bureaucratic palms and bribing officials—even before leaving their homes. It was a life-saving device often repeated later in crossing borders en route to embarkation points.[13]

Decisions about what to take proved to be especially heart-wrenching. Most belongings, of course, had to be left behind, as baggage was limited to just what they could carry with them. What should they do with priceless legacies that had been handed down from generation to generation, with cherished possessions from dowries, with treasured *tchatschkas* that so much in their daily lives?

Most noteworthy is what so many finally did bring. They brought pillows and featherbeds. They brought soup kettles and mixing bowls to make bread. In a word, like millions of other immigrants from all over Europe, they brought the bare necessities to establish new homes in America. But they brought more. They brought their *siddurim* and their *chumashim*—their prayer books and their Bibles. They brought *talaisim* and their *t'fillin*—their prayer shawls and their phylacteries. They brought their Torah scrolls and their volumes of the Talmud. And they brought their bent and beat-up Sabbath candlesticks—still used today by their descendants, and residing prominently and adoringly in breakfronts and on mantels in St. Louis Jewish homes.

This strong emphasis on their religiosity was a significant characteristic of turn-of-the-century Russian immigrants. In contrast, many of the German Jews who came earlier to the United States had sought to distance themselves from their Old World religious practices, as attested by the large numbers who either led secular lives or who turned to the less traditional new Reform Judaism. Even those who retained their Orthodoxy such as early United Hebrew and B'nai El Congregations—modified their religious practices to acculturate comfortably to their American environment. But eastern European Jews conscientiously and steadfastly brought their ancient religion with them, resolved to practice its tenets virtually unchanged in their new environment. This comes as no surprise for who had always been observant in their traditional

Orthodoxy. But often overlooked is that large numbers of Russian Jews, like many of their German coreligionists in central Europe, were only minimally observant and except for basic life-cycle events—a *bris* or a *bar mitzvah* or a wedding or a burial—they otherwise led very secular lives. Nevertheless, when any occasion called for some sort of religious observance, it was done according to the eastern European Orthodox Judaism in which they had been raised. Only after they came to St. Louis were they exposed to the liberalism of Reform or Conservative Judaism, which indeed many did turn to later, especially their children. But the first generation of eastern European Jewish immigrants adhered overwhelmingly to Orthodoxy, whether they were totally committed or just minimally observant. As the eastern, European/Orthodox population increased in St. Louis, its cultural and religious inclinations became a major factor in the overall configuration of St. Louis Jewry. Up to the turn of the century the city's Jewish community was predominantly German/Reform; in the 1900s the inexorable growth of the eastern European/Orthodox element resulted in a concomitant increase in its influence and power. It would bring about a major transformation within the St. Louis Jewish community.[14]

Though most immigrants made only one trip across Europe and the Atlantic to get from their Old World homes to St. Louis, some experienced rather circuitous travels. Max Weiss, later a prosperous sewing machine manufacturer in St. Louis, recalled that the Weiss family of Foczany and Galatz, in Rumania, sought refuge first in Turkey, where a group of Viennese Jews led by Theodor Herzl hoped to establish a Zionist farming community. The family managed to reach Vienna, but there Herzl informed them that he had run out of money helping so many aspirants for the project. So the Weiss family had to return to Rumania, except for the eldest son, who went alone to America and eventually to St. Louis. In the next few years the rest of the family followed, first mother Rebecca Weiss with some of the children, and then father Aaron Weiss with the remainder. (This piecemeal immigration was not at all unusual because of the prohibitive cost for all to go together.)[15]

Morris Atlas, another immigrant who finally settled in St. Louis, described how his family first went from Odessa to South America, part of a group sponsored by the Baron de Hirsch Fund aimed at establishing a Jewish haven in Argentina. Though he was only eight years old at the time, Atlas later recalled how hardships brought on by heat, drought and locust plagues drove his family after three years to return to Odessa. There the youthful Atlas joined a Jewish defense group to protect against anti-semitic Black Hundred gangs. Charged with concealing weapons, Atlas was exiled for three years to Cholmi-Gori in northern Siberia. When he returned to Odessa in 1914, war with Austria-Hungary and German was imminent, and he faced conscription into the Russian army. Rather than that, he joined members of his family still in Odessa in their trek to America.[16]

Perhaps the most precarious phase of the journey to America was crossing Europe and getting to the port of embarkation. Many cities serve. as ports—in Italy, in Belgium, in France, and in Germany. Some even crossed over to England and sailed from there. Hamburg in Germany and Antwerp in Belgium seem to have been the most popular for those whose eventual destination was St. Louis; perhaps that was because steamship companies that operated liners from those two ports advertised extensively in the St. Louis press, offering package deals for those seeking to help friends and relatives come over. But those bargains meant very little unless the travelers reached the embarkation points. The long journey across Europe was fraught with all sorts of hazards, some even life-threatening, but more often dangers were instigated by conniving and unscrupulous thieves and swindlers.[17]

Several St. Louis Jewish immigrants recalled some of those experience. One, of course, is Leon Lander, whose adventures already have been described. Harry Jacob Warshavsky hid in a load of hay to cross the Russian border, an experience replicated by many others. Israel Cohen encountered border officials on both sides of the Russo-Rumanian border, where it was necessary, as he later described it, to "buy our deliverance with gold."[18] Many emigrants found that scraping together enough money for steamship tickets left them unable to pay for passports, and they turned to "agents" who promised to sneak them across the border for a lesser cost. Morris Atlas described one such experience:

I had enough money to buy a third class ship's ticket, money for the agent, and twenty-five dollars that you were required to show at Ellis Island before entering the country. I came to a little town near the German border where I met seven others who were also on their way to the United States. It was a cold rainy night when the agent told us to get ready. In our group were three women, one with a child in her arms, the other two carried heavy bundles on their backs. I was carrying my "karazinka" [wicker trunk] on my back, as were the other three men. We were told to be very quiet. We marched on for about a mile, when we heard a whistle. The agent asked us to stop. He said, "We are in trouble. I had hoped that the guard would be hiding from the rain, but he isn't. However, don't worry, I can take care of him. I want each of you to give me seven more rubles so I can make the guard look the other way." The women began to cry and said they didn't have that much money. "All right," he said, "if you don't have seven, give me five." We settled the deal, and went on, finally reaching the other side.[19]

Fortunately, these harrowing experiences had some salutary counterparts. Jewish communities in many inland transportation centers established emigrant aid societies and *hachnosos orchim* (travelers' shelters) which provided invaluable services for those en route to seaports, services which included lodging, kosher meals, sorely needed medical assistance, and help in resolving all sorts of travel problems. When unscrupulous bureaucrats imperiled itinerants, local Jewish groups came to their rescue, often with money to bribe corrupt officials. Quite a few St. Louis Jews later recalled being recipients of these *g'milot chasodim* (deeds of loving kindness).[20]

Reaching the port of embarkation did not end the emigrants' perils. Living conditions in those seaports were described invariably as crowded and unsafe, filthy and unsanitary. Arrangements previously made—and even prepaid—frequently went awry, and correcting them inevitably led to unexpected and often lengthy room and board changes. Sometimes that necessitated revising sailing plans, forcing many to linger in ports of embarkation much longer than anticipated, straining already meager finances. Again local Jewish *hachnosos orchim* provided invaluable assistance. Nevertheless, unsophisticated emigrants from backward eastern European surroundings found themselves constantly at the mercy of ever-present swindlers, con men, and thieves. Women had to be on special alert against merciless white slavers, ruthlessly seeking to ensnare victims into their wretched lairs.

Ultimately, though, the long-awaited time came when they finally boarded ship for the sea voyage to America. Very few could afford decent accommodations; emigrants typically traveled in third-class steerage, all they could afford.[21] Reminiscences of those steerage crossings can be summarized in a few vivid words: miserable, squalid, filthy, deplorable, wretched, and unbearable. One St. Louisan wrote about his crossing as follows:

Our point of embarkation was the city of Antwerp, Belgium. We waited five days before we could board ship. The day of departure finally arrived and the anxiety among the third class passengers was so great that none of us could eat. . . . The night was stormy [when we departed] and the ship began to rock in the high winds. . . . We were taken below deck where out bunks were located. There was no ventilation, and the odor of luggage and engine oil was so oppressive that one could hardly breathe . . . I selected a top bunk because if your bunk mates became seasick, at least you were out of the way of their vomit. We had barely settled down when all of us began to be sick. The remedy for the awful nausea would have been fresh air, but we had been given strict orders to remain below because a storm was gathering. The man in the bunk below me was so ill that he begged to be thrown overboard. The storm lasted four days and nights and the very mention of food was enough to make our stomachs turn. . . . On the fifth day the storm subsided and I managed to climb on deck. I spent the next four days on deck because the sailing had become very pleasant. Besides, I could not abide the awful stench and filth in the steerage.[22]

Another St. Louis Jewish immigrant's description was equally graphic:

. . . The stink was terrible. People were sleeping in bunks three and four high. Some vomited from the top onto others. It was crowded and filthy, . . . people packed like chickens in a coop. They were in a great big room–it looked like hundreds of people packed in there. The bunks were so close that there was just enough room to pass through. Way at the end of the room there were about half a dozen long wooden tables where people eat or sit and talk. Whenever they could, though, they would go up on deck, where they could get a little fresh air. But down below it was filthy and smelly, and you could hardly breathe. Many people were sick, especially the little ones. I don't know how they managed to survive.[23]

But survive they did—or most of them. Food was atrocious; staples consisted of salted herring, stale brown bread, and putrid water. Privacy was virtually nonexistent. Churlish ships' crews considered young women fair game. Rats proliferated in the dirt and filth. Disease was rampant. One prominent immigration historian estimated a "normal" mortality rate of about 10 percent. Little wonder, then, that the sight of the Statue of Liberty generated pent-up elation and excitement among the miserable and we travelers.[24]

Nevertheless, yet another traumatic hurdle awaited them—Ellis Island. Immigrants carried with them all sorts of horror stories about tortuous encounters which they still had to endure in that mysterious and foreboding processing center—rigid medical examinations, especially those involving the eyes; children being lost or kidnapped; and all sorts of bureaucratic red tape. Those misfortunes meant that some had to undergo the heartbreak of being returned to Europe. Most, however, went through a hectic few hours or days and finally received their official approval to enter the United States.[25]

Some St. Louis Jewish immigrants later recalled unique experiences at Ellis Island. The more humorous usually involved name changes. The classic story is how a Russian Jew ended up with the untypical name of Shawn Ferguson. Advised to Anglicize his Hebrew name Yoel Reuven ben Avraham to Joel Abramson, he repeatedly practiced that new name during the entire crossing. But when he approached the appropriate clerk at Ellis Island, he became so flustered that all he could say was the Yiddish: *"Oy, Ich hab es shoin fargessen."* ("Oh, I have already forgotten it.") To which the clerk responded, "Shoin Fargessen-that would be Shawn Ferguson." And so Russian Jew Yoel Reuven ben Avraham entered the United States not as Joel Abramson, but with the delightfully Scottish name of Shawn Ferguson. Many a St. Louis Jewish family can point to comparable name modifications when their forebears came to this country.

A very poignant experience involved Leah Feldman and Ida Schneiderman, teenagers who befriended each other on board ship coming over. While going through Ellis Island, Ida frantically found herself short of the money needed for processing, and envisioned being sent back to the hovel she had left in Russia. Meanwhile, Leah and a younger brother who accompanied her had been cleared. As they were leaving the building, Leah stealthily slipped her own funds through a barred window to her despondent friend. Before long a jubilant Ida emerged through the exit gate, met Leah and her brother outside, and gratefully returned the money. After tearful and youthful farewells, the girls went their own prearranged ways. Some sixty years later, Leah Feldman Trattner and Ida Schneiderman Goldberg ran into each other one Friday evening at United Hebrew Temple. Neither had any inkling that the other had lived in St. Louis all those years since one teenager's concern had made it possible for a fellow immigrant to make it through Ellis Island. Needless to say, tears of joy flowed freely and profusely at the Oneg Shabbat that evening.[26]

Once through the processing center, eastern European Jewish immigrants moved to all parts of the country. Most, as we know, gravitated toward the urban Northeast. Why did many thousands end up in St. Louis? One obvious reason was that it was a large and important commercial center, offering a variety of economic opportunities—the very thing so many immigrants sought in the first place. By the turn of the century, St. Louis had become the fourth-largest city in the United States, ranking behind only New York, Chicago, and Philadelphia. Its population approximated six hundred thousand, including about forty thousand Jews, mostly German in origin. When the great wave of eastern European Jews thronged into already crowded eastern metropolitan areas, two important relocation organizations—the Hebrew Immigrant Aid Society (HIAS) and the Industrial Removal Office—identified St. Louis, with its sizable and well-organized Jewish community, as a desirable place to send many of those new arrivals.[27] Well-established German Reform elements at first reacted quite negatively toward bringing in this totally different type of Jewish population. Eventually, though, basic Judaic concepts of *tzedakah* (charity) and *g'milot chasadim* (deeds of loving kindness) overcame those trepidations, and German Jewry in St. Louis and elsewhere contributed generously toward assisting their eastern European coreligionists. There is little doubt that many eastern European Jews would never have made it to St. Louis had it not been for the aid rendered them by German Jewry. Thus, when Ben Weiss arrived at Ellis Island with no particular destination in mind, relocation people in New York sent him to St. Louis. (Other members of the Weiss family later settled in St. Louis because Ben was already there.) During the early 1900s, Montefiore Bienenstock and S. H. Frohlichstein headed Jewish philanthropic groups that regularly met immigrants at Union Station and took them in tow. Indeed, as long as Jewish immigrants came into St. Louis, regardless of their origins and backgrounds, the Jewish community consistently helped them with such necessities as housing, employment, education, and medical aid. Of course, as with so many other immigrants, many settled elsewhere first, and later moved to St. Louis, usually for business reasons, but also to join friends or family there.[28]

As eastern European immigrants settled in St. Louis, they in turn became magnets who attracted others. Many later acknowledged unequivocally that they came specifically to St. Louis to join *"k'rovim und landsleit"* (relatives and former townspeople) already there. While this had been a factor earlier with some German Jews, it applied more widely to eastern European Jews, who generally were less urbane than their German counterparts and therefore more in need of things familiar. In fact, various *landsleit* organizations became distinctive institutions within the new immigrant populace. The Yampoler Society, for instance, numbered more than a hundred former residents of the small Ukrainian town of

Yampol. Groups such as the Bilhorodka Society, the Kurnitze Society, and the Wishnivitz Aid Society provided essential orientation and social outlets for their members. They also augmented Federation agencies in helping newcomers find housing, employment, education, and other basics of life. Often, too, they acted as small loan companies from which those in distress might borrow needed funds at little or no interest. In addition, several congregations grew out of *landsleit* associations. Brith Sholom Congregation, for instance, originated as the "Hungarische Shul." It was followed soon by "Ahavas Achim Anshei Romania," "Anshei Wolhynia" (Vohlyn province in the Ukraine), and "Bnai Yeshurun Anshei Galizian" (Galicia). Just as the Jewish community per se became an identifiable part of the larger St. Louis community, so one could discern within the Jewish community distinct elements based upon their geographic origins in eastern Europe—the Galizianer, the Yampoler, the Litvaks, and others.[29]

Even getting from Ellis Island to St. Louis proved to be quite an adventure. Many immigrants, of course, spoke no English, and HIAS people literally placed them on trains with directions pinned on their outer garments, relying on cooperative railroad conductors to shepherd bewildered itinerants through to St. Louis. Occasionally pranksters took liberties with "greenhorn" travelers, though mostly in fun. Normally the immigrants traveled by coach, "shlepping" baggage and food with them; several later recalled their awe at the luxurious dining cars and restrooms on American trains. One impetuous young man—fortunately traveling alone—concocted a roundabout way that he thought would be cheaper and faster to reach St. Louis. First he went by freighter to Norfolk, Virginia. There he took a train to Cincinnati and another to St. Louis. (Of course, it would have been faster and cheaper to go by train directly from New York to St. Louis, which he found out the hard way.) Arriving at Union Station with just one dollar in his pocket, he gave his sister's address to a policeman, who placed him on a streetcar and asked the conductor to drop off his passenger at a particular stop. There a friendly stranger directed him to an address only one block away, at Twentieth and Biddle where the wandering immigrant was joyfully and tearfully reunited with his sister, whom he had not seen for fourteen years.[30]

Poignant stories like these played out innumerable times during the early decades of the 1900s, as eastern European immigrants came to t United States and specifically to St. Louis in unprecedented numbers. World War I, of course, slowed that migration considerably, simply because of all sorts of wartime constrictions, but it picked up again after the war. This was especially true for Jews in Russia, where the communist revolution brought them no respite from their tortuous existence under the czars. Red and White forces contested furiously to control Russia, a situation made more dismal as local warlords maneuvered blood-thirstily for their own aggrandizement. Jews were frequently caught in the middle, often blamed for the widespread malaise, and a new wave of pogroms and virulent suppression drove many more to seek asylum in America. Just how many ended up in St. Louis cannot be determined accurately from census statistics. One thing, though, is certain: probably by 1914, but certainly by 1921, eastern European Jews outnumbered German Jews St. Louis. This was, of course, a dramatic—and traumatic—demographic change. Inevitably it would be reflected in the power structure within the Jewish community.[31]

The great influx of Jewish immigrants into St. Louis came to an end in the mid-1920s. This is not the appropriate place to detail American immigration policy. Suffice it to say that many forces had stimulated immigration from the very beginning of American history: the availability of huge expanses of land; the need for labor; the expansion of commerce and industry; democratic idealism; and other "pull" factors. At the same time, though, self-aggrandizing and nativist elements—predominantly white, Anglo-Saxon, and Protestant—had long objected to "different" and "objectionable" people "diluting" American society with their "strange" and "foreign" ways. Many European prejudices and hatreds, including antisemitism, were transplanted to America. The huge increase of southern and eastern European immigrants in the late 1800s and early 1900s only intensified anti-foreign animus. At the same time, racist theories that certain people were genetically more "fit" than others attracted many adherents, in both Europe and the United States. Writings of social scientists Madison Grant, Herbert Baxter Adams, John W. Burgess, and other academics tended to legitimize bigotry for many Americans. This ferment was compounded when certain political and racist and nativist elements equated criticism of capitalism's defects with subversion of Americanism. Those who saw even the slightest good in socialism or communism or any other form of collectivism or anarchism were arbitrarily and maliciously labeled as un-American. World War I and its aftermath crystallized all these forces into a strong anti-foreign movement. The result was a series of legislative restrictions on immigration, the centerpiece of which was the National Origins Act of 1924, which set severe quotas on the numbers who might immigrate into the United

States, especially from those countries in eastern Europe from which so many Jews were seeking to escape. What had been an open door to immigrants from all over, regardless of their religious or national backgrounds, now became but a tiny crack through which only a few could enter.[32]

The inevitable question, of course, is this: while that door was open, where did the eastern European immigrants who settled in St. Louis come from? Clearly, they came from many places, and they came as both individuals and as small family groups. Some, in fact, had settled first in other American communities—Belleville, Peoria, and Pekin, Illinois; Frankfort, Kentucky; Mobile, Alabama—and then moved to St. Louis. Most, though, left their European homes behind with St. Louis as their chosen destination. To most it was a place about which they knew absolutely nothing; it was simply "St. Louis, America." Some came from large cities such as Kiev, Odessa, and Kishinev, and found big city urban life not too unfamiliar. Most, though, came from small towns and villages with populations ranging from a few hundred to a few thousand. These were located usually in the rural countryside along railroad lines or crossroads, where the communities served as small local commercial centers. Jews in those places normally lived in segregated *shtetl* areas and associated very little with non-Jews, usually only for business purposes. Included among those communities were places such as Bilorodka, Stuchin, Kalyitz, Lenkovitz, Mogilev, Yampol, Proskurov, Wishovitz, Kurtitze, Glukhow, Kamenetz, Lachowy, and Kornitza. Some were located in the Hungarian part of Austria-Hungary; some in Rumanian Carpathia and Moldavia. Most, though, were situated in the "Pale of Settlement" the western extremity of the Russian empire extending from the Baltic Sea on the north to the Black Sea on the south, which included the Ukraine, and was heavily populated with Jews. And why did they come to St. Louis? Based upon what they and their descendants have said, primarily for one of two reasons (or both): to join family and *landsleit* already living in St. Louis, or to seek economic opportunities in one of the most dynamic cities in the United States.[33]

How many Jewish immigrants came to St. Louis from eastern Europe? Census figures do not break down that neatly, nor did mobility of people into and out of St. Louis make counting them any easier. Nevertheless, unofficial estimates of the total Jewish population of St. Louis—including both German and eastern European Jews—put the figure at between fifty-five thousand and sixty thousand in the 1920s. It has remained at approximately that level ever since.[34]

Endnotes

1. Author's interview with Audrey Klausner Montague, St. Louis, June 30, 1997; *Modem View* (St. Louis), June 13, 1913; *St. Louis Globe-Democrat,* October 1, 1948, October 27, December 19, 1949, February 3, 1950; *St. Louis Post-Dispatch,* October 1, 1948, September 25, October 27, November 4, December 19, 1949; *St. Louis star-Times,* October 27, December 19, 30119491 February 4, 1950; *Jewish American* (New York), July 1, 1949; *National Jewish Post* (Missouri Edition), December 23, 1949, February 17, 1950; *Alumni News of Saint Louis University* (October 1949): 3; John Conner, "Well Done, Sir," *Collier's* (June 10, 1950): 18–19 ff.; *Time* (February 13, 1950): 73.

2. A "graf" was an individual, usually a nobleman, to whom the Russian government granted special real estate or commercial favors or franchises.

3. Author's interviews with Nolan DeWoskin, St. Louis, July 28, 1997, and with David M. Krem, St. Louis, July 29, 1997; David M. Krem, "History of the DeWoskin Family," manuscript copy dated July 1994 in possession of author. See also *St. Louis Jewish Light,* December 14.1983. and December 21. 1988.

4. Leon Lander, "My Autobiography," manuscript copy given to author on May 21, 1981, and in his possession. With Lander's permission, the author made copies of that manuscript available to the St. Louis Jewish Community Archives, the Missouri Historical Society (St. Louis), and the American Jewish Archives (Cincinnati).

5. The following are but a few of many documented accounts of individual St. Louis Jews detailing why and how they left longtime European homes and emigrated to America: Senturia Family File, David Katz File, and Jeanette W. Bernstein, "The Grateful Thread: A Family Journey," all in American Jewish Archives (Cincinnati); "Atlas Writings" File, in office of Director of Community Relations, Jewish Center for Aged, St. Louis; Max Weiss, "The History of My Family," manuscript copy provided by Mr. Irvin Fagin of St. Louis and in possession of author; "Simon Joseph Ehrlich Interview" tapes, Western Historical Manuscript Collection, Thomas Jefferson University of Missouri-St. Louis; *Jewish Voice* (St. Louis) (hereinafter referred to as *Voice),* January 23, 1903, September 14,1906, January 12,1912.

6. *Voice,* March 27, 1908.

7. Ibid., September 14, 1908.

8. Morris David Marcus, M.D., "Memoirs from the St. Louis Ghetto," undated (about 1980), manuscript copy in possession of author. A published edited version appears in the Missouri Historical Society's *Gateway Heritage* (winter 1997–1998): 42–49.

9. It should be noted that many non-Jews protested against antisemitic depredations in eastern Europe. Prominent among those who came out publicly and in supporting humane treatment for Jews in Russia and Rumania were St. Wells, Rev. S. J. Nicholls of the Second Presbyterian Church, Otto L. Teichmann, president of the Merchants Exchange, brewer Adolphus Busch, attorney Oscar Whitelaw, and others. *Voice,* November 17,24,1905, March 4,1910

10. See particularly Martin Olevitch, "Interview with Anna Olevitch, September 26, 1982," transcript in possession of author; "Simon Joseph Ehrlich Interview" tapes, Western Historical Manuscript Collection, Thomas Jefferson Library, University of Missouri-St. Louis; and Senturia Family File, American Jewish Archives (Cincinnati).

11. Many excellent histories deal with late nineteenth and early twentieth century life of the Jewish people in eastern Europe. Among others, they include Howard Mor-

ley Sachar, *The Course of Modern Jewish History;* Robert M. Seltzer, *Jewish People, Jewish Thought;* and Solomon Grayzel, *A History of the Jews.*

12. Oscar Handlin, *The Uprooted.* See also Gary R. Mormino, *Immigrants on the Hill: Italian Americans in St. Louis,* 1882–1982,28–55, for comparable experiences among Italian immigrants.

13. Illustrative of assistance provided for Jews in St. Louis who wanted to help their friends and relatives come to America is an interesting article in the local Yiddish newspaper entitled "Voss Men Dahrf Vissen Ven Men Vill Ariber-bringen K'rovim"—"What One Must Know When You Wish to Bring Over Relatives." *Jewish Record* (St. Louis), December 3, 1920 (herein referred to as *Jewish Record).*

14. Israel Treiman provides one example of an eastern European Jewish family that went from Orthodox to Reform after living for a time in St. Louis. Treiman, who became a prominent St. Louis attorney, recalled how he was raised in a strictly Orthodox home in the South Broadway neighborhood, and that later in his adult life he joined a Reform temple. Author's interview with Israel Treiman, St. Louis, September 8,1982. Albert Radinsky made a similar observation. He even wore a *tallis koton* until his late teens.

Author's interview with Albert Radinsky, St. Louis, October 21,1997.

A generalization about eastern European Jewish immigrants comparable to that of their religious practices applies to their societal and cultural characteristics. These immigrants were, after all, part of an eastern European Slavic society influences of culture upon religious practices—and vice versa—it was often difficult to separate Judaism as a religion from Jewishness as a cultural and sociological phenomenon. In any event, major differences distinguished eastern European Jews from Germanic peoples of central and western Europe, including the latter's Jews. Reform Rabbi Moritz Spitz, editor of the *Jewish Voice,* often decried the animosities engendered by those cultural differences, pointing out that whether of German origin, whether Reform or Orthodox, they were all Jews, and therefore there should be more unity than divisiveness. See especially his editorials in *Voice,* January 2, February 18, 1909, March 4, 1910, and May 12, 1911.

15. Max Weiss wrote in his family history: "The object of this trip was that the rich community of Jews in Vienna would send us all to Es Geshier, Turkey, where we would become farmers." Es Geshier was in Palestine, at that time under Turkish control, and the project which the Weiss family wanted to join apparently was a farming community established by the new Zionist movement. Although Weiss wrote this memoir in 1970, he made no reference to Zionism. Max Weiss, "The History of My Family," manuscript copy in possession of author.

16. Atlas Writings" File, Jewish Center for Aged, St. Louis.

17. The Hamburg-American Line, with offices at 901 Olive, advertised that it would make all travel arrangements for immigrants "directly to St. Louis." *Voice,* February 26, 1904, July 27,1906. John Elman and Company, at 1507 Franklin, advertised as "agents for all steamship lines." Ibid., March 28,1913. Jacob Mellman, steamboat agent with offices at 406 Olive and 5500 Easton, advertised: III represent over 20 companies . . . Closed on Shabbos." *Jewish Record,* November 29,1920.

18. *Voice,* March 21, 1908. See also Gloria Rudman Goldblatt, "From the *Shtetl* to St. Louis in 1912:" in Howard Schwartz and Barbara Raznick, eds., *First Harvest,* 177–79.

19. "Atlas Writings" File, Jewish Center for Aged, St. Louis.

20. The term is from *Ethics of the Fathers,* chapter 1, verse 2. For one example see Martin Olevitch, "Interview with Anna Olevitch, September 26, 1982," transcript in possession of author.

21. Teenager Helen Rudman and her younger brother Morris had prepaid first-class tickets, but porters on the SS *Pennsylvania* put them in steerage anyway. Goldblatt, "From the *Shtetl* to St. Louis in 1912," 178.

22. "Atlas Writings" File, Jewish Center for Aged, St. Louis.

23. "Simon Joseph Ehrlich Interview" tapes, Western Historical Manuscript Collection, Thomas Jefferson Library, University of Missouri-St. Louis.

24. Handlin, *The Uprooted,* 50–54. See also Pamela S. Nadell," The Journey to America by Steam: The Jews of Eastern Europe in Transition," 269–84. Ellis Island opened as the first *federal* processing center in 1892. Prior to then, each state regulated immigration individually. Castle Garden, at the southern tip of Manhattan, had served that purpose in New York. Other ports through which immigrants came included Boston, Baltimore, Philadelphia, Norfolk, Charleston, Savannah, Mobile, New Orleans, Galveston, San Francisco, and Seattle. Some also entered through Canada via Montreal. Most, though, came through Ellis Island.

25. The renovation of Ellis Island as a national monument in the late 1980s spawned a number of fascinating books depicting how more than twelve million immigrants came through there to become Americans. Typical is Susan Jones, ed., *Ellis Island: Echoes from a Nation's Past.*

26. The late Leah Feldman Trattner was the author's mother-in-law, and he witnessed that emotional reunion at United Hebrew Temple that evening.

27. Jewish immigration far exceeded what relocation officials had anticipated, and many immigrants, lacking funds to go elsewhere, found themselves trapped in already overcrowded northeastern cities, especially New York. Settling them somewhere else became a high priority; hence efforts to move as many as possible to St. Louis and other interior cities. One aspect of this problem is sometimes referred to as the "Galveston Program." It entailed two measures. The first was to encourage immigrants to use Galveston, Texas, instead of Ellis Island as their point of entry, Galveston being a lot closer to ultimate inland destinations. The second was an effort to establish a number of agricultural communities so that Jewish immigrants might become farmers and break away from urban industrial life. Successful for a while, these efforts eventually failed. An excellent scholarly study of the Galveston Program is Uri D. Herscher, *Jewish Agricultural Utopias in America, 1880–1910.* See also *Voice,* July 24,1908, and Jack Glazier, *Dispersing the Ghetto: The Relocation of Jewish Immigrants Across America.*

28. See, for example, Weiss, "History of My Family," manuscript copy in possession of author; *Voice,* January 23, 1903, May 11, 1906, July 24, 1908, and March 10, 1916; Ferdinand S. Bach, "The Federation of Jewish Charities," in *Modern View,* 25th Anniversary Edition (1925),32–35; and various annual reports of the Jewish Charitable and Educational Union and the Federation of Jewish Charities, copies in the St. Louis Jewish Community Archives. Cited as being active in St. Louis relocation activities were Hyman Cohen, Rabbi Jacob Mazur, Rabbi Adolph Rosentreter, Reverend Nathan Blitz, Gilbert Harris, Rabbi Samuel Thurman, Rabbi Abraham E. Halpern, Samuel J. Russack, Sam Hamburg, Max G. Baron, Frank Dubinsky, Dr. Moses I. DeVorkin,

David Baron, Harry Felberbaum, Michael Novak, I. Goldberg, Morris Shapiro, Sam Rudman, Harry Roven, Leon DeWoskin, and J. Weinstein. *Modern View,* December 8,1922. Two later waves of Jewish immigrants, although much smaller, received St. Louis Jewish community beneficence: refugees from Nazi depredations and refugees from the former Soviet Union. Today the Jewish Federation continues this important service through such constituent agencies as the Jewish Family and Children's Service Resettlement Office, the Metropolitan Employment and Rehabilitation Service and the English Language School. For a brief overview of these agencies, see *St. Louis Jewish Light,* March 31, 1971.

29. *Modern View,* May 1,1925, October 4,1929, October 21,1937; *Jewish Record,* December 28,1917, March 15,1918, May 28,1920. Those *landsleit* organizations gradually disappeared as first-generation immigrants passed away. However, the singular popularity of genealogy in the 1980s and 1990s, along with a concomitant interest in Holocaust studies, created in many descendants a unique interest in the lives of their ancestry and virtually resurrected some of those old *landsleit* groups, primarily to exchange research discoveries.

30. "Atlas Writings" File, Jewish Center for Aged, St. Louis.

31. Most published accounts of mistreatment of Jews in eastern Europe deal with czarist antisemitism. Even though many Jews favored the overthrow of the czar, communist antisemitism proved to be no less oppressive. For how this new wave of depredations influenced Jewish emigration from Russia, see, among others, "Simon Joseph Ehrlich Interview" tapes, Western Historical Manuscript Collection, Thomas Jefferson Library, University of Missouri-St. Louis. For relations between the United States and Russia dealing specifically with Jewish immigration matters, see Gary Dean Best, *To Free a People: Jewish Leaders and the Jewish Problem in Eastern Europe,* 1890–1914; also Cyrus M. Adler and Aaron W. Margalith, *American Intercession on Behalf of the Jews in the Diplomatic Correspondence of the United States,* 1840–1938, Naomi W. Cohen, *Not Free to Desist,* and Joseph Samuel, *History of the Baron de Hirsch Fund.*

St. Louis's eastern European Jews may have outnumbered the city's German Jews even earlier than 1914. See *Modern View,* March 6, 1914, and *Voice,* March 10, 1916. But there is no doubt that by the early 1920s the composition of the St. Louis Jewish community had undergone this major change. An interesting sidelight is that at that time only New York, Chicago, Philadelphia, Cleveland, and Boston had more Jewish residents than St. Louis. *Modern View,* March 6, 1914, April 22, May 13, 1921.

32. Many excellent scholarly studies analyze changes in American immigration policy in the post-World War I era. One of the most concise is William S. Bernard's essay, "Immigration: History of U.S. Policy," in Stephan Thernstrom, ed., *Harvard Encyclopedia of American Ethnic Groups.* Others include Thomas J. Curran, *Xenophobia and Immigration,* 1820–1930; Roger Daniels, *Not Like Us: Immigrants and Minorities in America,* 1890–1924; Leonard Dinnerstein and David M. Reimers, *Ethnic Americans: A History* of *Immigration;* Robert A. Divine, *American Immigration Policy,* 1924–1952; John Higham, *Strangers in the Land;* and Maldwyn A. Jones, *American Immigration.* Myron Bennan, *The Attitude of American Jewry Towards Eastern European Jewish Immigration,* 1881–1914, and Sheldon M. Neuringer, *American Jewry and United States Immigration Policy,* 1881–1953 focus on American Jewish attitudes. The entire December 1986 issue of *American Jewish History* focuses exclusively on that topic.

33. The spellings of towns are phonetic, and may not appear as such on a map. Some, in fact, no longer exist, having been obliterated in the fighting of World War I and World War II. The area of the Pale of Settlement at one time had been part of greater Poland into which the Polish government actually had welcomed Jews because they could be a buffer against expanding Russia. Many of those Jews came from the Rhineland area to escape mistreatment there. In the late 1700s, though, a now weak Poland was forcibly partitioned among Russia, Prussia, and Austria. The territories most heavily occupied by Jews came under Russian control. As a result of long-standing anti-Jewish sentiments in Russia, a royal ukase issued in 1794 restricted Russia's Jews to living in the Pale.

The publication of Alex Haley's *Roots* has led to a renewed enthusiasm for researching family history and genealogy. The Jewish Genealogical Society of St. Louis has provided valuable assistance and resources for many whose ancestors came over as immigrants.

34. Estimates in the early 1900s placed the St. Louis Jewish population at about forty thousand. By 1921 that figure had risen to fifty thousand, and in 1925 to fifty-five thousand. It has remained between fifty-five thousand and sixty thousand since then. *Voice,* January 21,1902, March 17,1905, March 10,1916; *Modern View,* March 6, 1914, November 12,1915, August 30,1918, April22, May 13,1921, August 5,1927. A demographic study of St. Louis Jewry in 1995 estimated the number to be sixty thousand. Gary A. Tobin, *Jewish Federation of St. Louis Community Study, Summary Report,* 1995,5, copy in possession of author. This would suggest that once immigration ceased to bring additional Jews to St. Louis, the normal birth rate within St. Louis Jewry has remained at a level that just barely sustained itself. It indicates also that the post-World War II "influx" of immigrants from Germany and from the Soviet Union was not very large.

Jeff Friedman
The Poem of the Family

The poem of the family is a poem of loss. The poem that remembers the family has lost the family. The poem that depicts the dysfunctional family is also a poem of loss, lamenting the loss of the ideal family.

But the poem of the family is also about power and powerlessness. Who sits at the head of the dinner table? Who eats first? Who gives the gifts and who gets them? The emotions are always complicated, ambivalent. Why was I given what was I given? Why wasn't I given more? My parents loved me too much; they didn't love me enough.

Recently I was discussing the work of a contemporary poet in a poetry writing class. Graphically detailed, her book contained a long sequence of poems about a father who was sexually and emotionally abusive. The speaker was the daughter, and the poems told the stories of the speaker and her father, the speaker and her mother, the speaker and her husband, the speaker and her daughter, and the speaker and her son. Interspersed among the family poems were poems about teachers who abused their power and about poets. So the book covered victims and victimizers. I'm not trying to belittle the book by describing it this way. The poems created a world of complicated emotional responses.

One of the writing students challenged the subject of the poems: "But doesn't everybody write about the family. Aren't there are a thousand poems just like these?"

The answer to that is probably yes. That's what a tradition is, generations of poems spawned from the same family tree. But every good poem is unique, a world unto itself. so a tradition is rich with differences, rich with pattern and variation.

The family poem has become quite popular in the last fifty years, but if we look back before that time we have very few poems that deal with the family with such particularity. I can only think of Stanley Kunitz's "My Father and I" and Hart Crane's "My Grandmother's Letters." Then in the late 50s and the 60s we get Lowell's *Life Studies,* Snodgrass's *Heart's Needle,* Ginsberg's *Kaddish,* the poems of Sexton, Plath, Stern, Levine, Etheridge Knight and many others. Then from the 70s on we get a vast outpouring of these poems. Poets have always written about the family—consider Oedipus, Antigone, Lear and Hamlet. What's different or new is the emphasis on the personal and private home life as an explicit subject matter.

The student was trying to say something and finally said it: Who wants to read bunch of poems where the poet whines about his family problems?

It's true in recent years American poets have written a large number of poems that center on the injured self coping in a dysfunctional family. But poets have also written just as many poems memorializing and celebrating the family.

Most people have very strong feelings about their fathers, mothers, brothers and sisters, so why shouldn't the family offer us a fertile ground for the imagination. Why shouldn't we write about the problems since problems frequently provoke the strongest response?

In the poem of the dysfunctional family, usually the injured self has been injured by someone and that someone is often a loved one. The speaker is often the victim, and the victim is the hero of the poem, which means the victimizer, the loved one who has refused to give love in the right way, becomes the villain. In the more complex poems each emotion triggers its opposite: a great love requires a great hate. The injured self is heroic because of the depth and violence of its emotions.

In the poem that memorializes the family, the poet wants time to stand still. He wants to hold the moment in memory forever. He wants to be young again and relieve it all, so he remembers and reinvents the family. He fixes what couldn't be fixed. He recreates his father, mother, brothers and sisters. In this portrait love and death walk hand in hand. The poet must find the right light, the right composition, or the picture will be too soft in focus, too nostalgic, too sweet.

In both cases, if these poems fail to move us deeply, it is because they don't reach beyond the limits of the ego or the individual case.

In the best poems the individual's experience coping with life, suffering, love and death is transformed into the experience of the group, the tribe, the nation or the culture.

Discussing James Wright's poem "The Life" in his essay "Poetry, Personality and Death," Galway Kinnell states," whatever is autobiographical—and the reference in the first stanza must have its origin in something very personal and particular in Wright's life—is transmuted, opens out as the inner autobiography of us all."

Later in the essay, Kinnell adds this: The voice is a particular recognizable voice; at the same time it mysteriously sheds personality and becomes simply the voice of a creature on earth speaking."

Wordsworth said it this way: "Aristotle, I have been told, hath said that Poetry is the most philosophic of all writing: it is so: its object is truth, not individual and local, but general, and objective; not standing upon external testimony, but carried alive into the heart by passion." So poetry must bring us the truth, not individual and local, but general through passionate expression.

For a moment, let's take the tale of the Binding in *Genesis*, sometimes referred to as the sacrifice of Isaac. Abraham takes his son to Mount Moriah to sacrifice him. The son goes with the father unquestioningly, but when they set up the altar, he asks, "where's the lamb?" He's to be the lamb, the sacrifice. To satisfy his God, the father who has been granted this child late in life raises his knife, ready to kill his son. Is there a story more heartbreaking in Western culture? Is there a story about a family that is more dysfunctional than this? The emotions are primal. All individual details have been shed. The story is about faith, the binding of the covenant, the continuation of a race.

Phil Levine's poem "Zaydee," opens with three pressing, unanswerable questions: Why does the sea burn? Why do the hills cry? Where did my father go in my fifth autumn? The questions echo throughout the poem. The individual loss is framed within a larger universe, a universe of suffering where the sea burns and the hills cry. The opening questions come from Job. Instead of the father telling him the story of his ancestors, it is the grandfather telling him the story of his father. As in Genesis the poet is creating his own genealogy, his own myth of the father. The poem memorializes both the grandfather and the father.

In Nelly Sachs' poem "The Dead Child," she uses the persona of a dead child. The dead child describes his mother leading him to his death. The knife of parting is an allusion to the Isaac story. As the poem progresses, the child details his last moments of life, the inevitability of his death. We soon realize that the poem is informed by historical reality, the Holocaust. The speaker in the poem is a single child, but also a representative child. He is Isaac. By the end of the poem the child speaks for all the dead children, indeed for all those who were sacrificed; the voice of the poem is the voice of six million who died, and finally it is the voice of lamentation.

Pinchas Giller
Recovering the Sanctity of the Galilee: the Veneration of Sacred Relics in Classical Kabbalah

Relics, namely the preserved remains or paraphernalia of a saint, are venerated in Christianity by being made the object of a chapel. Ideally, they serve as the catalyst for miracles. Peter Brown has documented the "translation" of relics in Christian piety, the phenomenon by which the presence of relics conferred sanctity on a particular locale. He observes that:"The graves of the saints–whether these were the solemn rock tombs of the Jewish patriarchs in the Holy Land or, in Christian circles, tombs, fragments of bodies or, even, physical objects that had made contact with those bodies—were privileged places, where the contrasted poles of Heaven and Earth met."[1] Lionel Rothkrug and Lewis Lancaster have studied the interplay of sacred relics, sanctified texts and the sanctification of images in post-reformation Christianity and classical Buddhism. Relic-based traditions promoted a phenomenon that Lancaster and Rothkrug call "fixed sanctity." In this phenomenon, the holiness of the relic is transferred to its locale. When removed from its locale, the relic loses its efficacy. The locale, in turn, confers sanctity on the nation as a whole and even on its monarchy.[2] According to Rothkrug, in medieval Germany, supernatural powers were understood as emanating from a place, a *locus sanctus*. Shrines that embody this fixed sanctity tend to be bastions of religious conservatism. Their "earth-bound" holiness is often a reaction to religious reform. By contrast, there are religious movements that emphasize "portable sanctity," that is often based on the veneration of sacred texts.[3]

In Judaism, portable spirituality is manifest in the history of the Diaspora, and its movements of text veneration. The academies of the Diaspora were constantly relocated according to the upheavals of history. The resilient portability of text veneration, from its inception in the first Babylonian exile, was able to sustain Diaspora culture. Thus has traditional Judaism understood Yochanan ben Zakkai 's legendary request to Vespasian:"Give me (the academy at) Yavneh and its sages."[4]

However, relic-veneration has always been present in Jewish practice. Even as it declined in some Diaspora cultures, it flourished upon return to the Holy Land. This phenomenon reached its doctrinal peak in the teachings of the Zohar, the classical work of Jewish mysticism, and in the application and refinement of the Zohar's ideas among the Galilean mystics in sixteenth century Safed.

Scripture taught that ritual impurity would result from any contact with death. Jews of the first and second Temple periods buried their dead in caves, in order that this ritual impurity would not pollute the general community. Burial took place in two stages: an initial burial followed by the bones of the deceased being re-buried in ossuaries.[5] In order to contain the spread of ritual impurity generated by the corpse, the Jews of antiquity dug thousands of limestone burial tombs. These tombs dot the rocky hills and punctuate the weave of valleys and gullies that wind among the mountains of the Galilee. During the middle ages, gravesites associated with Biblical, Talmudic or mystical heroes came to serve as centers for prayer[6] and the development of communities.

This relic-veneration affected the subsequent history of Jewish settlement in the Holy Land in ways that are germaine to Lancaster and Rothkrug's research. The bold return to relic-veneration in late medieval Judaism led to a concurrent veneration of the land that housed the relic. This shift from text-oriented, portable sanctity to the veneration of the relic and its locale affected the development of subsequent Jewish movements from the medieval period to the present.

The Gravesite Shrine in Judaism

Gravesites are referred to in the Hebrew Bible and the knowledge of their whereabouts is assumed for the Biblical reader. The cave of *Machpela*, in Hebron, was a pilgrimage site as early as the Roman period.[7] This is the primary gravesite in Jewish tradition, by virtue of the Patriarchs' and Matriarchs' primacy and its indisputable authenticity and antiquity. Mystical traditions identifed *Machpela* as the gate to the Underworld.[8]

The identities of other gravesites are clearly etiological, particularly in cases where Biblical figures are buried in Hellenistic tomb structures. The present day tomb of King David is a Hellenistic memorial from Roman Jerusalem, the Bible, of course, records that the once and future king was actually buried far below Mount Zion "in the city of David."[9] Similarly, the *Yesha* crossroad, some twenty miles north of Safed is considered the Biblical *Kadesh* and Naftali, that in turn is linked to the Biblical judges Deborah, Barak, Yael and Chever.[10] The site is clearly a lavish Hellenistic gravesite, long since plundered. Even more fanciful are the Galilean locations of the gravesites of Mordechai and Esther, the prophet Ovadiah, various Babylonian *amoraim* and the medieval poet/philosophers Yehudah ha-Levi and Solomon Ibn Gabirol.

Major figures were often buried at the places where they were most active, or at sites are evoked by their names, or even at places with linguistic similarities to the sound of their names.[11] The house of the charitable Shunnamite woman who housed the prophet Elisha was identified at the village of Shunnam. The graves of Rabbi Yishmael, the legendary "High Priest," and R. Shimon Shazuri[12] are revered by the local Druze who bury their own dead from Israel's wars in their proximity.

Biblical figures who are buried at high places are usually so identified because the name of the place literally means "height." This is the case with Samuel, who is buried at *Ramah*, literally "the height."[13] The saint's presence may be evoked melodramatically, so that R. Yochanan ben Zakkai lies buried between Eliezer and Yehoshua, the two students who spirited him out of the besieged Jerusalem.[14] Similarly, Rabbi Akiva's grave is closed up, as, according to legend, it was sealed by Elijah the prophet.[15]

The circumstances of the physical site could also effect the traditions surrounding the figure. Sometimes the grave is marked by a large, ancient stone, such as those of Meir Ba'al ha-Nes, Ishmael ha-Amorah or Rabbi Tarfon. The only part remaining might be a heap of stones,[16] or a cave with burial chambers.[17] Some figures have multiple gravesites, particularly Biblical figures who are revered by various religions. The prophets Habakuk and Jonah have three gravesites, and one in the Galilee, one in the Judaean hills and one in Babylonia.[18] Maimonides has a tomb in Tiberias and also in Cairo.[19]

A shift in general opinion regarding the veracity of a site is not uncommon. The gravesite of Hannah and her seven sons has been relocated in the popular mind, in accordance with early descriptions that have come to light. It was long considered to be a large grave of several compartments at the bottom of the Safed graveyard, but popular opinion today places it at the military cemetery and monument in the main part of the town.[20] The major figure of the kabbalistic revival in Safed, Isaac Luria, insisted that the site was inauthentic, but popular opinion has not accepted his view and it continues to be venerated as Hosea's grave.[21] Luria also identified the sites of the *Idrot.*, the Zohar's climactic convocations, and attempted to re-enact them with his disciples.[22] Until recently, the site of the *Idrot* was popularly identified with a large burial cave of some thirteen chambers that sits at a bend in the road between Safed and Meron. A structure over the cave was built by the Israel Ministry of Religious Affairs some years ago. In recent years, however, local kabbalists have relocated the *Idra* site in the vicinity of a number of other graves at Ein Zeitim.[23]

Maintaining accurate traditions was always a struggle. The Palestinian *amora* Shimon ben Lakish would "mark the burial places of the Rabbis."[24] The Jewish mystics of sixteenth-century Safed entrusted the beadle of a certain synagogue with recording the gravesite locations for posterity.[25] A conservative attitude prevailed with regards to the authenticity of various sites, so that whatever had been accepted from generation to generation continued to have credibility.

Ultimately, the identification of gravesites was a function of Jewish memory. For instance, Rachel's tomb is always pictured, in Jewish art, as a small, forlorn building on an empty road. This reflects the tragedy of Rachel's death in childbirth and her exclusion from the cave of Machpelah.[26] In a phenomenon Rothkrug has noted in post-Reformation Europe, "the saint's name referred as much to the place—as in the name of a village—as it did to his person,"[27] as when a bus-driver, upon coming to Meron or Tiberias, will call out the name of the occupant of the shrine, saying "*Rabi Shim'on, Rabi Meir Ba'al ha-Nes!*"

Certain sites are acknowledged as holy to both Judaism and Islam, particularly those related to primordial figures from the Pentateuch. Moses' father-in-law Jethro was, according to the Koran, an early incarnation of *hidud*, the light of the creator. The esoteric Shi'ite Druze sect celebrate their major festival at the elaborate grave of Jethro, their *Nebi Shwieb*, in the early spring.[28] Elijah's cave in Haifa is but one of a series of sites associated with *Al Chadr*, a similarly immortal saint of Islam, and the Christian Saint George. There are mosques at the Cave of Machpelah, the grave of the prophet Joel in Gush Chalav and the prophet Jonah in Kefar Kannah.[29] The ancient Temple of Pan at the Bannias spring at the foot of the Golan Heights is associated with the burial place of the mysterious prophet Iddo, as well as being a Druze site for a shrine to Al Chadr. Jews and Moslems revered a site on the northwestern slope of Mount Hermon as the location of the *brit bein ha-betarim*, the covenant of the split carcasses made between Abraham and God.

At all of these sites, funerary practices are often shared among Jews, Muslims, Christians and Druze. Rocks may be left at the grave as tokens of a visit, or brought back as amulets.[30] Candles are traditionally lit at the gravesite, particularly at the gravesites of Shim'on bar Yochai, Eliezer, Yitzchak Napchah and King David. Visitors to the Western wall are familiar with the practice of writing names and requests and placing them between the stones of the structure. These notes (yiddish: *k'vitlakh*) are commonly found at gravesites as well. It is a custom among Palestinian Arabs to coat the grave with henna and keep a tray of coals burning on which incense may be placed. The Jews also burned incense at the gravesite, as evidenced by Karaitic writing and sixth century Christian reports.[31] The practice of cutting an infant's hair for the first time as part of a gravesite pilgrimage has its antecedents in pagan practice.[32]

The tree by the grave is often associated with the holiness of the deceased.[33] Often there is a single, ancient tree at the gravesite. Such trees have been venerated since Canaanite times; the terebinths of Mamre, near Hebron, were venerated until their destruction during the Roman period.[34] Palestinean Arabs tie handkerchiefs to the surrounding trees. These places are called *um shratit*, "with rags," (Heb. *smartut*) in Arabic, after this practice. Specific graves were associated with women's practices.[35]

Gravesites played a central role in times of drought and famine. Jews would gather to pray for rain at the the cave of Machpelah in Hebron and the grave of the legendary thaumaturge Choni ha-Ma'agel in Far'am.[36] The appearance of water in the grave of Hillel, at Mt. Meron in the upper Galilee, was considered propitious for the year's rainfall.[37] Curative powers were ascribed to water brought from Maimonides' grave, as well as the aforementioned graves of Hillel and Shammai. Later, when the grave of Shim'on bar Yochai became the focal point of activity in Meron, the kabbalists would gather there in times of drought.[38]

In the present day, the grave of Yonatan ben Uzziel, translator of the prophets into Aramaic during the Roman period, is a popular pilgrimage site. Recent traditions identify him as a matchmaker, and I have heard him described, by pilgrims, as interceding between families just as he interceded between the reader and the Divine text. Today, young men and women in various stages of desperation will leave keepsakes on the grave.[39] In the last eight years the site has been appropriated by several religious communities of Sephardic origin who have funded the construction of a synagogue over the site, with a high and opaque barrier between the men and women. The woman's side is also festooned with scraps of cloth, in the Arab fashion, much as is the grave of Yehoshua de-Sichnin, where Palestinean Arabs tie handkerchiefs to the surrounding trees, *um shratit*.[40]

Christian and Roman historians of the Byzantine period indicate that sacred graves, such as the cave of Machpelah[41] and the tombs of Aaron, in Petra[42] and Rachel, in Bethlehem[43] were venerated in late antiquity. In fact, the location of Rachel's tomb was a matter of some dispute as early as the Biblical period.[44] In the Mameluk period, after centuries of obscurity, travellers began to include laconic references to gravesites and religious practices associated with them.[45] The sixteenth century saw the advent of the *moreh derekh* (road guide) literature.[46] These were pamphlets, often written in various Jewish vernaculars, describing the location of the Holy sites and salting the accounts with mythic and homiletical materials.

The Restless and Malevolent Dead

And yet, in the literature of classical exoteric Judaism, it is hard to find justification for these traditions and practices. Relic veneration is not a natural outgrowth of rabbinic Judaism, and it is not easily reconciled with the ritual status of the grave in Judaism's legal structure. Moreover, the Rabbis of the period of the Talmud were ambivalent about the nature of the gravesite because they were ambivalent about the nature of death itself.

Talmudic tradition records the practice of prostration (*hishtatchut*) in supplication before the gravesite. Rabbinic texts portray *hishtatchut* as accompanying periods of crisis, when the protagonist in a tale goes to a gravesite in order to engage in petitional prayer. Aggadic accounts refer to this practice among Biblical figures, *tannaim*, and *amoraim*.[47] These accounts may not imply that the act of *hishtatchut* was anything more than reverential bowing before the deceased *tzaddik*.[48]

Nonetheless, the Rabbis had not arrived at one doctrinal conclusion about the distinction of the soul and the body, the nature of the afterlife or its relationship to the bodily resurrection that would accompany the onset of the messianic age. A number of rabbinic speculations about the afterlife are collected in a long passage in the Babylonian Talmud.[49] The earliest opinions portray the dead as passive and unconscious. They "know their own pain but not the pain of others,"[50] and mutely await the resurrection. Although they may be unconscious, it is worthwhile to avenge their honor and do mischief on their behalf.[51] Other opinions see the dead as intercessors in human affairs. They are active, restless spirits, as described in this influential account described tactive restlyess spirits, who leave the grave on the night of the Day of Atonement, in order to rise up "behind the *pargod* (curtain)" to "see what misforturne shall be this year." The protagonist, meaningfully described as a *hasid*, or pietist, profets from his communion with the dead, until he hears the admonition "Put these things aside, for what passed between us has been heard by the living."[52]

This folkloristic image of the wandering spirit led to two poles of belief as to the nature of the afterlife. One understanding saw the spirits of the dead and their abode as beneficent towards the living. The other opinion reflected and expanded on the horror of the gravesite as the source of death impurity. A horror of the gravesite is evident in the traditions of the *chasidei Ashkenaz*, pietists who populated the Rhineland in the twelfth and thirteenth centuries. For the German *chasidim*, the world of the dead was an abode of dread and danger.

This dread is expressed in the widely circulated ethical will of Yehudah ha-Chasid, the leader of the movement. According to that document, the dead were liable to try to lure the living over into the netherworld. Therefore, Yehudah instructed his community not to kiss their deceased children,[53] grieve excessively[54] or return habitually to the grave.[55] When the dying refer to absent events and objects, the living were not to acknowledge the reference,[56] or accept gifts from the dead in a dream visitation.[57] Were this to happen, the deceased must be confronted at the gravesite, as illustrated in this injunction from the major popular work of the *chasidei Ashkenaz*, *Sefer Chasidim*, or "The Book of the Righteous:"

> The spirits of the dead wander the world, hoping to hear the Divine decrees. Sometimes they induce the living to join them. If one humors them, then he or one of this family will soon die. Rather one should say to them, "because of the Blessed Holy One, I refuse to go with you or with another other dead person." The next day he should go out to the graveyard and prostrate himself on the that person's grave, saying, "for the sake of the Holy Blessed One who desires life, you and your messengers must desist from following me, my children or any other Jew, for I desire this world and not the other."[58]

For Yehudah ha-Chasid, the dead reacted to any slights or breaches of honor connected with their own burial, and would bring reprisals for them. Graves were not to be left open and unfilled[59] and caskets were not to be stacked on top of one another. Following the rites of purification, the body was always placed at the entrance to the house.[60] The dead of a certain town were apt to take offense if one declined to bury ones kin near them.[61] This horror often translated into the classical superstitions of medieval Europe. Women who were suspected of killing and eating children had to be watched carefully at the time of burial. If their jaws slipped open, their mouths were to be filled with earth lest they rise from the grave to kill more children.[62] Clearly, for the German chasidim, the living were to be protected from the machinations of the dead.

The Zohar

The image of the dead as restless and malevolent did not remain central in Medieval Judaism. Another understanding came to challenge it, one that viewed the gravesite as hallowed ground and its relics as soteric instruments. This doctrinal shift came about as one result of the ascent of the Zohar, the classic work of the Kabbalah. The Zohar's portrayal of Rabbi Shimon bar Yochai's mystical fellowship was set in the Galilee of the second century, C.E.. It was there that the protagonists shared their contemplative visions and had their adventures, often among the more marginal elements of society.

The Zohar teaches a doctrine of a tripartite soul. The three parts of the soul are the *nefesh* or physical soul, the *ruach*, or emotive soul and the *neshamah*, the transcendent spark of the Godhead that resides in the upper reaches of the believer's soul.[63] These three aspects of the soul separate at the moment of death. At that time, the *ruach* and *neshama* leave the *nefesh* at the gravesite. The *ruach* rises up to the celestial garden of Eden, a paradise where it passes eternity in the company of the *tzaddikim*, or righteous saints, who rejoice nightly in the celestial Garden of Eden.[64] The *neshamah*, having always been a spark of the Divine that had merely sojourned in the human soul, ascends and is lost within its source in the Godhead. This process takes place more easily depending on the spiritual attainments of the deceased.

The *tzaddik*'s *nefesh* is an active presence at the gravesite, a listening ear ready to relay messages upward to the *ruach* and *neshamah*. The soteric relic is not the decaying body, but the *nefesh*, whose aura suffuses the gravesite.[65] In times of emergency, the community goes to the graveyard to beg the *tzaddikim* for their intercession. The *nefashot* of the righteous then gather and plead the case of the living with God.[66] Gravesite pilgrimages often climax a period of fasting and personal mortification, that are then presented as offerings: "Israel goes (to the gravesite) bringing only their repentance before God, with fasting and contrite hearts, in order that their holy souls may beseech mercy for them. Therefore we learn that the righteous man, even when he departs from this world, does not really disappear from any world, since he may be found in any of them more than in his lifetime."[67] The dead are almost more alive in death than in life, for they say: "If not for us, the dead, who intercede before the angel of the grave for the living, the living would not remain alive for even half a day."[68]

The Patriarchs,[69] in particular, "ask for mercy for their children," in the earthly Garden of Eden, "where the souls of the righteous sit wearing crowns of light."[70] Pilgrimage to the Cave at Machpelah is a model for the general practice of gravesite pilgrimage. So it is that: "When the world requires mercy, the living go and inform the spirits of the *tzaddikim* and weep over their graves, in order that soul may cleave to soul, and the souls of the righteous come together and tell the sleepers of Hebron[71] of the pain of the world, then all enter the gates of Paradise. These spirits, who are crowned in Paradise like celestial angels join them. They tell the *neshamah*, who tells the Blessed Holy One, then God has mercy on the world for all of their sins."[72] The influential Safed kabbalist, Chayyim Vital, echoed this sentiment: "One should never imagine that the Righteous, on their passing . . . are idle from service. Were it not for the prayers of the dead, the living could not continue living!"[73]

In Safed

The desire to recreate the experiences of the Zohar's protagonists propelled them to the Galilee, where they projected the Zohar's romanticism onto its mysterious, demanding terrain. This projection of the Zohar's lore was to transform the spiritual image of the region.

There are reports as early as the thirteenth century of Jews going to the gravesite of Hillel and Shammai at Mt. Meron, in the Northern Galilee to pray for rain.[74] Subsequent reports note the presence, at Meron, of Shimon bar Yochai's study room, probably at the site of an ancient synagogue. Eventually the graves of Rabbi Shimon and his son Eliezer were located on Mount Meron's lower slope.[75] Isaac Luria had a vision of Shimon bar Yochai at the gravesite, sealing the authenticity of the site forever.[76] An important commentator on the Zohar, Avraham Galante, financed the construction of the building complex over the grave.[77] In this way, the original focus of Meron changed from an emphasis on the presence of Hillel and Shammai to a preoccupation with the etiological cult of Shimon Bar Yochai. The presence of Shim'on bar Yochai's grave was also a catalyst for medieval settlement in the neighboring town on the opposite mountaintop, Safed.

As a result of this settlement, gravesites in the area became centers for pilgrimage, particularly during the religious festivals. Joseph Caro built a *sukkah* on the gravesite of Shimon bar Yochai, a practice that has continued to this day.[78] Presently, there is a mass pilgrimage to Meron on the thirty-third day of the *Omer*, the traditional date of Shimon bar Yochai's coming out of hiding from Roman persecution.[79] The chasidim of the Breslav sect customarily spend the New Year and Day of Atonement at Meron. These practices are at variance with the Zohar's doctrines, that taught that the righteous depart the gravesite during the festivals.

Moshe Cordovero and his teacher, Shlomo Alkabetz sought inspiration wandering through Safed and its environs, stopping at gravesites and sites that were increasingly coming to be associated with specific events in the Zohar. These ramblings, or *gerushim* (literally "exiles"), were a conscious imitation of the picaresque journeys of the Zohar's protagonists.[80] In terms of kabbalistic symbolism, his footsteps represent the penetration of Divine union, the archetypal realm called *yesod*, into the *Shekhinah*, who is symbolized by the land of Israel.[81]

The most striking religious figure of this period, Isaac Luria, made the veneration of the sacred grave an important part of his mystical teaching. Prior to Luria, the living had petitioned the dead with traditional prayer. The pilgrim set out to wake up the sleeping *tzaddik* at the gravesite and send him to intercede with the Divine. Lurianic texts often based themselves on the Zohar's vision of whole communities beseeching the righteous in times of crisis:

> Cleaving to the *zaddikim* and prostrating oneself at the gravesite, cleaving spirit (*ruach*) to spirit and soul to soul (*nefesh*) is as described in the Zohar (III 70b): *when the world is in need of mercy and life they go out and inform the tzaddikim, weeping on the gravesite of those who it is appropriate to inform, conforming to their will and cleaving soul to soul*, to purify with great purification and to sanctify them with great sanctity and to delight greatly, to behold the kindness of God, to know that his path and his actions are illuminated with the light of God's presence. [The *tzaddik*] tells him true things and does not lead him astray, on the condition that he behaves with holiness and humility and fear of sin, keeping God's great and terrible name before him always, to unify the name of the Blessed Holy One always, with love and fear . . .[82]

In Luria's world, the living and the dead mingled. He boldly identified various gravesites with figures from the Bible, Talmud and Zohar.[83] From the hill overlooking Safed, he observed a whole society of the dead, in the shrines and tombs in the area. He could recognize the *nefesh* of the departed saint hovering over the site. Sometimes his pronounced opinions were at variance with prevailing traditions.[84] As well as identifying the inhabitant of the gravesite, Luria was aware of the deceased's fate in the afterlife. Sometimes, because of some outstanding transgression, the dead transmigrated into inanimate objects for an unspecified period of limbo.[85]

With his identification of many new gravesites, Luria helped shape the emerging mythos of the Galilee.[86] Chayyim Vital's son, Samuel, included most of the sites linked to Luria in chapter thirty-eight of his *Sha'ar ha-Gilgullim*, that acts as a guide to the tiny communities surrounding Safed: Ein Zeitim,[87] Biriah, Avnit, Akvarah, Gush Chalav and others. Luria even identified Jesus' grave at Ein Zeitim, off the Safed-Meron road. Contemporary Franciscan monks in the area knew of this tradition. This gravesite probably figures in one account of a harrowing experience that occurred to Vital at the grave of a certain "dead gentile." The malevolent spirit, "dead more than a thousand years,"[88] took possession of Vital, propelling him in flight over the graveyards of Safed, till Luria was compelled to revive him from his coma.

The accounts of Luria's wanderings remain open to interpretation after centuries. How complex it is, from the vantage point of centuries of withering history and climate, to follow the route suggested in this account in Vital's *Sha'ar ha-Gilgullim* (c. 1580):[89] "When one walks from the village of lower *Dahariah*, to the west of Safed, when descending to the river where there is a mill. Descend further, continue in the same direction until the water is barely visible, at the point of descent from one spring to another. On the left side of the road is a small path between the rocks. To the south of this path is a high boulder, like a small wall, and this is the grave of Hiyya as is mentioned in the *Idra* in *Parashat Naso*."

Luria's method of prostration, or *hishtatchut,* consisted of his literally lying prone across the gravestone, with his face at the face of the deceased, so as to align all the levels of his soul with that of the departed *tzaddik*.[90] According to Vital: "Whenever he desired to speak with a certain prophet or sage, he would go to his grave and lay himself down upon it, with outstretched arms and feet . . . He would bind his soul, spirit and super-soul [*nefesh, ruach* and *neshamah*] to those of the *tzaddik* and bring about supernal unification."[91]

In this bold instance of prostration, soteric energy is clearly drawn from the relic. The horror of the gravesite is replaced by a desire to cleave to the deceased, an experience that is understood as nurturing and restorative to the living. This was the act of *yichud*, or "unification." In the *yichud*, the deceased acts, or is used, as an instrument for mystical union. The intention of the gravesite pilgrim was not to have a noetic experience, but to repair the rupture of the upper worlds.[92] Lurianic theorists eventually come to consider the *yichudim* to be as profound as Torah study.[93]

A central premise of Lurianic doctrine is that every reincarnated soul derives from a specific root, that itself comes from the world progenitors, Adam, Cain and Abel.[94] The soul root's journey can be traced back through prior generations, which tend (in the case of the Safed kabbalists) to include significant rabbinic and prophetic figures. One's forebears in the soul root generally embodied a common inner quality. Shimon bar Yochai was identified as having the lineal soul root of Moses.[95] Chayyim Vital stoically bore the karmic burden of his past lives as the *amora* Abbaye, the Zohar's Yeiva Saba,[96] Rabbi Akiva, Yochanan ben Zakkai, Hezekiah the king of Judah, and the prophet Samuel.[97]

The success of the *yichud* depends upon whether the soul roots of the departed *tzaddik* and that of the visiting kabbalist were the same.[98] The kabbalist absorbs the soul of the departed saint in an act of mystical ascent and theurgic arousal, lost in the soul of the departed saint: "In every act of unification, one should intend to raise up one's own soul and the soul of the *tzaddik*, bound together, with ones own soul absorbed into the other's soul."[99] Vital was clear about the intention of the practitioner: "At the *yichud*, through gravesite postration, one must intend the *tzaddik* to lay forth his soul, to shed the bones that are in the grave and return to life . . . This soul is that which remains in the grave . . . It is as if that *tzaddik*, at that very moment, is alive . . . In every act of unification, one should intend to raise up one's own soul and the soul of the *zaddik*, bound together, with ones own soul absorbed into the other's soul."[100] All the mobility of the *tzaddik*'s soul, with all of its connections in the upper worlds, is transfered to the petitioner,[101] who loses his soul in the soul of the departed saint.[102]

The practitioner could judge the success of the *yichud*. For instance, one of Luria's principal students, Joseph Ibn Tabul, was instructed in the practice of *yichudim* at the gravesite of the *amora* Abba Shaul. "But I forgot them," he wrote, "yet I re-learned them after Luria's death in a dream and I tested them on the gravesites of the *tzaddikim* and they are true and his words are true."[103] Clearly, an initiate could test the power of a gravesite and the spiritual aura of its occupant.

The Safed kabbalists considered different times and circumstances as propitious for *yichudim*. The *yichud* should be performed after midnight on weeknights, though on the Sabbath it could be before midnight. Sabbaths and festivals have no petitional prayers. Hence, petitional *yichudim* are therefore inappropriate for those times, although they can be performed on the intermediary days of the festivals.[104] The eve of the new moon and the full moon are propitious times. On those nights the Divine light, symbolized by the light of the moon, is either wholly blocked or wholly absorbed, so that extraneous demonic forces are unable to steal it.[105]

For the kabbalists, the New Year, with its theme of the Divine decrees, is suffused with a mood of pathos and uncertainty. According to the Zohar,[106] the souls of the righteous await the people Israel's petitions at the New Year. Eventually, the eve of the New Year came to be considered a propitious time for visits.[107] Vital also specified a *yichud* for the penitential month of Ellul.[108]

Prior to the *yichud*, the adept would undergo a rigorous process of soul-searching. The kabbalist had to atone for all his sins and practice mortifications for the graver ones. The practitioner was expected to to avoid anger, to refrain from all inessential speech, to cultivate an attitude of humility, and to atone for his sexual offenses.[109] Ritual immersion was also required prior to the gravesite visit, so that one might remain in a constant state of ritual purity.[110] The role of the gravesite is thus transformed from that of a place that generates pollution to a place whose purity and sanctity were to be preserved.

The scrupulous performance of the required daily liturgy was essential, including the special midnight prayers bewailing the destruction of the Temple, that had been instituted by Cordovero and Luria. The adept was also required to maintain his studies in Jewish law, in addition to his study of mysticism.[111] Qualities of sensuality and pride wouild disqualify one from performing the *yichud*, as they would negate the necessary qualities of holiness, humility and fear of sin.[112]

These practices were necessary, for the gravesite *yichud* was not without psychic risks. The kabbalist's soul could be possessed by a *maggid*, or incarnate spirit of the deceased. This practice has been documented in the case of Joseph Caro and elsewhere in the Safed community.[113] When cleaving to the soul of the deceased, the Rabbi was apt to emerge in a state of Shamanic trance.[114] The practice of the *yichud* was really meant for the fully fledged spiritual adept. If the practitioner was unready for the experience, he would be paralyzed by the confrontation with the *mysterium tremendum* and would be unable to accomplish anything, as Vital described:"One who has begun to attain a certain degree: the spirit rests upon him, but he lacks the wholeness to resolve the voice of prophecy and the holy spirit on his lips, and his tongue does not speak. At the time of the *yichud*, he feels his hair stand on end, his body and limbs shake, his lips move, but his mouth has no power to speak."[115] The transition to a possible loss of ones "self" and absorption into the soul and mentality of the dead could only be practiced by the spiritual elite. Hence the morifications and penitential acts were intended to purify the body so that it would be a pure vessel for the *nefesh* of the deceased. This aspect of the *yichud* practice seems not to have survived among contemporary kabbalists.

Besides the intensity of the experience, the practice of the *yichudim* also involved certain hazards due to the dangers of the site. This was especially the case were the pilgrim reckless enough to visit the site alone. Even Shimon bar Yochai's grave was not entirely safe.[116] Reflecting this apprehension, some Lurianic theorists who spoke against the gravesite visit as the proper context for *yichudim*. Such was the case in a decidedly Lurianic work, Emanuel Chai Ricci's *Mishnat Chasidim*. According to Ricci, the gravesite is haunted by demons that have been created by nocturnal emissions.[117] As even the righteous are tormented by nocturnal emissions, these demons are "waiting to cleave to the holiness and corrupt it." On the basis of this problem, Ricci argued for confining the practice of *yichudim* to the home.[118] Yisrael Meir of Radin, in his popular commentary to the Code of Jewish Law, echoed this concern, writing that ". . . one should not go within four cubits of even a Jewish gravesite for there is a danger of extraneous forces."[119] Vital, however, had been adamant that the gravesite was by far the optimal place for the *yichud*, maintaining that: "It is best to perform the *yichud* on the gravesite . . . because it awakens the *tzaddik* who dwells there. However, if one performs the *yichud* in one's house, this is also unification, but it requires more 'smoothing' (the path) in order for his soul to cleave to the *tzaddik*, while prostration on the grave arouses the *tzaddik* and informs him of the matter at hand."[120]

Despite these potential dangers, gravesites remained charged locales in the communal mind. The incarnate presence of the souls of the righteous infused the land with a new degree of sanctity and spiritual possibility. Aharon Berakhiah of Modena, in his masterful anthology *Ma'avar Yabok*, considered the existence of a physical site a defining aspect of the state of the soul of the departed *tzaddik*. Those who have a recognizable gravesite are considered to be in the *Almah de-itgalyah*, the revealed world, while those who don't are considered to be in the *Almah de-itcasiyah*, the hidden world. This teaching may have originated with the traditions brought to Italy by Israel Saruq, as its main source seems to be Naftali Zvi Bacharach's influential *Emek ha-Melekh*.[121] Vital felt that the more desolate a gravesite was, the more likely it would provide an effective *yichud*: "It is a good thing to go to the gravesites of the righteous, to pray upon them. Indeed, when the gravesites of the righteous are unknown and hidden from society, except for a few individuals . . . then those prayers that a person prays on them are more acceptable to God, and more likely to be heard."[122]

Gravesite pilgrimage, without specifying mystical prostrations, is mentioned several times in the exoteric legal tradition. The *Shulchan Arukh*, or code of Jewish law, recommends pilgrimage to gravesites at certain times.[123] This relationship to the gravesite is echoed by the eighteenth century German codifier Judah Ashkenazi, in popular and altogether un-kabbalistic terminology: "The graveyard is the resting place of the righteous, a holy and pure place where prayer is more fully received. Whosoever prays at the gravesite of the Righteous should not make the dead the object of his prayer, but rather the blessed God, may He have mercy through the merit of the righteous who dwell in the earth."[124]

Even this arbiter of the popular religion portrays the gravesite as a place of soteric, or redemptive possibilities, a place sanctified by the presence of its sacred relic. The pilgrim may pray conventionally in the presence of the *tzaddik*, or prostrate himself in the Lurianic *yichud*, in an attempt to bring about the redemptive *tiqqun*, or repair of the world. In either case, the grave, its structures and the land where it is situated are all charged with the presence of that exemplar of Judaism.[125] The map of sacred gravesites makes up an esoteric map of the spirituality of the region.

In the mystical understanding, the veneration of the grave led to the union with the departed *tzaddik*. This itself was like union with the Divine presence, a repair of the world, that would lead, inevitably, to the restoration of the land and the restoration of the world. This linking to the righteous is intrinsic to classical Judaism. The first business of the

thrice daily petitional prayer instituted by the Pharisees is to link the petitioner to the founding forefathers, (and, recently, the fore-mothers) of
Judaism. According to Meroz: "The essence of the living *tzaddik* prostrating himself on the gravesite in a kind of death, is nonetheless a way of
obtaining the true life. His prostration on the gravesite brings the dead
person to life, even though it temporarily lowers the state of his
neshamah, that is itself a kind of death."[126]

The practice of wandering among the gravesites continued subsequent to Luria's death. The renowned Chayyim ben Atar (c. 1742), author
of the popular work *Or ha-Chayyim*, a commentary on the Pentateuch,
was known to have practiced *gerushim* with his student, Chayyim Yosef
David Azulai (ChYDaH). The founder of Chasidism, Israel Ba'al Shem
Tov, in a letter to his brother, Gershon Kitover, pleaded that his name be
mentioned in the course of any gravesite pilgrimages "for only there is it
possible to configure the 'Holy sparks' properly." [127] A recent account portrays an obscure circle of kabbalists centered around R. Yosef Shlomo
Dayan and R. Shlomo Voltoch, who, up to the last decade, practiced
gravesite prostrations throughout the Galilee and even in the perilous districts of Shechem and Hebron.[128]

Scholars such as Yoram Bilu,[129] Issachar Ben-Ami,[130] and Norman A.
Stillman[131] have documented the establishment of new sacred sites, particularly in development towns in Israel. These studies have, as well,
tended to emphasize the activities of the Moroccan community, both in
Morocco and Israel, as a particularly rich source of religious traditions.
Bilu has documented the phenomenon of the "translocation of a saint
from Morocco as well as through the discovery or renewal of a sacred
place in the locality on the basis of folk beliefs and local traditions."[132]
These sites may be indicated through visitational dreams to one or more
humble members of the community.[133] Bilu views this phenomenon as
an expression of local identity among new immigrants from Middle eastern countries. Such communities were often marginal and econmically
dependent, their members psychically "displaced." This phenomenon
would account for the upsurge of veneration of the grave of Choni ha-
Ma-aggel in Chatzor, a struggling development town. Certainly the construction of a synagogue over Yonatan ben Uzziel's gravestone and the
recent sanctification of the grave of the Morrocan saint Baba Sali, who
had made his home in Netivot, are examples of dispossessed communities claiming the land and thereby validating their presence in the community.

Relics, Texts and Images

With the exception of its maniestations among the Moroccan and Chasidic communities, Judaism's tradition of relic veneration is intimately connected to the return to the Holy Land. Jewish pilgrims and settlers projected the content of their sacred texts onto the blank topography of their land. The graves of the righteous have soteric possibilities. To be gathered around the grave of one *tzaddik* is comparable to being gathered around one spiritual leader or progenitor, producing a tendency to monolithic belief that is foreign to the pluralistic nature of the Talmud and Rabbinic Judaism. Classical Jewish literature quells the cult of personality through values of pluralism and literary decentralization. The Talmudic literature did not devote itself to any one Rabbi over others; there is no cult of Hillel or Akiva in spite of their enormous influence.

The personality cults and social movements of the late middle ages and modernity have their origins in the Zohar, a work of imagination and romance. The cults surrounding Isaac Luria, Shabbatai Tzevi and Moshe Chayyim Luzzatto and the early Chassidic mastersare recreations of the Zohar's cult of Shim'on bar Yochai. In Chasidism, the spiritual master performs the same function as the sacred relic, while the disciple must simply belong to a community that follows a living *tzaddik*. Emotional linkage with the *tzaddik* is the act of unification. The *tzaddik* may himself be performing *yichudim*, or he may simply be a personal intercessor by virtue of force of personality and saintliness. The eros of this mystique of proximity underlay the great social movements that have defined late medieval and modern Judaism: Shabbateanism, Chassidism, Zionism. The Chassidic movement spearheaded a wave of resettlement of the Holy land.

There are further implications in this study that are beyond the scope of this paper. In Rothkrug and Lancaster's formulation, relic veneration leads to the veneration of the land and the veneration of the monarch, and, eventually, to the monarch's image. Judaism has been ambivalent about the role of images, as a result of its aversion to idolatry and the fertility rituals of the Canaanites. While the Romans were saturating their empire with images of Augustus and Hadrian, the coins of the Jewish revolt portrayed citrons, palm fronds and the decorative pomegranates of the Temple. Even a sympathetic governor such as Agrippas symbolized his reign with a cluster of wheat sheaves.

The popular portraits of the great rabbinical figures are late in origin and include many frauds and forgeries. The popular representation of the Ba'al Shem Tov, the founder of chasidism, is actually that of a notorious

Sabbatean of eighteenth century London. The popular representation of Shim'on bar Yochai has no basis in reality, nor does the image of Maimonides reproduced on writing tablets since the nineteenth century. The late ascendance of the image in Judaism dovetails with the wide circulation of disposable reading materials, photography and nationalist aspirations, for the image has best been purveyed by Zionism. Israel's leaders: Herzl, Ben Gurion, Begin, Golda Meir and Moshe Dayan have lent themselves to being transformed into archetypes and icons. Pictures of wonder-working Rabbis such as the Baba Sali of Netivot and the Rebbe from Lubovitch have appeared in traditional Jewish households.

The veneration of gravesites also found its way into the Zionist community. Israel's national anthem *Ha-Tikvah*, composed by Naftaly Hirtz Ember, includes the verse "as long as the blood courses through our veins and the drops of dew collect on the gravesites of our forefathers, as long as throngs of our people still go to the gravesites of the Patriarchs, *Od lo 'avdah tikvatenu*, to return to the land of our fathers."[134] Judaism, after all, had always been cut off from its relics by violence and despair, not by a volitional move away from attachment to the relic and the sacred land that housed it.

So it is that the role of relic veneration in classical Judaism is not exactly as Peter Brown observed: ". . . holy graves existed in both Judaism and Islam. But to exist was never enough. Public and private, traditional religious leadership and the power of the holy dead never coincided to the degree that they did in Western Europe."[135] Perhaps not, but the coincidence does exist on a perhaps more profound level. As Rothkrug has written: "To have the dead enter into the affairs of the living is to have people converse with departed souls."[136] In the case of Judaism, perhaps the order should be reversed: when people converse with departed souls, then the dead enter into the affairs of the living.

Endnotes

    1. *The Cult of the Saints: Its Rise and Function in Latin Antiquity.* Chicago, 1981. p. 3.

    2. See Rothkrug, "German Holiness and Western Sanctity in Medieval and Modern History" *Historical Reflections 15*, No. 1, (1988) : 162; "Popular Religion and Holy Shrines" in *Religion and the People 800–1700* ed. James Obelkevich (Chapel Hill, University of North Carolina Press, 1979) pp. 20–86; "Holy Shrines, Religious Dissonance and Satan in the Origins of the German Reformation," *Historical Reflections 14* (1987):147–286.

3. In Rothkrug's words, this portable sanctity gives rise to "an efflorescence of figurative expression, especially metaphor, (that) allowed people to imagine a world which they previously thought they had somehow *embodied.*" (Rothkrug, "German Holiness and Western Sanctity . . ." : 164). In the Europe of the Reformation, the contrast between fixed and portable sanctity was such that that "regions with few, often no shrines to saints turned Protestant, whereas lands rich in saints' shrines remained Catholic. There are no important exceptions; the correlation is virtually perfect." (Ibid :165). The Reformation was a text-based phenomenon, stressing the ideas of Luther and the soteric effects of reading the Bible. The Catholicism of the Counter-Reformation emphasized the sacred relic, while sanctifying many sites in connection with sacred events and objects. Many *umritte,* places where Jewish communities were massacred in blood libels and accusations of Host desecration, were designated and sanctified during this time. Lewis Lancaster has pointed out that in Hinayana Buddhism's spread through Asia was limited by its requiring the presence of a sacred relic at the base of the Stupa. Mahayana Buddhism placed sacred texts at the base of the stupa. Since these texts were replaceable, their portable sanctity lent itself to Mahayana Buddhism's evolution into its various east Asian forms.

4. *Gittin* 56a–b

5. Rothkrug, "German Holiness and Western Sanctity . . ." :218–222.

6. Ze'ev Vilnay, *Matzevot Kodesh be-Eretz Yisrael* (Holy Monuments in the Land of Israel) (Henceforth "Vilnay") (Jerusalem: HaRav Kook 1951; revised: Ah°iavar 1991) Vol. I, pp. 29–32.

7. See Vilnay I pp. 100–147; Elkan Nathan Adler, ed. *Jewish Travellers: A Treasury of Travelogues from 9 Centuries* (New York: Hermon Press 1966) p. 193; Peter Brown, *The Cult of the Saints* p. 3.

8. Zohar I 127a, Avraham Azulai, *H°esed le-Avraham* (Jerusalem 1991) p. 115; H°ayyim Vital (henceforth "Vital"), *Etz H°ayyim Shaar Tziur ha Olamot* 95c. Quotations from Vital's rendition of the Lurianic canon, the *Shemoneh Sha'arim* (Eight Gates) and the *Etz H°ayyim* (Tree of Life) are from the comprehensive edition of Yehudah Ashlag (Tel Aviv 1962), unless otherwise noted.

9. Kings I 2:10. See Vilnay I, pp. 298–326; See also Elkan Nathan Adler, *Jewish Travellers* p. 119.

10. Vilnay I, pp. 274–276.

11. Vilnay I, pp. 71–72.

12. Vilnay II, pp. 223, 226–228.

13. Samuel 1 25:1; the verb roots RM and GV', that denote "height," color the names of the whole area, the Palestinean *Ramalla h* and the Hebrew *Ramot,* whick overlook *Gibe'a* and *Giv'on.* Today the site of Samuel's grave is a major pilgrimage site for Arabs and Jews in the Jerusalem area. See Elkan Nathan Adler, ed. *Jewish Travellers-* p. 193.

14. Vilnay II, pp. 79–81; Elkan Nathan Adler, *Jewish Travellers.* p. 147.

15. Vilnay II, pp. 87–92.

16. Vilnay I, pp. 49–51.

17. The rabbis were familiar with the unhappy fact of grave looting, as is the case with the graves of Yehudah bar Ilai, Yehudah ben Babba, and the Yenukah (the wonderchild of the Zohar). (*Semah°ot* 13:9). See Vilnay I, pp. 51–53.

18. Elkan Nathan Adler, *Jewish Travellers* p. 97.

19. Sometimes historical mysteries are resolved by these folk traditions. For instance, there is a tradition that the vessels of the Temple were hidden away in a particularly inaccessible ridge of the upper Galilee. Nineteenth century accounts tell of

catastrophes that occurred to those reckless enough to tamper with them.

20. Vilnay II pp. 19–22

21. Vilnay I, p. 21. See Vital, *Sha'ar ha-Gilgullim*, p. 181.

22. c.f. Vital, *Sha'ar ha-Gilgullim* p. 132:

23. The original *Idra* site could not be ignored, so these same kabbalists have re-identified it as the family mausoleum of one of the founders of medieval Safed, Yosi Sargossi.

24. Babba Batra 58a

25. Vilnay I 22–23.

26. Ibid, pp. 147–166.

27. Lionel Rothkrug. "German Holiness and Western Sanctity in Medieval and Modern History":167

28. Michael Ish Shalom, *Matzevot Kodesh* (Holy Tombs—A study of Traditions Concerning Jewish Holy Tombs in Palestine) (Jerusalem:Mosad ha-Rav Kook 1948) p. 86; Elkan Nathan Adler, *Jewish Travellers* p. 125.

29. Ish Shalom *Matzevot Kodesh* p. 76.

30. Vilnay II, 331–335.

31. Vilnay I, p. 37.

32. Vilnay I, p. 43.

33. c.f. Gen. 35:8

34. c.f. Gen. 18:1; There is, additionally, a tradition of oracular trees and groves on mountains in the book of Judges. Deborah sits under her palm (Judges 4:5), while an angel attends the oak at Oprah (Ibid 6:11).

35. Vilnay I p. 23, 147–166, 363–369.

36. Vilnay II 69–74, Ish Shalom *Matzevot Kodesh* p. 135. See also Alex Weingrod, *The Saint of Beersheba* (Albany, SUNY Press 1990) pp. 94–95. Weingrod errs, however, in assuming that the identification of the grave is recent, as it was identified as early as 1210 by R. Shmuel ben Shimshon, in an account that agrees with the geographical relationship of modern H°atzor to the site of Yonatan ben Uzziel's grave at *Amukah* (Elkan Nathan Adler, *Jewish Travellers* p. 107).

37. As reported by Rav Patah°ia in 1180 (Vilnay II p. 54, Elkan Nathan Adler, *Jewish Travellers* pp. 87, 148)

38. c.f. Yosef Karo's *Maggid Mesharim* (ed. 1880, p. 35b)

39. Vilnay II p. 68; Ish Shalom *Matzevot Kodesh* p. 152; Elkan Nathan Adler, *Jewish Travellers* p. 107, Avraham Levi, *Od Yosef H°ai* (Joseph Yet Lives!) (Jerusalem 1986) pp. 83–85.

40. Vilnay I, p. 23.

41. Ibid p. 106

42. Ibid p. 220

43. Ibid p. 149.

44. Genesis 35:19–20 locates Rachel's burial place as by the road in Bethlehem, in the territory of the tribe of Judah, while 1 Samuel 10:2 locates it on the border of the tribe of Benjamin, further north. See Vilnay 1, 147–148. Some comtemporary archeologists are of the opinion that Samuel's grave is actually the Benjaminite tomb of Rachel.

45. Benjamin of Tudela visited the Holy Land in 1170 and described its sacred places. His description is augmented by the accounts of Petah°ia of Regensburg (Ratisbon ?) (1180), who also alluded to Persian traditions that posit the gravesites of 550 "prophets and Amoraim." Petah°ia also identified many gravesites in Persia that are venerated by Jews to this day. They are further augmented by the accounts of Samuel ben

Samson (1210) and Menah°em ben Peretz ha-H°ebroni (1215). Menah°em made a point of relying on local traditions and defending their antiquity (Vilnay I p. 12). An anonymous student of Nah°manides (c. 1272) wrote on gravesites, as did Ashtori ha-Parh°i (early 14th century), Ya'akov ben Natanel ha-Cohen (early fourteenth century and Moshe Basula (c. 1522).

46. The first, compiled by one Uri Ben Shim'on, became the widely distributed *Yih°us ha-Avot*. In Cassalle, Gershon Ben Asher of Shkarmiel took material from *Yih°us ha-Avot*, augmented it with homiletic material and reissued it under the name *Yih°us ha-Tzaddikim* (1561). It is the first published work on the gravesites of the saints, and was translated into Arabic and Ladino. Another missive, published by "the messenger of Zion and the paupers of Jerusalem" (1626), was published in *Zikhron Yerushalayim* (1743). The letter was also translated into Yiddish in 1700, and is also included in the famous work *Ma'aseh Book*. Another such missive, form one Gershom ha-Levi Segel, was published in 1624, and in Yiddish in 1635. This edition was burned by the Catholic Church. Classical works in this mold include Gershom ben Asher's *Sefer Yih°us shel ha-Tzaddikim* (Mantua, 1561), Moshe Reicher's *Sha'arei Yerushalayim* (1863), the descrptions of Joseph Sofer (1762) and Simh°a Yehoshua of Zalozitz (1765), Moshe Hagiz' *Parashat Eleh Masai* (1738) and H°ayyim ha-Levi Horovitz' *H°ibbat Yerushalayim*. which dates from the nineteenth century (Vilnay I p. 24).

The great geographer and folklorist Ze'ev Vilnay's *Matzevot Kodesh be-Eretz Yisrael* (Holy Monuments in the Land of Israel) (Jerusalem: HaRav Kook 1951; revised: Ah°iavar 1991) provides an overview of the entire field, presented in rather popular terms, as does Michael Ish Shalom's *Matzevot Kodesh* (Holy Tombs—A study of Traditions Concerning Jewish Holy Tombs in Palestine) (Jerusalem:Mosad ha-Rav Kook 1948), Presently, the Commitee for the Restoration of Ancient Graves in the Land of Israel has produced its own popular guide, with maps and photographs: *Sefer Kadmoneinu* (Jerusalem: 1989). The contemporary kabbalist Yosef Eliyahu Deitsch in his *Even ha-Shoham VIII* (Jerusalem: Mosdot Anshei Ma'amad, 1990) produced a popular commentary on the thirty-seventh chapter of Vital's *Sha'ar ha-Gilgullim*. A number of medieval reports have been translated in *Jewish Travellers-A Treasury of Travelogues from 9 Centuries*, Elkan Nathan Adler, ed. (New York: Hermon Press 1966).

47. Caleb is described a prostrating himself at the Cave of Mah°pelah in order to gain strength (*Sotah* 34b), Rav Mani prostrates himself and beseeches his deceased father to cast a spell on the Patriarch's household (*Ta'anit* 23b)and an unworthy adventurer in mystical speculations is struck blind and is cured after prostrating himself at the gravesite of R. H°iyya (*Babba Metzia* 85b).

48. The Karaite Segel ha-Matzliah° and Yehudah haDasi also complain about the the pagan aspects of the practice. The Muslim writer Muhammed Albuh°ari in his *Aljemi Azahiah* (1863, brought in Vilnay I p. 51.) wrote "All curses on the Jews, who turn their gravesites into places of worship."

49. *Berakhot* 18a–20a

50. Ibid 18b

51. Ibid 18a–20a

52. Ibid 18b

53. Will of Yehudah ha-Hasid #4, published in preface to *Sefer H°asidim* (Bologna, rep. 1870) Similar customs regarding death and burial from this period are discussed in Joshua Trachtenberg's classic *Jewish Magic and Superstition* (Philadelphia: Jewish Publication Society) pp. 174–180.

54. Ibid #13, #16, *Sefer H°asidim* #236.

55. Ibid #12

56. Ibid #15

57. Ibid #13

58. Ibid #9

59. Ibid #1

60. Ibid #3

61. Ibid #11

62. Ibid #5

63. See also Gershom Scholem *Zohar: The Book of Splendor* (New York: Schoken 1949) pp. 42–43, 96–97, Tishby and Lachover. *The Wisdom of the Zohar*. Translated by David Goldstein Oxford: 1991, pp. 703–714, Werblowsky, R.J. Zwi, "Philo and the Zohar." *Journal of Jewish Studies 10* (1959): 37–44, 112–35. Moshe De Leon, *Sefer ha-Rimmon*. Edited by Elliot Wolfson (Atlanta: Scholars Press, 1988) pp. 305, 328; *Sefer ha-Mishkal*. edited by Jochanan Wijnhoven. (PhD. thesis, Brandeis University, 1964). pp. 38–47; Brakha Zak, "Le-Mekorotav shel Sefer H°esed le-Avraham leR. Avraham Azulai." *Kiryat Sefer 56* (1981) :166.

64. Zohar I 72a, 80b, II 176a, III 168a

65. Zohar II 141a, 142a; III 170a, see Vital, *Etz H°ayyim I* (Tel Aviv 1962), p. 254.

66. Zohar III 70b

67. Zohar III 71b

68. Zohar II 16a–b.

69. The *Merkavah* text *Sefer ha-Heikhalot*, presages the Zohar in portraying the Patriarchs as intercessors with the Divine; c.f. *Sefer Heikhalot:Seder ha-Mah°anot*, in Jellinik, *Beit ha-Midrash 5* (Jerusalem: Wahrmann 1967), pp. 186–187.

70. Zohar I 225b

71. i.e. the Patriarchs: Abraham, Isaac and Jacob, and possibly the Matriarchs, Sarah, Rebeccah and Leah, who are buried at the cave of Mah°pela in Hebron.

72. Zohar III 70b

73. Vital, *Sha'ar Ruah° ha-Kodesh* p. 110

74. Ish Shalom, *Matzevot Kodesh* pp. 129–132; Elkan Nathan Adler, *Jewish Travellers* p. 123.

75. Vilnay II, pp. 118–146, Ish Shalom, *Matzevot Kodesh* pp. 178–179.

76. Vital, *Sha'ar ha-Kavvanot* II p. 191

77. H°ayyim Yosef David Azulai, *Shem ha-Gedolim-Ma'areket Gedolim* 1:37

78. Vital, *Sha'ar ha-Kavvanot II* p. 191, Immanuel H°ai Ricci, *Mishnat Hasidim, Mesekhet Iyyar ve-sivan*, pp. 5–6; *Pri etz H°ayyim* p. 530; *Ateret Zekenim* (on *Orakh H°ayyim* 493); Naftaly Tsvi Bacharach, *Emek ha-Melekh* (Amsterdam, 1653), 12d. See also *Even ha-Shoham VIII* p. 69.

79. Yoram Bilu and H. Abramovich, "In Search of the Sadiq: Visitational Dreams Among Morrocan Jews in Israel" *Psychiatry 48*: 84–85.

80. In his *Book of Gerushim* (Jerusalem 1962), Cordovero recounts visiting the grave of Yossi Daman Yukrat (p. 4), Yehudah bar Ilai (p. 11), Shimon bar Yoh°ai and his son Eliezer (p. 20), and the legendary thaumaturge H°oni ha-Ma'agel (P. 51). See also Lawrence Fine, "Purifying the Body in the Name of the Soul: The Problem of the Body in Sixteenth-Century Kabbalah," in *People of the Body*, Howard Eilberg-Schwartz, ed. (Albany: SUNY 1992). pp.123–124.; Brakha Zak, "Le-Mekorotav shel Sefer H°esed le-Avraham leR. Avraham Azulai." *Kiryat Sefer 56* (1981) :171.

81. See Cordovero, *Tomer Devorah* 5:9, *Or Yakar* 1:57–58, 2: 112–116. The kabbalistic principle embodied here, that of the union of the sefirah yesod, appears also in the text "The Footsteps of our Father Abraham" (Vital, *Sha'ar Ma'amarei RaZa"l* p. 49.)

See also Elliot Wolfson "Images of God's Feet: Some Observationson the Divine Body in Judaism" in *People of the Body*, Howard Eilberg-Schwartz, ed. Albany: SUNY 1992. pp.170–173; Brakhah Zak. "The Exile of Israel and the Exile of the Shekhinah in R. Moshe Cordovero's *Or Yaqar*" (Hebrew) in *Jerusalem Studies in Jewish Thought* 4, Jerusalem: Magnes 1982: 176–179.

82. Vital, *Sha'ar Ruah° ha-Kodesh* p. 109.

83. Among Biblical gravesites, he identified those of Edino ha-Atzani (A hero of the Davidic period, see 2 Samuel 23:10, Vlinay I p. 346), the prophet Joel ben Putiel, King David's general Benyahu ben Yehoyada, and his father Yehoyada' ha-Cohen. The latter two are referred to a number of times in the Zohar (Vital, *Sha'ar ha-Gilgullim* pp. 141, 181). See also Avraham Levi, *Od Yosef H°ai* (Joseph Yet Lives!) (Jerusalem 1986) pp. 89–90.

84. Vilnay I p. 18. He took issue with the relevant view regarding a number of sites, among them Nah°um Ish Gamzo, Pinchas ben Ya'ir, Neh°emiah ha-Amsoni. He also cast aspersions on the veracity of Yoh°anan ben Zakkai's being flanked by his students R. Eliezer and R. Yehoshua (*Sha'ar ha-Gilgullim* p. 185).

85. Vital, *Sha'ar ha-Gilgullim* p. 59.

86. Vital, *Sha'ar ha-Gilgullim* p. 181.

87. Elkan Nathan Adler, *Jewish Travellers* p. 125; Vital, *Book of Visions* (Jerusalem 1990) p. 32.

88. Vital, *Sha'ar ha-Gilgullim* p. 158, *Book of Visions* (*Sefer Hezyonot-Shivh°ei R. Hayyim Vital*) (Jerusalem 1988) pp. 18–19.

89. p. 181

90. See Menashe Ha-Levi Horowitz *Shivh°ei ha-AR"I* #5, Naftaly Tzvi Bacharach, *Emek ha-Melech* 11d Vital, *Sha'ar ha-Yih°udim* (Jerusalem, Mekor H°ayyim reprint 1970) 4b.

91. *Shivh°ei ha-AR"I* #5, brought in Lawrence Fine, "The Contemplative Practice of Yih°udim" in *Jewish Spirituality* p. 89 in *Jewish Spirituality II*, Arthur Green, ed. (New York: Crossroads 1987, pp. 64–98).

92. Vital, *Sha'ar Ruah° ha-Kodesh* p. 75, 111; *Sha'ar ha-Gilgullim* p. 11

93. Vital, *Sha'ar ha-Gilgulim* p. 131. *Sha'ar Ruah° ha-Kodesh* p. 74. See Fine "The Contemplative Practice of Yih°udim." p. 89 c.f. Vital, *Sha'ar ha-Yih°udim* 3d: "In any case it is good to perform these *yih°udim* everyday, and it is more efficacious that preoccupation with the Torah, and through it the souls of the Righteous are drawn forth to impregnate through him. They desire these *yih°udim* very much; they cleave to this same *yih°ud*, drawing forth a great light, which they divide and return to the one who performed that *yih°ud*, revealing to him the secrets of the Torah . . ."

94. See Cordovero's commentary in Abraham Azulai's *Or ha-H°amma* 3:56a. See also Gershom Scholem, *On The Mystical Shape of the Godhead* (Nw York: Schoken 1991) pp. 197–250; Yehudah Liebes, *Peraqim be-Millon Sefer ha-Zohar* ;(Some chapters in a Zohar Lexicon) Ph.D. dissertation, Hebrew University, 1976, (Jerusalem: Hebrew University, 1982) pp. 294–296; Lawrence Fine, "Maggidic Revelation in the Teachings of Isaac Luria" in *Mystics, Philosophers and Politicians: Essays in Jewish Intellectual HIstory in Honor of Alexander Altmann* Jehudah Reinharz, Daniel Swetschinnski, Kalman Bland, eds. (Durham: Duke University Press 1982) p. 146–148.

95. Meir Poppers, *Zohar ha-Raki'a* (Siget, 1875, 22d) *Sefer Limudei Atzilut* 34a, Vital, *Sha'ar ha-Gilgullim* p. 123.

96. Zohar II 114a

97. c.f. Vital, *Sha'ar ha-Gilgullim* p. 149. See also Vital's *Book of Visions* (*Sefer Hezyonot-Shivh°ei R. Hayyim Vital*) (Jerusalem 1988) pp. 2, 18.

98. Vital, *Sha'ar Ruah° ha-Kodesh* p. 108, after Zohar III 71a, See also Cordovero's *Or Yaqar 13* p. 65. Meroz (*Redemption in the Lurianic Teaching*, p. 287) attributes the doctrine of the "soul root" to Vital, who developed and incorporated the idea into the Lurianic system only after Luria's death.

99. Vital, *Sha'ar Ruah° ha-Kodesh* p. 109.

100. Ibid, see also Vital, *Sha'ar ha-Gilgulim*, p. 141.

101. Vital, *Sha'ar ha-Yih°udim* 3c, *Sha'ar Ruah° ha-Kodesh* pp. 75, 109.

102. Although finding a *tzaddik* with the same soul root was desirable, the deceased *tzaddikim* could appear to anybody, whether they had the same soul root or not (Vital, *Sha'ar Ruah° ha-Kodesh* p. 75) If the adept and the deceased were related in some way, a father and son or master and pupil, then success was much more probable(.*Ma'avar Yabok* p. 274; Vital, *Sha'ar ha-Yih°udim* 3d, Vital, *Sha'ar Ruah° ha-Kodesh* p. 109). In *Sha'ar ha-Gilgullim* p. 176, Shmuel Vital writes: "Everything that happened to my father and teacher with his teacher (Luria) from the day he came to know him until the day he passed on to the World to Come, similarly happened to me with my father and teacher on the day of his passing. He told me to fear nothing, to petition him for all my wants at the gravesite, and thus it was . . ."

103. Vilnay I, p. 21. One explanation of gravesite devotions is ended with the ascription "thus I have copied from my teacher's manuscript." (*Sha'ar Ruah° ha-Kodesh* p. 111; *Sha'ar ha-Kavanot* pp. 143, 152.) ; See also Meroz, *Redemption in the Lurianic Teaching* pp. 70–71.

104. *Orah° H°ayyim* 288:9. See Meroz, *Redemption in the Lurianic Teaching*, p. 288. Vital, *Sha'ar ha-Gilgulim* p. 132, *Sha'ar ha-Yih°udim* 5a See also *Even ha-Shoham VIII* p. 47; See also *Mishnat H°asidim, Mesechet Yih°udim* 1:1, Moshe Cordovero *Or Yaqar 9* p. 94.

105. Vital, Sha'ar Ruah° ha-Kodesh pp. 107–108

106. Zohar II 141b

107. *Orah° H°ayyim* 581:4, see Aharon Berachiah de-Modena *Ma'avar Yabok* (Vilna, 1860)p. 276c.f. Gloss to *Orah° H°ayyim* 581:4

108. Vital, *Sha'ar Ruah° ha-Kodesh* p. 126. See Emanuel H°ai Ricci, *Mishnat H°asidim Mesechet ha-Yih°udim* 1:1, Vital, *Sha'ar ha-Yih°udim* 5a,, *Sha'ar ha-Gilgulim* p. 132, *Pri Etz Hayyim* pp. 178–181 (on the rhythms of the Moon). See also Yosef Eliyahu Deitsch, *Even ha-Shoham VIII* (Jerusalem: Mosdot Anshei Ma'amad, 1990) p. 43.

109. Vital, *Sha'ar ha-Yih°udim* 4d

110. Vital, *Etz H°ayyim II* p. 393, *Sha'ar ha-Yih°udim* 5a.

111. Vital, *Sha'ar ha-Yih°udim* 5a

112. Vital, *Ibid* 4d, *Sha'ar Ruah° ha-Kodesh* p.109

113. Vital, *Sha'ar Ruah° ha-Kodesh* p. 10. Joseph Caro's practices are described in Solomon Schechter, "Safed in the Sixteenth Century" *Studies in Judaism* (New York: Atheneum 1958) pp. 240–245 and R.J. Zwi Werblowsky, *Rabbi Joseph Karo, Lawyer and Mystic* (Philadelphia: Jewish Publication Society 1977) pp. 148–188. For an overview of the phenomenon in the Safed community, see Lawrence Fine, "Maggidic Revelation in the Teachings of Isaac Luria" in *Mystics, Philosophers and Politicians: Essays in Jewish Intellectual HIstory in Honor of Alexander Altmann* Jehudah Reinharz, Daniel Swetschinnski, Kalman Bland, eds. (Durham: Duke University Press 1982) pp. 141–157.

114. Such was the case when Luria was possessed by the spirit of the *tanna* R. Yannai, as Vital recounted (*Sha'ar ha-Gilgullim* p. 126.): "On the first of the intermediate days of Passover I went with him to the village that is called *Akvarah*, and through an orchard we entered the tomb of Rabbi Yannai. A spring flowed out of the entrance of the cavern,

and the entrance was very narrow . . . And there (Luria's) soul cleaved to the soul of Yannai. And through his speech he said to him, "I am Yannai, the master of this site. God has said to you, 'Go and say to your disciple, H°ayyim Vital, that he must avoid all slander and idle gossip and random conversation, and that he should be very humble, and I will be with him in every place.'"

115. Vital, *Sha'ar ha-Yih°udim* 5a. See *Sha'ar ha-Yih°udim* 4a–b, *Even ha-Shoham VIII* p.10.

116. Hayyim Vital, *Sha'ar ha-Mitzvot* p. 8.5

117. See Marc Saperstein *Jewish Preaching 1200–1800: An Anthology* (New Haven: Yale University Press 1989) p. 326 n.65.

118. *Mishnat H°asidim; Mesekhet Yih°udim* 1:4. This is in contradiction to Vital, *Sha'ar ha-Yih°udim* 4b.

119. Lit. *h°itzonim*, in the *Mishnah Berurah, Orah° H°ayyim* 559:10:42.There are also legal writings that advise one not to go to gravesites except for funerals; see *H°oshen Mishpat* 427: 57–58, 60–62

120. *Sha'ar ha-Yih°udim* 4b

121. *Ma'avar Yabok* p. 447. See *Emek haMelekh* 11a; see also Gershom Scholem, "Was Israel Sarug a Student of the AR"I?" (Hebrew) *Tziyyon 5*, 1940: 214–243, Ronit Meroz. "Was Israel Sarug a Student of the AR"I?—New Research" (Hebrew) *Da'at 28*, 1992 : 41–56.

122. Vital, *Sha'ar Ruah° ha-Kodesh* p. 76.

123. *Orach H°ayyim* 568:10, 481:4, 505:1. Moshe Isserlis, in his glosses to the Code (Orach H°ayyim 559:10), writes: "(On the ninth of Av) we go to the graveyard immediately upon leaving the synagogue."

124. *Be'er Hetev* to *Orach H°ayyim* 581:17

125. For an example of the application of Eliade's notion of the sacred center to the living Jewish saint, see Arthur Green, "The Tzaddiq as *Axis Mundi* in Later Judaism." *Journal of the American Academy of Religion 45* (1977): 327–347.

126. Meroz, *Redemption in the Lurianic Teaching*, p. 289

127. Vilnay I p. 26

128. Avraham Levi, *Od Yosef H°ai* (Joseph Yet Lives!) (Jerusalem 1986) pp. 65–102. Full body prostration was apparently not practiced by this group.

129. Yoram Bilu and Eyal Ben-Ari "Saint's Sanctuaries in Israeli Development Towns: On a Mechanism of Urban Transformation" *Urban Anthropology Vol 16(2)* 1987: 243–272.

130. I. Ben Ami, "Folk Veneration of Saints Among Moroccan Jews", with S. Morag and N. Stillman, eds. *Studies in Judaism and Islam* (Jerusalem: Magnes Press 1981), also *Folk Veneration of Saints Among Jews of Morocco* (Jerusalem: Magnes 1984).

131. c.f. "Saddiq and Marabout in Morocco," in *The Sepharadi and Oriental Jewish Heritage: Studies*, ed. I. Ben-Ami (Jerusalem 1982) pp. 489–500, and (with Yedidah Stillman) "Pulh°an Me'arot ve-Kivrei Kedoshim be-Aspaqlariyyat Sefrou, Morocco (The cult of Burial Caves and Holy sites in the World-view of Sefrou, Morocco)" in *Shalom Zohar Memorial Volume*, ed. I. Be-Ami (Jerusalem 1991).

132. Ibid : 244.

133. Ibid : 253. See Yoram Bilu, "Dreams and the Wishes of Saint" in *Judaism Viewed from Within and from Without* Harvey Goldberg, ed. New York: N.Y.U. Press pp. 285–313.; Yoram Bilu and H. Abramovich, "In Search of the Sadiq: Visitational Dreams Among Morrocan Jews in Israel" *Psychiatry 48*: 83–92. See also Alex Weingrod, *The Saint of Beersheba* (Albany, SUNY Press 1990).

134. The original text has two redactions: Barkai, Jerusalem 1886 p. 10, New York, 1904, p. 58

135. *The Cult of the Saints: Its Rise and Function in Latin Antiquity.* Chicago, 1981. p. 10.

136. Lionel Rothkrug. "German Holiness and Western Sanctity in Medieval and Modern History" :163

Hillel J. Kieval
Pursuring the Golem of Prague:
Jewish Culture and the Invention of a Tradition

Introduction

The Babylonian Talmud, Sanhedrin 65B, reads:
Rava said: If the righteous wished, they could create a world, as it is written [Isaiah 59:2]: "It is your iniquities that have separated you from your God" (i.e., made a distinction between you and God). Rava created a man and sent him to Rabbi Zera. Rabbi Zera spoke to him but he [the man] did not answer. Then he [Rabbi Zera] said to him: You are from the companions (i.e., a creature created by the rabbis). Return to your dust.

Rabbi Hanina and Rabbi Oshaia spent every Sabbath eve studying the Book of Creation (*Sefer Yeẓirah*); a third-grown calf was created for them, and they ate it.

An observation:
Prague's oldest existing synagogue, the thirteenth-century Altneuschul (Staronová Synagoga) follows an idiosyncratic—and apparently unique—liturgy during Friday evening services. Psalms 92 (The psalm for the Sabbath day) and 93 are said in their entirety and then *repeated* before the cantor issues the formal call to prayer (*Barekhu*).

A modern rendition of the Golem story reads:
Der Golem
During the reign of Rudolph II there lived among the Jews of Prague a man named Bezalel Löw, who, because of his tall stature and great learning, was called "der hohe" [the Great] Rabbi Löw. This rabbi was well versed in all of the arts and sciences, especially in the Kabbalah. By means of this art he could bring to life figures formed out of clay or carved from wood, who, like real men, would perform whatever task was asked of them. Such home-made servants are very valuable: they do not eat; they do not drink; and they do not require any wages. They work untiringly; one can scold them, and they do not answer back.

Rabbi Löw had fashioned for himself one such servant out of clay, placed in his mouth the Name (a magic formula), and thereby brought him to life. This artificial servant performed all of the menial tasks in the house throughout the week: chopping wood, carrying water, etc. On the

Sabbath, however, he was required to rest; therefore, before the day of rest had begun, his master removed from his mouth the Name and made him dead. Once, however, the rabbi forgot to do this and calamity ensued. The magic servant became enraged, tore down houses, threw rocks all around, pulled up trees, and carried on horribly in the streets. People hurried to the rabbi to tell him of the situation. But the difficulty was great; the Sabbath was already at hand, and all labor—whether to create or to destroy—was strictly forbidden. How, then, to undo the magic? The rabbi's dilemma with his Golem was like that of the sorcerer's apprentice and his broom in Goethe's poems. Fortunately, the Sabbath had not yet been consecrated in the Altneu synagogue, and since this is the oldest and most honorable synagogue in Prague, everything is set according to it. There was still time to remove the Name from the crazy youth. The master hurried, tore the magic formula from the mouth of the Golem, and the lump of clay dropped and fell in a heap. Alarmed by this event, the rabbi did not wish to make such a dangerous servant again. Even today pieces of the Golem are to be seen in the attic of the Altneu synagogue.[1]

★ ★ ★

The oft-cited passage from the Tractate Sanhedrin, many scholars have argued, constitutes the literary core of the Golem legend in Jewish culture, the tale of the artificial being, created from earth and clay, and brought to life through the miraculous combination of letters.[2] The anecdote concerning Rava and his colleagues is embedded within a larger discussion, which sets forth permissible versus non-permissible forms of magic. It is apparent from the tone of the story, as well as from more explicit statements that follow, that the Talmud views the activities of the rabbis in question as being perfectly acceptable. Righteousness, one might infer, involves more than moral perfection. Ultimately, it constitutes both a striving after and an imitation of God, which for the truly righteous has no limits. The rabbis have extended the sentiment in Isaiah, that human sinfulness erects a barrier between God and his creatures, to suggest the obverse: that in the absence of sin, individuals can in fact become God-like, even to the extent of creating life. Apparently, however, even the most righteous would-be creators of life suffered a major limitation to their art. Though their creatures could apparently understand the spoken word, they were denied the power of their own speech. Thus when Rabbi Zera could not get Rava's creature to respond to him, he immediately suspected that it was in fact an artificial creation made by one of his colleagues and ordered it to "return to its dust."

The Golem motif has undergone a long and meandering evolution from antiquity to our own times, when the tale seems to speak of cybernetics and aritificial intelligence while retaining strong elements of doom that hark back to Faust and Frankenstein.[3] What we know as the *Book of Creation (Sefer Yezirah)*—one of Judaism's earliest mystical texts, dating anywhere from the third to the sixth century C.E.—may or may not be the work referred to in Sanhedrin 65b. In seeking to understand the secrets of creation, it proposes "thirty-two paths of wisdom," consisting of combinations of the ten basic numerals and the twenty-two letters of the Hebrew alphabet.[4] At least one modern scholar argues that the *Sefer Yezirah* is not merely a speculative work but rather has as an underlying goal the actual creation of artificial life.[5] This conclusion may remain a controversial one for some time. It is eminently clear, however, that a number of medieval Jews who read the work understood it in this practical light. The most prominent example of this trend is the 12th and 13th century rabbi Eleazar of Worms, one of the exemplars of German-Jewish pietism. Eleazar's commentary to *Sefer Yezirah* went so far as to enumerate instructions for the actual creation of a Golem. The kabbalistic writings of Abraham Abulafia of Spain and the so-called *Pseudo-Saadya*—a 13th century text of French-Jewish origin—similarly testify to the interest of medieval Jewish mystics in the "practical" arts of creation.[6]

Among early-modern Jews tales of the creation of life by pious individuals seem to have been most common in Poland, where, beginning in the 17th century, an important, new motif was added. Now the creature of the rabbis is understood to be not only a servant, who performs all sorts of physical labor for his master, but also a source of danger. One of the earliest literary depictions of this theme comes from a non-Jewish source, Christoph Arnold, who reports in a letter written in 1674 on the practice of Golem-building among Polish Jews.

> After saying certain prayers and holding certain fast days, they make the figure of a man from clay, and when they have said the *shem hamephorash* [the explicit—and unmentionable—name of God] over it, the image comes to life. And although the image itself cannot speak, it understands what is said to it and commanded; among the Polish Jews it does all kinds of housework, but is not allowed to leave the house. On the forehead of the image, they write: *emeth*, that is, truth. But a figure of this kind grows each day; though very small at first, it ends by becoming larger than all those in the house. In

order to take away his strength, which ultimately becomes a threat to all those in the house, they quickly erase the first letter *aleph* from the word *emeth* on his forehead, so that there remains only the word *meth*, that is, dead. When this is done the Golem collapses and dissolves into the clay or mud that he was [. . .] They say that a *baal shem* [literally, master of the Name (of God)] in Poland, by the name of Rabbi Elias, made a Golem who became so large that the rabbi could no longer reach his forehead to erase the letter *e*. He thought up a trick, namely that the Golem, being his servant, should remove his boots, supposing that when the Golem bent over, he would erase the letters. And so it happened, but when the Golem became mud again, his whole weight fell on the rabbi, who was sitting on the bench, and crushed him.[7]

That Arnold's report is based either on the first- or second-hand testimony of Polish Jews is supported by the individual details of the account as well as its reverberations in the Hebrew literature of the period.[8] The Rabbi Elias in question is Elijah of Chelm (d. 1583), an important talmudic scholar, kabbalist, and wonder worker, who possessed secret knowledge of the "Holy Names" of God. It is not surprising that Jews should have attributed to popular healers (*ba'alei shem*) the ability to create life, since both healing and the act of creation, according to the mystical tradition, involved the purposeful manipulation of words and letters. Zevi Hirsch Ashkenazi, a descendent of Elijah of Chelm, told a similar story to his son Jacob Emden (1697–1776), the leading German rabbi of the 18th century. Yet this tale, recorded by Emden in his autobiography and elsewhere, omits the wordplay that had occupied a central position in the accounts of Christian Hebraists (i.e., *emeth* and *meth*) and also allows a less drastic fate to befall his ancestor Rabbi Elijah. In Emden's version, the Golem does not crush and kill his unfortunate creator but only renders him cut and bruised.[9]

Sometime between the 17th and the 19th century—precisely when is not clear—the Golem tradition among European Jews appears to have taken a decisive turn, attaching itself to the life and career of Prague's most famous Jew after Franz Kafka, Rabbi Judah Löw ben Bezalel (ca. 1520–1609), known in western literature as "The Great (*der Hohe*) Rabbi Löw," and in traditional Jewish culture by the acronym *Maharal*. Judah Löw's activity in Prague fell during the reigns of the Habsburg emperors Maximilian II (1564–1576) and Rudolf II (1576–1612), a period often referred to as the "Golden Age" of Czech Jewry, during which time imperial policy demonstrated remarkable tolerance toward Jews and Protestants alike, Jewish cultural life flourished, and the Jewish population—particularly in Prague—grew significantly.[10] The Maharal presided over one of Europe's great talmudic academies; pioneered important reforms in Jewish education; and produced a large literary oeuvre that bestowed pride of place to Judaism's homiletical tradition ('aggadah or narrative). But no evidence suggests that he ever engaged in activities associated with the creation of a Golem. While he does appear to have had an interest in the speculative side of Jewish mysticism, Judah Löw is not known for having been a dévoté of the so-called "practical kabbalah"; and, unlike Elijah of Chelm, Judah Löw was not a ba'al shem.[11]

Nevertheless, virtually every literary evocation of the Golem legend since the first half of the nineteenth century has incorporated two new elements: Judah Löw is understood to be the Golem's creator and Prague's Jewish Town is portrayed as the locus of events. Precisely, it is the Prague of Rudolph II that is recalled, the capital city of one of Europe's most eccentric, cosmopolitan, and tolerant monarchs, patron of the arts and the occult sciences, supporter of the astronomers Johannes Kepler and Tycho de Brahe, and suspected Protestant sympathizer.[12] When Rudolph became emperor in 1576 he moved the imperial court from Vienna to Prague, which now, in the words of Frances Yates, "became a center for alchemical, astrological, magico-scientific studies of all kinds. [. . .] Prague became a Mecca for those interested in esoteric and scientific studies from all over Europe." It was, again in her words, "a melting pot of ideas, mysteriously exciting in its potentiality for new developments."[13]

It is possible that the modern version of the Golem tale settled on Prague as the locus of events because of a "general knowledge" that it was there during the age of Rudolph that occult science and magic, humanistic pursuits and textual study, appear to have coexisted in a creative mix the likes of which were rarely scene—even in Renaissance Europe. To posit this hypothesis, however, is to answer very little. The Golem tale, after all, is one of many built around the life and personality of Judah Löw. Rudolph may represent little more than the rabbi's alter-ego; he may simply be the Gentile king in a story created by and for Jews. And one still would like to know where this version of the legend originated. Did it constitute a piece of the "local knowledge" of Prague Jews, generated in Bohemia and recounted as a form of self-understanding; or was it shared simultaneously by a number of different local cultures? Did both Jewish and Gentile communities "know" and transmit—hence remember—the tale?

The only "hard" piece of evidence we have linking the Maharal to the intellectual universe of Rudolph's court is a brief entry in a Hebrew chronicle written by the Maharal's contemporary and fellow resident of Prague, David Gans, in 1592.[14] A student of both the Cracow luminary, Moses Isserles, and Judah Löw, Gans had taken the unusual step for a Jew of his era of devoting himself mainly to the "secular" sciences: mathematics, astronomy, geography, and history. Around the year 1600 he made the acquaintance of two of Europe's leading astronomers—the Dane Tycho Brahe and the German Johannes Kepler—both of whom were living in Prague at the time and enjoying the patronage of the imperial court. Gans managed to visit the two in their "observation rooms" on at least three occasions, and he wrote about the encounters in his own work on astronomy, *Neḥmad ve-Na'im* (Delightful and Pleasant).[15] His chronicle of world history, *Ẓemaḥ David* (The Offspring of David) was completed in the aftermath of a century of cataclysmic events that included the expulsion of the Jews from Spain, the rise of the Ottoman Empire, the Protestant Reformation, and wars of religion in Central Europe; the book ended with a summary of the year 1592 and with profiles of some of Prague's luminaries. It is in this context that he wrote the following:

> Our lord the emperor [. . .] Rudolph, may his glory be exalted, in the full measure of his graciousness and correctness sent for and called upon our master Rabbi Löw ben Bezalel and received him with a welcome and merry expression, and spoke to him face to face [literally, *peh 'el peh*, mouth to mouth] as one would to a friend. The nature and quality of their words are mysterious, sealed, and hidden [*setumim, ḥatumim, ve-ne'elmim*]. This took place here in the holy community of Prague on Sunday, the third of Adar, 352 [1592].[16]

In view of the fact that the encounter in question involved a member of Gans's own community and purportedly took place not only in his own lifetime but in the months preceding the completion of his work, it would be reasonable to suppose that Judah Löw and Rudolph II did meet on at least one occasion. The nature of the interaction and the content of their discussion, however, cannot be retrieved. Judah Löw may have preferred to keep the details confidential, or he may have been enjoined by the imperial court to do so. It is also conceivable that Gans wished to intimate with his choice of words—"mysterious, sealed, and hidden"—a topic of conversation relating to mysticism and the occult sciences, whether Jewish or gentile. Any conclusions are necessarily speculative. But there is no evidence to suggest that Gans's account of the royal meeting encouraged, in the short run, a *local* tradition tying the Maharal to practical kabbalistic arts.

Precisely when a body of legend and popular wisdom developed around the figure of the Maharal remains largely an enigma, but the degree of our indecisiveness depends to a large extent on the methods we use to attack the problem. If one were to proceed as a literary historian (following the lead of Gershom Scholem, Moshe Idel, Sigrid Mayer, et al.) what one would look for are paper trails—formal, written stories linking the Maharal to the creation of a Golem. On this point the record seems clear enough: nothing appears during the Maharal's lifetime; nor are they found in the seventeenth and early eighteenth century, when tales of Golem making circulate among both Jews and non-Jews, but mainly in connection with Elijah of Chelm.

When Moses Meir Perles (1666–1739), a descendent of the Maharal, produced the first biography-cum-genealogy of his illustrious predecessor, Megilat Yu?asin, in 1727, the theme of Golem-making was likewise absent—although Perles did include other traditions associated with the life of the Maharal.[17] The first written source that gives voice to a Maharal Golem legend does not appear until 1841, about which more will be said later. All of this leads the literary historian to conclude that the story of the Golem of Prague is a quite modern creation. It could not have existed before 1730 (or Perles would have known about it), yet we can be fairly certain that it enjoyed popular currency in Prague before 1840. Thus, as Gershom Scholem writes, the Golem legend "was transferred from R. Elijah of Chelm to R. Löw at a very late date, apparently during the second half of the eighteenth century."[18]

The rough coincidence of timing and geography has led Vladimír Sadek to speculate that is was Polish Hasidism that generated the modern connection of the Golem legend to the Maharal and to Prague.[19] He observes that the Beshtian Hasidim and their pietistic predecessors venerated the Maharal and saw him as a spiritual precursor. Ze'ev Gries relates, moreover, that some of the same publishing houses that were responsible for the diffusion of Hasidic books in the the late-eighteenth and early-nineteenth century also reissued the works of Judah Löw. The Koznitzer Rebbe, R. Israel ben Shabbetai, is a case in point. An enthusiastic publisher of works on *halakhah* and midrash and a great admirer of the Maharal—whose works had been out of print for generations—R. Israel reprinted many of these accompanied by his own commentaries.[20]

It is one thing, however, to acknowledge an elective affinity between Polish Hasidism and the Maharal and quite another to establish a role for Hasidism in the Golem saga. One major obstacle to making such an argument is the fact that the Prague Jewish community (as opposed to that of Moravia, for example) appears to have been largely cut off from and immune to Hasidic influence until the First World War. Although pre-emancipatory Czech Jewry enjoyed close ties to a number of Polish-Jewish centers, none of these was in areas dominated by Hasidism. The first documented appearance of Hasidim in Bohemia occurs after 1914, when refugees from Galicia—among them the entourage of the Belzer Rebbe—stream into the country.[21] More problematic still is the relationship of Hasidism to the theme of Golem-making. Moshe Idel calls our attention to the "obvious absence of the golem legend" in the formative years of Polish Hasidism. "Hasidic literature," Idel writes, "richer in legends than all the Jewish mystical literature, ignored this peculiar type of legend." Tales of Golem-making may have been excluded from Hasidism's early repertoire, he suggests, because of the assumption that lies at the core of Hasidic thought that spiritual perfection is attainable— not through miracle or magic—but through the mystical performance of prayer and the *miẓvot*. When R. Menahem Mendel of Kotsk was told about the wondrous powers of a wonder-worker, he is said to have responded, "Can he also make a Hasid?"[22]

An alternative to the literary-historical approach might be found in ethnography and the study of folklore. What the ethnographer wishes to know is not when literary texts were produced, but what a culture "remembers" and recounts, especially through oral transmissions. But how to get at these acts? Communal and family traditions can often be inscribed in decorative art, tombstone carvings, communal record books, family Bibles, and the like; if one cannot always work backwards from these sources to original expressions of beliefs or ideas, one nevertheless can see in them evidence for the presence of a given motif in the general culture of the community. One "window of opportunity" for ethnographic observation was opened up in the 1720s when the Prague Jewish community embarked on a renovation of the Maharal's tombstone and, more or less simultaneously, a rabbinical descendant of Judah Löw— Isaiah Katz, who served as rabbi of Ungarisch Brod (Uherský rod) in Moravia—instructed the secretary of the Prague Jewish community,

Moses Meir Perles, to write the family chronicles.[23] As noted earlier, Perles' work, *Megilat Yuḥasin*, makes no mention of a Golem tradition; and, although legends involving the Maharal's grave may already have been in circulation at the time, the decorative accompaniments to the new tomb do not allude to a Golem theme.

I should also mention two other folkloristic possibilities that have yet to yield much fruit. One was brought up by Vladimír Sadek in the context of his argument in favor of a Hasidic origin to the Maharal-Golem tale. Sadek observes that Hasidim accord the gravesite of the Maharal the same treatment that they would give the final resting place of any *zaddik*, making pilgrimages to it and placing on it prayers and petitions.[24] Anyone who has visited the old Jewish cemetary in Prague knows that this is true. But it is no less obvious that thousands of non-Hasidim—both Jewish and Christian—also visit Judah Löw's grave every year and engage in comparable behavior. The problem is that we do not know when this practice began or who started it. It is possible that the folklorists are right in looking to the early eighteenth century, sensing that the renovation itself was either an indication of a kind of "Maharal cult" or an act of "invented tradition." But it may also be the case that the Maharal's grave did not attract pilgrims until the early twentieth century, when Jewish refugees from Eastern Europe reminded Prague Jewry of its own cultural history by seeking out the graves of numerous rabbis, all of whom were part of the living memory of Polish orthodoxy—if no longer of Czech Jewry.

To date neither enthnography nor literary history has succeeded fully in explaining the convergence of the Golem legend with Prague and the Maharal. Admittedly, Scholem and Idel have established the Polish tradition associated with Rabbi Elijah of Chelm as the most likely, immediate predecessor of the Prague venue. And folklorists are probably correct in guessing that some type of new, or renewed, veneration of the Maharal took root in Prague around the 1720s or 1730s. This was during a period of rapid growth and development of the Jewish community: the Jewish Town made up nearly half the population of Prague's Staré Město (Altstadt), and about 28 percent of the city's five districts combined, during the first decades of the eighteenth century.[25] It was also a time in which David Oppenheim (1664–1736) consolidated unprecedented political and religious authority, occupying—at various points and in combination—the positions of *rosh yeshivah*, Chief Rabbi of Prague, and Chief Rabbi of Bohemia. The rabbinical establishment in Prague during the second, third, and fourth decades of the eighteenth century appears to have been deeply implicated in kabbalistic studies. Frederic Thieberger claims that Oppenheim himself was a kabbalist, but one can point to other figures as well: Naftali Kohen, a great-grandson of the Maharal and former Chief Rabbi in Frankfurt am Main, who moved to Prague after 1711; and Jonathan Eibeschütz (1690–1764), a charismatic preacher and Rosh Yeshivah, who was known to have dealt in amulets and who, later in life, stood accused of being a secret follower of the "false Messiah," Shabbetai Zevi.[26]

But there are crucial connections that have yet to be drawn. It may well be that rabbinic elites in Prague in the 1720s and 1730s—in particular the students and faculty of the city's *yeshivot*—fostered a magical-kabbalistic reinterpretation of the life of the Maharal. If this was, indeed, the case, then it is to the traffic between Poland and Prague in students and teachers that one needs to look for the transmission of the early-modern Golem tale to the Bohemian capital. Continued human and intellectual commerce after 1740 might explain the internalization of Maharal traditions within Polish Jewry—especially Hasidism—which one finds by the nineteenth century. A venue of the 1720s or 1730s would also imply that the elite circles in Prague, in producing a Maharal cult, actually were engaged in a process of historical projection, in which the mystical pursuits and cultural fashions of the present were attributed to an earlier, heroic age and to an older historical figure.

And what does one make of the custom maintained by the Alt-neuschul to repeat the 92nd Psalm on Friday evening? The skeptical impulse—probably correct—would lead one to view the practice as relatively recent (i.e., post-sixteenth century), the justification for which was sought in the evolving cult of the Maharal. It is possible that the repetition originated from practical, perhaps even *halakhic*, considerations. Here I am drawn to the claim made by the ethnographer and biblical scholar J.J. Schudt in his compendium *Jüdische Merckwürdigkeiten* (1714–18), purportedly on the basis of Jewish testimony, that Prague's Altneuschul possessed an organ.[27] If this claim is true, and assuming that it was generally agreed that the *halakhah* did not permit the playing of an organ on the Sabbath, the practice in the Altneuschul may have been to allow musical accompaniment for the introductory Pslams on Friday evening (95–99 and 29) but not once the Sabbath had formally begun. Pslam 92, which is introduced as "A Song for the Sabbath Day," might well have been viewed as a liturgical demarcation between the sacred and the profane—

sung once to the accompaniment of the organ and once without, as the prayer which marked the start of the Sabbath in the synagogue.[28]

The crucial point seems to be that, while the organ eventually was removed from the Altneuschul—possibly during the rabbinate of Ezekiel Landau (1713–1793)—the custom of repeating Psalm 92 remained. Landau, who was born and raised in Opatów (Poland), and who assumed the Chief Rabbinate of Prague in 1754, may have played a dual role in the reinvention of the Golem tradition: insisting on the removal of the synagogue organ and reinforcing the connection between Polish and Bohemian rabbinic culture. By the time ethnographers set out to collect the stories that Prague Jews told about themselves, in the 1830s and 1840s, the community had "mythologized" the practice, locating its justification in a heroic narrative, a legend associated with the venerable rabbi of the Prague Renaissance.

I readily admit that the limb on to which I have just climbed is unsteady and that a more research is needed before feelings of vertigo can reasonably be eliminated. A proper research agenda might take the following tacts: a reexamination of Jewish communal records in Prague in the eighteenth century, particularly as they relate to Yeshivah life and the rabbinate; a rereading of the writings of Oppenheim, Eibeschütz, and Landau; and a new effort to get at the popular culture of both Jewish and non-Jewish Bohemians. The opening up of libraries and archives in East Central Europe in the last few years should be helpful to a certain extent. But much of what is called for involves a new reading of old materials with an eye to a new set of questions.

What we do know is this: the first literary records of the Golem of Prague come to us by way of nineteenth-century ethnography and folklore, relatively new fields of inquiry in the 1830s, inspired by a mixture of Enlightenment criticism, Herderian anthropology, and budding romantic nationalism. Jakob Grimm, of the famous brothers who were among the major practitioners of these arts in Germany in the early part of the century, published a version of the Polish legend in the journal *Zeitung für Einsiedler* in 1808. He was, however, apparently unaware of any association of the Golem theme with the city of Prague.[29] Berthold Auerbach is to be credited with the first literary attribution of the Golem legend to the Maharal, having included it in his 1837 historical novel *Spinoza*.[30] But the first individual to transmit in written form a *tale told by Prague Jews* concerning the Maharal and a Golem of his creation was the non-Jewish

journalist and folklorist Franz Klutschak (1814–1886). He published his
story in 1841 in a Prague monthly devoted to the investigation of world
cultures, which went by the name of *Panorama des Universums*.[31]

Omniverous in its interests, *Panorama* offered cultural/anthropologi-
cal pieces on Europe and Austria (separate rubrics), Asia, Africa, America,
and Oceania, as well as examples of "narratives, legends, and folktales"
from different parts of the world. In 1838 Klutschak had published a set
of short pieces on the "Old Jewish Cemetery of Prague and Its Legends,"
the opening story of which also dealt with the Maharal, though not as
the creator of a golem.[32] His story "Der Golam [*sic*] des Rabbi Löw,"
which appeared three years later, formed one of four tales which
Klutschak offered under the heading: "Legends, Fables, and Stories from
Bohemia. Partly newly told, partly retold, by F.K."[33]

A Jewish physician by the name of Leopold Weisel (1804–1873), who
grew up and lived most of his life near the town of Domažlice in south-
western Bohemia, worked at the same time as a kind of partner in arms
to Klutschak. Weisel's career is testimony to the fact that the self-
conscious recovery of oral traditions is a decidedly *modern* act in which
secular intellectuals, in the throes of social and cultural change, seek to
save something of the traditional society that is fast slipping away for ever.
He acquired his medical education in Prague—probably from about
1824 to 1830—during which time he lived in the Old Jewish Town and
supported himself as a private tutor for a number of Jewish families. Sensing that he stood at a historical turning point, he took it upon himself to
capture the rich folk traditions of the ghetto, apparently by interviewing
older residents and recording their stories.[34]

Weisel occupied himself in the 1830s and 40s with the collection and
dissemination of the folk wisdom of Jewish Prague, publishing his earliest efforts alongside those of Klutschak in *Panorama des Universums*. In
1838 his "Pinchasgasse: Eine jüdische Volkssage" appeared, a tale about a
poor peddler who lived in Prague "over two hundred years ago," who
traced the streets of the city with a pack over his shoulder by day and
"studied the law" by a dim lamp in his dirty room at night.[35] The story
was reprinted in 1847, together with four other tales collected by Weisel,
as "Sagen der Prager Juden" in the immensely popular collection *Sippurim: Eine Sammlung jüdischer Volkssagen*, published by Wolf Pascheles.[36]
Among the five stories retold here by Weisel was his own version of the
golem legend, a minor classic of brief fiction and the benchmark for subsequent retellings to the eve of the First World War.

These two modern renditions of the golem tradition were published six years apart; yet they build upon rather different narratives. Interestingly, Klutschak's is the longer and more elaborate of the two, written with an eye for descriptive detail in lyrical German prose. By contrast, Weisel's rendering is sparse and unembellished. The Klutschak tale proceeds as a prose piece that is annotated with ethnographic and scholarly observations, and punctuated with "insider" information and terminology.[37] Thus the designation "der Hohe Rabbi Löw" alternates in the text with the more homey (and Yiddish) "Rabbi Liwa"; the Altneuschul, the narrator tells us—"as is well known"—was built by the Angels immediately after the destruction of the Temple in Jerusalem. Though the story clearly is narrated in a distinct voice, it is equally apparent that the storyteller has his informants within the Prague Jewish community. The tale is offered as an example of authentic Prague-Jewish folk tradition.

The story is also remarkable for the completeness with which it accounts for circumstances and motivations in the golem narrative. Klutschak offers a compelling explanation, for example, for the Faustian element of power run amock, which occupies a central position in all modern versions of the Prague account. With one foot in the practical kabbalah and the other in popular psychology, he writes that "fortunately, the Golem was not aware of his magical powers," and that Rabbi Löw was able to devise ways to keep his creature under control.

> He prepared for each of the seven days of the week a talisman, which held the strength of the Golem in check and directed its will only toward good; and when the Rabbi went to the synagogue in the evening [lit., in the evening at the start of the day], he would remove the old *shem* (talisman) from the mouth of the Golem and exchange it with a new one.[38]

Similarly, Klutschak's narrative accounts for Rabbi Löw's absence from the synagogue on that critical Friday evening, the reason for the rabbi's ordering first the stopping and then the repetition of Psalm 92, and the fact that the Sabbath had not yet officially begun. Relying, once again, on one layer of Jewish folk tradition to explain another, Klutschak has the cantor urging an early start to the Friday evening service so that the souls in purgatory might cool themselves off in the brooks and streams whose enjoyment was prohibited to Jews on the Sabbath day.[39] Attending to a sick and dying daughter, Rabbi Löw had decided not to pray with the community that evening, but was brought running to the synagogue when the cries of people watching the Golem start to tear apart the building reminded the rabbi of his failure to provide the Golem with a new talisman. The reason for the violence lay in the simple fact of consciousness: the creature was becoming aware of his own power.

By the time the Maharal arrives at the Altneuschul, the Golem is tearing at its walls; the doors to the Holy Ark (which, Klutschak knows— and makes certain that his readers know that he knows—rested in the eastern wall of the Altneuschul) have fallen off; and the candelbra has fallen to the ground, so that all is darkness "as though the end of the world were approaching." At this point, practicality reigns. The Maharal orders the prayers halted so that he can put the proper talisman in the mouth of the Golem. Once peace is restored and the candles rekindled (which can only be done on a weekday), the Jews "laud the wisdom of Rabbi Löw, who has saved them from destruction, and pray more ardently than ever the first [sic] Psalm and the Sabbath prayers; [they] send a prayer to Jehovah with such fervor for the recovery of the great Rabbi's daughter, that Jehovah calls upon the Angel of Death ["malach Hama-wod" (sic)], whom He already has sent to the Rabbi's house, to return."[40]

Leopold Weisel's "Der Golem," though spare and impoverished com-pared to Klutschak's tale, is the better-known of the two and appears to have served as the basis for subsequent borrowings. For all of its brevity, the author does provide a few bits of extraneous information, which afford the reader a small window on to his self-conceived ethnographic mission. When he writes, in a brief introduction to "Sagen der Prager Juden," that "countless tales are attached to the old synagogues and the narrow streets; and nearly every tombstone in the large, old cemetary offers up material to one tale or another," he betrays his own indebted-ness to the romantic movement. At the same time, he assures the reader that he transcribed the stories as he heard them "from the mouth of the old," thus attesting to his reliability as a transcriber of folk traditions.[41]

Weisel introduces his story with a tantalizing aside that relates directly to my inquiries in this essay: he excuses the brevity of the story that is to follow with the observation that this "popular tale" [*Volkssage*] has already been used by various writers. "It seems to me superfluous," he writes, "to rework such a well-known story. I shall present it briefly if only so that one not think that I did not know it."[42] Weisel clearly means to indicate that *this particular* Golem story enjoyed wide circulation in his day, both as a piece of literature and as a tale told by the Jews of Prague. He hardly deemed it worthy of reproducing because it already was widely acknowledged as belonging to the folkloristic treasury of Jewish Prague. Weisel's statements in this regard make me more confident in assigning a date for the provenance of the Prague tale that is a good deal earlier than what most literary historians have allowed up to now.

★ ★ ★

The efforts of Weisel and Klutschak to retrieve—and ultimately recast—Jewish Prague's folk traditions in literary language echoed beyond the confines of the Jewish community. The writer Václav Bolemír Nebeský, a romantic poet of the Byronist mold, published a Czech version of Prague Jewish tales for the literary journal *Květy* in 1844.[43] Nebeský had formed close ties to Jewish university students in both Prague and Vienna and had become convinced of the desirability of recruiting Jews to the cause of Czech nationalism. His collection of Jewish legends in the Czech language appeared in the same year in which he joined forces with Siegfried Kapper (1821–1879) and David Kuh (1818–1879)—both Prague Jewish writers—to launch a newspaper campaign in both the Czech and German press designed to create a Czech-Jewish cultural alliance.[44] The effort to "capture" Jews to the cause of Czech culture and politics achieved only moderate success before the 1880s. Nevertheless, the various literary codifications of Czech folklore that occurred in the nineteenth century, including Josef Svátek's *Pražksé pověsti a legendy* and Alois Jirásek's *Staré pověsti České*, reserved an important place for the Jewish stories that the writers–cum–ethnographers of the 1830s and 40s had so assiduously collected.[45]

What united these various endeavors was the desire to uncover and disseminate the "cultural memory" of the Czech nation, to put forward a "usable past" that could be employed in the service of the construction of a collective identity. A cultural program of this type inevitably combined anthropological investigation and creative embellishment, with equal importance ascribed to the oral traditions of the older generation and to the literary imagination. In adopting Weisel's "Legends" for their own rewritings of Czech folk culture, the modern authors of the Czech nation were, in effect, claiming "Jewish Prague" as part of their own inheritance. Why did they do this? Did non-Jewish Czechs have their own "memory" of Judah Löw and Prague's "Golden Age"? Did they "remember" the Golem tradition in the same way that the Jews of Prague did or differently? Did this adoption of Jewish lore as something that was simultaneously Jewish and Czech indicate the existence of a significant area of shared culture? Perhaps, in appropriating part of Prague's Jewish past the Czech nationalist writers were deepening their own claim to Bohemia itself, thereby strengthening their challenge of German cultural, economic, and political domination. When seen as part of the process of creating a "useable past," the "discovery" of the Maharal and his Golem among the oral tales of the Czechs themselves added to the antiquity and legitimacy of the Czech national position. Both the Jews and the Czechs were "there" before the Germans; they shared the same wise men, the same legends, the same monsters.

The recovery of myth and legend in the nineteenth century provides evidence for the fact that oral traditions can in a very real sense *follow* literary traditions—even invented ones. The stories of the modern Czech masters were avidly read—their renderings of the Jewish past "remembered"—and over the ensuing decades both assimilating Jews and educated Gentiles literally recounted the same legends. Thus, when the Czech sculptor Ladislav Šaloun was commissioned to erect statues outside the newly-constructed Town Hall in Prague's Staré Město, or Altstadt, in 1912, he produced two figures, both drawn from the folklore of the city. One was a knight—the so-called Iron Knight—of Czech lore. And the other was the Maharal, Rabbi Judah Löw, depicted in a frankly modernist (and unlikely) pose flanked by his granddaughter (unclothed). The granddaughter is handing Judah Löw a flower in allusion to a well-known Czech—and Jewish—tale concerning the master's ultimate demise at a very advanced age: death, whose designs the Maharal had been able to thwart for so long, hides in the fragrance of the rose.[46]

And a final example of the role of literature in the production of popular wisdom: the story that *everyone* knows about the Maharal and the Golem (and reproduced in film and in plays and even in contemporary Czech anthologies) is the newest of them all. In the decade immediately preceding the First World War, the Jewish world was treated to a series of publications based on sensational manuscript "discoveries," said to have been uncovered at the "Imperial Library" of the city of Metz in eastern France. The first such work, *Sefer goral ha-ʻassiryot* (Book of Lots of Tens), which appeared in 1904, purported to describe a system whereby people were able, through various manipulations of Hebrew letters, to receive oracular answers to their queries. This was followed in 1905 with the publication of a commentary to the Passover *Haggadah* said to have been written by the Maharal. The work that elicited the most interest, however, appeared in 1909 under the title *Sefer nifla'ot Maharal 'im ha-golem* (Book of the Wonders of the Maharal with the Golem). The publisher of each of the "manuscripts" was Yudel Rosenberg (1859–1935), a Hasidic rabbi and dayyan living at the time in Warsaw. Rosenberg claimed to have received all three manuscripts from one Hayyim Sharstein, whom he later described as a relative, and even reproduced letters, purported to have been written by Sharfstein, in the introductions to two of the works—letters which described the difficulties that he had had copying by hand from the worn and faded pages of the forgotten works and which alluded to other "discoveries" that he would soon make available to Rosenber. Not surprisingly, perhaps, there is no "imperial library" in Metz and there was no Hayyim Sharfstein. The author of all three works in question (including the oft-reprinted *Haggadat ha-Maharal*) was Yudel Rosenberg himself.[47]

Rosenberg claimed that both the Haggadah commentary and *Sefer Nifla'ot Maharal* had been written down by the Maharal's son-in-law, R. Isaac Katz (Isaac ben Samson ha-Kohen, d. 1624). In fact, much of the Haggadah commentary (which went under the names *Divrei negidim* and *Leshon limudim*) was derived from the Maharal's work on the exodus from Egypt, *Gevurot ha-Shem*; the rest was Reb Yudel's.[48] As far as *Sefer Nifla'ot Maharal* is concerned, the narrative is laced with historical innacuracies, improbabilities, and terms and concepts that make sense only in a *Polish* context.[49] This story, too, is Reb Yudel's, yet people continue to read and remember it, not only as a "genuine" account, but as the *only* account of the creation of the golem that they know! Subsequent twentieth-century authors have adopted Rosenberg's forgery wholsesale. The Hebrew writer and folklorist, Micha Yosef Ben Gurion, anthologized it in is *Mekor Yehuda* [Fountain of Judah]. The Galician-born writer, Chaim Bloch, adapted Rosenberg's stories (or should we say Rabbi Isaac Katz's stories?) to German prose, a project which *he* claimed to have produced through "ethongraphic research" on the Russian front. Bloch's collection was soon translated into English and was widely distributed in the U.S. for many years under the title *The Golem: Legends of the Ghetto of Prague*.[50] *Nifla'ot Maharal* was aslo adapted by the Yiddish poet H. Leivick for his drama entitled "Der Goylem." As recently as 1980, Judaica Press of New York published a work by the Brooklyn-based writer Gershon Winkler entitled *The Golem of Prague*, an unabashedly romantic and pious rewriting of Yudel's "invented tradition," which promoted itself as "a new adaptation of the *documented* stories of the Golem of Prague" (my emphasis).[51]

What has gone largely unnoticed in the almost automatic acceptance (and retransmission) of Rosenberg's twentieth-century rendering of the golem legend is the fact that this version constitutes a radical rewriting of the tale. Here the story of the creation and adventures of the artificial being is embedded within a larger narrative of Christian accusations of Jewish "ritual murder." The motif of the blood libel is inscribed in the book's subtitle: "Lekhol ha-'otot veha-moftim asher pa'al ha-ga'on ha-gadol Maharal mi-Prag 'al yad ha-golem 'asher bara lehilaḥem neged ha-'alilat [sic] dam" (All of the signs and wonders, which the great and wise Maharal of Prague effected with the aid of the Golem, which he created [in order] to battle against the blood libel).[52]

I suspect that most contemporary readers of these tales do not appreciate the irony, that the supposed need to build a monster out of clay in order to defend the Jews against popular violence inspired by the Christian accusation of Jewish ritual murder would *not* have made much sense to a Jew living in the Prague of Rudolph II and the Maharal. The Jewish community in Rudolph's capital at the end of the sixteenth century simply did not face any serious accusations of ritual murder, and I know of no evidence to suggest that the Maharal dispensed much, if any, energy defending his people against this libel. The salience of the ritual murder motif, which serves as the architectural underpinning of the entire collection of stories—and, indeed, which constitutes Yudel Rosenberg's chief literary contribution to the legend—is the strongest evidence by far of the work's twentieth-century provenance. It was the Europe of Reb Yudel, not of the Maharal, that witnessed a proliferation of accusations—and even of formal, criminal trials—against Jews on the charge of ritual murder. Starting in 1882 in Hungary and continuing down to the eve of the First World War, Central and Eastern Europe served up a half-dozen sensational murder trials, each prosecuted by agencies of the modern state, in which the case against the Jewish defendants hinged on a modern reworking of the old canard that Jews require the blood of innocent Christians for their religious rites.

Viewed, then, from the perspective of the twentieth-century, Yudel Rosenbeg's rendition of the golem tale functions—on two levels—as a sort of wishful thinking. The Maharal's creature of clay does not act as a mere servant, to perform menial tasks at the bidding of his master. Like the superheroes of our own comic-book culture, the golem rescues the community from powerful enemies who would do it harm. Beyond the wish for a supernatural resolution to human conflict, Rosenberg's *Nifla'ot*

Maharal gives expression to another pious hope. As the long-lost manuscript of R.Yitzhak Katz, it is supposed to silence all of the modern "doubters" within the Jewish fold, the rationalists and sceptics, who had cast doubt on the authenticity of the folkloristic accounts of the Maharal's powers.[53] Rabbi Yitzhak's Maharal is a Jew of the "old school," unsurpassed in wisdom, adept at the secrets of *kabbalah*, dignified in his dealings with the non-Jewish world, and a strict defender of *halakhah*. He personifies for Yudel Rosenberg the bedrock faith of our fathers and mothers, and he, too, is a redeemer of Israel.

In the well-known version, the Golem does his job, saving the Jews of Prague from the certain catastrophe that would have resulted from a false accusation of ritual murder. But the purpose of this story was not to instill hope and confidence in its readers. It was a cautionary tale of a type quite different from the original legend. At least as far back as the seventeenth-century Polish rendition, the source of danger had always been understood to reside within—within the confines of community; in the very process of the creation of artificial life. Throughout the twentieth century, the tale has been remembered as a distortion, as if it had always been concerned with the danger posed by the outside world. Much has been lost, I think, in the translation; much can also be inferred with regard to the changing nature of the Jewish-Gentile relationship in East Central Europe.

Endnotes

1. Leopold Weisel, "Der Golem," in *Sippurim: Eine Sammlung jüdischer Volkssagen, Erzählungen, Mythen, Chroniken, Denkwürdigkeiten und Biographien berühmter Juden,* edited by Wolf Pascheles, Erste Sammlung, 4th ed. (Prague: Pascheles, 1870), pp. 51–52 (all subsequent citations are to this edition). All translations, unless otherwise indicated, are mine.

2. On the theme of the Golem in the history of Judaism, see: Gershom Scholem, "The Idea of the Golem," in his *On the Kabbalah and Its Symbolism* (New York: Schocken Books, 1965), pp. 158–204; Moshe Idel, *Golem: Jewish Magical and Mystical Traditions on the Artificial Anthropoid* (Albany: SUNY Press, 1990); idem, "The Golem in Jewish Magic and Mysticism," in Emily D. Bilski, ed., *Golem! Danger, Deliverance and Art* (New York: The Jewish Museum, 1988), pp. 15–35; and Byron L. Sherwin, *The Golem Legend: Origins and Implications* (Lanham, MD, 1985).

3. On the importation of the Golem motif to general European culture, see: Sigrid Mayer, *Golem: Die literarische Rezeption eines Stoffes* (Bern and Frankfurt a.M., 1975); Arnold L. Goldsmith, *The Golem Remembered, 1909–1980: Variations of a Jewish Legend* (Detroit: Wayne State University Press, 1981); Beate Rosenfeld, *Die Golemsage und ihre*

Verwertung in der deutschen Literatur (Breslau, 1934); and Emily Bilski, "The Art of the Golem," in Emily D. Bilski, ed., *Golem!*, pp. 44–111.

4. On *Sefer Yezirah*, see Scholem, "The Idea of the Golem," passim, and esp. pp. 167–173.

5. See Idel, *Golem*, pp. 9–21.

6. Scholem, "The Idea of the Golem," pp. 171–93; Idel, "The Golem in Jewish Magic and Mysticism," pp. 20–30; and Idel, *Golem*, pp. 56–61, 81–86, 96–104.

7. Christoph Arnold to J. Christoph Wagenseil, 1674. Letter appended to Arnold's *Sota hoc est Liber Mischnicus de uxore adulterii suspecta*, pp. 198–99. Translated in Scholem, "The Idea of the Golem," pp. 200–201; reproduced here with minor revisions.

8. Moshe Idel has found what appears to be an earlier reference to the creation of a Golem by R. Elijah of Chelm in the manuscript testimony of a Polish kabbalist contained in Ms. Oxford 1309. The Polish kabbalist, writing perhaps between the 1630s and 1650s relates the following:

> I have heard, in a certain and explicit way, from several respectable persons that one man, [living] close to our time, in the holy community of Chelm, whose name is R. Eliyahu, the master of the name, who made a creature of of matter [*Golem*] and form [*zurah*], and it performed hard work for him, for a long period, and the name of *emet* was hanging upon his neck, until he finally removed, for a certain reason, the name from his neck and it turned to dust. (Quoted in Idel, *Golem*, p. 208.)

9. Jacob Emden, *Megillath sefer* (Warsaw, 1896), p. 4; his *Responsa*, II, No. 82; and his *Mitpahat Sefarim* (Altona, 1769), p. 45a). See also Scholem, "The Idea of the Golem," pp. 199–201; and Mayer, *Golem*, pp. 25–30.

10. A survey of Bohemian Jewish history during this period, and a description of the career and writings of the Maharal can be found in my *Languages of Community: The Jewish Experience in the Czech Lands* (Berkeley: University of California Press, 2000), pp. 10–36. See also the following works: Otto Muneles, ed., *The Prague Ghetto in the Renaissance Period* (Prague, 1965); and Anna Drábek, "Die Juden in den böhmischen Ländern zur Zeit des Landesfürstlichen Absolutismus," in *Die Juden in den böhmischen Ländern* (Munich and Vienna, 1983), pp. 123–43; Frederic Thieberger, *The Great Rabbi Loew of Prague: His Life and Work and the Legend of the Golem* (London, 1955); A. F. Kleinberger, *Ha-ma?shava ha-pedagogit shel ha-Maharal mi-Prag* (The Pedagogical Thought of the Maharal of Prague [Jerusalem, 1962]); and Vladimír Sadek, "Rabbi Loew—sa vie, héritage pédagogique et sa légende," *Judaica Bohemiae* 15 (1979), 27–41; and Byron Sherwin,; and Byron Sherwin, *Mystical Theology and Social Dissent: the Life and Works of Judah Loew of Prague* (London and Toronto, 1982).

11. Cf. Thieberger, *The Great Rabbi Loew*, pp. 8–44; and Sherwin, *Mystical Theology*, passim.

12. On the life and policies of Rudolph II, see R.J.W. Evans, *Rudolf II and his World: A Study in Intellectual History, 1576–1612* (Oxford, 1973); idem, *The Making of the Habsburg Monarchy* (Oxford, 1979); and Frances Yates, *The Rosicrucian Enlightenment* (London and Boston, 1972).

13. Yates, *The Rosicrucian Enlightenment*, p. 17.

14. A second, purported, contemporaneous account, said to have been written by Judah Löw's son-in-law Rabbi Isaac ben Samson Ha-Kohen, discovered in the latter's

"Venitian Bible," and published in 1872 in the Hebrew periodical *Ha-Maggid*, is—I am convinced—a modern forgery.

15. On Gans's scientific interests, see George Alter, *Two Renaissance Astronomers: David Gans, Joseph Delmedigo* (Prague, 1958). On Gans's activity as a historian, see Mordechai Breuer, "Mavo" (Introduction) to *Sefer Ẓemaḥ David le-rabi David Gans* (Jerusalem: Magnes Press, 1983), pp. i–xxxiii.

16. *Sefer Ẓemaḥ David* [1983 ed.], p. 145.

17. Meir Perles, *Megilat Yuḥasin* (Warsaw, 1864); German trans. by S. H. Lieben, "Megillath Juchassin Mehral miprag," in *Jahrbuch der Jüdisch-Literarischen Gesellschaft* 20 (1929): 315–336.

18. *Encyclopaedia Judaica* (Jerusalem, 1972), 7:755; also Scholem, "The Idea of the Golem," pp. 202–03. Here he dates the transferral of the legend from Poland to Bohemia "toward the middle of the eighteenth century."

19. Vladimír Sadek, "Stories of the Golem and their Relation to the Work of Rabbi Löw of Prague," *Judaica Bohemiae* 23, 2 (1987): 86; also idem, "Rabbi Loew," p. 36, where he likens the popular pilgrimages to the gravesite of the Maharal to those undertaken by Hasidim to the graves of their Zaddikim.

20. Ze'ev Gries, *Sefer, sofer, ve-sippur be-reshit ha-ḥasidut* (Tel Aviv: Hakibbutz Hameuchad, 1992), p. 56.

21. On the presence of Galician refugees in Prague, see Hillel J. Kieval, *The Making of Czech Jewry: National Conflict and Jewish Society in Bohemia, 1870–1918* (New York and Oxford, 1988), pp. 174–178.

22. Moshe Idel, "The Golem in Jewish Magic and Mysticism," p. 35.

23. On the possible significance of these two events, see: Sigrid Mayer, pp. 33–34; and Goldsmith, pp. 30–31.

24. Sadek, "Rabbi Loew," p. 36.

25. Anna Drábek, "Die Juden in den böhmischen Ländern," pp. 127–28.

26. Thieberger, *The Great Rabbi Loew*, pp. 77–79; see also the entry by Gershom Scholem on Eibeschütz in *Encyclopaedia Judaica* 6: 1074–76.

27. "Es ist auch recht was merckwürdiges, und wohl sonst nirgends in der Welt anzutreffen, daß die Juden zu Prag in der Alt-Neuen Synagog, wie sie dieselbige nennen, eine Orgel haben, die sie aber zum Gottes-Dienst weiter nicht brauchen, als nur, wann sie Freytags Abends das Bewillkommungs-Lied des *Schabbes* singen, und darbey ein Jud diese Orgel schalget. . . ." (Johann Jacob Schudt, *Jüdische Merckwürdigkeiten* [Frankfurt and Leipzig, 1714–18], 1:218.)

See also ibid., 2:284–85: "Jedoch gar viele glaubhaftige Juden, die lang in Böhmen gewesen, haben mich für gewiß versichert, daß zu Prag in der Alt-Neuen *Synagoge* eine Orgel seye, die man aber weiter nicht brauche, als zu dem Gesang dieses Liedes (zu Bewillkommung des instehenden *Sabbaths*) in der Neuen *Synagoge* aber, wie auch an Theils andern Orten habe man zu denen Stimmen der Sänger auch allerhand *musicalische Instrumenten.*"

Schudt explains that "Kabbóles Schabbes" means "die Empfangung oder Bewillkommung des Sabbaths" (p. 284). It is unclear from this description, however, whether the "Bewillkommungslied" refers to the *Kabbalat Shabbat* service in general or specifically to the liturgical poem "Lekha Dodi."

28. I have never seen this explanation offered for the Altneuschul practice. It has,

however, been suggested to me by Alexandr Putík, that if the Altneuschul did possess an organ, it was not used on the Sabbath, and that the instrument itself was probably removed from the synagogue during the tenure of Ezekiel Landau. David Ellenson, in a recent article, notes that the precedent of the "Prague organ" occupied a prominent position in the controversy between Orthodoxy and Reform in Hamburg in 1819. (David Ellenson, "A Disputed Precedent: The Prague Organ in Nineteenth-Century Central-European Legal Literature and Polemics," *Leo Baeck Institute Yearbook* 40 [1995]: 251–64.)

29. Jakob Grimm, in *Zeitung für Einsiedler* (1808); reprinted in his *Kleinere Schriften*, vol. 4 (Berlin, 1869) as well as in Beate Rosenfeld, *Die Golemsage*, p. 41.

30. Berthold Auerbach, *Spinoza: Ein Denkerleben*. 2 vols. (Stuttgard, 1837), ch. 12. I am indebted to Shnayer Z. Leiman for this reference. See Leiman, *The Adventure of the Maharal of Prague in London: R. Yudl Rosenberg and the Golem of Prague*. Fourth Annual Lecture of the Victor J. Selmanowitz Chair of Jewish History. (New York: Touro College, 2000), p. 18.

31. The full title of the journal was *Das Panorama des Universums zur erheitenden Belehrung für Jedermann und alle Länder* (Prague, 1834–1848). Klutschak was later to become editor-in-chief and then publisher of the Prague German newspaper *Bohemia*. (See Heribert Sturm, ed., *Biographisches Lexikon zur Geschichte der böhmischen Länder*, [Munich, 1984], 2:186; and *Österreichisches biographisches Lexikon 1815–1950* [Graz-Cologne, 1965], 3: 426.)

32. *Das Panorama des Universums* 5 (1838): 292–95. (Knihovna Národní Muzea, Prague.)

33. *Das Panorama des Universums* 8 (1841): 75 ff. Of this collection of four tales, "Der Golam des Rabbi Löw" is the only one to deal with a specifically Jewish theme. It has been reprinted in Hillel J. Kieval, *Languages of Community: The Jewish Experience in the Czech Lands* (Berkeley: University of California Press, 2000), pp. 231–233.

34. See Jana Doleželová, "Questions of Folklore in the Legends of the Old Jewish Town Compiled by Leopold Weisel (1804–1870 [sic])," *Judaica Bohemiae* 12 (1976): 37–50; also S. Winninger, *Große jüdishce National-Biographie* (Czernowitz, 1925–36), 4:610.

35. Leopold Weisel, "Die Pinchasgasse: Eine jüdische Volkssage," *Das Panorama des Universums*, 5 (Prague, 1838): 328–332.

36. The original title of the 1847 collection was: *Gallerie der Sipurim* [sic], *eine Sammlung jüdischer Sagen, Märchen und Geschichten als ein Beitrag für Völkerkunde*. It incorporated legends, tales, and biographical sketches from Biblical, rabbinic, and popular sources, and drew on the literary efforts of a number of writers other than Weisel, including Siegfried Kapper (1821–79) and Salomon Kohn (1825–1904). The collection was reissued unchanged in 1851 (following the 1848 Revolution) and then in numerous editions to the end of the nineteenth century—three between 1853 and 1864 alone. A German edition in Hebrew type appeared in 1860. A popular version was published by Jakob B. Brandeis, Pascheles' son-in-law and successor, in 1887, which itself ran through three editions in 20 years (1909). (See Peter Demetz, "Nachwort" to *Geschichten aus dem alten Prag* [Frankfurt a.M. and Leipzig, 1994], pp. 361–76; and Otto Muneles, *Bibliographical Survey of Jewish Prague* [Prague, 1952], passim.)

A word of caution regarding the widely-diffused 1921 edition (*Sippurim: Prager Sammlung jüdischer Legenden. In neuer Auswahl und Bearbeitung.* [Vienna and Leipzig:

R. Löwit, 1921]): Wholesale changes have been made to the nineteenth century editions: titles have been altered; stories have been rearranged and abridged; new wording has been substituted; and, in some instances, incorrect authorship attributed.

37. Parenthetic remarks inform the reader that the Hebrew *shem* is to be understood as "talisman"; *golam* as "servant"; *godolah* as "adult," and so forth. A footnote explains to the reader the practice in which Jewish women light candles on the eve of the Sabbath. Characteristically, the explanation is neither *halakhic* nor textual, but folkloristic, based on a popular midrash concerning the consumption of the forbidden fruit in the Garden of Eden.

38. Klutschak, "Der Golam [*sic*]des Rabbi Löw," *Panorama des Universums* 8 (1841): 77.

39. Klutschak explains this point with a footnote:

> "According to the beliefs of the Rabbis, the souls in purgatory also observe the Sabbath; as soon as the celebration of the Sabbath begins in the synagogue, they leave the place of their suffering and flee to the nearest water in which they bathe and cool off until the Sabbath ends. For this reason the Jews are not allowed to drink or draw from brooks and streams on the Sabbath, so as not to disturb the souls during their refreshment." (Ibid.)

40. Ibid., p. 78. As to the misidentification of the Psalm, I can only surmise a reason. It is possible that on this occasion Klutschak's informants failed him. It is also possible, though less likely, that the practice in the Altneuschul was to *begin* the Friday evening prayers with Psalm 92, omitting the previous six.

41. Weisel, "Der Golem," in Pascheles, *Sippurim*, pp. 50–51.

42. "Diese Volkssage ist oft schon von verschiedenen Schriftstellern benützt worden—und es scheint überflüssig, eine so bekannte Sage nochmals zu bearbeiten; damit man aber nicht glaube, ich hätte sie gar nicht gekannt, will ich sie hier nur in der Kürze anführen" (ibid., p. 51).

43. "Pověsti židovské," *Květy*, 6 August 1844.

44. See Kieval, *Languages of Community, pp. 65–94*.

45. Josef Svátek, *Pražské pověsti a legendy* (Prague, 1875). Alois Jirásek, *Staré pověsti české* (Prague, 1893).

46. The Maharal was either eighty-nine or ninety-seven at the time of his death, depending upon what one accepts as his date of birth: 1512 or 1520.

47. On Yudel Rosenberg's authorship of the works in question, see Ira Robinson, "Literary Forgery and Hasidic Judaism: The Case of Rabbi Yudel Rosenberg," *Judaism* 40, no. 1 (Winter 1991): 61–78; Eli Yassif, "Introduction" to Yehuda Yudel Rosenberg, *Ha-golem mi-Prag u-ma'asim nifla'im aherim* (The Golem of Prague and Other Wonderous Deeds) by Yehuda Yudel Rosenberg (Jerusalem: Mosad Bialik, 1991), pp. 7–72; Abraham Benedict, "Haggadat Maharal o 'aggadat Maharal" (The Haggadah of the Maharal, or the Aggadah [i.e., Legend] of the Maharal)? *Moriah* 14, no. 3–4 (1985): 102–113; and, most recently, Leiman, *The Adventure of the Maharal of Prague in London*.

48. Rosenberg was able to attach approbations from two leading Warsaw rabbis, Petahia Hornblum and Isaac ha-Kohen Feigenbaum, to his edition of the *Haggadah* commentary. For the most part, he succeeded in passing the work off as genuine. It was published in many editions, both by Rosenberg and by others, and has also been accepted

by a number of rabbis as an halakhic authority "relative to the laws and customs of the Passover Seder." See Robinson, "Literary Forgery," p. 68.

49. Thus, for example, Rosenberg identifies the Cardinal in Prague at the time of the Maharal as "Jan Sylvester." No such bishop existed in the city. (Jan Sylvester was the name of a sixteenth century Christian Hebraist.) I also doubt if there was in fact a "priest-sorcerer" in Prague named Thaddeus (Polish: Tadeusz?) who spread the accusation of Jewish ritual murder.

50. Chayim Bloch, *The Golem: Legends of the Ghetto of Prague.* Trans. from the German by Harry Schneiderman (Vienna, 1925).

51. Gershon Winkler, *The Golem of Prague.* Illustrated by Yochanan Jones (New York: The Judaica Press, 1980.)

52. The inscription is more elaborate on the inside title page of the Piotrków edition: "This is the book of miracles of the Maharal . . . in which he miraculously performed great deeds and wonders through the golem, which he created through the wisdom of the Kabblah to fight against the blood libel, which was widespread in his day, and to make clear to the eyes of all the truth that the Jews are innocent of this charge." Rosenberg, *Sefer nifla'ot Maharal* (Piotrków, 1909).

53. Rosenberg explains his introduction to *Nifla'ot Maharal* that while many knew and spoke of the ability of the Maharal to fashion a creature out of mud and clay (*tit ve-ḥomer*), this knowledge had weakened with the passage of time. Some "maskilim" even wished "to deny and uproot everything," to say that it was only a legend (*ki akh mashal hi zot*). For a while, Rabbie Ezekiel Landau had set the record straight by venturing, himself, to the attic of the Altneushul, where the remains of the golem were said to rest (and thereafter forbidding anyone else to enter this space). But "many people have begun to doubt the matter again." And, Rosenberg adds, "and all because this whole episode had not been inscribed in writing in Jewish chronicles" (*vekhol zeh ba'avur shelo nehkak ba-sefer kol ha-'inyan bein korot hayehudim*).

Now, the definitive truth has been revealed. "Now all of Israel will know that it all was recorded in writing by the son-in-law of the Maharal, the great Gaon R. Y. Katz, zz'l." (Introduction to *Sefer nifla'ot Maharal*, Piotrków, 1909.)

Robert E. Kohn
Spinozan Judaism

In one of the books on his concentration camp experiences, Primo Levy remembered a terrifying period in which the Nazis called out a list of names each day of inmates that were being removed from the barracks. It was well known that these men had been selected for the gas chambers. There was one man who would pray each day that his name not be called, and then, when it was not, would thank God profusely for saving his life. Levy's remark "I spit on that man's prayers" would inevitably come to my mind when I asked God for some favor, until I stopped asking, or even giving thanks. One becomes a different kind of Jew when he stops believing in God.

Several years ago I happened to read in George Alexander Kohut's 1939 edition of *Nathan the Wise* by Gotthold Ephraim Lessing that the playwright, a Lutheran, saw in his cherished friend, Moses Mendelssohn, who was his model for the pious Nathan, "a second Spinoza, who would do honor to his [Jewish] nation" (43). It was only after Lessing had died, that Mendelssohn

> "suffered a mortal hurt when he learned [. . . that Lessing] had openly professed Spinozism. To one who ardently cleaved to the idea of a personal God, Providence and the immortality of the soul, it seemed almost inconceivable that a dear comrade, who had never hidden the thoughts of his heart, should have dissembled his convictions" (72).

If, then, Benedict Spinoza did not believe in a God that he could talk to, who would protect him when he was most vulnerable, and would keep faith with him in death as in life, what could he have believed in that was affirmative?

In 2000, G.H.R. Parkinson published a new translation of Spinoza's *Ethics*. The 17th century philosopher unambiguously quashed the idea of a personal God when he wrote that

> "Some people imagine God in the form of a man, consisting of body and mind, and as subject to passions [; . . .] how far these people stray from a true knowledge of God" (86). "God is without passions, and is not affected by any emotion of pleasure or of pain" (299).

Spinoza was equally negative with regard to a provident God, insisting that "neither intellect nor will belong to the nature of God"(91). As far as an afterlife is concerned, "Our mind [. . .] can be said to endure, and its existence can be defined by a certain time, only in so far as it involves the actual existence of the body"(304). These are the negatives; the positive attribute of Spinozism is that

> "[T]he omnipotence of God has existed actually from eternity, and will remain to eternity in the same actuality"(92). "[T]here can exist no thing which is in itself and outside God"(93). "[A]ll things were produced by God with supreme perfection; for they have followed necessarily from a given most perfect nature [. . . and] could not have been created by God in any other way or in any other order"(103, 104).

Through Spinoza's writing, I have discovered a God that I can believe in. Science tells us nothing about the universe before the "big bang" but my intellect tells me that there was an original Creator, and Spinoza respected "The idea of God which exists in us [as] adequate and perfect"(299). In the Shema, we acknowledge the eternity of God's kingdom, which is consistent both with Spinozan Judaism and with modern scientific judgment.

However, I must pick and choose my way through synagogue services. Most of the prayers in the *siddur* presume a personal and provident God and some seem to promise life after death—I balk at those prayers. Besides the *Shema,* there are three notable exceptions, quoted here from the *Siddur Sim Shalom* (The United Synagogue of Conservative Judaism, New York, 1998). First there is the *Ma'ariv* prayer, which is recited every evening immediately prior to the *Shema*:

> "Praised are You, Adonai our God, who rules the universe, Your word bringing the evening dusk. You open with wisdom the gates of dawn, design the day with wondrous skill, set out the succession of seasons, and arrange the stars in the sky according to Your will. *Adonai Tz'va-ot*, You create day and night, rolling light away from darkness and darkness away from light. Eternal God, Your sovereignty shall forever embrace us. Praised are You Adonai, for each evening's dusk"(28).

This prayer celebrates the perfection of God's creation that Spinoza extolled. That it was ordained billions of years ago, and that it continues on its own each day as the *Ma'ariv* prayer asserts, affirms that God "is the

immanent but not the transitive cause of all things"(Spinoza 93). I prefer
to think that the original creation was perfect and that its apex was and
is human creativity, notwithstanding the fact that some of this world's
most regrettable failures are unwanted by-products of that creativity.

The second prayer is the *Adon Olam*, written in Spain in the 11th
century by Solomon ibn Gabirol, which has been part of the morning
service since the 15th century:

> "Before creation shaped the world, / eternally God reigned alone;
> but only with creation done / could God as Sovereign be known.
> When all is ended, God alone / will reign in awesome majesty.
> God was, God is, always will be / glorious in eternity.
> God is unique and without peer, / with none at all to be compared.
> Without beginning, endlessly, / God's vast dominion is not shared.
> But still—my God, my only hope, / my one true refuge in distress,
> my shelter sure, my cup of life, / with goodness real and limitless.
> I place my spirit in God's care; /my body too can feel God near.
> When I sleep, as when I wake, / God is with me; / I have no fear"(187).

The first six lines could have been written by Spinoza as well as by his
Sephardic predecessor. The last four lines imply a provident God, and I
accept them only as an expression of humanity's love for God. "The person who understands himself and his emotions clearly and distinctly feels
pleasure," wrote Spinoza, "and this is accompanied by the idea of God
[. . . So that] he loves God, [. . .] the more so, the more he understands
himself and his emotions"(298, 299).

This love for God may be better understood in the context of the
third prayer, the Mourner's *Kaddish*:

> "May God's name be exalted and hallowed—*Yitgadal v'yitkadash sh'mei
> raba*—throughout the world that He created, as is God's wish. May God's
> sovereignty soon be accepted, during our life and the life of all Israel. And
> let us say: Amen.
> May God's great name be praised throughout all time.
> Glorified and celebrated, lauded and worshipped, exalted and honored,
> extolled and acclaimed may the Holy One be, praised beyond all song and
> psalm, beyond all tributes that mortals can utter. And let us say: Amen.
> Let there be abundant peace from heaven, with life's goodness for us and for
> all Israel. And let us say: Amen.
> May the One who brings peace—*Oseh Sholom bi-m'romav*—to his Universe
> bring peace to us and to all Israel. And let us say: Amen."(184).

It is one of the sacred precepts of Judaism that the Mourner's *Kaddish* says nothing about death and everything about honoring God. As someone who has lost his brother and mother within the last year, this paradox has been puzzling. Perhaps, Spinoza has some explanation for it—when we honor God we honor our loved ones, for their existence was "conceived through the very essence of God"(303). Given that the "love for God must occupy the mind most of all (299)" and that "[t]he more an image is joined to several others, the more often it flourishes (298)," the *Kaddish* intensifies both our love for God *and* for those whom we have lost" This is perhaps the most comforting message of the *Kaddish* and Spinoza.

Spinozan Judaism may not be as spiritually fulfilling as Judaism that is further enriched with faith in a personal, provident God. However, it is more satisfying to be a Spinozan Jew than to be a secular Jew. What Moses Mendelssohn derided as Spinozism might rescue some of those, like myself, who might otherwise fault themselves for being unfaithful to the religion passed down through the millennia by their forbearers.

Acknowledgments

I am grateful for help from Daniel B. Kohn, my rabbi son; from Avi Katz-Orlow, rabbi of St. Louis Hillel; and from Bea Sorkin, secretary of BSKI Synagogue, none of whom has read this essay and can be criticized for its content. I also want to thank Richard and Rita Gram, Mildred and Bob Kaufman, Carol Portman, Martha and Bob Senior and my wife Martha for their participation in an earlier discussion of Spinoza's excommunication at a Chavurah meeting at our home.

Susan Koppelman
Why (Jewish) Women's Short Stories
are My Sacred Literature

Five anthologies of Jewish women's stories are treasures worth having on your shelf. They are Joyce Antler's *America and I* (Boston: Beacon Press, 1990), the issue of *Sinister Wisdom* that was published as a book called *The Tribe of Dinah, The Woman Who Lost Her Names* edited by Julia Wolf Mazow, Irene Zahava's *Speaking for Ourselves: Short Stories by Jewish Lesbians, Her Face in the Mirror: Jewish Women On Mothers and Daughters* edited by Faye Moskowitz (Beacon Press, 1994). The editors were broadly representative in their choices of stories not only in terms of types of literary styles and sub-genres, but in the variety of Jewish women's voices. In these collections, Jewish women are sincere and crafty, well-meaning and selfish, politically feisty and politically indifferent, "normal" like "regular" (read: non-Jewish) Americans and intensely committed to living an identity that is exotic in the United States. They are heterosexual and lesbian, married, mothers, single, dreamers, hard working, in conflict over the distance between the generations of immigrants (read: assimilation, the end of the *frum* life). They are hungry for learning, hungry for justice, hungry to understand, and sometimes just plain hungry.

Many of the stories feel like family history to me, give me a sense of familiarity that no other literature has for me. They touch on all the aspects of my own identity. But the anthologies published thus far don't show all of us. No anthology could. We need more.

I miss those missing Jewish women and their stories. I miss the peasant women, like the narrator in Martha Wolfenstein's "Chayah." I miss women like the Biblical Sarah, women who joke around with God, like the narrator in Wolfenstein's story about "Genendel the Pious" who suddenly stops praying when finally her luck gets good. I miss women who ask questions of God's creation in the spirit of the Kabbalah, like the aunt in Joanna Greenberg's "Certain Distant Suns" who stops believing in gravity. I miss family stories like Carol Carr's about a typical Jewish father whose heart is broken when his daughter marries a Martian—because the purple man isn't Jewish. I miss portrayals of immigrant Jewish women as the heroines of their families, as the saints of our tradition.

So, who am I that I claim the stories in these anthologies as my own and also long for those that are missing? Does it matter who a reader is when she reports on her responses to a body of literature? I think it does. So here is who I am as a reader:

> I am a voracious reader and an old-fashioned literary scholar. I read with the sense of being a student and a lover of Literature, which I capitalize in the old fashioned Serious Way. I am a Jew. I am a Jew who had a pretty decent (for the post-WWII period in Conservative Jewish education) Religious School education and I learned in Temple about the holiness of Books. I am a woman. I learned how to be a grown-up woman by paying close attention to my mother and her many, many friends, some relatives, some neighbors, some from her grade school years, some she met while performing her many mitzvot. I learned that the joys of being a good woman included reading and sharing books and knowledge with other women and the ethics of being a good woman included protecting other women. I am a feminist. This fourth flowed naturally in my life from the first and the second and the third.

Thus, I am a feminist second-generation American Jewish woman reader.
or (the long version)

1. I am a Passionate Reader. I am an old-fashioned literary scholar. I read with the sense of myself as a scholar, as a lover of Literature, a word I capitalize in my mind in the old fashioned Serious Way that people did in the nineteenth century before they learned to be afraid of being thought "sentimental," when they weren't embarrassed to acknowledge with due seriousness, worshipfulness, respect, awe, the things they believed were Holy. I imagine that I "get permission" to feel this way about books because I am a Jew who had a pretty decent Religious School education and I learned in Temple about the holiness of The Book.

2. I am a Jew. I am a Jew whose parents sent her to Religious School from pre-kindergarten until I was confirmed at the age of sixteen. I chose to continue through high school. Considering that I only went to religious school three hours a week, and only during the secular school year, and not during the Jewish holidays and holy days, and not during the times when gentiles closed the public schools for their holidays and holy days, I had a good Jewish religious education. I learned in Temple about the holiness of The Book. I learned that The Book was not just the five books of Moses, the Torah, but the whole Bible. (Ours, not theirs.) Then I learned that there were the written commentaries, The Talmud. Then I

learned about the Midrash. It wasn't just one book, or even the collected voices of one tradition, but a collection of different tradition's collections of commentary. And then there were the commentaries on the commentaries. The Mishna and the Gemarrah. I don't remember the names of any more of the Special Books, but this is enough to remind myself how I learned that Books are Holy.

Because I am a somewhat educated Jewish woman, I learned that there are books that are holy to Jews. But I also learned that the Jewish holy books weren't meant directly for *me*. I didn't like a lot of what they had to say anyway.

The holy books weren't really for *me* because I was a girl. The Holy Books were just for the boys. Boys *had* to study for their *B'Nai Mitzvot*. There was no such ritual (in my youth) for girls. I would never get a chance to know which part of the Holy Books was especially mine, mine because it came on my birthday. I would never be expected to become an expert on the meaning of that passage. I would never be asked or expected to make a public commitment to the study of the Holy Books. I was a girl. I wasn't one of those who could grow up to be a scholar. I would never be valued in the Orthodox tradition for doing what *I* wanted to do, which was to sit and read all day and talk with my friends about what the reading meant, about what the implications of the words might be. While I never had penis envy, I certainly did have *portion* envy.

The Orthodox Rabbi across the street used to talk with me sometimes, try to answer my questions about the illogic of being forbidden to boil a kid in its mother's milk but being allowed to boil the shell-less eggs from the belly of the shabbos chicken in the soup made with its mother's body. Why was one wrong and the other right? I had lots of questions like that. Such inconsistencies outraged me. Were chickens less God's creation than cows? Was the motherhood of chickens less motherhood than the motherhood of cows?

He would talk with me for a while, trying to answer me, trying not so much to answer me as to satisfy me in a way that would turn me away from curiosity, from this constant questioning. And then finally, when he had run out of time or answers, he would smile and caress my hair for a minute and say, "You're a pretty girl, and smart. You'll make a good *rebbitzen*."

A *rebbitzen*! Me? Not *me*! I *wanted* to be a rabbi! A scholar! I wanted to spend my life finding out about all this stuff, talking with other people who were spending their lives finding out about this stuff. I didn't want to do housework!

Clearly, those books were not meant for me.

"All right," I consoled myself; "I don't want to spend my whole life reading the same books over and over anyway. If they don't want me to read *their* books, I'll read *other* books. I'll read *all* the other books!"

"And anyway," I pouted, "I don't really *like* their books. They tell awful stories, stupid stories, unfair stories. And they're not written in *my* language."

So many of the stories from the Holy Jewish boy Books I listened to in Religious School and at services made me start with surprise! There was so much unfairness in them. Mostly it was unfairness to girls and grown-up women.

But sometimes, like with the killing of the first-born sons of the Egyptians, or the killing of the Jewish boy babies mandated by the Egyptians, or the attempted killing of Isaac by his father, the stories were unfair to some group of little boys.

Those stories weren't about a Good god. A good god would be fair and good: else how would we know that it was God? How would we know it was important to be the way god was or told us to be? Why should we let somebody so mean and unfair make all the rules? If we had been created in the image of god, and we knew we were supposed to be good and fair, then god had to be good and fair. It was fair that way; it made sense. But there were so many stories that weren't fair.

For instance, many people took the story of Job seriously, but, not to mention for the moment that this god was a gambler, nobody seemed to care that when god tested Job's faith by killing his wife and children and Job didn't lose faith and, in fact, passed a number of other equally awful tests and trials, all ridiculous and cruel, and god decided that Job had proved his loyalty enough, and he gave Job back all the stuff that he had taken away, god did not give Mrs. Job and the children their lives back.

Was one wife supposed to be the same as another? Would my father be just as happy with another woman as he was with my mother? And what about the children? *I* was a child. Was this the way I wanted to be treated? Killed and replaced at a whim? Wasn't it supposed to matter that I was I, and not just "a child?" What kind of god was this?

And then there was the one about Eve being blamed for everything bad in the world just because she wanted knowledge, wanted to know the difference between good and evil. Well, if she didn't know the difference between good and evil in the first place, then how could she have known that it was evil or wrong to eat the fruit just because she had been told not to. Why should she assume that someone had the right to tell her what to do? Why shouldn't she do what she wanted to do? And besides, who said that doing what someone else wants you to do instead of what you want to do or know is right, is a good thing? If someone told you to jump in the lake, would you? My mother always asked me that question when I said that I wanted to do something because some other kid was doing it. Her question made me think seriously and I realized that I wouldn't jump in the lake if someone else did or told me to. Lake Erie was dangerous and dirty. Why should I jump in the lake just because someone told me to? I knew it was a stupid, dangerous thing to do.

And, conversely, why should I not eat a piece of fruit or learn about good and evil if I wanted to just because someone told me not to? Especially if there's lots of fruit and no one will go hungry because I have eaten. And why should Eve take god more seriously than she took the snake? I'm sure the snake was friendlier. And aren't we supposed to be friendly? Isn't it better to be friendly than to be a bully always making people do what you want them to? What was the difference between god and a bully? And what was the difference between the snake and a friend?

Eve was in a garden full of fruit trees, all of which she had eaten from, except one; she wanted to taste the fruit on *that* tree. God told her in his bully voice that she shouldn't eat any. Snake told her in a friendly voice that if she wanted some, she should go ahead and eat some. Why shouldn't she do what she wanted to?

"What," she probably wondered (I would have), "is this knowledge of good and evil? Why shouldn't I have this knowledge? Besides, the fruit looks good. Why shouldn't I eat this fruit? All the other fruit I've eaten has been good. I'm sure this will be, too. Why should I let some bully say I can't have it. If Adam took all the grapes and said I couldn't have any, would I put up with that?"

"And why is Adam so content to do what that bully says? It's because he doesn't really *care* about the knowledge of good and evil. And he isn't interested in tasting something he's never tasted, either. He always wants the same thing for dinner every night, over and over. And he never has much to talk about because he doesn't *think* about anything. Adam is *boring*! I'm glad that snake has been around lately; he's much more interesting."

I had some boy cousins and some boy neighbors and some boy class
mates who were like that. They were sort of dull-witted; they weren't
interested in anything. They never talked about *anything* interesting.
Mostly they hung out, played the same stupid ball games that they weren't
very good at anyway over and over. They seemed to be smart enough if
they wanted to be, but the thing was, they didn't really care to be: they
had no curiosity. They were boring. They weren't unpleasant or unkind.
But that didn't make them interesting. I figured that's what Adam must
have been like. Not interesting.

And what about Leah? How do you suppose *she* felt when her father
made her marry the guy who was in love with her sister? How awful!
How humiliating. And what if there was some other guy *she* wanted to
marry? We never hear her side of it, but it can't have been good for her.

And what about one of the worst things of all! That god told Abraham to kill his and Sarah's son and Abraham was willing to do it! What if
my father started hearing voices that told him to kill me? What if someone tried to kill *my* son? Was I supposed to just let it happen? What kind
of father was Abraham that he would let some voice in his head tell him
to kill his son? Whose voice, inside or outside of his head, could be
important enough for him to do what it told him to do when it told him
to do something so horrible as to kill his child? That story sickened and
scared me. No god that I'm ever going to have anything to do with
would want to have someone on his side, representing him to the world,
who would be so awful as to kill his own child.

And what about Sarah? It was the same story as Mrs. Job all over
again. What she might have wanted or thought or felt or deserved just
didn't count.

And how was I supposed to learn how to be a good grown-up
woman? Was I supposed to sleep with strange men to protect my husband, like Sarah did for Abraham, or my people, like Esther did and Judith
did; was I supposed to tell my sons to die rather than say "Uncle" the way
Hannah did?

And what about Esther? What if she didn't want to have that awful
mean drunk old Ahashuarus touch her? Yuck! Would you want him to
touch you? If she was heroic because she let that man touch her, am I
heroic if I let drunk old cousin Joe grope me in the coatroom?

And so, like sensible, brave, thinking people, Eve ate the fruit and
gained the knowledge of good and evil and Lillith refused to be pushed
around and Vashti refused to let her husband treat her badly and Mrs. Lot

refused not to say "good-bye" to her home and the world she had always known.

And for this, they are BAD? They deserve punishment? Ridiculous!

3. I am a woman. I learned how to be a grown-up woman by paying close attention to my mother and her many, many friends. They all read books and shared their books. I have written elsewhere about how I hid under the table to listen to them talk and laugh and to learn from them when I was young. I learned that the ethics of being a good woman included reading and sharing books and all kinds of knowledge and information with other women and it also included protecting each other.

I listened, I watched, I asked questions, I was given advice, and finally, when I was thirteen, I was invited to sit at the table with them.

I knew my mother was good; I knew I was supposed to be good. I knew adults were different from children. Therefore there had to be a different way to be a good adult woman than the way of being a good little girl. I could find out how to be a good adult woman by learning from my mother and her friends.

When I told the women, my mother and Aunt V. and whoever else was at the table at the Party Center that Cousin J. was *touching me* (I didn't say where—I couldn't speak the word "breasts" yet) they all sort of laughed and waved it off, "Joe does that to all the women. Don't let it bother you. And don't make a fuss because it would really be awful for I. (his wife) to have to hear about it. Just make sure he can't get to you. Don't go places alone when he's around."

This was a lesson. But what was the lesson? Was this the lesson: it was more important for a grown-up woman like I. to be spared the embarrassment of having it become public knowledge that her husband did things like that than it was important to get him to stop doing those things to me, to others. Did it mean what he did wasn't important enough to *us* (who were "us," was it the community of women, of adult women?) to violate what was evidently one of the ethical values of this community—that one woman's comfort and safety was more important that letting one man's behavior bother you; i.e., *she* was more important then *he* was.

I knew that it didn't mean I was less important than she was, but rather that he was less important than either of us. That particular thing he had done wasn't worth worrying her about and I shouldn't let it matter to me, I shouldn't be hurt by it. To be hurt by it was to grant it and him more importance than they deserved. It was like being emotionally damaged in some way by a mosquito bite.

If that was the lesson, then what a curious lesson in values. Are these *women's* values? Are they Jewish women's values? Are these the values of people who are oppressed and have developed an ethics that allows them to make choices—about their attitudes towards their oppressors, about how much they will allow their oppressors to intrude on their senses of self.

Whatever the lesson was meant to be, I didn't learn it right. I couldn't help feeling damaged, dirtied, frightened by what he did to me and I couldn't help feeling dismissed, disregarded, and unprotected by the women I had turned to in my shock and discomfort and fear. And I wound up not only being hurt by him, but hurt by them, and ashamed of myself because I wasn't whatever it was they were that would allow me to dismiss what he had done with a casual wave of my hand and a laugh.

4. I am a feminist. This fourth flowed naturally in my life from the first and the second and the third.

To repeat: I am a reader and an old-fashioned literary scholar. I read with the sense of being a student and a lover of Literature, which I capitalize in the old fashioned Serious Way. I am a Jew. I am a Jew who had a pretty decent Religious School education and I learned in Temple about the holiness of Books. I am a woman. I learned how to be a good grown-up woman by paying close attention to my mother and her many, many friends. I learned that one of the joys of being a good woman included reading and sharing books and knowledge with other women and the ethics of being a good woman included protecting other women. I am a feminist. This fourth flowed naturally in my life from the first and the second and the third.

Thus, I am a feminist Jewish woman reader.

I began to read stories, "real books," by which I mean adult fiction, when I was very little, probably nine years old. [I have since learned that this is a tradition with writing women, especially in the nineteenth century. I have learned that this impulsion in me to immerse myself in other people's lives while also living my own—I was a comparativist even then—characterizes certain kinds of women who share certain mental or imaginative characteristics and various other attributes. I have known many women like this in my life, women like me in this way, and they are all intellectuals and writers of some sort.]

I read because it the most absorbing activity I had learned. The most fun, even when it made me scared or made me cry or made me mad. I wanted to learn about life and people. I wanted to know *how to be.* I thought I could find out by reading about other lives and learning how different people lived those other lives. I knew that the most important rock-bottom value of life was being a good person. I believed that if there were a heaven and an ultimate judgment day, what we would be judged *on* was if we had been good. It was more important than anything else about us. It was more important than pretty or smart or rich or anything else.

[I had no idea what happened if you hadn't been good. Nor did I speculate about what happened if you had been good. I think I thought about it as some sort of school exercise: at the end of life, which was sort of like the end of your years in a particular school you always knew you would eventually graduate from, you would get a report card. It was best to try and get all A's. The subjects were all aspects of goodness. I knew I would never fail, because I was a hard worker and a good student. But I didn't want just not to fail, just to pass; I wanted to get *good* grades. Maybe straight A's. That was sort of like planning to get 800s on the SATs. It was supposed to be impossible. But you could get awful close to 800, maybe 795. So my friends and I all aimed for 800s and it was all a game. I think that's how I thought about life. It was a game with serious results. It was more interesting than the sports games, games at which you were richly rewarded if you did it really well, if it was a popular kind of sport, and if you were a boy. I didn't worry about not being a boy, because if I had been me but a boy, I still would have been lousy at ball games. I was always afraid the ball would hit me in the face and break my glasses.]

Because I thought of literature, Real Books, Story Books, as being of the same nature as the Holy Books and because passages from the Holy Books in my tradition constitute an occasion for commentary, whether it be drawing a moral lesson (parables), understanding something about divine (authorial) intention, or discerning the meaning of what has come before us (history), so too were passages, stories, from Real Books occasions for similar exercises. In other words, if the Bible and its adjuncts existed to tell men how to live, then all *other* books existed to tell me and other women how to live. Especially books by women.

I felt simultaneously excluded as a woman by the Holy Books and yet stimulated as a Jew to ask certain kinds of questions and define problems and look at them from certain kinds of perspectives.

The kinds of questioning I was stimulated to engage in are well represented by one of the passages in small print that was never read aloud from the old Chase and Sanborn *Hagaddah* that was used at the seder tables of my childhood. I always read it to myself during one of those times when we were supposed to be praying silently, which I never did, and pondered it by myself, although over the years my attitude towards it changed. And this passage engaged my attention fully year after year.

What does it mean, the Rabbis wondered, debated, when it says that God led the Jews out of slavery with a variety of appendages variously enumerated? Does it mean there were twelve appendages being extended—two hands and ten fingers? Or ten appendages—eight fingers and two hands, but no thumbs. Or is the number of appendages only eight: first it says hands, meaning fingers but not thumbs; but then, for those who didn't understand that, in an attempt to clarify, fingers are specified so that the reader will know fingers but no thumbs constituted the outstretch hands because after all, when the fingers are extended *out* the thumbs are extended in a different direction. And what are the implications of each of these possible different answers in terms of what god might be offering or threatening with those outstretched appendages. If it only means eight, does that mean that god was not giving as much as he could have given using ten or twelve? If so, why not? Does god not give more than is needed, or does god give less than needed to inspire the recipient to get the rest independently—sort of like matching grant strategy? Or does god want to keep the recipient always in need. . . .

In other words, how much is enough, and *is* enough enough? Or is enough too much?

As a woman I was stimulated to ask particular kinds of questions. As a woman I asked woman questions of Jewish texts. As a Jew I asked Jewish questions of secular texts.

For instance, one of the Ten Commandments (for men) is not to covet thy neighbor's wife. Also, the coveting of the neighbor's ass and mule are out. Now not coveting the neighbor's wife can have relevance for heterosexual men or lesbians—although I didn't know about lesbians when I was a little girl having this conversation with myself, but what does it have to do with me, if I am a heterosexual woman? And if the commandment to not covet wives excludes me, does that also mean I am recused from coveting my neighbor's ass and mule? Does that mean it's okay for women to covet? Or does that mean that somewhere else is written the rules about what *women* aren't supposed to covet? How will

I find them? Will I recognize them when I find them? Is coveting something that women don't do by nature or is it something so different for women and for men that it can't be talked about in relation to both kinds of humans at the same time? That's just a for instance.

When I discovered the stories of American Jewish women writers, I discovered Real Stories in which the questions being asked were those I was asking as a woman and the perspective on the questions was that of a Jew and the parables to be drawn for instruction were parables that spoke to me as a Jewish woman.

Mary Antin's portrait of Malinka in her wonderful story "Malinka's Atonement"—in czarist Russia, at that time, in that place, this young woman was almost old enough to be getting married at which point she would have become a hard-working domestic slave with more children than she could care for and feed well and educate, but she would have to struggle and struggle and struggle. But what *Malinka* wants is to *study,* to learn. She risks her eternal soul, as the Christians would say, and I'm not sure how the Jews would say it—I know we talk about *neshoma,* soul, but I've never heard that term used to describe something that could be lost; it was just something that is there. At any rate "Malinka's Atonement" is a sort of Faustian story.

Viola Brothers Shore's story "Tradition" which will be reprinted when I publish my own anthology of Jewish women's stories, is about women caught in that struggle between assimilation and keeping faith with the old values, about making a choice of life style when you chose your husband. A story like this educates young women reading it to realize that you can't just choose with the hankering of your loins, as the Americans advise with their romantic love myths. It's dangerous not to listen to the advice of your elders and make a choice, or allow them to make a choice for you, that will be good for a lifetime, not just a couple of nighttimes.

Martha Wolfenstein's "Chayah," included in my 1984 anthology *The Other Woman: Stories of Two Women and a Man* makes the same point about marriage, mating, choosing a life partner. Pay attention to those who are older, wiser, who know and love you and really do want for you what is best for you. And who are also convinced that what is best for you is best for the Jewish people, for survival of the tribe.

The stories in my collection will focus on three strands of American Jewish women's lives.

(1) How have we dealt with the issue of assimilation? For women, that issue has most forcefully presented itself to us in the form of inter-

marriage. There are two kinds of intermarriage that have concerned Jewish women in our fiction. The first is the kind that comes most obviously to mind—marriage between a Jewish woman and a non-Jewish man. There is almost no Jewish woman writer I have read who does not deal in fiction at some point in her oeuvre with the questions, the problems, inherent in this subject. The second kind of intermarriage is one that presents more subtle problems, but problems none the less demanding, excruciating, and basically insoluble. Those are the marriages between "old world" and "new world" Jews, between those who brought up in the old world and with the values of tribal people and those from the new world, those who have shed the extended family ties and obligations as well as the orthodox life style. One of the most moving stories exploring that conflict is Fannie Hurst's "A Boob Spelled Backward" which I've included in my 2004 collection of *The Stories of Fannie Hurst*.

(2) What has been the relationship of American Jewish women to traditional Judaism, traditional Jewish religious and spiritual life? The problem here is how do women either reared in or who have adopted the principles of individualism, pragmatism, secularism, and gender equality relate to a tradition that excludes or excuses (depending on whose midrash you believe) women from religious obligation, a tradition which ties one's Jewish righteousness so closely to one's narrowly prescribed gender-role that to struggle for gender-role freedom seems to equate with rejection of the religious tradition? Do women retain a connection to Jewish spirituality even if or after they have abandoned Jewish religious practices?

(3) What has been the impact of the Holocaust on the imaginations of American Jewish women? These stories are numerous enough to fill half a dozen books. I included one of them, Edna Ferber's "No Room at the Inn" in my collection *"May Your Days be Merry and Bright:" Christmas Stories by Women*. What a story that one is!

In Jewish tradition, the saint is not a virgin martyred for her faith; our saints are mothers who martyred themselves for their children's' health and safety and education and happiness. Despite the ignorant self-hating Jewish male (P. Roth et al.) betrayals of our mothers, making them into laughing stocks for the gentiles, most of the children of these strong Jewish mothers turned out fine, and love their mothers and were good and caring parents in their turn. I love to read about those generations of women loving and tending each other in their roles as mothers and daughters and sisters and aunts and grandmothers, always in and out, but mostly *in* each other's lives, in the stories written by Merrill Joan Gerber.

And in the stories of Fannie Hurst I find the heroic struggles to survive in the urban sweat shops called department stores and theaters of young first generation American Jewish women—how to survive in this New World? Hurst tells the stories of that struggle for women early in the last century. Some of them are success stories, some of them are stories of women who don't make it: all of the stories are real. There are stories of women struggling with the pull towards bonding with the generations of women behind them by sharing in the life of observance they lived and the pull towards living like your neighbors in this day and place—when your neighbors are all gentile and go to church and put up Christmas trees and eat ham sandwiches—like the story Grace Paley tells part of in "The Loudest Voice" which I also included in my collection *"May Your Days be Merry and Bright:" Christmas Stories by Women*.

There is "The Fast," the story Edna Ferber tells of a young woman flirting with and finally embracing the responsibilities of a Jewish adult—fasting on Yom Kippur—her own assumption of the estate of being *Bas Mitzvah*, a child of the Covenant. It is a story of the struggle for faith and Jewish identity in the exile of the Diaspora—in a small town in Wisconsin.

The Holocaust stories by Esther Broner and Andrea Dworkin not only move me more than most other stories I have read, they help me sort out things in my life that are accounted for no where else. Who among us that is conscious that she is a Jew is not haunted by the Shoah, does not know that it meant *her* as much as any other Jew, that she is a survivor, too—not of the death camps, but of the death sentence? Which of us does not understand how narrowly we escaped to this country, the Goldene Medina, how recent was the historical accident that brought us here, where we survived, instead of kept us there, in the Old Country, where we would not have survived?

These are wonderful stories; these are wonderful Jewish stories; these are wonderful women's stories: these are wonderful Jewish women's stories.

Irving Litvag
"Hello, My Friend!"

Memories of Isaac Bashevis Singer

In truth, I cannot claim to have been a close friend of Nobel laureate Isaac Bashevis Singer, whose birth centennial was recently observed. But we were warm acquaintances. He usually didn't remember my name, but whenever we saw each other over the years, he would look over at me, his intense blue eyes would light up, and he would call out, "Hello, my friend!" Each time this happened, I felt as if I had been knighted.

He was a guest several times in our home in Creve Coeur and my wife Ilene and I visited him and Mrs. Singer in their apartment on Manhattan's Upper West Side and their oceanfront condo in Surfside, a suburb of Miami Beach. We took our two small children with us to Surfside and the Singers graciously gave each of them a children's book as a welcome gift.

I first met him in the mid-1960s. I supervised the weekly Assembly Series lectures at Washington U. and I brought in Singer as a guest speaker. He was not yet a world literary celebrity, but generally was considered the greatest Yiddish writer of modern times. His writings, translated into English, were finding a steadily increasing general audience. I thought it would be interesting to expose his talents to WU students and faculty. I met him and his wife, Alma, at Union Station (in those days, he was afraid to fly) and thus began three delightful days as his host and sponsor.

Somewhat to my surprise, WU's Graham Memorial Chapel was packed for his talk. I had wondered how Singer would come across as a speaker with his heavily Yiddish-accented English. The audience loved him. His gentle wisdom and modest humor were a big hit. I remember some of the lines he was to use often over the years: "Some people say I speak Yiddish with an English accent" . . . "I am a vegetarian for health reasons—the health of the chickens."

After the lecture, he and I went to a lunch with a group of faculty members. The group included a few of the much-acclaimed campus writers and some were plainly not fans of Singer's literary approach. But he easily held his own in the discussion and gave as good as he received. Only a couple of times did he become riled and turn those blue-burning laser eyes on an impudent questioner. He was not cowed by this assemblage of PhDs.

That first visit to St. Louis had only one sour note. As we stopped for refreshments at Union Station while awaiting the train back to New York, Singer quietly asked me what I had paid for his lecture services. I had made the arrangement through a New York lecture bureau and I learned that Singer never before had worked with this agency. When I told him the fee was $900, Singer turned white with anger. The lecture agent had told Singer that the fee was $400, of which two-thirds would go to the writer. Singer was furious that the agent had scammed him and there was little I could do to assuage his sense of betrayal.

As the years passed, we kept in touch. I heard from him occasionally via letters written by Alma. I don't think he wasted much time in casual correspondence and she took care of it for him. I met with him on his periodic lecture stops in St. Louis and, as mentioned, we visited each other's homes. It took a few years, but I finally found the courage to address him by his first name. (His wife usually called him "Bashevis.")

In 1972, my first book—*Singer in the Shadows: The Strange Story of Patience Worth*—was published. Knowing of Isaac's interest in mysticism, angels, demons, etc., I asked the publisher to send him a set of galley proofs for a possible jacket comment. My book was about an occult case that occurred in St. Louis and caused a world-wide sensation in the early 20th century. To my great joy, Singer not only read the book, he was fascinated by it. Alma Singer told me later that for several nights running, her husband read the proofs until very late, until she forced him to turn off the light and get to bed.

In his quote for the jacket of my book, Singer referred to it as "a masterpiece of research and presentation." He never got straight the name of the ghostly entity in the story, but whenever we met thereafter, he would ask me more questions about "Patience Hope," as he called her. The mystery of the case, still unsolved, always intrigued him.

When the news came in 1978 that Singer had been awarded the Nobel Prize for Literature, we sent congratulatory telegrams to both his homes, not knowing where he might be at the time. We watched proudly on TV when he received his award in Sweden. Although he looked uncomfortable in his white tie and tails when he received the award from the King of Sweden, later he spoke in his Nobel lecture with poise and conviction about his pride in Yiddish:

"The high honor bestowed upon me by the Swedish Academy is also a recognition of the Yiddish language—a language of exile, without a land, without frontiers, not supported by any government, a language which possesses no words for weapons, ammunition, military exercises, war tactics; a language that was despised by both gentiles and emancipated Jews. The truth is that what the great religions preached, the Yiddish-speaking people of the ghettos practiced day in and day out. They were the people of The Book in the truest sense of the word . . .

"There are some who call Yiddish a dead language, but so was Hebrew called for two thousand years. It has been revived in our time in a most remarkable, almost miraculous way. . . . It is a fact that the classics of Yiddish literature are also the classics of the modern Hebrew literature. Yiddish has not yet said its last word. It contains treasures that have not been revealed to the eyes of the world. It was the tongue of martyrs and saints, of dreamers and Cabalists—rich in humor and in memories that mankind may never forget. In a figurative way, Yiddish is the wise and humble language of us all, the idiom of frightened and hopeful humanity."

I loved talking literature with Isaac because he confirmed most of my own beliefs, opinions that were (and are) out of favor in most academic and other high-brow literary circles. He declared firmly that a fine novelist must also be a superb storyteller, that compelling stories were the basis of all great literature. He had little patience with current literary fashions that proclaim language or style—the choice of words—to be the hallmark of excellence in fiction, with story a secondary and almost useless asset. "The worst crime that a writer can commit," Isaac would say, "is to be boring."

He always insisted that a writer must entertain his or her readers, but he also affirmed writing as a moral force in the world. Singer began his Nobel Lecture, two days after he received his Nobel Prize, with these words:

"The storyteller and poet of our time, as in any other time, must be an entertainer of the spirit in the full sense of the word, not just a preacher of social or political ideals. There is no paradise for bored readers and no excuse for tedious literature that does not intrigue the reader, uplift him, give him the joy and escape that true art always grants. Nevertheless, it is also true that the serious writer of our time must be deeply concerned about the problems of his generation."

He wrote a number of very successful books for children and devoted about half of his brief speech at the Nobel Banquet on December 10, 1978, to his reasons for writing for children. These few lines encompass much of his literary philosophy and they are still worth reading for all aspiring writers:

"There are five hundred reasons why I began to write for children, but to save time I will mention only ten of them. Number 1) Children read books, not reviews. They don't give a hoot about the critics. Number 2) Children don't read to find their identity. Number 3) They don't read to free themselves of guilt, to quench the thirst for rebellion, or to get rid of alienation. Number 4) They have no use for psychology. Number 5) They detest sociology. Number 6) They don't try to understand Kafka or *Finnegan's Wake*. Number 7) They still believe in God, the family, angels, devils, witches, goblins, logic, clarity, punctuation, and other such obsolete stuff. Number 8) They love interesting stories, not commentary, guides, or footnotes. Number 9) When a book is boring, they yawn openly, without any shame or fear of authority. Number 10) They don't expect their beloved writer to redeem humanity. Young as they are, they know that it is not in his power. Only the adults have such childish illusions."

Singer demanded that his work be treated with respect. Both he and his wife hated Barbra Streisand's musical film *Yentl,* an adaptation of one of his best-known short stories. He refused even to speak about it, but Alma conveyed his disgust to all. Paul Mazursky's film adaptation of Singer's novel, *Enemies: A Love Story* found greater favor in their eyes.

I once asked Isaac the name of his favorite American writer. Expecting to hear a name from the Pantheon of such writers—Twain, Hemingway, Steinbeck, perhaps Bellow—I was surprised to hear him reply without hesitation: "Conrad Richter." I had heard of Richter, of course; he had won the Pulitzer Prize and other major literary awards, but he died in 1968 and, so far as I knew, had been largely forgotten since. Most of his novels were about pioneer life in the U.S.

Out of curiosity I began reading Richter. Ever since, I have been grateful to Isaac for that recommendation. He had introduced me to a master writer, whose work glowed with genius. Richter's trilogy of historical novels, *The Trees, The Fields,* and *The Town,* later published together as one volume, *The Awakening Land,* might well be the "great American novel" that for so long has been the Holy Grail of American literature. Some day it will get the recognition it deserves.

Recently, a writer in the *Forward* (ironically the same Yiddish/English newspaper in New York that was the first publisher of many of Singer's stories and novels) described him as a "nasty man." He had a powerful ego—what great artist doesn't?—and it broke through sometimes. But in my own meetings with him in diverse settings, among different types of people, I saw almost always a man of kindness, openness, and patience. I can only judge by what I myself saw and heard, and nastiness was notably absent. Even during the years when his fame and income multiplied and even after his Nobel Prize, Isaac continued to list his address and phone number in the Manhattan telephone directory so that he would be accessible to those who wished to contact him.

Isaac died in a Florida nursing home on July 24, 1991, just 10 days after his 87th birthday. Alma had devotedly cared for him through the several years of dementia that preceded his death. We got a letter from her a couple of years after his passing. She described herself as "very lonely" and asked us please to write her. We answered her with a long, consoling letter and urged her to keep in touch with us. We never heard from her again. Alma died in Miami in January, 1996, at the age of 89.

Isaac Bashevis Singer began as the quasi-private treasure of Yiddish readers, but his genius was too powerful to be thus limited. His prolific writings went forth into the world and readers everywhere came to love his work. He was one of the few writers to receive the approval of both the literary intelligentsia and also millions of average readers, gentiles and Jews alike.

Isaac once quietly commented to me about Saul Bellow's *Herzog,* a book celebrated upon its publication as a literary masterpiece, "I do not think this book will live."

I am no authority for sure, and I am biased because of my feelings for the man, but I believe the writing of Isaac Bashevis Singer *will* live, and will be read and savored for a long time to come, perhaps for as long as words endure.

Jerred Metz
Drinking the Dipper Dry Twenty-five Years Later

Listening to the elders, what is it like?
It is like eating ripe grapes and drinking aged wine.
                    Pirke Avot
                    R. Jose ben Yehudah

Twenty-five years after *Drinking the Dipper Dry* appeared all the people whose stories the book tells are gone. A source of stories of a Jewish generation is gone, too. The five who appear here were born between 1986 and 1906. The youngest would have been ninety-nine in 2005.

In 1977 CEMREL's Arts for Older Adults asked me to teach creative writing at the Jewish Center for the Aged and Webbe Senior Citizen Apartments. Even the first night some of the people told interesting stories about their lives, and told them well. So instead of teaching creative writing, with the permission of Arts for Older Adults, I taped and edited our conversations. The project officially ended after ten weeks. I could see that there was the possibility of a book of their lives if we continued meeting and talking. I told the people this. They were eager to keep on. From our weekly conversations over the next two years came *Drinking the Dipper Dry*. Being with these people, hearing and working with their stories, then giving readings and lectures about it over the years led me to many discoveries, many insights and lessons.

What the Book Taught Me

Lesson One:
None of these people considered themselves storytellers. They did not have a reputation as storytellers. As far as they were concerned, we talked, passed many pleasant hours, though they knew that what they said was going to be in a book.

Along the way, some expressed a purpose in telling their stories. After a particularly moving account, Sophie Dricker said, "Do you know why I wanted to tell you this? So when you write this down and when I die I want my grandchildren to read it in a book."

Lesson Two:
The elders see from a perspective that comes with the passage of time. They see how things began, worked out, and ended. While people

may grow and change in particular facets of their lives, the essential character forms early in life and persists. So we can see the way the person
was in youth and what they came to be, what happened to them that they
find worth talking about. Their stories demonstrate this. Point of view is
not just a literary convention. We are points of view. How we see things
is specific to the seer.

Lesson Three:

From the stories of fleeing European persecution we can begin to
appreciate the travails, terrors, and sacrifices. Many left behind beloved
family, never to see them again. Most underwent great hardships and pri-
vations. They all stood at the brink of death in escaping the Old World.
What these everyday people endured is amazing.

Lesson Four:

Life stories portray the joys of life as well. Family, celebration, friendship, good work, jokes, conversation, games, entertainment, religious
community, mealtime, raising a family, the way life was—many mores and
customs have radically changed in our modern world—are a delight to
hear about. . Their life stories help us consider that the frail old man or
old woman we see in homes for the aged and nursing homes often lived
rich lives.

Sophie Dricker:

> One day I called up my boss at seven o'clock in the morning and I
> say to him, "Sidney, I don't think I'll be able to work today. I'm very
> sick. "
>
> He says, "Well, if you got sick so take the day off."
>
> I belonged to a club. We used to play poker. We all went, the
> ten of us. We went on the Admiral at ten o'clock. I only had ten dol-
> lars with me. The minute we came on the boat we started to play. We
> had lunch. And I lost my ten dollars. I didn't even have a dollar the
> next day to go to work.
>
> When I came back to work the next day my boss said, "Did
> you have a bad day?"
>
> I said, "Did I have a bad day? I was very, very sick."
>
> I was sick because I lost my ten dollars.

Frank Fershter:

> In our town where I grew up the Jews and the Ukranians, they were all together. We used to go to their weddings. They used to go to our parties. There was no distinction among either one. Of course, some people thought they were better than other people. They just didn't care for any company. The people that didn't care for any company didn't care for their own nationality or any other.

Lesson Five:
When someone gives an example, shares an anecdote, illustrates a point with an instance, the speaker is on the verge of a story. Embellish a point and a story emerges, the best being of first-hand experiences. As these stories show, well told, a story makes a point, teaches a lesson, explains, accounts for, or justifies. It is a testimony. A record. An account.

Frank Fershter:

> Hoover told us that he'll give us a chicken in every pot and a machine in every garage. By the time he got through, we broke the pots looking for the chicken and we burned the garages for coal. He said that prosperity was just around the corner. We didn't know what corner to look for it.

In matters of plot, incident, phrase, descriptive detail, and characterization of people and events, the book's speakers' stories flow as easily as water in a brook. These people are particularly skilled at this, as if telling a story is second nature.

Lesson Six:
The storyteller watches and listens. Inflection, tone of voice, accent, volume, and gesture make their way into the words and express a rich palette of sound and meaning. Through cadence of phrase and sentence the written words recreate essential, nearly-perfect voices, duplicating the effect the spoken word had on me as I listened.

Lesson Seven:
What counts as a story in *Drinking the Dipper Dry*? Anything from autobiographical sketches, to aphorisms, vignettes, folk wisdom, parable,

sermon, monologue, and conversation. The stories are brief and pointed, the language plain. Thus the book's subtitle: *Plain-Spoken Lives*.

Lesson Eight:

The manners of simple life guide the essential feelings and speak a plain, emphatic language. There is a daily beauty in the people who live such lives. Entwined in the fabric of the stories" events and words, this beauty pictures active yet simple virtues within the grasp of each person:

Sophie Dricker:

You know what the Rabbi says to me? If everyone will feel the same way and do the things like I do then the world would be beautiful.

★ ★ ★

If we are fortunate we have each found ourselves in the presence of a spellbinding storyteller, someone who enthralls, enchants, transports us to realms of picture and circumstance, to the story-teller's experience. The speaker's words meet the listener's mind's eye and intellect. As the rabbi says, "Ripe grapes and aged wine." Maturity and perfection. Like wine, wisdom ripens with age. Not all old people are wise, but those who are, are a treasure.

These first-hand accounts give us a glimpse into a by-gone world. Twenty-five years after the book appeared I still find a drink from the dipper of wisdom enlivening, refreshing, thirst quenching.

Howard Schwartz
The Role of Jewish Lore
in the Children's Stories of I. B. Singer

Isaac Bashevis Singer began his career as a writer of children's stories with the publication of *Zlateh the Goat* in 1966, thirty-three years after the publication of his first novel, *Satan in Goray*. Even though Singer was a Yiddish writer renown (and, in some circles, infamous) for passionate, sensuous stories and for invoking the world of the supernatural, he immediately demonstrated the ability to address himself to children in a direct, natural way, without the least hint of condescension. Any reader, young or old, of the exquisite story "Zlateh the Goat" will confirm that Elizabeth Shub did the world of children's literature a great service in convincing Singer to turn his talents to stories for children.

As is well-known, because of his upbringing as a yeshivah student, the son of a rabbi, Singer was steeped in the Jewish literary tradition. Indeed, it was second nature to him. In all his writings, Singer draws upon these sources, but in his children's stories, in particular, he makes them the focus of many tales. Perhaps because writing for children brought him back to his own childhood and to the texts that were so much a part of that time in his life, he often drew on models that he studied as a Yeshivah student and that were part of the oral lore of Eastern European Jewry.

One of the most intriguing questions about Singer's writings, and especially about his children's stories, one that has intrigued me for many years, concerns the ways in which Singer makes use of these traditional sources. Does he simply retell them or weave them into his stories, or does he find some other way to draw these sources into his fictional world? It is obvious that, despite his disclaimers, Singer is a very Jewish writer, but how exactly does he draw on Jewish tradition? This is one of the primary issues for us to consider.

An examination of the body of Singer's children's stories indicates that despite Singer's extensive use of Jewish sources, he rarely simply retells an existing tale. One exception to this rule is "Elijah the Slave." Here Singer draws on an 11th century collection of folktales compiled in Judeo-Arabic by Nissim ben Ya'akov ibn Shahin, later the basis of a well-known Hebrew collection, *Hibbur Yafeh me-ha Yeshuah*.[1] Like the original, Singer's version is the story of Elijah—the most popular figure in all Jewish folklore—having himself sold into slavery so that a poor man might profit from the proceeds. While the poor man in the original does not have a name or a profession, in Singer's story the poor man is identified as a scribe, Tobias, who lost the use of his right hand and thus lost his profession. In both stories the plight of the poor man and his family becomes desperate, in both Elijah presents himself to the poor man and insists he be sold as a slave, and in both Elijah is freed once he completes building a palace for his new owner. Like the original, Singer's story reads like a pithy folktale, and other than giving the poor man a name and a profession, Singer does not really change the story.

It is important to note, however, that the kind of retelling Singer does here is the exception. Even when he undertakes to work with very well-known stories, such as that of the Golem or the life of the Ba'al Shem Tov, Singer does not hesitate to take considerable liberties with these popular legends. But the fact that Singer felt compelled to reimagine them testifies to his need to put his own imaginative mark on these famous stories, and to his refusal to serve simply as a storyteller who transmits existing tales. Thus the first conclusion that can be drawn is that Singer rarely simply retells traditional tales. Even when he works with well-known folk narratives, he insists on making them his own.

Further evidence of Singer's approach can be found in his stories about the city of Chelm, such as "The Fools of Chelm and the Stupid Carp," "Shlemiel the Businessman," and "Dalfunka, Where the Rich Live Forever." While Singer certainly builds on the existing lore about this city of fools, he creates new narratives set in Chelm and does not retell the existing tales, which are really extended jokes. This approach—putting his stories within a traditional context but then creating new narratives rather than retelling existing ones—is Singer's most consistent method.

Thus Singer is more likely to make use a rabbinic or folk model or theme rather than an existing narrative. Among the stories based on rabbinic models is "Why Noah Chose the Dove." Here all of the animals, responding to a rumor that Noah would only take the best of the them, beg Noah to take them on the ark. Each one makes a case for himself, except for the dove, who remains silent. Noah assures the animals that he'll take all of them on the ark, and he rewards the dove's modesty by making it his messenger. The moral of this story is clear: it is better to be modest than to promote yourself.

Readers familiar with traditional sources will quickly recognize this story as being closely parallel to the myth best-known for the version found in the *Zohar* about the letters of the alphabet: "When God wished to fashion the world, all the letters were hidden away. For two thousand

years before creating the world, God contemplated them and played with
them. When God was about to create the world, all the letters presented
themselves before Him, from last to first." Each letter then makes its case
that God should create the world through them. Tav, for example, argued
that God should create the world with it, since it completes the word
emet, "truth," which is God's seal. God eventually decides to create the
world with the letter Bet, since it stands for *berakhah*, "blessing." And God
rewards aleph, who alone among the letters did not offer itself, by making it the first letter of the alphabet.[2] A parallel midrash is found about
the mountains competing for God to choose one of them to be the one
on which the Torah will be given. In this case, God selects Mount Sinai
because no idol worship had taken place there.[3]

Singer has clearly drawn the model for "Why Noah Chose the
Dove" from these rabbinic sources. In addition, Singer first changes the
biblical narrative a bit by making the animals anxious about whether
they'll be included on the ark. He then poses a midrashic-type of question—why did Noah choose the dove to be his messenger? He finds the
answer by taking an existing traditional model about a competition
among personified letters or mountains and changing it into a competition among the animals over who will be permitted to board the ark.
Thus Singer creates an entirely new narrative, but it is closely modeled
on biblical and rabbinic sources.

In some cases Singer works directly from existing rabbinic texts. His
story "The Wicked City," about a visit that Abraham pays to his nephew
in Sodom, draws heavily on the midrashim about Sodom, especially those
found in *Sefer ha-Yashar*.[4] In both accounts the wickedness of the inhabitants of Sodom has no limits. In the midrashim we learn that if a short
stranger seeks to spend the night in Sodom, he is given a long bed, and
his feet are stretched until they fit, while a tall stranger is given a short
bed, and his feet are cut off to make them fit. In a similar vein, anyone
caught giving bread to a beggar is stripped naked, tied down in public,
smeared with honey, and offered as food for the bees.

Singer's description of Sodom in "The Wicked City" is equally
malignant: "Strangers were banned from Sodom by law. The people were
even forbidden to sell food to travelers. In those rare cases where a for-
eigner was allowed inside, he was usually killed during the night. Such
was the custom of this sinful city." In the biblical account, *The men went
on from there to Sodom, while Abraham remained standing before the Lord* (Gen.
18:22). It is here that Abraham bargains with God about whether Sodom

deserves to be saved if some righteous men can be found there. Thus Abraham does not accompany the two angels who set out for Sodom. Singer, however, imagines that Abraham makes just such a visit, accompanied by the two angels, who are here described as his servants Gabriel and Raphael, the names by which the two angels who visited Sodom are identified in *Bereshit Rabbah*[5] and other sources. Thus Singer has fearlessly changed a biblical narrative, using the same kind of narrative freedom found in the Midrash. In Singer's version, Abraham's visit not only brings great distress to Lot and his family because of the views of strangers in Sodom, but because Abraham makes things worse by calling on the people to repent of their sinful ways. Needless to say, repentance is the last thing in their minds. Yet, despite the considerable changes Singer makes to the biblical narrative, it is clear that "The Wicked City" is firmly built on the existing biblical and rabbinic traditions about Sodom.

In addition to his formal study of the Talmud, Singer was exposed to an exceptionally rich tradition of oral lore, including superstitions and folkways of every kind, which he drew upon in his writings at least as extensively as the rabbinic sources. Many of these superstitions warned of dangers from evil beings—witches, imps, demons and devils—who were blamed whenever things went wrong, as they often did. Indeed, life for humans was viewed as an eternal struggle against the dark forces that surrounded them on all sides. In the 12th century Rabbi Judah the Pious stated that there were 10,000 demons at a person's right hand and a 100,000 at the left (right representing the side of good, left the side of evil). This view persisted into the modern era among most Eastern European Jews. Singer seems to have been exceptionally attuned to the presence of these evil forces, but rather than focus on keeping them at bay, he was not afraid to invoke them in his stories, and sometimes even to portray them as beings with their own, almost-human needs. For this he was harshly criticized, but for Singer the key issue was always how to write a compelling story, and he understood well that the demons know where a good story can be found. Thus Singer did not hesitate to draw upon the bounty of superstition and folklore that he learned as a boy.

Singer's attraction to the supernatural is well-known. In his adult stories, such as "Taibele and Her Demon" and "The Mirror," demons are treacherous and seductive beings, but in his children's stories, such as "Tsirtsur & Peziza," he focuses on less dangerous supernatural figures, such as imps and goblins. In the latter story Peziza is an orphan imp who makes her home behind a stove, obviously a figure children could identify with and not be frightened of. She is the daughter of Lantuch the imp, a type of goblin who plays tricks on people but doesn't really harm them. In this Singer is following the oral tradition. In *Tsefunot ve-Aggadot* M. J. Berditchevsky includes an Eastern European folktale about a family of demons.[6] They sneak around after dark, making strange noises and frightening children who are trying to go to sleep. Or they hide inside mirrors and trick children into thinking they've turned into strange creatures. And they are easily chased out of a house by an old rabbi reading the Psalms out loud. Singer's orphan imp is completely compatible with this folktale about a family of demons.

The best examples of the kinds of oral folklore Singer was exposed to as a child are the oral stories collected by Y. L. Cahan in *Yiddishe Folkmaayses* (Vilna: 1931) and *Yiddishe Folklor* (Vilna: 1938). In his essay "What is Jewish About the Jewish Folktale?" Professor Dov Noy of Hebrew University writes about these seminal collections:

> When the fine Jewish folklorist Y. L. Cahan published the first annotated collection of genuine Jewish folktales from Eastern Europe over half a century ago . . . the collection was vehemently attacked by Jewish writers and critics. They claimed that except for the language, there was nothing particularly Jewish about the collection. The most vituperative criticism was directed at the universality of the tales' supernatural motifs and the "superstitions underlying them" . . . . Accordingly it was asserted, Jews have a "natural" aversion to the mystical and fantastic. The minority (among whom was Cahan) who represented fantasy literature as normative to Jewish culture, were harmful, even dangerous, insofar as such literature represented Jews as irrational and superstitious people to the outside world.[7]

Those familiar with the kind of angry responses provoked by Singer's supernatural stories—which still exists in some circles even today—should recognize the mindset that rejected the authenticity of Cahan's folktale collections. It is true that many the stories that Cahan collected are universal tales, variants of the kinds of stories collected by the brothers Grimm, in contrast to the explicitly Jewish tales most often found in rabbinic sources. But Cahan had made a profound discovery: that the Jewish oral tradition had kept alive a bounty of universal tales, especially fairy tales, that had never been deemed worthy of inclusion in the "sacred" collections. Here you will find Jewish variants of classic stories such as "Cinderella" and "The Golden Bird," as well as fairy tales about imprisoned princesses, wishing rings, and encounters with demons.

Many of these tales are strongly echoed in Singer's children's stories. This echo adds a ring of authenticity to them, for we recognize that they are only one step removed from a rich tradition of oral lore. Thus Singer's story "Mazel and Shlimazal" finds a strong parallel in *Yiddishe Folklor* in a story about a man who escaped misfortune. In both stories bad luck is personified. In the folktale, misfortune takes the form of a talking raven who follows a man wherever he goes. In Singer's story, Mazel, good luck, and Shlimazel, bad luck, are identified as spirits, but are personified, respectively, as a young man with a feather in his cap and as an old man with angry eyes wearing a long black coat.

But Singer being Singer, he does not simply create new stories that resemble the old ones. Instead, he does not hesitate to combine rabbinic and folk models in ways that are not found in either tradition. In the story "Menaseh's Dream," for example, he combines rabbinic and folk models in ways that are unique. In this story, one of Singer's most beautiful, a young orphan, Menassah, leads a lonely life in the forest. He has one book, *Alone in the Forest,* which he reads over and over, just as he lives the isolated life described in that book. At a time when things look especially desperate, he falls asleep and has a wonderful dream of journeying into heaven and being reunited with his family there. So too does he explore the heavenly realm, including its wonderful treasuries, and in this way he is reassured that in the time to come he will be reunited with his family for good. Further, at the end of the story Manasseh is woken from his dream by a young girl who clearly is intended to be his future companion, ending his long period of loneliness and isolation. Thus we see that the story follows the folk pattern of moving from sadness to happiness, as Manasseh's lonely days come to an end.

If we examine the frame of this story, we can see that it has strong echoes of Jewish lore. There are a great many tales about lonely shepherds in Jewish tradition, starting with the young King David. Singer's story connects directly to this tradition, and seems completely at home within it. Although Manasseh is not a shepherd, he spends his time in the forest, as do shepherds, and like them he has a lonely existence. Often these stories about isolated young shepherds are a starting point for fairy tales. In *Midrash Tehillim*, the Midrash on Psalms, the young shepherd, David, is said to have come upon a sleeping *re'em*.[8] The *re'em* is a horned mythological creature of great size, similar to a unicorn or a rhinoceros. Thinking it was a mountain, David climbed upon it. Before long the *re'em* awoke and rose up, and David, astride its horns, was lifted as high as the heavens. Then God caused a lion to appear, coming toward the *re'em*. When the *re'em* saw the lion, the king of beasts, it knelt down in fear. David was also afraid, so God caused a gazelle to come along, and as the lion sprang after it, David descended the horn of the *re'em* and escaped. The purpose of this imaginative tale is to explicate the meaning of the words of Psalm 22:22: *Deliver me from a lion's mouth, rescue me from the horns of the re'em.* Like the young shepherd David, Manasseh is also lifted up to heaven, but in his case the miracle takes place in a dream.

In addition, even though it may not be obvious at first, the frame of this story owes a great deal to "Hansel and Gretel." Here, however, instead of Hansel and Gretel being together from the first, the boy, Manasseh, does not find his Gretel until the end of the story, and then, it is suggested, his loneliness will have come to an end.

Now, while the frame of this story is very much in the tradition of fairy tales, the rest of the story owes a great deal to a completely different tradition, that of heavenly journeys. This is a rich tradition with sources in the Bible, in the ascent of Elijah into heaven in a fiery chariot (2 Kings 2:1–12). So too are there elaborate descriptions of the ascent of Moses into heaven to receive the Torah. Above all, there are the traditions connected with the ascent of Enoch found in the pseudepigraphal books of Enoch. This tradition is elaborated on in the Hekhalot texts, which describe journeys into heaven in great detail. These texts, dating between the 1st and 8th centuries, were created by Jewish mystics who sought greater knowledge of God by ascending on high. But one result of these texts and others found in rabbinic, kabbalistic and hasidic sources, is a considerable expansion of the map of heaven. We learn that there are seven heavens, with gatekeepers posted before every one. In the highest heavens we find not only God and the angels, but other figures, including the Messiah and the *Shekhinah*, the Bride of God, as well as strange mythological creatures called *hayyot* who hold up the Throne of Glory. Furthermore, heaven has a great many palaces, one for each of the patriarchs and great sages, where they teach Torah to the souls of the righteous. In this way it is possible for the righteous to study Torah with Rashi, Maimonides, Moses and even Abraham. Further, there are a great many treasuries in heaven—treasuries of rain and snow, the treasury of prayers, the treasury of merits, the treasury of gifts and the treasury of souls, the treasury of peace, the treasury of blessings, the treasury of dew with which God will revive the dead.

Readers of "Manasseh's Dream" will recognize these treasuries, which Manasseh explores in his dream, during his heavenly ascent, and will realize that Singer is working well within the traditions about heaven described in these earlier texts. This is absolutely characteristic of Singer: while he invents his own narratives, they are usually based on existing Jewish traditions, and when it comes to the details about heaven or hell or other supernatural realms or beings, Singer draws on the existing traditions and, in fact, is quite faithful to them.

Another story with pronounced fairy tale elements is "The Fearsome Inn," where the witch Doboshova has enslaved three young women and plans to enslave three young men who turn up in a snowstorm. However, Leibel, one of the young men, is returning home from a faraway city where he has been studying Kabbalah, which Singer describes as "the ancient Hebrew books that reveal the mysteries of heaven and earth." He has been given a precious gift by his master, a piece of magic chalk. "If you draw a line around man or beast with this piece of chalk, it will imprison them in a circle." Naturally the young man uses this chalk to save himself and the other young men and the three maidens, drawing a circle around the witch and her devil, Lapitut, who try to imprison them. The witch and devil turn into shadows and vanish behind the Mountains of Darkness, themselves a familiar presence in Jewish folklore, "where there is neither day nor night and dusk is eternal."

Even though the frame of this story strong resembles a fairy tale like "Hansel and Gretel," where two children are imprisoned by a witch, it is filled with echoes of Jewish folklore. The circle that the student of Kabbalah draws around the witch and her devil is a common device in Jewish folktales, such as one from *Maaseh Nissim* about Asmodeus, the king of demons, trying to steal a bride-to-be from her groom, who, assisted by a wise rabbi, draws a magic circle around her that even Asmodeus cannot enter.[9] Here, then, we can see a story which has combined elements of universal fairy tales with specific elements of Jewish folklore and magic.

At one point in "The Fearsome Inn," after the witch and demon have been captured, the devil Lapitut begs for his pipe, in order to smoke a mandrake root. Leibel, the student of Kabbalah, is not foolish enough to permit this—perhaps because he is familiar with the story of Joseph della Reina, the kabbalist who captured Lilith and Ashmodai on Mount Seir but permitted them to sniff incense, which gave them all the power they needed to break the chains in which they had been bound.

Indeed, the young Singer was fascinated with the story of Joseph della Reina. In "Growing Up" Singer tells his friend that "I was possessed by the spirit of Joseph della Reina, a saint who centuries earlier had captured Satan and put him in chains. Had Satan remained so confined, Rabbi Joseph could have brought the Messiah at that time, but he had taken pity on Satan, who had cried and bemoaned his fate and pleaded with Rabbi Joseph for something to eat or drink, or at least for a pinch of snuff. When Rabbi Joseph gave him the snuff, Satan broken into hellish laughter and two sparks shot from his nostrils. Right after that, the chains crumpled from his body and he flew away along with ten thousand demons to Mt. Seir near Sodom, where the dark powers hold sway. I told Feivel that Rabbi Joseph's soul had entered my body and I was destined to carry out what he had commenced." In this amazing passage Singer retells the famous story of Joseph della Reina, adding his own changes—Asmodeus into Satan, the incense into snuff, the linkage of Mt. Seir and Sodom, the ten thousand other demons—and acknowledges that as a child he felt possessed by the soul of a holy heretic: "I would become a heretic, and while I rode horseback on the Sabbath he, Feivel, would follow behind and listen to his wisdom." Here he not only identifies with Joseph della Reina, but with Aher, Elisha ben Abuyah, the talmudic heretic who rode on horseback on the Sabbath while accompanied by his disciple, Rabbi Meir. The grown Singer, as well, was something of a holy heretic, who pursued his own path in literature with the kind of single-minded determination of Joseph della Reina, and with a power that borders on the supernatural.

In an autobiographical story, "A Hanukah Eve in Warsaw," we have a glimpse into the imagination of the young Singer. Here he recalls walking through the streets of Warsaw when a powerful wind began to blow. "A fear came over me—I was lost! . . . . That which I had always feared had apparently happened—the evil spirits had turned their wrath on me. . . . I knew where the gale sought to carry me—to Sodom, to beyond the Mountains of Darkness, to Asmodeus's castle, to Mt. Seir." These fears of the young Singer, for whom the truth of Jewish lore was a fact of life, prepared the way for the Singer the storyteller, who was able to convey his vivid experience of these traditions in stories that keep them alive in the imaginations of young readers fortunate enough to encounter them.

Endnotes

1. This Judeo-Arabic text is the basis of the well-known Hebrew text *Hibbur Yafeh me-ha-Yeshuah* 88a. It is interesting to note that there is no talmudic source for this story.

2. One version of this story is found in *Alphabeta de-Rabbi Akiva* in *Otzar Midrashim*, p. 424. The best-known and most extensive version, and the one quoted here, is found in *Zohar* 1:2b.

3. *Genesis Rabbah* 99:1.

4. *Sefer ha-Yashar, Va-Yera*, 35b–38a.

5. *Bereshit Rabbah* 50:2. Gabriel had been sent to destroy the sinful cities and Raphael to save Lot.

6. *Tsefunot ve-Aggadot* edited by Michal Joseh Bin Gorion (Berditchevsky). Tel Aviv: Am Oved, 1957.

7. "What is Jewish About the Jewish Folktale?" by Dov Noy. Foreword to *Miriam's Tambourine: Jewish Folktales From Around the World* (MacMillan, 1986), p. xiii.

8. *Midrash Tehillim* 22:28. This legend about King David explains the enigmatic meaning of Psalm 22:22, *Deliver me from a lion's mouth rescue me from the horns of the re'em*, by offering an account of the young shepherd David escaping both from the *re'em* and a lion. In *B. Zevahim* 113b the wandering sage Rabbah bar Bar Hannah reported seeing a *re'em* in one of his journeys. He described a one-day old *re'em* as being as large as Mount Tabor.

9. *Maaseh Nissim*. See "The Bride of Demons" in *Lilith's Cave: Jewish Tales of the Supernatural* (Harper San Francisco, 1987), edited by Howard Schwartz, pp. 25–28.

Laya Firestone Seghi
Glimpsing the Moon:
the Feminine Principle in Kabbalah

And God made two great lights: the greater light to rule the day, and the lesser light to rule the night . . .
Genesis 1:16

Jewish legends tells us that even before the first man and woman were created, the dynamic tension that exists between them was foreshadowed. The cosmic events of the fourth day of creation parallel the subsequent ordering of the male-female relationship within the Jewish system. According to biblical lore, the sun and the moon were actually created on the first day and at first enjoyed equal powers and privileges. It was on the fourth day, the legend relates, that the heavenly spheres were assigned their places after the following conversation between the moon and God. The moon asked why the world was created with the letter *bet* (numerically equivalent to the number two). God replied, "So that My creatures will know that there are two worlds." The moon questioned further: "Which of the two worlds is larger—his world or the world to come?" And God replied, "The world to come is larger." The moon persisted: "You created two worlds, one greater and one lesser. You created the heaven and earth, the heaven exceeding the earth; You created fire and water, the water stronger because it can quench the fire; and now You have created the sun and the moon. It would be fitting that one should be greater than the other." Then God spoke to the moon: "I know you would have Me make you greater than the sun. As a punishment, I decree that you may keep but one-sixtieth of your light."

A less vindictive version of the legend has the moon asking God, "Is it possible that two kings can share the same crown? "God replies, "Go, make yourself smaller." The moon responds, "Is it fitting that when I raise a reasonable question, I must diminish myself?" God says to her: "Go, you will rule both by day and by night." In yet another version, a more promising one, God says, "In the future world I will restore your light so that your light will again be as the light of the sun."[1]

Regardless of which version of the legend is told, these stories together can be understood as early Jewish attempts to grapple with the duality of the *masculine* and *feminine* principles. The sun and moon symbolize, not only in Jewish myth but for people around the world, complementary but opposite modes of being that man and woman have come to personify .Before beginning to explore the feminine principle in Jewish mysticism, therefore, it is important to recognize that the terms *masculine* and *feminine* are difficult to disentangle from their natural identification with gender. Although the masculine and feminine principles represent psychological qualities present in both men *and* women, the terms are often expressed with reference to the biological and traditional social roles that men and women have assumed.

Considering the cultural context that produced the literature of Jewish mysticism—a patriarchal system in which gender stereotypes were accepted as the norm—the masculine and feminine principles were seen as being inherent in the nature of men and women respectively.[2] Therefore, while reading the passages ahead, bear in mind that the qualities considered to be masculine and feminine exist within every psyche, male or female. At the same time, we need not lose sight of the fact that the Kabbalistic identification of the masculine with the positive quality of love or mercy of God and the feminine with the negative quality of God's stern judgment perpetuated the already existing social polarization of the sexes within Judaism.

So, although according to the Bible the moon rules the night, the Jewish attitude toward that nocturnal light and the feminine mode of being it symbolizes reflects Judaism's deep ambivalence about women. That ambivalence is understandable, considering that in order to establish itself as a separate religion, Judaism had to differentiate itself from pagan cultures that worshiped female deities. For those seeking to resolve the tension of the opposites, however, the Jewish legend of the creation of the sun and moon provides hopeful indications. As in our own individual development–in which we begin life in an embryonic state of wholeness, then struggle to differentiate our identities, and finally, toward the end of life, if all goes well, arrive at a state of renewed wholeness–the legend tens us that in the future the sun and moon win once again be restored to their original state. To hasten the restoration of that mythical state of harmony, the legend of the sun and the moon draws us to reevaluate the diminished power of the moon and the feminine, which has been relegated to the night.

In seeking out the lesser feminine principle in Judaism, one may notice how it emerges obscurely, intermittently. One catches it as if glimpsing the moon amid the clouds. Hidden in the predominantly male storyline and perspective of the biblical texts, the voluminous rabbinic commentaries, the mystical interpretations of the Kabbalah, and the vast variety of Jewish folklore and ritual, the feminine principle repeatedly makes its appearance. Depending upon the context in which it emerges, related to a variety of historical factors, that principle is either negated and dismissed or enhanced and embellished, reflecting the waxing and waning of the feminine principle in Judaism.

The female biblical characters and Talmudic commentaries about them and other women offer a rich area in which to explore the undervalued feminine in Judaism. The narratives about the flesh-and-blood characters of Sarah, Rebecca, Tamar, Miriam, Ruth, Devorah, and Judith, for example, or the stories about Hannah and her seven sons, Rabbi Akiba's wife, Rachel, or Rabbi Meir's wife, Bruria, provide a wealth of information about how the feminine expresses itself. The ability to see into the future, to execute a mission with purpose, the instinctive drive to reproduce, to lead, to follow, to love-all these aspects of the feminine are embedded in the Jewish collective unconscious. In studying these Jewish stories of the feminine, we confront universal archetypal motifs that have been shaped within a particular Jewish frame. Those powerful feminine qualities that have not been given conscious value, representing neglected aspects of the psyche evoke considerable ambivalence in Jewish sources. Women are generally portrayed either as praiseworthy and virtuous or as dangerous and to be shunned.

It is in the realm of Jewish mysticism, however, that the *essence* of the feminine has been sought. In Kabbalah, both the positive and negative polarities of the feminine can be seen at their most extreme. It may come as no great surprise, therefore, that the feminine as described in the Kabbalah has the same essential attributes as the Great Goddess of the universe, that archetype of the Great Mother which appears repeatedly in numerous religions and cultures, guised in a variety of myths, fairy tales, and even individual dreams. As Joseph Campbell, the popular scholar of mythology, described her:

> She is the paragon of all paragons of beauty, the reply to all desire, the bliss-bestowing goal of every hero's earthly and unearthly quest. She is mother, sister, mistress, bride . . . the comforting, the nourishing, the "good" mother. . . . She encompasses the encompassing, nourishes the nourishing, and is the life of everything that lives. She is also the death of everything that dies. . . . She is the womb and the tomb. Thus she unites the "good" and the "bad," exhibiting the two modes of the remembered mother, not as personal only; but as universal.[3]

Those archetypal feminine qualities, both positive and negative, are of supreme significance throughout the complex web of interpretive commentaries that constitute the Kabbalistic literature. Even though the origin and development of Kabbalistic ideas continues to be debated,[4] there is no question that the power of the feminine is essential in the Kabbalistic understanding of the divine creative process and our own human potentialities.[5]

Rather than enter into questions of scholarly debate, I will take the concepts and images of the feminine in Kabbalah that scholars of Jewish mysticism have already raised for discussion and explore them from my perspective as a woman and a psychotherapist. For it is an irony to reflect on that the spiritual object of so much attention in Kabbalah—the Mother archetype in one form or another—has been kept at such a distance from the actual physical source of the concept: women. The study of Kabbalah, after all, has traditionally been an exclusive one, reserved for men only, and more specifically, for men over forty, those who have mastered the study of traditional Jewish texts and have also grounded themselves with the responsibilities of marriage and children. On the whole, the perceptions and experiences of women themselves have not been included.

Nevertheless, despite centuries in which the Jewish religious authorities condemned anything remotely resembling ancient fertility cults and sacred prostitution, despite the elimination of women from any official role in the Temple and the disparagement of their participation in Torah studies, the feminine principle managed to reemerge with force. From a psychological point of view, the reemergence of the feminine in Judaism is not only understandable but inevitable. As a result of being buried in the unconscious, idolatrous worship of the Universal Mother having been virtually erased from consciousness, the energetic value attached to the feminine became even more powerful. The swing of the pendulum in the direction of patriarchal values against the background of the pagan world propelled an equally forceful swing in the opposite direction at a later time. Thus, during the earliest writings (the Kabbalists through the subsequent innovations of Lurianic Kabbalah in sixteenth-century Safed and beyond, an erotic mythology developed in which feminine imagery was personified, giving expression to the awe and terror inspired by the primal power of the female. And now again, in our time, there is a renewed interest in Jewish mysticism and the expression of the feminine in Judaism.

In grappling with the full, dynamic range of experience—male and female, physical and spiritual, good and evil—the Kabbalah addresses the ALL that is God. The sacred marriage of Masculine and Feminine at the core of its system of sexual symbolism pointed the way back to the primordial state of wholeness in God and the Garden of Eden, and forward to a goal not yet achieved: the coming of the Messiah. The personal goal in striving for that mythic union is a living experience of the divine in everyday life, a state of wholeness transcending masculine and feminine, where the war between opposites can find peace. By developing a mythic system in which the Feminine in all her aspects could be conjoined with her opposite, the mystical tradition in Judaism pointed to a redemptive means for full spiritual and psychological integration.

As we examine the multiple expressions of the Feminine in Kabbalistic literature from the perspective of depth psychology, we assume that the mythic figures represented there are not isolated entities developed solely within the Jewish psyche. Rather, this approach begins with the premise that Carl Jung pioneered, in which all mythic content represents universal expressions of the collective unconscious.[6] The distinctly Jewish versions of the feminine archetype emerge from the particular language of Jewish history and experience, yet the core content—that of the Universal Mother—reflects collective elements of the human psyche. In this view, the mythic content that the Kabbalah elaborates is similar to that elaborated in the history of many cultures and religions, signifying the "truth" as the psyche knows it.

The archetype of the Universal Mother, as represented in a wide array of mythic and cultural material, thus mirrors a universal psychic fact, that of the primary condition of human life. The symbiotic union of the infant with the mother is the equivalent of the initial developmental stage of consciousness, in which the unconscious world of instincts reigned supreme.[7] In the Kabbalistic myth of the exile of the Feminine, this universal human condition, clothed in the particulars of the Jewish collective unconscious, represents not only the inevitable separation of the individual from the paradisal state of union with the mother, the source of life, but also the collective suppression of the Divine Mother in favor of the patriarchal values of law and spirit.

In the following pages we will take a closer look at the two polarized mythic figures of the Feminine as expressed in Jewish mystical literature. The Shekhinah and Lilith, in all the fine gradations of their various manifestations, as the Compassionate Mother, the Seductive Temptress, and the Devouring Mother, together constitute the wholeness pattern of the archetypal Feminine. So let us attend to the Universal Mother archetype, both Good and Terrible, as she surfaces repeatedly in Kabbalistic texts.

SHEKHINAH

In early rabbinic literature, the term Shekhinah, although grammatically feminine in Hebrew, referred to a neutral concept of "God's glory," the essence of God's "indwelling presence." With the mystical literature of the Kabbalah, however, came the dramatic innovation that recontextualized the term into a feminine concept. As the image of the yearned-for opposite as well as that which had been consciously rejected, the Shekhinah came to refer to the feminine aspect of the divinity. A primary feminine figure in the Kabbalah, she shared many of the same traits as goddesses described in other religions and mythologies. She also came to be identified with a host of concepts and images that had previously been associated in Jewish texts with the Feminine.

The Shekhinah, therefore, is not one clear-cut image, but rather an ever-changing entity, depending on her context and purpose. Like the different aspects of the tripart Goddess, represented variously as Maiden, Mother, or Crone, the Shekhinah has been personified alternately as a daughter, sister, mother, queen, bride-consort, and old woman. Figurative associations and conceptual associations were also attached to the Shekhinah. Just as in the variations of the Mother archetype described by Carl Jung, the Shekhinah was variously associated with the Earth, Moon, Night, Well, Sea, Garden, Pearl, Discarded Cornerstone, Heavenly Jerusalem, Kingdom of God, and Community of Israel, among others.

When the Shekhinah emerged as a separate mythic entity within the Kabbalah, some of the concepts that had previously been linked with the Feminine were incorporated into it. The figure of Wisdom (Hokhmah, or Sophia in Christian theology) in the first ten chapters of Proverbs, for example, had a distinctly feminine association, as for example in the verse "Say unto wisdom: 'Thou art my sister'" (Prov. 7:4), or "Wisdom crieth aloud in the street, /She uttereth her voice in the broad places," (Prov. 1:20), or when she appears as the first of created beings, "The Lord made me as the beginning of His way ,/The first of His works of old" (Prov. 8:22).

The notion that the feminine Wisdom was present before human creation foreshadows later Kabbalistic ideas about the role of the Sefirot in creation. The Sefirot represent the ten creative powers or primordial energies by which God is manifest. Through a series of gradations, the limitless, formless, eternal and unknowable divine essence—the Ein Sof—becomes manifest by degrees from the top Sefirah, Keter/Crown, signifying the most transcendent force, down to Malkut/Kingdom, the lowest and most physical manifestation of God's presence. The third highest Sefirah, Binah, the Supernal Mother, along with the second, Hokhmah, as the Supernal Father, are the first creative processes, which initiate the "lowering" of the ineffable divine essence down to a level accessible to us. As Binah, the Mother, the Shekhinah is linked with the positive, life-giving aspect of the Universal Mother, which was honored in ancient times.

But the Shekhinah was associated not only with the overflowing Supernal Mother Binah, but also with her daughter Malkut, the final Sefirah, that feminine receptacle that brought the divine essence down into the world of physical form. As the feminine element of God's dynamic nature, the Shekhinah was thus portrayed both as an idealized being and as one in need of transformation. Similarly, it is interesting to note that even in the early, positive image of Wisdom as a feminine figure, the bipolar nature of the Feminine emerged. For in Proverbs, Wisdom's shadow sister Folly is never far away:

> My son, attend unto my wisdom;
> Incline thine ear to my understanding;
> . . . For the lips of a strange woman drop honey;
> and her mouth is smoother than oil;
> But her end is bitter as wormwood,
> Sharp as a two-edged sword.
> Her feet go down to death;
> Her steps take hold on the netherworld . . .
> (*Prov.* 5:1–5)

The negative aspect of the feminine, portrayed in Proverbs as Folly, bears some resemblance to the final Sefirah, Malkut. Referred to as the "depth of evil," Malkut is the feminine aspect of God that descends into the earthly plane, that realm of the physical with all its attendant dangers. As the receptacle of God's goodness and light, the Shekhinah as Malkut is in itself the *absence* of God's light. As with Folly in Proverbs, with whom she is later identified in the *Zohar*, Malkut heads toward the netherworld, in the opposite direction from God.

Just as the primordial figure of Wisdom was absorbed into the femi-
nized notion of the Shekhinah, so was the image of a compassionate,
ever-loving mother. A particularly poignant image drawn upon was that
of the foremother Rachel:

> A voice is heard in Ramah,
> Lamentation and bitter weeping,
> Rachel weeping for her children,
> She refuseth to be comforted for her children
> Because they are not.
> (Jer. 31:15)

Kabbalists developed this long-suffering figure of a mother hovering
over Israel into an independent mythic figure. In a similar vein, the image
of Jerusalem or Zion as the Mother of Israel, which appears repeatedly in
biblical and subsequent literature, lends the positive feminine association
of the Good Mother to the Shekhinah figure. In one legend, for example, Jeremiah sees a woman dressed in black who finally identifies herself,
"I am thy Mother Zion." The hardships suffered by the people of Israel
during their periods of exile evoked the tender image of a grieving
mother who mourned for their suffering and identified with them in
their exile. This image did not need to be stretched too much further to
become the lamenting Shekhinah, that compassionate feminine figure in
Kabbalah who was herself suffering in exile.

In a similar fashion to that of Zion as a maternal figure, the identification of the Community of Israel (Knesset Yisrael) as a feminine being
had emotional power. In describing the desired relationship between
God and Israel, the metaphor of marital fidelity was used, implicitly in the
Bible and explicitly in the Prophets, with tremendous personal resonance. Given the more positive value attributed to masculine characteristics in Judaism, it is not surprising that God is represented as the
Husband and Israel as His Wife. The resulting poetry in which God
promised to "allure her, and bring her into the wilderness, and speak tenderly unto her" achieved great emotional depth:

> And I will betroth thee unto Me forever;
> Yea, I will betroth thee unto Me in righteousness, and in justice,
> And in lovingkindness, and in compassion.
> And I will betroth thee unto Me in faithfulness;
> And thou shalt know the Lord.
> (Has.2:19–20)

The metaphor of the Community of Israel as God's wife was developed further in later biblical literature. Nowhere, however, was the metaphor of a loving couple more erotic than in the Song of Songs. Rabbi Akiva ben Joseph, (ca. 50–132 CE) the most prominent *tanna* (teacher of Mishnah, the oral law) and leader of his time, who had himself successfully probed the secret Orchard of esoteric mysteries, argued forcefully for the inclusion of Song of Songs in the biblical canon. With his famous statement, ". . . all of Scripture is holy, but the Song of Songs is the Holy of Holies," he designated the work as a sacred love poem between God and His consort.

This rich allegory of Husband and Beloved Spouse, representing God and the people of Israel, was the most powerful symbolic seed that germinated within the Kabbalah. In the mystical tradition, the rabbinic interpretation of the Song as an allegory was transformed into a dramatic myth. Whereas the rabbinic commentaries identified the Song as being about the love between God and Knesset Yisrael, the Kabbalists identified Knesset Yisrael with the Shekhinah. Thus, for the Kabbalists the Song was an expression of love between the masculine and feminine elements *within* God.

The sexual union of male and female powers within God, the holiest of mysteries, was the central metaphor of Kabbalah. The holy state of unity between the masculine and feminine elements—that is, the dynamic essence of God—was seen as the mystical symbol for the ultimate source of creation. But despite the Jewish mystics' monotheistic insistence that male and female elements were *symbols* for processes taking place *within* God, the distinct descriptions of those elements as separate personalities allowed for the development of a mythology of the "divine family" very close in composition to the "divine tetrads" of numerous other religions.

According to the Kabbalistic myth, the Heavenly Father and Mother are eternally conjoined: "Never does the inclination of the Father and the Mother toward each other cease. They always go out together and dwell together. They never separate and never leave each other. They are together in complete union" (*Zohar* III, 29ob). The result of the union of the Divine Parents are the Son and Daughter, who, like many a brother and sister in mythical divine families, are also to be conjoined in marital union. The Temple in Jerusalem was to serve as the nuptial chamber for God the King and His wife Matronit, who were a "lower" version of the "upper" couple of the Father and Mother united.

But, as is all too well known, the glorious state of marital bliss between the King and the Shekhinah was not destined to last. Depending on which strand of myth one follows, the separation between God and His Wife occurred either because of a cosmological flaw in the creative process or because of human sin, or both. In some versions the separation occurred because of Adam's sin, in that he mistook the last Sefirah, Malkut, for the totality of God and thus shattered the unity; or, insofar as the Community of Israel was identified with the Shekhinah, the sins of Israel contributed to the exile. According to the Lurianic myth of the "breaking of the vessels," the separation of the feminine element of the divinity from God occurred on the cosmic level when the lower Sefirot were unable to contain the power of the upper lights. Regardless of the mythic interpretation, the final result was a breakdown in the primordial wholeness, with a rift between the masculine and feminine elements of God.

This overlap and blurring of mythic motifs, resulting in the striking parallels between the metaphysical exile occurring on the ultimate spiritual plane—within the Divinity itself—and the exile of Adam and Eve from the Garden of Eden, and/or the people of Israel from their Holy Land, is a commonplace occurrence in the development of mythic material. It serves as a reminder that the very source of myths is our own psychic makeup, with the various symbolic images drawn from the deepest level of the collective unconscious. But, it must be emphasized, this acknowledgment is intended not to psychologize the nature of God or the metaphysical realm, but rather to assert that our human ability to interact with the Divine must necessarily flow from our own psychic nature. We can only "know" what our psychic structure permits us to apprehend and understand of the divine power .

Rabbi Akiva's statement, "Wherever Israel was exiled, it is as if the Shekhinah were exiled with them," summarized the identification of Israel's suffering with God's wife, who was also in exile. As the tenth Sefira, Malkut, the one furthest removed from the highest source of divine light where all is One, the Shekhina was portrayed as also wandering in a state of exile. This significant mythic motif of exile took on a particularly dramatic quality after the expulsion of the Jews from Spain. For the painful exile that the Kabbalists themselves experienced evoked a deep emotional resonance: just as they had been sent out wandering, so had the Shekhinah. As a feminine figure wandering in this earthly realm, carrying the divine light but far removed from the source of that light, the Shekhinah thus represented a manifestation of God that can be apprehended in the world: God's divine immanence—in everything—as perceived right here and now in living matter.

In this sense, the Shekhinah was also closely linked to the concept of soul *(neshamah)*, for the twin myths of union and exile explained not only the nature of God and the creation of the universe, but also the nature of the individual. Just as the cosmic origin of the world and of God was absolute unity, so the individual was understood to be a cosmic being that contains the whole world in itself. As the cosmic process of creation mythologically heralded the world of duality and the exile of the Shekhinah, so Adam's sin, which symbolized human nature, indicated the inevitable separation of the spiritual soul from physical being.[8] The spiritual goal of restoring the full structure of one's spiritual potentialities is the process of *tikkun*, restoration. On the personal level this means bringing the soul home, letting the unconscious, instinctual side regain its harmonious balance within the psyche. On the collective level, *tikkun* is restoring the original unity of the masculine and the feminine principles, which will result in the long-awaited redemption.

As a figure embodying the soul, the Shekhinah appeared to Kabbalists in dreams and visions as well as auditory experiences.[9] Throughout most of his long life, Joseph Karo (1488–1575), the author of the *Shulchan Aruch*, the code of Jewish law, experienced a personal *maggid* (literally "sayer" or "teller") that he identified with the Shekhinah.[10] This channeled personal spirit, who identified herself at times as the Mother, the Shekhinah, the Matronit, and the Mishnah, spoke to him and gave him practical and personal advice, interpreted secrets of the Kabbalah, and generally was the creative muse stimulating him to write his halachic (legal) works.

Although more rare than such auditory experiences, visionary appearances of the Shekhinah have also been documented. In Hayyim Vital's *Sefer ha-Hezyonot* (Book of Visions), for example, he reports a dream in which the Prophet Elijah took him to a mountaintop, where a ladder stood leading up to heaven. Once there, Elijah disappears. .

and behold a dignified woman, beautiful like the sun, was standing on top of the ladder. And I thought in my heart that she was my mother. And she said. "What is it, my son Hayyim, why are you crying? I heard your tears, and came to help you." And she stretched forth her right hand, and lifted me up to the top of the ladder. And I saw, and behold, there was there a big round window, and the flame of a great fire came out of it, sweeping back and forth like the appearance of lightning, with great strength, and it bummed everything that was there. And I called out with bitterness of soul to that woman and said to her: "My mother! My mother! Save me from this fire so that it should not burn me!" And she said: "Nobody can save you from this flame but you yourself! Therefore I shall advise you what to do. . . ."[11]

Like the feminine Anima figure that Jung identified as an archetype of the collective unconscious, the Skekhinah presented herself to the Kabbalists as an inspiration for their own spiritual evolution.

Thus mediating between the earthly realm and the divine, the Shekhinah holds a double position. She receives the emanations from the upper Sefirot, but she must transmute them into form to allow them expression. In one allegorical rendering of this concept, the forms are described as the "garments of the Shekhinah." And so we see that it falls to the realm of the Feminine to give form to the ultimate majesty of the divine essence. Just as goddesses were personifications of the energy that gives birth to forms and nourishes them—the energy of Mother Earth—so the Shekhinah was that which allowed God's undifferentiated total-ity—the most transcendent Ein Sof—to be manifested in the world of matter.

According to the *Zohar*, however, the process of containing the divine energies naturally entailed some sort of residue. Thus, according to this Kabbalistic interpretation, evil is a natural by-product of the creative process.[12] For consider the negative aspects of bringing life energy into form: as in the birth process, which naturally takes place in the womb of the feminine, the harsh and punishing contractions of labor are necessary to bring forth new life. As the various divine energies were expelled by Malkut into the world of form, they left an outside shell *(kelipah)*, like an afterbirth, that in itself did not house the divine energy but was capable of containing it and of retaining a residue.

Through such mythic motifs—the contraction *(tzimtzum)* of God, the breaking of the vessels, the falling of the shells *(kelippot)* into the realm of the evil Other Side *(sitrah acherah)*, the exile of the Shekhinha, Adam's sin of separating the Tree of Life from the Tree of Knowledge of Good and Evil—the dark side of the Feminine and the world of the Mother (the *material* world) were confronted. In the world of form, which con-stitutes the "garments" of the Shekhinah, death is the other side of life. For the Kabbalah to reflect *all* aspects of the human condition, the Feminine had to be presented in its entirety—not just the positive side as life-giving and loving, but the cruel and dangerous side as well.

LILITH

The ancient myth of Lilith, queen of demons, was an ideal vehicle to represent the dark aspects of the feminine as a devouring mother and sensual seductress. Reconstituted within the Kabbalistic framework to personify the negative threat from the evil Other Side, Lilith embodied a universal fantasy of a powerful wild woman that incites both fear and libido. With her dual aspect of child-strangler and dark-haired seductress, Lilith offered a Jewish version of the seductive and terrifying facets of the universal Mother, that primal force that gives life but also takes it away.

Interestingly, because of her exile into the lower world, the darker face of the Shekhinah was at times not too far from that of Lilith herself. In her state of exile, the Shekhinah and the scattered sparks she carried within her came under the influence of the evil Other Side and needed the conscious intention of mystics to redeem her.[13] With proper intentionality, the Shekhinah could be raised from her manifestation on the earthly plane to a spiritual essence, through ritual enactment. But if the feminine were to be encountered without the proper intention, or if the intention were misdirected, the frightening aspect of the feminine—Lilith, the terrible mother and seductive temptress—might emerge. Thus the two polarities of the Feminine, the Shekhinah and Lilith, as in other universal portrayals of the dual Mother, were linked mythologically to mirror the ambivalence inherent in the feminine principle.

In other historical and religious traditions, both among Semitic and non-Semitic peoples (the Babylonians, Assyrians, and Arabs, as well as the Sumerians and Hittites) , the demonic goddess that Lilith represents occurs in various guises.[14] The story of Lilith that has been pieced together from diverse Jewish sources includes the malevolent traits described in those myths but places them within a Jewish context. The *Alphabet of Ben Sira*, for example, a medieval work that fleshes out prior sporadic references to Lilith in the Talmud and post-Talmudic literature, portrayed Lilith in terms similar to the Babylonian Goddess Lamashtu, preying on women with the intention of causing harm to their children; In this Jewish text, however, Lilith's malevolence was given its root cause in the biblical verse in the first chapter of Genesis, "In the image of God He created him, male and female He created them" (Gen. 1:27). According to this explanation, before his rib was fashioned into a helper fit for Adam, the Eve described in the second chapter of Genesis, Adam and Lilith were created simultaneously. But—and this is the source of her resentment and malice—Lilith was not given equal treatment.

In the imagination of the Talmudic period, Adam's first wife, Lilith, was not willing to take a subservient position to him. When Adam wanted to have intercourse with her, she spoke up: "Why should I lie beneath you when I am your equal, since both of us were created from dust?" And when Adam attempted to overpower her, she incanted God's magic name, rose into the air, and flew away to the Red Sea. There she supposedly engaged in unbridled promiscuity and bore a demonic brood of a hundred a day. When God sent the three angels, Senoy, Sansenoy, and Semangelof, to bring her back, she refused to return. When they threatened to drown her in the sea, she finally conceded, swearing in the name of God that she would harm no child when she saw the angels or their names or images on an amulet. Moreover, she agreed to the death of her own children day after day.

The composite myth of Lilith, of which this excerpt is but one example, is the product of the collective Jewish imagination spanning centuries. The dual aspect of Lilith, as both an object of sexual fantasy and a threat to childbearing women and newborn infants, constitutes a merging of the archetypal motifs of lust and terror that the archetypal Mother has long evoked. From the early depictions of Lilith as the "first Eve" in the Talmud, the emotionally charged Jewish attitude toward the Feminine is apparent. And understandably so. Jewish culture struggled to assert male dominance in the midst of neighboring cultures that recognized the inherent power of the female, attributing power to feminine deities. To compensate for the relatively insecure position of male domination during the establishment of Judaism, the value of the feminine traits was ignored or, as in the story of the *original* woman, negative traits were emphasized.

From the standpoint of both men and women, the thought of one who would willfully cause harm to the most vulnerable self—a child— is horrific. And yet every child, male or female, by the very nature of being innocent and vulnerable, is faced with the possibility of harm. Since the primary caretaker of the child has traditionally been the mother, the horror of that threatening exposure to harm is represented by a "terrible mother," in this case portrayed by Lilith in her child-destructive mode. Not just males, but females too, perhaps to an even greater extent than males because of the betrayal by their own gender, experience the fear of being subject to an aspect of the Feminine that is willfully malicious.

So where did this malicious Feminine, feared by male and female alike, originate? Numerous versions of her birth have been recounted. In one version, Lilith was created before Adam, on the fifth day of Creation. She was the "living creature" with whose swarms God filled the waters. In another version, as discussed earlier, she was fashioned from the earth like Adam, but instead of clean earth, God took filth and impure sediments from the earth, and out of these he formed a female. In a third version, the female was attached to Adam's side, but God sawed his creation into two and Lilith flew off to the Cities of the Sea. In yet another, Lilith emerged out of the aspect of God, Gevurah or Din, that manifests in divine acts of judgment.

Whatever her origins, Lilith's existence was closely connected to the mysterious dark side, the opposite of all that is holy and acceptable. That Lilith's activities were involved with acts of malice and lust is understandable. For in representing the destructive side of the Feminine and the unconscious, Lilith personified a dangerous complex of buried instincts. Her image was so dreaded that for centuries, and in traditional circles even in our time, incantations, rituals, and amulets were devised to protect women in childbirth from her power. On a psychological level, one might say that the more something is repressed, the greater its emotional power. According to this gauge, Lilith's power to harm and seduce may be considered in direct relation to the degree to which the feminine principle has been repressed.

Sexually, this equation is easy to follow. When appreciation of the Feminine is lacking, an unconscious counterattack from the Feminine may be likely. This cause and effect can be demonstrated in the medieval myth of Lilith and Adam. It was told that when Adam understood that death came into the world because of Cain's murder of Abel, he separated from Eve and slept alone. For 130 years, the myth goes, Adam did not draw near to Eve. But during this period of abstinence, Lilith used to come and lie with him, and from their union, demons and spirits were born.

It is just such abstinence and denial of the natural that makes one vulnerable to the seduction of Lilith. The more the conscious being is identified with all that is good and virtuous, the more the unconscious will be identified with everything that is consciously rejected. By not acknowledging his natural sexuality, Adam opened the door to Lilith's seduction.

The *Zohar* described Lilith's seductive activities:

She roams at night, and goes all about the world and makes sport with men and causes them to emit seed. In every place where a man sleeps alone in a house, she visits him and grabs him and attaches herself to him and has her desire from him, and bears from him. (*Zohar* I, 19b)

It was not just the solitary and abstinent male that was vulnerable to Lilith's seduction, but even the married man. For, according to the Kabbalistic view, the sexual mystery between a "man and his wife" is the holiest of mysteries, reflecting the mystery on high.[15] When practiced in holiness, with the proper intentions, the Shekhinah, the Divine Presence, was understood to join the couple during sexual union[16] and to derive joy from the fulfillment of their religious obligation.[17] And just as sexual union practiced "below" honored the heavenly union "above," whatever aspect of the sexual union did not conform to the strictest standards of "holiness" was subject to the entrance of Lilith.[18]

And so it also can be seen how sexual fantasy provided a likely entry point for Lilith. This apparently was the case with Rabbi Joseph della Reina, a Spanish Kabbalist who attempted to bring the Messiah toward the end of the fifteenth century. Having failed, he is said to have turned to the forces of the evil Other Side and succumbed to the temptations of Lilith. The subject of numerous versions of folktales, Rabbi Joseph is described in a recent retelling:

Once, long ago, he had been a sage and had even been regarded as a holy man. But fate had dragged him to the other side, and now he was wedded to Lilith, the Queen of Demons. For it was none other than Lilith herself to whom he spoke, for she instructed him in the ways of Black Magic. . . . he wished to possess the most desirable woman in the world. Nor was Lilith jealous of this; on the contrary, she encouraged him to fulfill his every lust. . . .[19]

Rabbi Joseph's degradation epitomizes human vulnerability in the face of earthly temptation. In his case, although he had aspired to spiritual heights in hopes of bringing the redemption, he did not redeem the "sparks" of divinity from the earthly realm, but rather was held "captive" by the dark forces of the Other Side. Had his sexual urges been fulfilled by the holiness of marital union, the Shekhinah would have been called forth instead of Lilith.

As disturbing as the fall of a spiritual aspirant might be, dismay of a much greater magnitude results from Lilith's triumph on high. For it is in the domain of God's heavenly union with Lilith that the well-known esoteric principle "as above, so below" finds its most perverse application. It is told in the *Zohar* that after the destruction of the Temple in Jerusalem, God exiled the Shekhinah (Matronit) and took Lilith as his consort in her place:

> The King (i.e. God) sent away the Matronit and took the slave-woman [Lilith] in her place. . . . And this slave-woman was destined to rule over the Holy Land of Below, as the Matronit formerly ruled over it. (*Zohar*, 11169a)

Rabbi Shlomo Alkabetz, the sixteenth-century Kabbalist from Safed, famous for his authorship of the Sabbath song "Lekha Dodi," elaborated on this idea in his mystical writings. Describing the shame of the Shekhinah poignantly, Alkabetz aimed to inspire his readers:

> . . . her rival [Lilith] angers her greatly, and she sobs and sighs because her husband [God] does not throw his light upon her. . . . Her joy has fled because she sees her rival in her house, deriding her, to the extent that the mistress became the handmaid, and the handmaid mistress. And when our Father sees our Mother lying in dust and suffering because of our sins, He too becomes embittered in his heart and He descends to save her and make the strangers cease violating her. And now, can there be anybody who sees those things without rending his heart to repent and thus to bring back our Mother to her place and to her palace? (*Brith Ha-Levi,* chap. 7)

In this passage, we are led to recognize that even on the most elevated mystical plane, the union of the Masculine and Feminine must take into account *both* sides of the Feminine, Lilith and the Shekhinah, the dark side as well as the light. Although in traditional mystical texts, the polarities of the Feminine are personified by Lilith as evil and the Shekhinah as good, the psychological relationship of the two is not directly addressed. For the universal Mother, like other archetypes, has a two-sided nature. When either aspect of that nature is denied, it magnifies in strength. Thus, when the active power of the feminine is shunned or denied, it looms as a disproportionate threat, as exemplified by the aggressive and seductive qualities of Lilith.

In contrast, one might imagine that if feminine qualities are acknowledged, both active and passive, dark and light, they can assume their rightful place within a harmonious whole. The key to that harmony is conscious awareness and acceptance of the opposites. Modern literary interpretations of early biblical myths have reimagined the feminine polarities in this way.[20] Judith Plaskow, for example, has written of the reconciliation of Lilith and Eve. In her telling, Adam is puzzled by the bond of sisterhood that grows between the two women when Lilith reenters the garden. He seeks counsel from God, but even God is confused: "'I am who I am,' thought God, 'but I must become who I will become.' And God and Adam were expectant and afraid the day Eve and Lilith returned to the garden, bursting with possibilities, ready to rebuild it together."[21]

As we allow ourselves to imagine the reconciliation of the two poles of femininity, we can begin to imagine the harmonious state in which the masculine and feminine powers may also both receive mutual respect and recognition. But for the feminine life-and-death-dealing force to be valued in equal measure with the masculine principle of law and reason, there has to be an appreciation of living matter and the cycles of nature, both the waxing and the waning.

And so we come full circle to the moon as a symbol of the feminine. The Kabbalists interpreted the "lessening of the moon" as a symbol of the Shekhinah's exile, just as the renewal of the moon had been previously associated with redemption.[22] To bring about that messianic state of redemption, in which all wounds are healed and all wrongs are made right, would require spiritual scrutiny on a global level. For to restore the moon to her original position, with a status equal to that of the sun, the Feminine must once again be accorded due honor. On the collective level, inasmuch as we have denied the sacredness of life in all of its varied manifestations and have abused the earth, which constitutes the "lower realm," we have suppressed the universal Mother. And on a personal level, the denial of the Feminine for men and women alike involves negation of the human qualities of receptivity, nurturing, and connectedness, of instinct, and of the dark and light cycles of creative life.

That feminine principle, which has long been repressed or exiled in the patriarchal Jewish tradition, is once again being sought both by men and women with hope for personal and collective renewal. Some Jews, therefore, have turned to paganism, neo-paganism, witchcraft, and Goddess spirituality as a way of reconnecting with the feminine principle and the immanence of the Divine in nature.[23] In fact, "women's spirituality" has emerged as a movement in itself, with women reconnecting to the source of their own sacred experience rather than to that which men have traditionally defined. Today, in many different places, closely knit circles of women gather to share the mystery of the sacred in their own lives and to give voice to their own unique experiences.

In *The Feminine Face of God: The Unfolding of the Sacred in Women*, one of the authors describes a dream that initiated her collaboration on the book. In the dream, she gains entrance to a temple where an old man, Melchizedek, greets her and has her lead the way into an empty room with a built-in cabinet. She approaches and pulls open the doors:

> Then I notice something unusual. Instead of a mantle of velvet covering the scrolls, or a simple ribbon holding them closed, the Torah has been sealed shut by a dark round blot of red wax. I look at Melchizedek. "This is a very special Torah," he says. Pulling out his dagger, he breaks the seal and rolls open the scrolls. They are absolutely blank. "The Torah is empty," he says, "because what you need to know now is not written in any book. You already contain that knowledge. It is to be unfolded from within you."[24]

In the dream, the author asks, "What is this Torah for?" Her question unleashes a sequence of events that culminate in celebration. The long—bearded patriarchs Moses, King David, King Solomon, and Abraham, Isaac and Jacob appear and join in dance. When the dancing stops and she asks, "What is this all about?" Melchizedek answers, "We are celebrating because you, a woman, have consented to accept full spiritual responsibility in your life. This is your initiation as one who will serve the planet. . . . And you are not the only one. Many, many women are coming forward now to lead the way."

The dynamic nature of Judaism, which has absorbed and integrated countless movements over the centuries, has in the last few decades encountered the momentum of feminism. Externally, in the practical and political sphere, this has resulted in greater inclusion of women at different levels of participation, from the synagogue to official positions in organizations to rabbinical positions within the non-Orthodox denominations. On the internal dimension, however, the dimension that is the heart of mysticism, reevaluation of the Feminine has only just begun, again. By returning to the teachings of Kabbalah with a modern sensibility—bearing in mind the historical subordination of women, the destruction of our environment, and the workings of our own human psychology—we may renew the value of the Feminine as essential not only for our own mental well-being but for the well-being and perpetuation of life on our planet.

The Kabbalistic formulations designed to unite the essence of both the masculine and the feminine aspects of God, while laden with the cultural bias inherent in an archaic context, nevertheless mapped the path to a more wholesome spirituality. In reviewing the mystical teachings of the Divine Androgyne in Kabbalah, we may deepen our under—standing of the Divine as well as our own psyches. In the sense that we are made "in the image of God," unraveling the products of our own ongoing imaginative and mythmaking ability may serve not only to penetrate the divine mysteries, but to break through the mysteries of our own human existence. For just as we understand "the Lord is our God, the Lord is One" to mystically signify the harmonious union of the Masculine and Feminine conjoined, so may study of the Kabbalah lead us to strive toward integrating our own masculine and feminine natures to achieve wholeness. In so doing, may we be blessed to hasten the redemption, both personal and collective, which we still await.

> Moreover the light of the moon shall be as the light of the sun, and the light of the sun shall be sevenfold, as the light of the seven days, in the day that the Lord bindeth up the bruise of His people, and healeth the stroke of their wound. (Isa. 30:26)

Endnotes

1. For collections of such legends, see Louis Ginzberg, *Legends of the Jews,* vol. 1 (Philadelphia: Jewish Publication Society, 1909), and the recently translated *Sefer ha-Agadah,* compiled by H. N. Bialik and Y. H. Rawnitsky, *Legends of the Talmud* (New York: Schocken Books, 1992).

2. In his paper "Woman: The Feminine as Other in Theosophic Kabbalah: Some Philosophical Observations on the Divine Androgyne," Elliot Wolf son questions the viability of using Kabbalistic literature to cull images of the feminine God without taking into consideration the cultural context of that literature. He argues, rightly so, that a basic tension lies at the heart of Kabbalistic speculation regarding the androgynous nature of the divine. In Laurence J. Silberstein and Robert L. Cohn, eds., *The Other in Jewish Thought and History: Constructions of Jewish Culture and Identity* (New York: New York University Press, 1994) , p. 168.

3. Joseph Campbell, "The Meeting with the Goddess," in *The Hero with a Thousand Faces,* Bollingen Series XVII (Princeton, N.J.: Princeton University Press, 1949), pp.

110–114. (I have merged quotations from Campbell's descriptions of the Goddess in various mythologies.)

4. For discussion of these subjects, see for example, Gershom Scholem, *Major Trends in Jewish Mysticism* (New York: Schocken, 1961), and *Origins of the Kabbala* (Philadelphia: Jewish Publication Society, 1987); Moshe Idel, *Kabbalah: New Perspectives* (New Haven: Yale University Press, 1988); Yehuda Liebes, *Studies in Jewish Myth and Jewish Messianism* (Albany: SUNY Press, 1993); Aryeh Kaplan, *Inner Space: Introduction to Kabbalah, Meditation, and Prophecy* (Jerusalem: Moznaim Publishing, 1990) ; and the ever expanding bibliographic references in the studies of Jewish mysticism.

5. Gershom Scholem has suggested both psychological and historical factors to explain the emergence of the "feminine element in Divinity ." See the chapter "Shekhina: The Feminine Element in Divinity," in *On the Shape of the Mystical Godhead: Basic Concepts in the Kabbalah* (New York: Schocken Books, 1991), pp. 160–161.

6. See Carl Jung, *Symbols of Transformation* and *The Archetypes and the Collective Unconscious*, vols. 5 and 9(i) of the *Collected Works*, Bollingen Series XX (Princeton, N.J.: Princeton University Press, 1956, 1959).

Further, it should be pointed out that to approach Kabbalistic mythology from the perspective of depth psychology does not necessarily entail psychologizing God or the symbolic content of the mystical systems. Although Jung himself felt obliged to write primarily as an empirical scientist rather than as a metaphysician, he understood that psychological truth did not exclude metaphysical truth.

7. For a full elaboration of this theme, see Erich Neumann, *The Origins and History of Consciousness* (Princeton, N.J.: Princeton University Press, 1970). Neumann outlines the archetypal stages of the evolution of consciousness and maintains that the individual ego consciousness has to pass through the same archetypal stages that determined the evolution of consciousness in the life of humanity.

8. For a discussion of the relationship between man's fall and the cosmic process, see Scholem, *Major Trends*, p. 279.

9. For a full discussion of this phenomenon, see Raphael Patai, "The Shekhina as *Maggid* and Vision" in Raphael Patai, *The Hebrew Goddess*, 3rd ed. (Detroit: Wayne State University Press, 1990), pp. 118–122.

10. See R. J. Zwi Werblowsky, *Joseph Karo: Lawyer and Mystic* (Philadelphia: Jewish Publication Society, 1977).

11. Hayyim Vital, *Sefer HaHezyonot*, ed. A. Z. Aescoly (Jerusalem: Mossad haRav Kook, 1954), quoted in Patai, *The Hebrew Goddess*, p. 215.

12. On the cosmological level, this restrictive energy of limitation is the feminine Sefirah of *Din/Gevurah*, representing God's judgment or severity, a necessary aspect of limitation. When separated from the totality of God's potency, i.e., not counterbalanced by all the other energies, that contracting energy of *Din* or limitation is the origin of the realm of evil, the *Sitrah Achera*, or the "Other Side," which assumed a mythological potency of its own. For a thorough discussion of the subject, see Gershorn Scholem, "Sitra Ahra: Good and Evil in the Kabbala," in On *the Mystical Shape of the Godhead*.

13. Reb Nachman of Bratslav (1772–1810), the great-grandson of the founder of Hasidism, Rabbi Israel Baal Shem Tov (1700–1760), told his Hasidim of the exile of the Shekhinah and other secret mysteries of the Kabbalah in allegorical form. The tale "The Lost Princess" recounts the exile of the Shekhinah who was held captive in the palace of

the "evil one," and the efforts to redeem her. The tale can be found in Meyer Levin, *Classic Hassidic Tales* (New York: Penguin, 1975), pp. 190–197, and Howard Schwartz, *Eliiah's Violin and Other Jewish Fairy Tales* (New York: Harper & Row, 1983), pp. 210–218. The original can be found in the Hebrew *Sippure Ma'asiyot,* edited by Rabbi Nathan Sternhartz of Nemirov (Warsaw, 1881).

14. For a thorough historical account of the Lilith mythology in Judaism and other traditions, see Siegmund Hurwitz, *Lilith, the First Eve: Historical and Psychological Aspects of the Dark Feminine,* trans. Gela Jacobson (Einsiedeln, Switzerland: Oaimon Verlag, 1992), and Raphael Patai, *The Hebrew Goddess.*

15. See, for example, Seymour J. Cohen (ed. & trans.), *The Holy Letter: A Study in Medieval Jewish Sexual Morality* (New York: Ktav Publishing House, 1976). In this thirteenth-century work, which has often been attributed to Nachmanides but is considered by scholars to be anonymous, the author explains what is meant by sanctification during the time of sexual intercourse.

16. For "according to the secret doctrine, the supernal Mother is together with the male only when the house is in readiness and at that time the male and female are conjoined." *Zohar: Basic Readings,* ed. Gershom Scholem (New York: Schocken, 1949), p. 36.

17. Actually, like many other commandments, the religious obligation to "be fruitful and multiply" is incumbent only upon the male. The obligation to fulfill his wife's conjugal needs, apart from childbearing, is also a Jewish male's religious duty. The same does not hold true for the female with regard to her spouse.

18. Patai quotes an ancient text to this effect: "And behold that hard shell [embodiment of evil], Lilith, is always present in the bed linen of man and wife when they copulate, in order to take hold of the sparks of the drops of semen which are lost—because it is impossible to perform the marital act without such a loss of sparks—and she creates out of them demons, spirits, and Lilith. But there is an incantation for this, to chase Lilith away from the bed and to bring forth pure souls." *Emek ha Melekh,* after Patai, *The Hebrew Goddess,* p. 234–

19. Howard Schwartz, "Helen of Troy," in *Lilith's Cave: Jewish Tales of the Supernatural* (San Francisco: Harper & Row, 1988), p. 42.

20. Another version of reconciliation is told by Jacov Lind. In his tale, Lilith comes back to haunt Adam as lust. Eve returns home to find Lilith and Adam united together in an embrace; she brings them food and drink. She then enters Lilith's body and kisses Adam, feeling his love as she had never known it before. Adam believes that Lilith will leave at dawn, but Lilith, who was Eve now, kissed him and said: "I wish this were so, but alas I cannot leave you. I will stay with you, because you are full of fire for this other woman whose body I have now taken over." "The Story of Lilith and Eve," in Howard Schwartz, *Gates to the New City: A Treasury of Modem Jewish Tales* (New Jersey: Jason Aronson, 1983), pp. 133–134.

21. "Epilogue: The Coming of Lilith," in Rosemary R. Ruether, (ed.), *Religion and Sexism: Images of Woman in the Jewish and Christian Traditions* (New York: Simon and Schuster, 1974), pp. 341–343.

22. See Gershom Scholem, *On the Kabbalah and Its Symbolism,* pp. 151–152, for a discussion of the rituals dramatizing the exile of Shekhinah. The Talmudists (Sanhedrin 42a) found a parallel between the renewal of the moon and messianic redemption in the

ritual blessing for the new moon. The Kabbalists shifted the emphasis from the new-moon ritual to the day *preceding* the new moon as a fast day, devoted to meditation on the themes of exile and redemption.

23. For more about the involvement of Jewish women in countercultural spiritu-ality, see Rahel Musleah, "When the Goddess Calls: Jewish Women Answer," *Lilith,* Fall 1993.

24. See Sherry Ruth Anderson and Patricia Hopkins, *The Feminine Face of God: The Unfolding of the Sacred in Women* (New York: Bantam Books, 1991), pp. 2–4.

Notes on the Contributors

Minnie Appel, born in Odessa, Russia in 1898, was a housewife and mother, and active in her synagogue.

Gloria Attoun has been calming her chaotic brain through writing and art for over 30 years. She primarily expresses herself by writing songs and is in a band called Augusta Bottoms Consort, which has recorded three cds and is currently working on a fourth entitled *Brand New World*. She graduated from University City High School's "High School of the Arts" program and from the University of Missouri at Kansas City. "The Darkness" is a song, from Gloria's cd *Bottomland*.

Nancy E. Berg is author of *Exile from Exile: Israeli Writers from Iraq* (SUNY, 1996) and *More and More Equal: The Literary Works of Sami Michael* (Lexington, 2005). A St. Louisan by choice, she does, however, occasionally long for the ocean. She has been a member of Nairobi Hebrew Congregation for almost twenty years, and has taught at Washington University since 1990.

Freda Berns, born in Poneviej, Lithuania in 1902, housewife and mother, was a prominent benefactor of Jewish organizations in St. Louis.

Leah F. Silberman Bernstein, self-described Meta-Denominational Jew, is a graduate of Columbia University and the Jewish Theological Seminary's Joint Master Social Work/Jewish Studies program. A St. Louis native, Leah writes in her spare time from parenting and from her work in the Jewish community.

Lorry Blath has written a novel, *No Promises*, set in the 1950s in Wheeling, West Viriginia, where she grew up. Grandmother of three, mother of two, wife of one, Lorry has lived in suburban St. Louis for 27 years and is working on more contemporary fiction set in St. Louis.

Stan Braude's writing ranges from articles in *Boys Life* and *Scientific American*, to the forthcoming textbook: *Understanding Ecology*. He has survived twenty field seasons in Kenya and fifteen years in St. Louis, where he teaches at UMSL and Washington University.

Marc Bregman has taught in Israel at the Hebrew Union College, the Hebrew University, Ben-Gurion University and the Schechter Institute. In America, Bregman has taught at Yale University, the University of Washington in Seattle, and at the University of Pennsylvania. In 2005, he was research fellow at Harvard University and teaching fellow at the Center for Advanced Judaic Studies in Philadelphia. He is the author of *The Tanhuma-Yelammedenu Literature: Studies in* *the Evolution of the Versions* (Gorgias Press, 2003). As of 2006, Bregman has been appointed the Bernard Distinguished Professor of Jewish Studies at the University of North Carolina at Greensboro.

Louis Daniel Brodsky is the author of fifty volumes of poetry and eight scholarly volumes on William Faulkner. His biography of Faulkner, *William Faulkner, Life Glimpses*, was published in 1990 by the University of Texas Press. His poetry has appeared in *Harper's*, *American Scholar*, and *Southern Review*. Recent publications include *The Complete Poems of Louis Daniel Brodsky: Volume Two, 1967– 1976, Shadow War: A Poetic Chronicle of September 11 and Beyond* and his latest book of fiction, *Rated Xmas*. Five books of Brodsky's poems have been published in French.

Jan Garden Castro is contributing editor for *Sculpture* and author/editor of five books, including *The Last Frontier*. She received a CCLM award as Editor of *River Styx* and has published in varied poetry journals including *New Letters* and *Exquisite Corpse* and the now-departed *Contact II, Greenfield Review*, and *Telephone*.

Michael Castro is the founder of the magazine and literary organization, *River Styx*. He is the author of six books of poetry, most recently *Human Rites* (2001). Since 1995 he has been working with Gabor Gyukics translating modern Hungarian poets. This has resulted in the anthology *Swimming in the Ground* (2001), and two forthcoming books, *A Transparent Lion: Selected Poems of Attila Jozsef* and *Gypsy Drill, Poems by Attila Balogh*. Castro teaches at Lindenwood University.

Robert A. Cohn, Editor-in-Chief Emeritus of the *St. Louis Jewish Light*, has been associated with the St. Louis Jewish community's newspaper since 1969. He has won numerous national awards for excellence in North American Jewish journalism. He is the co-editor, with Rabbi Mark L. Shook of Temple Israel, of *By Reason of Strength: the Life and Work of Rabbi Robert P. Jacobs*.

Allison Creighton, a St. Louis native, has worked as a music therapist, a high school English teacher, an academic support program coordinator, and as an editor, and currently teaches at St. Louis Community College at Forest Park. She recently completed her MFA at the University of Missouri–St. Louis, where she was awarded the Graduate Prize in Poetry for 2002

Sophie Dricker, born in Berschek, Ukraine in 1903, was active in Jewish affairs in St. Louis. She worked in the needle trades until her retirement.

Walter Ehrlich is Professor Emeritus of History and Education at the University of Missouri–St. Louis. He is the author of several books, including *Presiden-*

tial Impeachment: An American Dilemma, They Have No Rights: Dred Scott's Struggle for Freedom, We the People: Two Hundred Years of the Contitution and the two-volume *Zion in the Valley: the Jewish Community of St. Louis.*

Frank Fershter, born in Bonderova, Ukraine in 1896, was active in the labor movement and worked in the needle trades.

Barbara L. Finch has lived in St. Louis since 1965. She is a retired public relations consultant and a graduate of the Master's of Liberal Arts program at Washington University and the Florence Melton Adult Mini-School at CAJE. She is a member of Congregation Temple Israel.

Donald Finkel was Poet-in-Residence at Washington University for many years, until his retirement. He has published a dozen books of poems, including the recent *A Question of Seeing* and *Not So the Chairs: Selected and New Poems.* He has won numerous awards, including the Theodore Roethke Memorial Award and the Mortan Zabel Award from the Academy and Institute of Arts and Letters.

Merle Fischlowitz, a native St. Louisan, worked as a school counselor and psychologist in Israel, Maryland and Hawaii, before retiring in San Diego. He is an active volunteer in musical and Jewish community organizations. His book of poems, *From Dirt Paths to Golden Streets: Poems of Immigrant Experiences* was published in 1999.

Shelly R. Fredman has taught writing at the honors college of the University of Missouri–St. Louis and Washington University. She earned an MFA from Washington University. Her fiction and essays have appeared in *Best Jewish Writing 2002, First Harvest,* the *Chicago Tribune Magazine, Hadassah, Lilith, Natural Bridge* and the *Sagarin Review.* A St. Louis native, she now resides in New York City.

Jeff Friedman is the author of four collections of poetry: *Black Threads* (forthcoming from Carnegie Mellon University Press in 2006), *Taking Down the Angel, Scattering the Ashes* and *The Record-Breaking Heat Wave.* His poems and translations have appeared in many literary magazines, including *American Poetry Review, Poetry, The Antioch Review, The Missouri Review, New England Review, 5 AM, Natural Bridge, Literary Imagination, Poetry East, Columbia: A Journal of Literature and Art, The Forward, The Saint Ann's Review* and *The New Republic.* He is a core faculty member in the MFA program in Poetry Writing at New England College.

Pinchas Giller is a professor of Kabbalah at the University of Judaism in Los Angeles. He is the author of two books on the *Zohar, The Enlightened Will Shine* and *Reading the Zohar: The Sacred Text of Kabbalah.*

Naama Goldstein's first collection of stories, *The Place Will Comfort You*, was published by Scribner in 2004. Born in Boston, Naama was raised in the city of Petakh Tikva in Israel from the age of three, returning to the U.S. as a high school senior. She received her introduction to fiction workshops at Washington University in St. Louis, remaining in the city for seven years. She now makes her home in Boston with her husband and son, and is at work on a novel set in Israel and the American Midwest.

Rabbi James Stone Goodman serves Neve Shalom Congregation and the Central Reform Congregation in St. Louis, Missouri. He is a musician specializing in a spiritually based music integrating story and poetry. He plays guitar, oud, and percussion and is presently finishing his fifth CD, *The Book of Splendor*. He is a poet and is working on an MFA in poetry writing. His work is available on two websites: www.stonegoodman.com and www.neveshalom.org.

Felicia Graber is a speaker and docent at the Holocaust Museum and Learning Center. She is a retired teacher and the founder and co-chair of the Hidden Child/Child Survivor Group of St Louis. She is married to Rabbi Howard M. Graber, Executive Director Emeritus of the Central Agency for Jewish Education, the mother of two and grandmother of eight. Her entries are true stories based on her family's survival in Nazi-occupied Poland.

Julie Heifetz, writer/teacher/psychotherapist founded the Institute for Humanizing Healthcare since living in Philadelphia these past five years. As a consultant, she has worked with hospitals and nursing facilities to institute the use of stories into their clincical proceedures. In addition, she helps individuals suffering from traumatic brain injury, or with life-threatening illnesses write their stories to improve cognitively and emotionally and move on in their lives.

Maurice L. Hirsch, Jr. (Bud) is the author of two collections of poems, *Stares to Other Places* and *Roots and Paths* (both AuthorHouse, 2004). He gives readings of his work at the Gallery at Chesterfield Arts and Left Bank Books. Hirsch is Professor Emeritus of Accounting at Southern Illinois University Edwardsville, an avid horseman and photographer, and active in the arts and community. He is a St. Louis native and lives in Chesterfield

Allen Hoffman is a member of the English faculty and Permanent Writer-in-Residence of the graduate creative writing program in Bar-Ilan University, Ramat Gan, Israel. He was born and grew up in Clayton, Missouri. An award winning novelist and short story writer: *Kagan's Superfecta and Other Stories, Small Worlds, Big League Dreams, Two For The Devil*; he is currently completing the fourth novel in the Small Worlds series, *Instruments of Desire*.

Jane Ellen Ibur's recent work appears in *Lilith, Runes, Reflections on a Life with Diabetes, Teaching the Arts Behind Bars* and *Natural Bridge.* Ibur teaches in prison, homeless shelters, community organizations, is Lead Faculty for the Community Arts Training (CAT) Institute, co-director of the Gifted Writers Project, co-host of Literature for the Halibut on community radio KDHX, and received a Teacher Appreciation Award from the Missouri Scholars Academy in 2004.

Andrea Jackson is an MFA student at the University of Missouri–St. Louis. Her poetry and fiction have appeared or are forthcoming in *Margie, The Sow's Ear Poetry Review, The Eleventh Muse,* and *Periphery.* In a previous life, she practiced law for 20 years in Clayton, Missouri.

Ethel Kessler (deceased) was born to Russian immigrant parents in St. Louis in 1921. Ethel's freelance writing career included three regular newspaper columns, more than 350 published articles and an unpublished young adult novel. Her work appeared in the *San Jose Mercury News, Almaden Times, St. Louis Jewish Light, Japanese Poetry Journal, American Poetry Anthology, Gems and Minerals, Los Gatos Magazine, South Bay Weekly, Well-Being Journal,* and *Kids Kids Kids,* among others. This story was her first, winning an award and launching her writing career at age 63.

Hillel J. Kieval is the Gloria M. Goldstein Professor of Jewish History and Thought at Washington University in St. Louis, where he also chairs the Department of History. He is the author of three books: *The Making of Czech Jewry: National Conflict and Jewish Society in Bohemia, 1870–1918* (Oxford University Press, 1988); *Languages of Community: The Jewish Experience in the Czech Lands* (University of California Press, 2000); and a forthcoming work: *Blood Inscriptions: The "Ritual Murder" Trial in Modern Europe* (University of California Press).

Robert E. Kohn, Professor Emeritus of Economics at Southern Illinois University Edwardsville, resides with his wife Martha in Clayton. As an economist he wrote papers and books on environmental economics, but, since his retirement, he has switched to literary and art criticism. In his new field, he is publishing articles that reveal Tibetan Buddhist themes in novels by William Kotzwinkle, Thomas Pynchon, Robin Moore, William Gaddis, John Hawkes and Don DeLillo.

Susan Koppelman is a noted literary historian who has edited many collections of important women's writings, including *Women's Friendships: A Collection of Stories; The Strange History of Suzanne LeFleshe; The Other Woman: Stories of Two Women and a Man, The Stories of Fannie Hurst* and *Between Mothers and Daughters: Stories Across a Generation.* She currently lives in Tucson, Arizona.

Linda Kram is a teacher for Shaare Zedek Early Childhood Center and a Hebrew tutor for special needs children through the CAJE Kulanu program. As a professional storyteller, Linda tells each year at the St. Louis Storytelling Festival and other venues. She is pursuing a Masters Degree through Spertus College. Linda has studied Talmud and Avot with Rabbi Zimand of Traditional Congregation and is a graduate of the Florence Melton School for Adult Education.

Cissy Lacks is a writer, photographer and teacher. She has a master's degree in broadcast and film and a PhD in American Studies.

Lynn Levin is the author of two collections of poems, *Imaginarium* (Loonfeather Press, 2005) and *A Few Questions about Paradise* (Loonfeather Press, 2000). Her poetry has appeared in or is forthcoming in *Boulevard, Hunger Mountain, Kerem, The Jewish Women's Literary Annual, Poetica,* and *Tiferet,.* A St. Louis native, She teaches at Drexel University, where she is also executive producer of *The Drexel InterView.*

Irving Litvag is the author of two books, *Singer in the Shadows: The Strange Story of Patience Worth* and *The Master of Sunnybank: A Biography of Albert Payson Terhune* A free-lance writer for more than 50 years, his work has been published in national and regional magazines and in many newspapers. He has written radio drama and his stage plays have been produced by Washington University and the Webster Groves Theater Guild.

Edward M. Londe writes stories on Jewish themes, many of them based on his dreams. He has previously published works in the *St. Louis Jewish Light*, the *Sagarin Review* and *First Harvest*.

Cheryl Maayan teaches third grade at the Saul Mirowitz Day School–Reform Jewish Academy. She enjoys listening to family stories about the old days and writing with her students. *The Hole in the Pantry* is her first publication. Cheryl is the recipient of the Grinspoon-Steinhardt award for Excellence in Jewish Education and the Stuart I. Raskas Outstanding Day School Teacher Award for 2005.

Jerred Metz is a former St. Louisan who still visits several times a year. He lives in Columbia, SC. He is the author of four books of poetry: *Speak Like Rain, The Temerate Voluptuary, Angels in the House,* and *Three Legs up, Cold as Stone; Six Legs down, Blood and Bone.* He has also written three books of prose: *Drinking the Dipper Dry, Halley's Comet, 1910: Fire in the Sky,* and *The Last Eleven Days of Earl Durand.* The stories in this collection from Minnie Appel, Freda Berns, Sophie Drickes, Frank Fershter and Yetta Schneider first appeared in *Drinking the Dripper Dry.*

David Millman is a sculpture. He graduated from SIU and has a Master's from Pratt Instiute. He worked at ABC News as graphic artist for 29 years. He lives on St. Simon's Island, GA. In 1981 he received an Emmy in 1981 for Individual Outstanding Creative Achievement, and in 2001 he received the George Foster Peabody Award for coverage of 9/11.

Marcia Moskowitz, a retired English teacher, taught at Parkway West High School for 22 years. A resident of St. Louis for over 27 years, she has been an active member of Congregation Shaare Emeth and serves on the board of the Central Agency for Jewish Education. She chairs the Commission on Reform Jewish Education, is a Melton graduate, and continues to pursue her lifelong love of learning by taking Center for Adult Jewish Learning (CAJL) courses. She is the mother of Rabbis Steven and Michael Moskowitz.

Rabbi Steven Heneson Moskowitz is the rabbi of the Jewish Congregation of Brookville on Long Island, New York. Prior to this he served as the Assistant Director of the 92nd Street Y's Bronfman Center for Jewish Life in New York City. He is married to Rabbi Susie Heneson Moskowitz and is the proud father of Shira Yael and Ari Chanan. He is a disciple of Rabbi Jeffrey Stiffman and a former student of Mrs. Ida Stack. He learned a love of Torah from his parents, Carl and Marcia Moskowitz and continues to study every summer at the Shalom Hartman Institute in Jerusalem with his friend, Rabbi Mark Fasman.

Niki Nymark has been writing, performing, publishing and teaching poetry in St. Louis for the past thirty years. She is currently at work on a book of poems based on Torah, Midrash and her experiences in Israel.

Gerald T. Perkoff, M.D. was born in 1926 and raised in St. Louis. He attended Washington University in St. Louis and Washington University School of Medicine, receiving the M.D. degree in 1948. He and his wife Marian have three children and five grandchildren. After 16 years on the faculty of the Washington University School of Medicine, he moved to the University of Missouri School of Medicine in 1979 and retired there in 1991 as Curators Professor Emeritus of Family and Community Medicine.

Vicki E. Pickle, a native of St. Louis, is writing a collection of stories, prose and poems about her childhood years in University City. She works as an educator and academic tutor with an emphasis in language arts. Vicki and her husband, Bob, have 2 daughters.

Nancy Powers' poems have appeared in *Mankato Poetry Review, Fan Magazine, PMS (PoemMemoirStory), Small Spiral Notebook, Melic Review* and *Fugue*. She is a life-long St. Louisan, a working journalist and a member of the MFA program at University of Missouri–St. Louis, where she was named runner-up in the 2005 graduate poetry contest. Other prizes include the 2004 Wednesday Club Poetry Contest and the Arts in Transit award.

Marilyn Probe's work has been published in the *Poetry Anthology*, *Breathing Out*, *Messages from the Heart, CAJE and Kerf* journals, the *Soulard Culture Squad Review* and *Spirit Seeker* magazine. She has won the James H. Nash and also the American Society on Aging poetry prizes. As the founder of Elders-Probe-the-Arts, she develops and teaches in intergenerational poetry programs. She is a frequent poetry reader at Central Reform on High Holy Days .

Miriam Raskin is a St. Louis area writer, activist and perennial student. Some of her writings, largely poems and essays, have been published; most have not. Many reflect her childhood experiences as a refugee from Nazi Germany and her subsequent reactions to the War Against the Jews. She is currently studying Biblical Hebrew—at a leisurely pace.

Barbara Raznick has been the director of the Saul Brodsky Jewish Community Library for twenty years. She co-edited all of the issues of the *Sagarin Review: the St. Louis Jewish Literary Journal* and edited *First Harvest: Jewish Writing in St. Louis 1991–1997* with Howard Schwartz.

Ann Lesley Rosen is currently a student in the MFA program at the University of Missouri–St. Louis, with a concentration in poetry. Her work is forthcoming in *Sambatyon*. She lives in St. Louis with her husband.

Marylou Ruhe is a Holocaust survivor from the city of Lodz, Poland. She survived the Lodz ghetto, Auschwitz, Bergen-Belsen and the Labor Camp in Salzwedel, Germany. She is a docent at the St. Louis Holocaust Museum and Learning Center, a lecturer and writer.

Marc Saperstein served for eleven years as Gloria M. Goldstein Professor of Jewish History and Thought at Washington University. He is currently Chair of Judaic Studies and Charles E. Smith Professor of History at George Washington University. His books include *Decoding the Rabbis, Jewish Preaching 1200–1800: An Anthology, Your Voice Like a Ram's Horn: Themes and Texts in Traditional Jewish Preaching* and *Exile in Amsterdam: Saul Levi Morteira's Sermons to a Congregation of "New Jews"* (HUC Press, 2005). He has twice received the National Jewish Book Award.

Jane Schapiro is the author of the nonfiction book, *Inside a Class Action: The Holocaust and the Swiss Banks* (University of Wisconsin, 2003) and a volume of poetry, *Tapping This Stone* (Washington Writers' Publishing House, 1995). Her poems have appeared in journals such as *The American Scholar, The Gettysburg Review, Prairie Schooner, The Southern Review*, and *The Women's Review of Books*. In addition to writing, she tutors at George Mason University in Fairfax, VA.

Amy Scharff has been writing down her thoughts and experiences since she was a child, and became a professional business writer as an adult. She left business recently to become a high school teacher in St. Louis, her hometown, where she continues to work with words and inspire other people to do the same.

Yetta Schneider, born in Ronov, Lithuania in 1906, was a housewife and mother.

Steven Schreiner is associate professor of English at the University of Missouri–St. Louis. He is the author of *Too Soon to Leave*, and a chapbook, *Imposing Presence*. His poems have appeared in *Poetry, Prairie Schooner, Image, Colorado Review, Poet & Critic* and elsewhere. He has been awarded fellowships from The National Writers Voice of the YMCA and the Virginia Center for the Creative Arts. He is the founding and senior editor of *Natural Bridge*, a journal of contemporary literature.

Joan Schultz, a native St. Louisan, is a writer, poet, artist, photographer and musician. She shared her enthusiasm for her art through lectures, seminars and private piano lessons.

Henry I. Schvey is Professor of Drama and Chair of the Performing Arts Department at Washington University in St. Louis. He has written numerous scholarly articles on modern European and American theatre, directs, and has written plays and fiction, as well as poetry.

Charles Schwartz grew up in St. Louis, left for many years and then returned. He is married and lives in Chesterfield with his family. He works as a technical writer for a software development company.

Howard Schwartz is a professor of English at the University of Missouri–St. Louis. He has the author of three books of poetry, *Vessels, Gathering the Sparks*, and *Sleepwalking Beneath the Stars*, and of several books of fiction, including *The Captive Soul of the Messiah*. He has also edited a four volume set of Jewish folktales, and ten children's books. His book *Tree of Souls: The Mythology of Judaism*, was published by Oxford University Press in 2004.

Maury L. Schwartz is a practicing psychotherapist in Chicago, who worked for many years as Director of Education for congregations in Omaha, Kansas City and Miami Beach. His memoirs have previously appeared in *The Sagarin Review* and *First Harvest*.

Miriam Schwartz is a student at New College in Sarasota, Florida majoring in Anthropology and Religion. She is attending Hebrew University in Jerusalem for her junior year abroad. She is currently co-editing a child's book of Jewish mythology with her father, Howard Schwartz.

Shira Schwartz is a graduate of Oberlin College, Class of 2001. She received her bachelor's degree in both Jewish Studies and Women's Studies, with a minor in Religion. Her poetry has appeared in *Crescendo*, *Oberlin Alumni Magazine*, *First Harvest* and the *St. Louis Jewish Light*. Shira currently resides in West Palm Beach, Florida.

Tsila Schwartz is a native of Jerusalem who now makes her home in St. Louis. She is a Jewish folk artist who specializes in *Ketubot* (Jewish wedding contracts) and other Jewish texts. She has also illustrated the book, *Rooms of the Soul*, and her calligraphy appears in the book, *Elijah's Violin*.

Laya Firestone Seghi has published poetry, midrash and essays in a variety of publications. A former resident of St. Louis, having attended Epstein Hebrew Academy, University City High (1964) and Washington University (B.A., MSW), Laya currently lives in Miami Beach with her husband Tom and has a private practice in psychotherapy.

Jason Sommer is author of *Lifting the Stone*, from Forest Books, London, and from the University of Chicago Press, *Other People's Troubles*, and *The Man Who Sleeps in my Office*. He has held fellowships in Poetry at Stanford University, and at the Bread Loaf and Sewanee writer's conferences, and has read his work at the National Holocaust Museum. In 2001, Sommer received a Whiting Foundation Writer's Fellowship. He teaches at Fontbonne University in St. Louis.

Arlene Rubin Stiffman, Ph.D. is the author of 95 scientific publications and 6 edited books on adolescent mental health, addictions, high risk behavior and services; and the recipient of 20 National Institute of Health research grants. She is the Barbara A. Bailey Professor of Social Work at Washington University in St. Louis, and is very active in the St. Louis Jewish community. This is her first published poem.

Phil Sultz is an accomplished painter and writer who taught in the Art Department at Webster University in St. Louis for many years. He currently lives in Dennysville, Maine.

Maria Szapszewicz was born in Lodz, Poland and is a survivor of Auschwitz and Bergen-Belsen concentration camps. She is a docent and speaker for the St. Louis Holocaust Museum and Learning Center. She has published a cd of her poems, *Memories and Dreams: a Holocaust Survivor Remembers.*

Adina Talve-Goodman graduated from Clayton High School in 2005 and is attending Washington University in St. Louis, Missouri. In 2005, she was awarded the Hadassah Myrtle Wreath Award for activism in the area of stem cell research

Shlomo Vinner is a native of Jerusalem who teaches mathematics and science education at the Hebrew University. He spent a year teaching at the University of Missouri–St. Louis in 1975–76. He has received the ACUM Prize and the award of the Jerusalem Foundation for Literature for his poetry. Two of his books of poetry, *For a Few Hours Only* and *Jerusalem As She Is*, have been translated into English.

Jane O. Wayne is the author of *A Strange Heart* (Helicon Nine Editions) which received the Marianne Moore Poetry Award, *Looking Both Ways* (Univ. MO Press) which received the Devins Award and the Society of Midland Authors Award, and *From the Night Album* which is forthcoming in 2007. Her work has also appeared in magazines such as: *Poetry, The American Scholar, Ploughshares, The Iowa Review*, and *Boulevard*.

Nati Zohar graduated from Ladue High School and served in the Israel Defense Forces. He currently lives in Jerusalem, where he is a translator. Many of his translations of Hebrew poets have appeared in literary journals, and he has completed a book of these translations with the poet Jeff Friedman.

Credits

Steven Schreiner "Desolated" appeared in *The Crab Orchard Review*; "Barren" appeared in *River Styx*; "Backrub" appeared in *Passages North* and was later reprinted in the *Passages North Anthology*.

Laya Firestone Seghi "Glimpsing the Moon: The Feminine Principle in Kabbalah" appeared in *Opening the Inner Gates: New Paths in Kabbalah & Psychology* by Edward Hoffman (Shambhala, 1995).

Jane O. Wayne "Timed Exposure," "Bookmarks" and "A Quick Lesson" appeared in *JAMA, Journal of the American Medical Association*, which grants permission.